THE NEW INTERNATIONAL COMMENTARY
ON THE
OLD TESTAMENT

General Editors

The Books of
EZRA AND NEHEMIAH

by

F. CHARLES FENSHAM

WILLIAM B. EERDMANS PUBLISHING COMPANY
GRAND RAPIDS, MICHIGAN

2140 Oak Industrial Drive N.E., Grand Rapids, Michigan 49505 /
P.O. Box 163, Cambridge CB3 9PU U.K.

Printed in the United States of America

18 17 16 15 14 13   16 15 14 13 12 11

Library of Congress Cataloging-in-Publication Data

Fensham, F. Charles (Frank Charles), 1925-1989
The books of Ezra and Nehemiah.
(The New International Commentary on the Old Testament)
Includes indexes.
1. Bible. O.T. Ezra — Commentaries. 2. Bible. O.T. Nehemiah — Commentaries.
I. Title. II. Series.
BS1355.3.F36 1982 222′.7077 82-11434
ISBN 978-0-8028-2527-8

www.eerdmans.com

In memory of
Jacobus Arnoldus Theron,
in gratitude.

AUTHOR'S PREFACE

When requested to write a commentary for NICOT on Ezra-Nehemiah, I accepted only reluctantly because up to that time my research concentrated mainly on the early period of Israelite history. However, in my lectures on Biblical Aramaic I had occasion to study certain aspects of postexilic times. I immediately decided to dedicate attention to the study of the late period. And what a wonderful experience it was! The history of the Persians in the sixth and fifth centuries B.C., their customs, their legal system, their tolerant attitude against their subjects (although not all of them were so tolerant), their religion, and so on are interesting material to study. Furthermore, an examination of Old Persian opens a fresh view of the speakers of the language. The best way to understand a people, ancient or modern, is to understand their language. By applying the study of the Persians to Ezra-Nehemiah, one becomes aware more than once that those things which are regarded by some scholars as not of Persian origin, although ascribed to them, are perfectly in accordance with Persian customs.

In this commentary the footnotes cite as far as possible the latest views or the latest interpretation of older views. Older publications are cited only when absolutely necessary, because the latest commentaries incorporate all the more important older views.

While working on such an important project on the word of God, one becomes aware of the value of one's former professors. More than once I have thought of Prof. Adrianus van Selms, who wrote a Dutch commentary on Ezra-Nehemiah. He is a keen observer and has a brilliant mind. Also, as every student who studied under him, I will never forget the towering figure of Prof. William F. Albright, the most brilliant scholar I have ever met and one who had a profound influence on me. Naturally I do not want to place responsibility for any of the results of this study on them.

I want to thank Dr. Walter Claassen, Dr. Hannes Olivier, and Mr.

Paul Kruger for carrying a heavy load of work while I had my sabbatical to write this commentary. My heartiest thanks to Mrs. Hannetjie Louw, our secretary, for typing this book.

This commentary is dedicated to my father-in-law, Mr. J. A. Theron, who died while I worked on this project. His interest and love for the word of God were two of his distinctive characteristics.

F. CHARLES FENSHAM

CONTENTS

ABBREVIATIONS

AASOR	*Annual of the American Schools of Oriental Research*
AB	Anchor Bible
ABR	*Australian Biblical Review*
AfO	*Archiv für Orientforschung*
AHDO	*Archives d'histoire du droit oriental*
AHW	W. von Soden, *Akkadisches Handwörterbuch*
AJBA	*Australian Journal of Biblical Archaeology*
AJSL	*American Journal of Semitic Languages and Literatures*
ANEP	J. B. Pritchard, ed., *The Ancient Near East in Pictures* (^{2}1969)
ANET	J. B. Pritchard, ed., *Ancient Near Eastern Texts* (^{3}1969)
AO	*Der Alte Orient*
AP	A. Cowley, *The Aramaic Papyri of the Fifth Century B.C.*
ArOr	*Archiv Orientální*
AT	Alte/Ancien Testament
ATD	Das AT Deutsch
ATR	*Anglican Theological Review*
AUSS	*Andrews University Seminary Studies*
AV	Authorized Version (King James)
BA	*Biblical Archaeologist*
BASOR	*Bulletin of the American Schools of Oriental Research*
BHK	R. Kittel, ed., *Biblia Hebraica*
BHS	*Biblia Hebraica Stuttgartensia*
Bibl	*Biblica*
BiOr	*Bibliotheca Orientalis*
BJRL	*Bulletin of the John Rylands Library*
BKAT	Biblischer Kommentar zum AT
BMAP	E. Kraeling, *The Brooklyn Museum Aramaic Papyri*
BT	*The Bible Translator*
BWANT	Beiträge zur Wissenschaft vom Alten und Neuen Testament
BZ	*Biblische Zeitschrift*
BZAW	Beihefte zur Zeitschrift für die alttestamentliche Wissenschaft
CBQ	*Catholic Biblical Quarterly*
CTM	*Concordia Theological Monthly*
CV	*Communio Viatorum*
DISO	C.-F. Jean and J. Hoftijzer, *Dictionnaire des inscriptions sémitiques de l'ouest*
ErIs	*Eretz-Israel*
EstBib	*Estudios Bíblicos*
EvTh	*Evangelische Theologie*

ExpT	*Expository Times*
FRLANT	Forschungen zur Religion und Literatur des Alten und Neuen Testaments
GKC	E. Kautzsch and A. E. Cowley, *Gesenius' Hebrew Grammar*
GNB	Good News Bible (Today's English Version)
GTT	*Gereformeerd Theologisch Tijdschrift*
HAT	Handbuch zum AT
HSAT	Die Heilige Schrift des ATs
HTR	*Harvard Theological Review*
HTS	*Hervormde Teologiese Studies*
HUCA	*Hebrew Union College Annual*
IB	G. A. Buttrick, ed., *The Interpreter's Bible*
ICC	International Critical Commentary
IDB(S)	G. A. Buttrick, ed., *The Interpreter's Dictionary of the Bible;* Supplementary Volume, 1976
IEJ	*Israel Exploration Journal*
Int	*Interpretation*
JB	Jerusalem Bible
JBL	*Journal of Biblical Literature*
JNES	*Journal of Near Eastern Studies*
JNSL	*Journal of Northwest Semitic Languages*
JPOS	*Journal of the Palestine Oriental Society*
JQR	*Jewish Quarterly Review*
JSS	*Journal of Semitic Studies*
JTS	*Journal of Theological Studies*
KAI	H. Donner and W. Röllig, eds., *Kanaanäische und aramäische Inschriften*
KB	L. Koehler and W. Baumgartner, *Lexicon in veteris testamenti libros*
KS	A. Alt, *Kleine Schriften zur Geschichte des Volkes Israel*
LXX	Septuagint
MT	Masoretic Text
NAB	New American Bible
NBD	*New Bible Dictionary*
NCB	New Century Bible
NEB	New English Bible
Neot	*Neotestamentica (Die Nuwe-Testamentiese Werkgemeenskap van Suid-Afrika)*
NICOT	New International Commentary on the OT
NThT	*Nederlands Theologisch Tijdschrift*
NTT	*Norsk Teologisk Tidsskrift*
OLZ	*Orientalische Literaturzeitung*

Or	*Orientalia*
OTL	OT Library
OTS	*Oudtestamentische Studiën*
OTWSA	*Die Ou Testamentiese Werkgemeenskap in Suid-Afrika*
PEQ	*Palestine Exploration Quarterly*
PJB	*Palästinajahrbuch*
RB	*Revue Biblique*
RE	J. J. Herzog, ed., *Real-encyclopädie für protestantische Theologie und Kirche*
RevBib	*Revista Bíblica*
RGG	K. Galling, ed., *Religion in Geschichte und Gegenwart* ([3]1957-65)
RHPR	*Revue d'histoire et de philosophie religieuses*
RLA	G. Ebeling and B. Meissner, eds., *Reallexikon der Assyriologie*
RSV	Revised Standard Version
SAT	Die Schriften des AT
SSN	Studia Semitica Neerlandica
ST	*Studia Theologica*
T.B.	Babylonian Talmud
TDOT	G. J. Botterweck and H. Ringgren, eds., *Theological Dictionary of the OT*
THAT	E. Jenni and C. Westermann, eds., *Theologisches Handwörterbuch zum AT*
ThZ	*Theologische Zeitschrift*
TLZ	*Theologische Literaturzeitung*
UF	*Ugarit-Forschungen*
VD	*Verbum Domini*
VT	*Vetus Testamentum*
VTS	Supplements to *VT*
WMANT	Wissenschaftliche Monographien zum Alten und Neuen Testament
WUS	J. Aistleitner, *Wörterbuch der ugaritischen Sprache* ([3]1967)
ZA	*Zeitschrift für Assyriologie*
ZAW	*Zeitschrift für die alttestamentliche Wissenschaft*
ZDMG	*Zeitschrift der Deutschen Morgenländischen Gesellschaft*
ZDPV	*Zeitschrift des Deutschen Palästina-Vereins*
ZRGG	*Zeitschrift für Religions- und Geistesgeschichte*

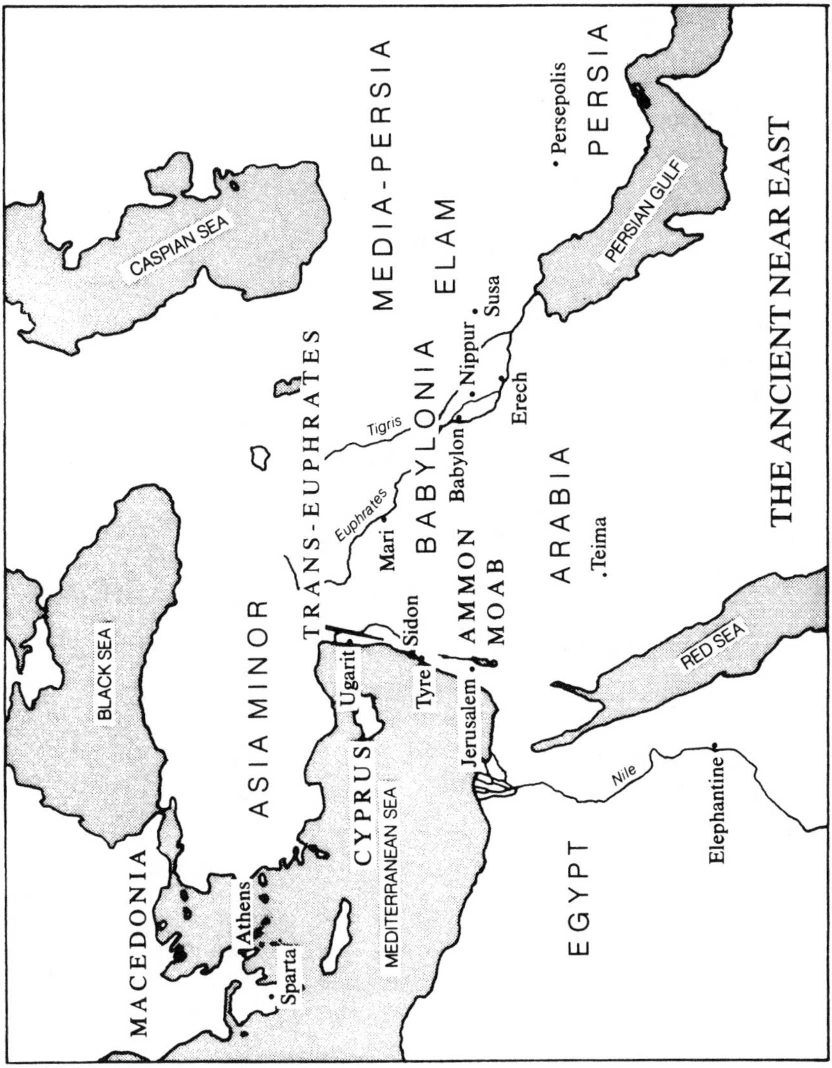
THE ANCIENT NEAR EAST
MACEDONIA
Athens
Sparta
BLACK SEA
ASIA MINOR
CYPRUS
MEDITERRANEAN SEA
Ugarit
TRANS-EUPHRATES
Sidon
Tyre
Jerusalem
AMMON
MOAB
Mari
Euphrates
Tigris
BABYLONIA
Babylon
Nippur
Erech
CASPIAN SEA
MEDIA-PERSIA
ELAM
Susa
PERSIAN GULF
Persepolis
PERSIA
ARABIA
Teima
RED SEA
EGYPT
Nile
Elephantine

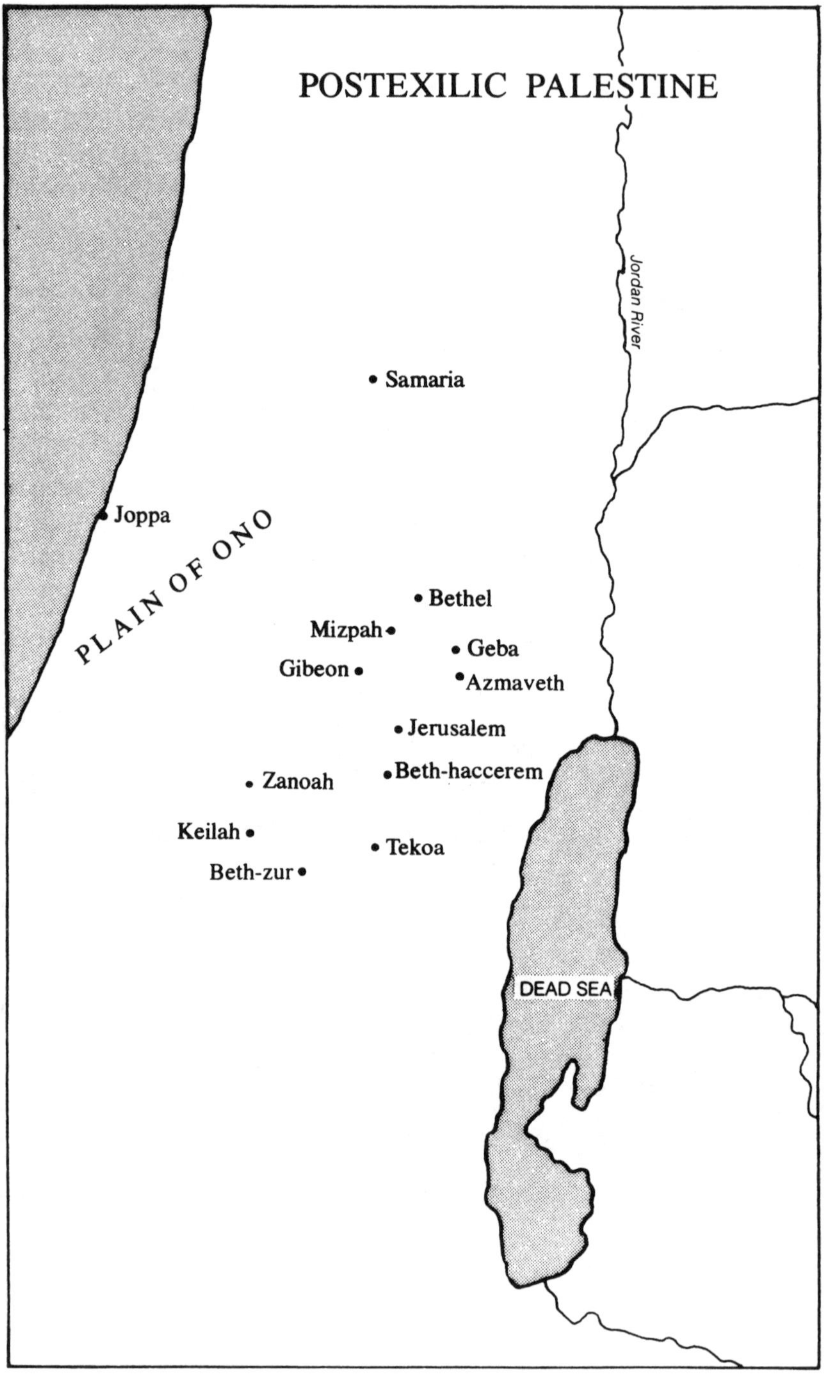
POSTEXILIC PALESTINE
Jordan River
Samaria
Joppa
PLAIN OF ONO
Bethel
Mizpah
Geba
Gibeon
Azmaveth
Jerusalem
Beth-haccerem
Zanoah
Keilah
Tekoa
Beth-zur
DEAD SEA

JERUSALEM IN THE TIME OF NEHEMIAH

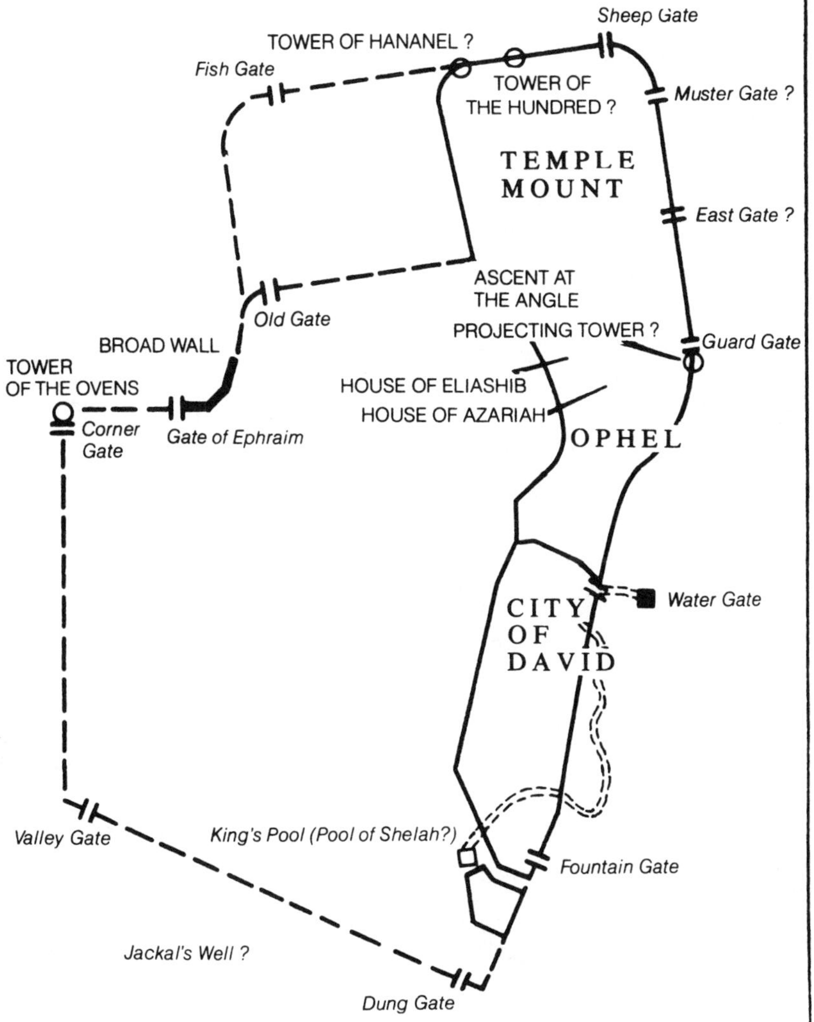

Sheep Gate
TOWER OF HANANEL ?
Fish Gate
TOWER OF
THE HUNDRED ?
Muster Gate ?
TEMPLE
MOUNT
East Gate ?
ASCENT AT
THE ANGLE
Old Gate
PROJECTING TOWER ?
Guard Gate
BROAD WALL
TOWER
OF THE OVENS
HOUSE OF ELIASHIB
HOUSE OF AZARIAH
OPHEL
Corner
Gate
Gate of Ephraim
Water Gate
CITY
OF
DAVID
Valley Gate
King's Pool (Pool of Shelah?)
Fountain Gate
Jackal's Well ?
Dung Gate

INTRODUCTION

I. ORIGINAL UNITY

The two separate books, Ezra and Nehemiah, were regarded in early times as a unity. Vestiges of this can be seen in rabbinic writings (T.B. *Baba Bathra* 15a) where the two books were regarded as a unity with Ezra as author. The same view occurs in the writings of Josephus and in Eusebius, who ascribed this position to Melito of Sardis (second century A.D.). Origen (third century A.D.) was the first to divide Ezra-Nehemiah into two books. Jerome acknowledged the division of Ezra and Nehemiah;[1] he used the same division in the Vulgate. A Hebrew manuscript dating to 1448 has the division of the two books, and it was likewise taken up in the Bomberg Bible in 1525. It is also of interest that the Masoretic notes of Ezra-Nehemiah were not placed after each book, but after Nehemiah, a proof that the Masoretes regarded Ezra-Nehemiah as a unity.[2]

In the Hebrew Bible Ezra-Nehemiah is placed before 1–2 Chronicles. This may show that Ezra-Nehemiah was received in the canon before Chronicles. The appellations Ezra and Nehemiah are appropriate, because the book of Ezra is devoted largely to the activities of Ezra and the greatest part of Nehemiah to Nehemiah's activities. Stylistic differences between the two books are also important to note.

II. AUTHORSHIP

This is one of the most difficult problems of OT research. In the exegesis certain problems are discussed that need not be repeated here. Rather, attention is drawn to the following more important views.

1. *Prologus Galeatus:* "Ezra, which itself is likewise divided amongst Greeks and Latins into two books" (E.T. 1954).
2. In the LXX the Greek (Apocryphal) Ezra occurs as 1 Esdras and the canonical Ezra and Nehemiah of the Hebrew Bible as 2 Esdras. 4 Ezra is the Ezra Apocalypse. See also below under "Text."

1. EZRA IS THE AUTHOR OF EZRA-NEHEMIAH AND 1–2 CHRONICLES

Originally stated in T.B. *Baba Bathra* 15a, this is the view held by W. F. Albright. He accepted with C. C. Torrey that the style of the Ezra memoirs and their viewpoint are identical with those of the Chronicler.[1] Thus Albright presumed that the Jewish tradition in the Babylonian Talmud was in principle correct. He accepted a date in the early fourth century B.C. for the Chronicler's final redaction.[2] But this theory is built on the assumption that Ezra started his work in 428 B.C., in the thirty-seventh year of Artaxerxes I and not in his seventh year as it stands in the MT (cf. Ezra 7:8 and Commentary). At the same time it ignores the role played by Ezra in the dedication of the wall (Neh. 12:36), which must have happened much earlier than 428 (cf. Commentary). Although Albright's view is a possibility, it is unlikely in the light of the overall picture created by the author of Ezra-Nehemiah.

2. EZRA AND NEHEMIAH WERE RESPONSIBLE FOR THEIR DISTINCTIVE BOOKS

In his survey of various viewpoints R. K. Harrison arrives at this conclusion.[3] The advantage of such a proposal is that the unique character of each of the books can be maintained. It is true that the styles of Ezra and Nehemiah are distinctively different, e.g., the tendency of Nehemiah to the short prayer, which is absent in Ezra. This difference, however, does not explain the editing of these books. As pointed out in the exegesis, traces of editing of the memoirs of Ezra and Nehemiah are clearly visible, particularly in the genealogical material; e.g., in Neh. 12:10–11 the high-priestly lineage is taken down to Jaddua, who lived in the late fifth and early fourth centuries. The switch from the first person in the memoir of Ezra to the third person also points to later editing.[4]

3. THE CHRONICLER WAS THE FINAL AUTHOR OF EZRA-NEHEMIAH

This view is generally accepted today by conservative as well as critical scholars. Opinions differ, however, on how much the Chronicler altered

1. "The Date and Personality of the Chronicler," *JBL* 40 (1921), p. 119; C. C. Torrey, *The Composition and Historical Value of Ezra-Nehemiah* (Giessen: 1896); *Ezra Studies* (1910, repr. 1970), pp. 240–48.
2. Albright, *JBL* 40 (1921), p. 112.
3. *Introduction to the OT* (Grand Rapids: 1969), pp. 1149–50.
4. See H. H. Grosheide, *Ezra-Nehemia I: Ezra*. Commentaar op het Oude Testament (Kampen: 1963), pp. 8–15.

the sources at his disposal. Some scholars, like Torrey and R. H. Pfeiffer,[5] hold the opinion that Ezra is a forgery of the Chronicler, but this extreme view is generally rejected in modern scholarship.[6] Other scholars are of the opinion that the Chronicler worked his own ideas into these books. Some accept that this was done on a grand scale, leading them to conclude that the Chronicler distorted many facts in his zeal to propagate the views of his time. Usually scholars refer to the Chronicler's preference for genealogies and his extolling of the role played by the Levites. Reference is also made to the Chronicler's anachronistic projection of the hostility of the Samaritans from his own time back to the first arrival of the exiles in 538 B.C. In the exegesis of the relevant passages we have tried to show that this view is greatly overemphasized. Many of these arguments are built on premises which are highly hypothetical.[7] Another approach would be to accept that the Chronicler compiled Ezra-Nehemiah while using some reliable sources, sometimes reproducing them verbally and other times rendering them in his own words. This positive approach of the final editing is taken, e.g., by H. H. Grosheide[8] and to a certain extent by J. M. Myers.[9]

But it is still not quite certain that the Chronicler had the final hand in the editing of Ezra-Nehemiah. Many of the arguments in favor of the Chronicler's authorship hinge on the presupposition that certain of his views are unique and wherever they appear they must be attributed to him. But our knowledge of Jewish views of the fifth century is so imperfect that no such assumption can be maintained with certainty. Indeed, the so-called typical views of the Chronicler might have been common among the Jews of that time. Thus it is not improbable that an unknown Jew, perhaps from the priestly or levitical circle, other than the Chronicler could have had the final word in Ezra-Nehemiah.

On the other hand, it still seems best to accept the Chronicler as the author of these two books, especially since 2 Chr. 36:22–23 presupposes Ezra 1. We accept with Albright that the Chronicler is basically reliable in his application of sources.[10] The Chronicler wrote a prag-

5. Torrey, *The Composition and Historical Value of Ezra-Nehemiah*; R. H. Pfeiffer, *Introduction to the OT* (New York: ²1948), pp. 813–838.

6. But cf. D. F. Robinson, "Was Ezra Nehemiah?", *ATR* 37 (1955), pp. 177–189.

7. It is thus heartening to see these presuppositions handled cautiously in two of the more recent Introductions to the OT, those of J. A. Soggin (E.T., OTL, 1976), pp. 420–25, and B. S. Childs (1979), pp. 624–638.

8. Grosheide, *Ezra*, pp. 34–35.

9. J. M. Myers, *Ezra. Nehemiah*. AB 14 (Garden City: 1965), pp. LI–LII, LXVIII–LXX.

10. W. F. Albright, "The Judicial Reform of Jehoshaphat," in S. Liebermann, ed., *Alexander Marx Jubilee Volume* (New York: 1950), pp. 61–82.

matic history, stressing certain religious themes,[11] but this tendency is typical of OT history writing. The religious message conveyed by the history is the most important aspect, a phenomenon also known from ancient Near Eastern historical texts.[12]

III. SOURCES

Although the more important problems in this connection are touched on in the exegesis, the position may be summarized as follows. Ezra 1–6 describes the history prior to the arrival of Ezra. The author had at his disposal certain sources, such as the edict of Cyrus and the receipt of the temple vessels in Ezra 1. Ezra 2 (= Neh. 7) contains a list of returnees, which could have been in the archives. For the differences between this list and that of Neh. 7 see the discussion of Ezra 2. As noted, the transmission of such a list and of the genealogies was difficult, and many textual-critical problems have developed. Ezra 3–4:5 might have been derived from an oral source of the early history of the exiles after their return from Babylon. We shall discuss in the exegesis the Aramaic source of Ezra 4:6–6:18. Too many uncertainties remain in the explanation of A. Klostermann, H. H. Schaeder, and lately Grosheide on the Tabeel theory[1] to accept it (cf. Commentary on ch. 4). It is clear, however, that the author had at his disposal the different documents from which he quotes. The reliability of these documents is accepted by a growing number of modern scholars. Ezra 7–10 constitutes the first part of the memoirs of Ezra. Some scholars contend that this whole portion was written by the Chronicler and that the occurrence of the "I-passages" is to be regarded only as literary fiction. Others accept that the Chronicler wrote this whole portion, but made use of certain historical sources. The best position is to accept with certain scholars that the "I-passages" are a verbal transmission of the Ezra memoir and that the "He-passages" are a rendering of the memoir in the words of the Chronicler.

That Neh. 1:1–7:72a comprises part of the memoir of Nehemiah

11. R. Mosis, *Untersuchungen zur Theologie des chronistischen Geschichtwerkes*. Freiburg theologische Studien 92 (Freiburg: 1973), pp. 41ff.

12. H. Cancik, *Grundzüge der hethitischen und alttestamentlichen Geschichtsschreibung* (Weisbaden: 1976), pp. 40ff.

1. A. Klostermann, "Esra und Nehemia," *RE* 5 (Leipzig: 1898), pp. 516–17; H. H. Schaeder, *Esra der Schreiber*. Beiträge zur historischen Theologie 5 (1930, repr. 1966), pp. 215–19; H. H. Grosheide, "Een geschrift van Tabeel?", *GTT* 50 (1950), pp. 71–79.

is generally accepted today.[2] Neh. 8–10 is the continuation of the Ezra memoir; the possible displacement of these chapters is unacceptable (see Commentary). The chronology is not at all clear, but quite probably the author brought these chapters into the book of Nehemiah to show that these events happened while Ezra and Nehemiah were both in Jerusalem. Neh. 11:1–13:31 takes up again the memoir of Nehemiah. It is possible that the final author inserted certain relevant material in this portion, e.g., 11:3–19, 21–24; 12:10–11.

Much has been written on the reliability of some of these sources. For example, a question mark is placed behind the reliability of sources such as Ezra 6:3–12 and 7:11–26, in which Darius and Artaxerxes give instructions that seem to be strongly influenced by Jewish conceptions. In the light of certain Persian inscriptions, however, these objections cannot be maintained (see Commentary). Unfortunately, extrabiblical sources are lacking to corroborate certain other sources in Ezra-Nehemiah. Nevertheless, a positive approach is to accept their reliability.

IV. HISTORICAL BACKGROUND

Material preserved in Ezra 1–6 provides a brief survey of the historical background of the books. Ch. 1 begins with the edict of Cyrus and reports the return to Jerusalem of the first group of Jews under Sheshbazzar c. 538 B.C. Ch. 3 describes the building of a new altar and the foundation of the temple, shortly after the arrival in Jerusalem of Sheshbazzar, Zerubbabel, and Jeshua, c. 537. Of special interest historically is the description in ch. 4 of the stern resistance from the Samaritans that immediately met these efforts. This opposition provided the author with the occasion to write down several more instances of Samaritan resistance to attempts by the Jews to rebuild the wall of Jerusalem. These incidents provide welcome historical material, although very compact and cryptic, on a period of which almost nothing is known, namely the time of Xerxes (c. 485) and the beginning of the reign of Artaxerxes I, c. 464. The description in Ezra 4:24–6:22 of the second attempt to rebuild the temple in the time of Darius (c. 519) shows that the overtures to Darius were successful and the temple was rebuilt and dedicated c. 516.

Thus it is clear that these chapters were not intended to provide a full account of postexilic Jewish history. Rather, the author recorded only

2. G. Widengren, "The Persian Period," in J. H. Hayes and J. M. Miller, eds., *Israelite and Judaean History*. OTL (Philadelphia: 1977), pp. 491–92.

certain instances which he regarded as important for understanding Jewish religious development in this period. Of primary importance for his purpose are those selected facts which emphasize the continual Samaritan opposition to the reconstruction of Jewish religious life and the reorganization of the religious community by the building of an altar and the eventual reconstruction of the temple.

In the remaining chapters, Ezra 7–Neh. 13, more complete information is given about the activities of the two most important Jewish leaders of the fifth century, Ezra and Nehemiah. The relationship between these two figures remains one of the most difficult problems of OT research.[1] Three explanations of the chronological sequence of Ezra and Nehemiah should be considered.

1. EZRA ARRIVED IN 458 B.C., BEFORE NEHEMIAH

This is the traditional approach and conforms with Ezra 7:8, which indicates that Ezra went to Jerusalem in the seventh year of Artaxerxes I. The impression created is that Ezra arrived in Jerusalem prior to Nehemiah. However, certain problems exist for ascertaining the precise relationship between Ezra and Nehemiah.

Nehemiah, the governor, is not mentioned in Ezra. This should not be surprising, because during the reforms carried out by Ezra (Ezra 7–10) Nehemiah had not yet been in Jerusalem. According to the traditional view he arrived approximately thirteen years later, in 445. In the second part of Ezra's memoirs (Neh. 8–10), Nehemiah is mentioned in connection with the reading of the law (8:9) and with the renewal of the covenant (10:2 [Eng. 1]). Ezra, however, is not mentioned in Neh. 10. Nor is Ezra mentioned in the first part of Nehemiah's memoirs (Neh. 1–7), but in the second part (Neh. 11–13) he is named in 12:36 in connection with the dedication of the wall. Some scholars, however, doubt the authenticity of the mention of Nehemiah in Neh. 8:9 and Ezra in Neh. 12:36 (see Commentary).

It is problematic that in the memoirs of Nehemiah Ezra is mentioned only once and nothing is said of his reforms of 458 B.C. However, it is clear from these memoirs that Nehemiah was to a certain extent self-centered in what he did. As evident from his short prayers, the aim of his actions was to satisfy God and to impress him with his good intentions.

1. The most recent assessment of the situation is P. R. Ackroyd, "The History of Israel in the Exilic and Post-exilic Periods," in G. W. Anderson, *Tradition and Interpretation* (Oxford: 1979), pp. 333–342.

The activities of other people were relevant only insofar as they opposed the good intentions of Nehemiah.

A few arguments have been directed against the traditional view. For example, Ezra 10 depicts the divorce from foreign women, but when Nehemiah arrived the problem had not yet been solved. Reference is also made to Ezra's vehement action against foreign marriages while Nehemiah's approach was milder (if one could call fighting and pulling out hair milder; cf. Neh. 13:25). The argument is then that the more rigid approach could only have developed later than that of Nehemiah. However, this does not take into account the various reasons for which the Jews were inclined to marry foreign women. When Nehemiah returned from Susa a few years later, he was shocked by the increase of foreign marriages. As Neh. 13 shows, even the cultic services at the temple had come to a standstill. This was one of the bleak moments in the history of Judaism, when the people were prone to forget the reforms of their leaders. If such regression could have happened in only the few years since Nehemiah had left Jerusalem (433–430), quite conceivably the same could have occurred after a thirteen-year interval from the start of Ezra's reforms (458–445).

One may envisage the events according to the traditional view as follows. Ezra arrived in Jerusalem in 458 with the sole aim—and by order of the Persian king—to promulgate a religious reform. He was at the head of a party of returnees who were typical of the various groups which had returned during the sixth and fifth centuries. Presumably, after his reforms Ezra returned to Susa.

Nehemiah arrived in Jerusalem in 445 as governor of Judah, appointed by Artaxerxes. As governor he had authority over all the Jewish activities, including all aspects of religious life. He succeeded in rebuilding the wall of Jerusalem despite the hostility of neighboring nations; he reorganized Judah economically (Neh. 5) and restored the cultic activities which had fallen into disuse after the departure of Ezra.

During Nehemiah's twelve-year stay in Jerusalem Ezra returned and supported Nehemiah's attempts to carry through his reforms. This reconstruction then explains why Nehemiah is mentioned in the second part of Ezra's memoir (Neh. 8–10) and why Ezra is mentioned in the second part of Nehemiah's memoir (Neh. 12). What became of Ezra after this is nowhere stated. Perhaps he returned to Susa. He is not mentioned in connection with Nehemiah's second arrival in Jerusalem, c. 430. Nor is what happened to Nehemiah after the reforms of his second term mentioned anywhere. The sources break off at c. 430. Nevertheless, the point is clear that the temple had been rebuilt, the wall of Jerusalem restored, the cultic activities properly organized, and the purity of the religion preserved.

2. EZRA ARRIVED IN 428 B.C., DURING NEHEMIAH'S SECOND TERM

Protagonists of this view accept that a scribal error had crept in at Ezra 7:8 and that the seventh year must be read as the thirty-seventh year of Artaxerxes I. They regard the events of Neh. 8–10 to have taken place during Nehemiah's second term. Ezra arrived with Nehemiah c. 428 and subsequently became active. This view is intended to explain certain difficulties of the traditional view, e.g., the mixed marriages, discussed above. The problem is that it presupposes a total reorganization of the material of Ezra 7–10 and the whole of Nehemiah. Moreover, it is strange that not a word is said of Ezra in Neh. 13 where the second term is expressly mentioned. If the failure of Ezra's radical reforms in 458 produces problems for scholars, the failure of Nehemiah's reforms described in Neh. 13 and the later actions of Ezra to carry through new reforms must be as problematic as the traditional view. Finally, this whole hypothesis is built on a textual error with no textual-critical evidence at all to support it.[2]

3. EZRA ARRIVED IN 398 B.C., IN THE TIME OF ARTAXERXES II

This view is built on the assumption that the activities of Ezra and Nehemiah must be separated completely. It accepts that Nehemiah arrived in Jerusalem in 445, but supposes that the Chronicler erred by suggesting that Ezra arrived in Jerusalem in the time of Artaxerxes I. Rather, his arrival should be in the time of Artaxerxes II. One of the main arguments for this view is based on Ezra 10:6, which reports that Ezra went to the chamber of Johanan (Jehohanan), the son of Eliashib (see Commentary). In Neh. 12:22 Johanan is called the grandson of Eliashib, who, it is then maintained, was high priest in the time of Nehemiah. His grandson thus could have lived only much later than Nehemiah, and the Elephantine papyri mention Johanan as high priest at the end of the fifth century.[3]

Although this hypothesis is very popular in modern research,[4] it is built on a very slender base. First, no proof whatsoever exists that the Johanan mentioned in Ezra 10:6 is the same person as the grandson of Eliashib. Indeed, Eliashib could have had more than one son, and one of them could have been called Johanan, for this was a fairly common name in the fifth century. Second, this hypothesis is built on the assumption that

2. P. R. Ackroyd, *Israel under Babylon and Persia*. New Clarendon Bible 4 (Oxford: 1970), p. 194.

3. *AP*, p. 114 (30:18).

4. O. Eissfeldt, *The OT: An Introduction* (E.T. 1965), pp. 552–53.

the mentioning of Nehemiah in the Ezra memoir and the reference to Ezra in the Nehemiah memoir must be regarded as later insertions when the Chronicler became confused about the chronological sequence of the two men. Such a mistake so close to the history it describes is extremely unlikely.

Although admittedly certain problems remain with the traditional view, it is by far the more satisfactory solution because the text as transmitted is kept intact and the sequence of the different chapters is accepted as a reliable guide to the chronology.

4. ANCIENT NEAR EASTERN HISTORICAL BACKGROUND

The historical background of the international politics at these times is very important. When Nebuchadnezzar finally demolished Jerusalem in 586 B.C. (or 587 according to some scholars), a large portion of the most important Jews, especially artisans and craftsmen, were carried to Babylon in exile. With the temple in ruins, the Jews left behind had no place to worship the Lord properly. Although an altar was erected on the site of the demolished temple, the official cult was for all practical purposes terminated. Jeremiah, belonging to a group who had warned the Jews not to rebel against the Babylonians, was left behind in Palestine. Archeological results have shown how utterly devastated Judah was. The Jews in Palestine were poor and thus not able to restore the damage done to their country. The Babylonians left after they appointed Gedaliah as governor, and the local Jewish population came out of their hiding places to try to make a living on their devastated land.

It is understandable that in these circumstances a rift appeared in Jewish circles. This rift must be described as a continuation of the difference of opinion about the feasibility of accepting Babylonian domination or looking to Egypt for salvation. Gedaliah was murdered because of his connections with the Babylonians. Although after his death a certain Johanan, a member of the Jewish Babylonian party, took over, he feared Babylonian reprisals. He and his followers decided to flee to Egypt and took Jeremiah against his wishes with them. So these Jews, together with other Jews who already had fled to Egypt, became part of a large group of Jews resident in Egypt, as also became clear after the discovery of the Elephantine papyri.

On the international scene we are poorly informed about the history of the Babylonians up to the time of Nabonidus. Only one text tells of a war between Nebuchadnezzar and the Egyptian king Amasis (570–526 B.C.). This happened c. 568 B.C. The text is too fragmentary to make any deductions from it, but it is clear that the enmity between Babylonia and Egypt did not cease. Certain cuneiform tablets on rations published by E. F. Weidner are also important.[5] From these tablets it is clear that Jehoiachin, the former Judean king, was well treated in Babylon. Later on, however, he probably fell into disfavor and was imprisoned by Nebuchadnezzar. It might have been that the hope of regaining independence flared up in Babylon and that Jehoiachin was somehow connected to it.

Evil-merodach (Amel-Marduk) became king after his father's death in 562 B.C. According to a fragment of a historical epic, Evil-merodach, that *enfant terrible,* went against anything his father Nebuchadnezzar did.[6] It is thus understandable that Jehoiachin was in these circumstances released (cf. 2 K. 25:27–30 and Jer. 52). In Babylonia instability set in when Evil-merodach was murdered by his brother-in-law, Nergal-sharusur. After his death Nabonidus took over, but he was more interested in religious activities than politics. He was in favor of the Mesopotamian god Sin instead of Marduk. The result was that the priests of Marduk became hostile to the king. He went to an oasis, Teima, in the Arabian desert and left the government of his country in the hands of his son Belshazzar.

The scene was perfectly set for a takeover by a foreign country. To the northeast, in the mountains of Iran, the young Persian king Cyrus succeeded in gaining control over the Indo-Arian Medes. The Persians and Medes became a formidable combination. Cyrus had great aspirations. He fought against the Lydians in Asia Minor and conquered their country. Afterward he moved into India with great success. Step by step he built up an empire and soon became strong enough to tackle the Babylonian empire. In the meantime Nabonidus constructed a wall north of Babylon to keep the marauding Persians and Medes out. Our sources on the fall of Babylon are very scanty indeed. It is clear, however, that Babylon and the Babylonian empire with it fell into the hands of Cyrus without any significant resistance in 539 B.C.

Cyrus was an enlightened and tolerant king. After his seizure of Babylon he released an edict in which he promised displaced peoples a return to their countries and the right to rebuild the sanctuaries of their gods. This is quite an opposite policy to that followed by the Babylonians. At the same time it was a realistic policy that would create the maximum amount of contentment among the peoples under the jurisdiction of the Persians. This created an excellent occasion for the exiled Jews in Babylon

5. E. F. Weidner, "Jojachin, König von Juda in babylonischen Keilschrifttexten," in *Mélanges Syriens offerts à M. René Dussaud* II (Paris: 1939), pp. 923–935.
6. A. K. Grayson, *Babylonian Historical Literary Texts* (Toronto: 1975), pp. 87–92.

to return to Judah and to rebuild the temple of the Lord in Jerusalem. This opportunity was taken up by Sheshbazzar and certain Jews.

Not all the Jews in Babylonia went back to Judah. A significant group stayed behind, because they had become prosperous and were satisfied with conditions in that country. They enjoyed a great amount of freedom and some of them concentrated with success on business. More than a century later the Murashu family, as we know from cuneiform tablets, started the first banking-house in human history.

Although financially assisted by their rich Jewish compatriots, the Jewish returnees were poor and ill equipped to shoulder their responsibilities in Judah. This might be one of the reasons that they stopped their work on the temple with the first signs of resistance from the local population.

After the sudden death of Cyrus during a campaign in the Indian mountains in 529 B.C., his son Cambyses took over. His greatest feat was the conquering of Egypt, which he invaded with a large army in 525 B.C. After the final submission of Egypt in 523 a rebellion broke out in Persia in his absence. A certain Gaumata (Pseudo-Smerdes) pretended to be the brother of Cambyses who had been murdered by him a few years earlier. Cambyses died in Palestine under mysterious circumstances in 522. It was probably shortly before the death of Cambyses that another group of Jewish returnees under Zerubbabel and Jeshua came back to Judah, but this is not at all certain (cf. Ezra 2 and Neh. 7).

One of the officers of Cambyses who fought with great success in Egypt was Darius, son of Hystaspes. After the death of Cambyses he took an oath to unmask Gaumata and to take control of the Persian empire. The ensuing war betwen Gaumata and Darius unsettled the Persian empire. Certain satraps (governors) of Persian provinces grasped the opportunity to become independent. In these uncertain times new hope flared up all over the ancient Near East among nations that they could become independent. It was at this time that the prophets Haggai and Zechariah inspired the Jews in Palestine to start work on the temple immediately. But Darius was a competent general. After the defeat of Gaumata and his death, Darius systematically subdued the rest of the Persian empire. By 519 B.C. he was completely in control and could give his attention to the internal affairs of his huge empire. He then ruled the whole of the ancient Near East, Asia Minor, Egypt, and even up to the Indus River.

Darius first gave his attention to the reorganizing and overhauling of the civil service and government of the Persian empire. Cyrus had laid the foundations of the Persian empire, which consisted mostly of large provinces with satraps (governors) in control who were directly responsible to the Persian king. The large province (satrapy) comprised smaller provinces with governors in control who were responsible to the satrap. But the satrap was not always in full control of them, i.e., they could be appointed or dismissed by the Persian king.

In this system of government Darius discovered certain weaknesses. A satrap of a large and powerful satrapy could revolt against the king and try to regain his independence. This happened in the uncertain times after the death of Cambyses. To counter this possibility Darius appointed only close friends as satraps, but even they could not be trusted. As a second measure of control he instituted the post of secretary of a province. This secretary was independent of the satrap and directly responsible to the king. If there was any sign of revolt from the satrap, the secretary could immediately report it to the king. A third measure of control was also built in. The king could send a state secretary at any time without warning to visit a satrapy to investigate government matters. With all these measures it became very difficult for a satrap to start a revolt. Darius thus exercised a tight control over his provinces. This tight control could be successful only if the king could appoint satraps and secretaries of high quality who would remain loyal in all circumstances. Later on in Persian history this was not the case.

A whole system of taxation was also developed. The satrap had to pay a certain amount of tax to the king and the central government. It is not clear how this amount was fixed. The satrap had to collect this royal taxation from the governors of the smaller provinces of his satrapy. The satrap and his civil servants were, however, not paid by the king; the satrap had to collect his pay and that of his civil servants from the provinces. Thus the governors of the smaller provinces had to collect taxation from their subjects for the satrap and for the king. But there was also a third category of tax. The governor of a smaller province had also to collect tax from his subjects for his own subsistence and for that of his civil servants. It was thus a threefold kind of taxation. As long as a tight control was exercised on the expenditures of the king, the satrap, and the local governors, taxation did not become too heavy a burden. Gradually, however, the king's court became so luxurious that expenditures grew to alarming heights, as in the time of Xerxes and Artaxerxes I. The moment this happened, discontent became rampant and the Persian empire was in danger.

Darius was not only an able organizer of the internal affairs of his empire, he was also a conqueror. In western Asia Minor Darius had jurisdiction over various Greek cities. This area was a real hornets' nest of unrest, stirred up by the Greek city-states in Greece proper. At the same time there had been a struggle for supremacy between the merchant fleets of Persia and Greece. Persia was fortunate enough to have at its disposal the fleet of the Phoenicians, seasoned sailors and merchants who had sailed all over the Mediterranean to sell their merchandise. Their strongest competitor was the Greek fleet, especially the one of Athens and its allies. One must keep in mind that Greece did not form a unity. The different city-states continually opposed each other and local wars often broke out. This was in favor of the Persians, and Persian gold was used to fan the flames of local Greek differences.

The situation came to a head and Darius decided to make an end to Greek influence. He set foot on European soil with an army of 700,000 men, the largest army up to that time, large even according to modern standards. He first attacked a number of cities west of the Black Sea, probably to cut off supplies of timber which the Greeks used to build their ships. But this was a complete failure, because the local population had fled deeper into the country after they had destroyed their crops. It was impossible for Darius to proceed any further without the loss of the largest part of his army through starvation. He then decided to attack Athens directly. Darius had previously sent a fleet of 600 ships to subdue the Greeks, but most of the ships were destroyed by a storm near Athos. A second fleet under Datis the Mede was dispatched. Datis was more successful and landed at Eretria. But here Datis made a diplomatic blunder. Within the city people disagreed about whether they should submit to the Persians. The city was taken by the Persians after an act of treason. After the city was conquered, Datis decided to demolish it completely and to take the whole population into slavery, even the people who were in favor of the Persians. The result of this blunder was that city-states which had been in favor of Persia rallied to the side of Athens. The huge army of the Persians was opposed by the Greeks on the plain of Marathon. Athens and its allies scored a resounding victory, even before the hesitant Spartans arrived to assist them. After this setback to Persian domination the Greeks were left alone for a while.

The biblical sources describe a situation at the beginning of the reign of Darius. In 519 B.C., as we have seen, Darius came in full control of the Persian empire. This is clearly reflected in the inquiries made by the governor of the province of Trans-Euphrates about the right of the Jews to rebuild the temple (Ezra 5–6). The edict of Cyrus that was discovered gave them that right and Darius honored it. The temple was completed and dedicated still in the early years of Darius. The king's positive attitude toward the Jews and Judah must be interpreted not only as continuing the policy of Cyrus, but also as being politically expedient for the king. Egypt was conquered only in 523 B.C., and it was necessary to have loyal subjects so close to Egypt, which was always a difficult country to dominate. We must also keep in mind that in those times Judah formed part of the whole system of Persian provincial government, including their system of taxation. After the rebuilding of the temple, it seems likely that the system of tithes was instituted to make the cult functional. This means that the Jews in Judah, already very poor, had to pay a fourfold tax, for the king, the satrap, the governor of the local province, and a tithe to the temple. This was indeed a heavy burden.

Darius was succeeded in 486 B.C. by his son Xerxes. His long reign up to 465 B.C. is reflected only in one verse in Ezra (Ezra 4:6) and in the story of Esther. Our knowledge of him comes mainly from Greek sources, which were hostile to him because he, like his father, had decided to attack Greece with a large army. He mustered a formidable army and collected a huge fleet to settle the issue with Athens once and for all. He easily overpowered the city-states north of Athens and then succeeded in conquering Athens. The last resistance on land was broken at the Isthmus near Corinth. But on sea the final victory was still wanting. At Salamis a sea battle was fought and ended in a great victory for the Greeks. With the supplies from the ships for the Persian army cut off they had to retreat as fast as possible. The result was that for the second time in ten years (Marathon in 490 and Salamis 480) the Greeks were victorious over the Persians. This victory did not mean that the Greeks were able to conquer Persian territory; they succeeded only in maintaining their independence and having a free hand in trade in the Mediterranean. At the same time they gradually undermined Persian influence, although the Persians still used their gold to keep the Greeks divided.

Xerxes inherited an established and organized empire from his father. Persian government and the civil service were functioning well. Xerxes, however, was an arrogant and fickle king, fond of extravagant parties. Occasionally trouble flared up in his harem. This was detrimental to the stability of the state. Xerxes also had a luxurious court, and taxes had to be raised to pay for it. Higher taxes resulted in dissatisfaction in the provinces. It was no longer easy to be a Persian subject. People could not understand why they should be taxed to pay for the extravagancies at court far away in Persia. But Darius had organized his state so well that a firm grip could be exercised on the provinces. Darius, however, was a just king who could be trusted; Xerxes on the contrary was fickle and unreliable. This was the beginning of the decay of an empire which had to suffer under unreliable kings, though it continued for more than a century.

Artaxerxes *(Longimanus)* became king in 465 B.C. and reigned until 424 B.C. Thus he was king, according to our analysis set out above, during the times of Ezra and Nehemiah. The whole effort of Artaxerxes during his long reign was to keep his empire intact. Occasionally he had to cope with internal unrest, caused mainly by his continuing the policies of his father. The court remained luxurious and expenditures rapidly increased. Herodotus, the Greek historian who visited Persia during the reign of Artaxerxes, gives us a list of taxation. Babylonia was detached from the province of the Trans-Euphrates and Cyprus was added to it. We must keep in mind that Judah formed part of this province. According to Herodotus the province of Trans-Euphrates had to pay to the royal court 350 talents of gold, a heavy burden indeed. The policy was then followed that what was left of the gold after the expenses of the court were deducted was stored up. The result was that gold became scarce and the empire had less gold to circulate. This was economically a bad policy.

It is thus understandable that unrest and revolt should develop. Artaxerxes had to cope with two revolts early in his reign, during the time of Ezra and Nehemiah. The first revolt broke out in Egypt, but was not unrelated to the Greek-Persian conflicts. In the Mediterranean there was still a struggle for supremacy of the sea trade. The Athenians under the leadership of Pericles had decided to attack the island of Cyprus, one of the Persian strongholds for control of the sea trade in the Mediterranean. Their aim was to break Persian domination of the eastern Mediterranean. Before they could accomplish this, a revolt broke out in Egypt with Inarus an Egyptian and descendant of the Saitic dynasty as leader. The Athenians then decided to assist the Egyptians in their struggle against the Persians. Initially, in the years 460 and 459 B.C., they had success against the Persians. In 459 only a small strip of land was still in Persian hands. It became clear to the Persians that the only way out was to divert the attention of the Athenians somehow. They succeeded in bribing the Spartans with gold to attack Athens. The immediate result was that the Athenians had to withdraw from Egypt to defend themselves against their archenemies. The Egyptians alone were not equal to the task of defeating a new large Persian army under the Persian nobleman Megabyzus. The Persians suppressed the revolt in 456. It was at this time of uncertainty, according to our opinion, that Artaxerxes sent out Ezra for his religious reform in Judah. It was politically the right attitude to pacify his Jewish subjects so close to the border of Egypt. Judah was in a certain sense a buffer state and thus very important to the Persians.

Out of this event developed the second revolt. Megabyzus, the general of the Persian army in Egypt, was at the same time the satrap of the province of Trans-Euphrates, the province bordering on Egypt. When he had defeated the Egyptians and a small Greek army left after the Athenian army had departed, Megabyzus generously promised the captured Egyptian Inarus and certain Greek generals their release after the war. This was in accordance with the tolerant policy of earlier Persian kings like Cyrus and, to a lesser extent, Darius. However, the king's mother, former wife of Xerxes, demanded their death. Artaxerxes was uncertain what to do, but finally he gave in to his mother's wish. This came as a blow to Megabyzus because he had given his word of honor to his enemies to release them. He went back to the Trans-Euphrates and eventually started a revolt against the Persian king in 449 B.C., a revolt that Artaxerxes was not able to put down. After a while Megabyzus decided that he had made his point and became loyal again. He was pardoned by the king and continued his work as a satrap.

It is important to note that shortly after the revolt of Megabyzus Nehemiah was allowed to go to Jerusalem to rebuild the wall and to organize the province of Judah. Nehemiah was a loyal subject of Artaxerxes and could be trusted. It was under the circumstances very important for Artaxerxes to have a loyal governor in one of his minor provinces.

It is thus clear that Artaxerxes had difficulties in keeping his empire intact. The Greeks were ready to make use of any occasion to undermine Persian authority. The heavy burden of taxation created unrest in the Persian empire. At court, intrigues abounded and murders were planned and executed. Slowly the way was opened for the great Macedonian Greek Alexander to conquer the Persian empire more than a century later.

V. THEOLOGY

In preexilic Israel the religious cult was organized around the temple in Judah and around sanctuaries in the north, notably Bethel and Dan. One of the most important functions of the temple was to provide opportunity to atone for sins by sacrifice (later aptly described in Heb. 9). On the Day of Atonement the high priest was required to enter the Holy of Holies to atone for his own sins and for those of his people. Throughout preexilic times, the Israelites were assured by this religious practice that their sins were forgiven by the Lord. Indeed, the prophets warned against a mechanical execution of this cult, but still the people were satisfied that the burdens of sin were lifted from their shoulders. As a religion with high ethical principles, Israelite religion, like Christianity, emphasized the guilt of the people. A sense of guiltiness developed that could only be removed by atonement of sins. With the destruction of the temple, this privilege had been taken away. This must be regarded as one of the major catastrophes which had overtaken the Jews.[1] Their whole religious life was disorganized by it. It is thus not surprising that the first act after the restoration was to build an altar and to begin reconstruction of the temple. Now for the first time since the Exile the Jews were able to atone properly for their

1. M. Schmidt, *Prophet und Tempel* (Zurich: 1948).

sins. The rebuilding of the temple was not simply an act of restoration of a venerable old building, but was of the highest religious significance. Similar activity followed the destruction of the Second Temple. The emphasis of the author of Hebrews on the eternal atonement by Christ the High Priest opened up a totally new view for the Jews about atonement for sins, and it became one of the cornerstones of Christianity.

As the prophets have shown, the continual atonement for sins could easily become mere custom and thus not a living reality. It was so easy to take a lamb to the altar as an offering yet live daily in disregard of all the religious principles implied in the religion of the Lord. The reforms of Ezra and Nehemiah, with their heavy emphasis on the law, are to be regarded as an attempt to counteract such a way of life. The lives of the Jews were to be in accordance with the principles of their religion, as laid down in these legal prescriptions. The reading and interpreting of the law confronted the people with their neglect of these principles. Certain festivals were reinstated, and the cult was reorganized to fulfil the requirements of the law. But this way of life organized by Ezra and Nehemiah was concerned not only with keeping legal prescriptions, but also with living in accordance with the ethical principles laid down by the Lord. Neh. 5 is a good example of how the ethical principles had been carried out. It is clear that only a merely formal keeping of the law was rejected. The religion of the Lord is a way of life and a living reality that grows out of a living relationship with the Lord. Ezra and Nehemiah were the first to set the example. Their prayers to the Lord give evidence of a realization of their relationship with the Lord and the acceptance that only through him could their ideals be fulfilled.

Thus it is not surprising that the covenant relationship is so heavily stressed in the memoirs of both Ezra and Nehemiah. The covenant was the vehicle that had given expression to the relationship between the Lord and his people since the time of the patriarchs. Before and during the Exile the covenant idea was more fully worked out, especially by Jeremiah.[2] An important aspect of the covenant was its promissory character and the expectations it created.[3] This was most important for the survival of the religion of the Lord, and must be counted as one of the reasons why postexilic Jewish religion has persisted under the most difficult circumstances. The covenant not only gave expression to a relationship with the Lord, but also described a relationship of the partners of the covenant, the Jewish people. It was therefore an important binding force. Love to God

2. J. Bright, *Covenant and Promise* (Philadelphia: 1976), pp. 140ff.
3. F. C. Fensham, "Covenant, Promise and Expectation in the Bible," *ThZ* 23 (1967), pp. 305–322.

and love to one's neighbor were equally important. At this stage the neighbor was regarded as the Jewish companion and not a member of any other foreign nation. It is in this light that the stern steps taken by Nehemiah against exploitation of fellow Jews must be understood (Neh. 5). The covenant relationship was clearly a living relationship, and the prescriptions of this covenant had to be kept in everyday life.

Against this background it is understandable that purity of religion is stressed in Ezra-Nehemiah. Sometimes this purity of religion seems to have been confused with purity of blood among the Jewish descendants. But one must keep in mind that the Jews were at that moment in history the carriers of the Lord's revelation. Contamination of their religion with foreign elements, which could alter considerably the orthodox conceptions, was regarded as such a danger that everything possible was done to combat it.

This should not imply that the world around the Jews exercised no influence on them. No one at any time of history could be totally free from the influence of environment. Rather, the emphasis on purity concerned mainly those things from the world in which the Jews lived that were incompatible with the principles of their religion. The most dangerous threat came from a surrogate of their religion, such as the Samaritan or Ammonite form. In opposition to this, Ezra and Nehemiah stressed the pure or orthodox form, a tendency already present, for example, in 1–2 Kings against the syncretistic religion of the northern kingdom. The Jewish exiles came to live in a Judah surrounded by all kinds of religions as well as surrogates of their own religion. They were poor and to a certain extent dependent on their foreign neighbors for their business. It was impossible to exclude foreign contact (cf. Neh. 13:16). In such circumstances the way of the least resistance would be to accept certain principles of the foreign neighbors in order to live in peaceful coexistence. But these principles might be incompatible with the principles of the Jewish religion, such as the sabbath law (Neh. 13:15–22). Once they had conceded on certain points, it would become more and more difficult to keep up the principles of their own religion. The next step would be to become so familiar and associate on such a friendly footing with foreigners that intermarriage became possible. The danger of this development was grasped fully by Ezra and Nehemiah. Once intermarriage was allowed, the purity of the religion of the Lord would be in jeopardy, because of the potential influence of foreigners on the children of such marriages.

Therefore, strong-minded leaders like Ezra and Nehemiah were necessary to take stern measures to protect the purity of the religion. Ezra and Nehemiah were not driven to these actions out of nationalistic feelings, but from a concern to protect the religious cult of the Lord. In a word, they were religiously motivated. They were also aware of the special call and task of the returned exiles to serve the Lord in accordance with the prescriptions of his law. They were an elect group with a special mission to serve the Lord in the context of a pure religion. It is amazing that such a small, poor group of people could have become the foundation for the development of one of the largest religions of modern times, Christianity. But in the religion of the Lord it is not numbers but purity of the heart that counts. This purity of heart is clearly discernible in the activities of Ezra and Nehemiah. Their piety, their devotion to God, and their sense of the living relationship with God stand out clearly.

Another feature discernible in the writings of Ezra and Nehemiah is what may be called the "religious-historical" approach. By "religious-historical" is meant not the theological discipline called by that name, but the OT tendency to interpret history in terms of the actions of God. He is the God of history, and his will is revealed through the historical process, as becomes evident in the three major prayers in Ezra-Nehemiah (Ezra 9; Neh. 1; 9). Everything that happened in the past to Israel is interpreted as the will of God; their moments of decline and their moments of success are ascribed to his will. Likewise, events in the time of Ezra and Nehemiah also are ascribed to him. The favorable disposition of Cyrus (Ezra 1; cf. also Isa. 45) and the friendly attitude of Artaxerxes are worked by the Lord (cf. Neh. 1:11). Hence, the Lord not only determines the history of his own people, but also fulfils his will through the mighty kings of foreign nations.

Also in this historical process is interaction between the acts of Israel and those of the Lord, as best described in Neh. 9. This prayer depicts the interaction of Israel's long history of infidelity to the Lord and his reaction against it. The prayer of Ezra 9 also was occasioned by such disobedience on the part of the returned exiles. Both Ezra and Nehemiah clearly accepted their responsibility for this disobedience by demonstrating their solidarity with their people, even with the sins and disobedience of their ancestors. At the end the returnees had nothing to offer to God to save them; only through his grace and covenant love could they be saved (cf. Neh. 9:33ff.). Thus in the stream of history is the undercurrent of the will of God that steers the history of his people in a given direction, guided by his grace and love for his people. He directed their history and brought them into new situations such as that in Judah after the Exile. This was the starting point of a new form of religious life known as Judaism, which found its consummation in the coming of Christ and a totally new direction in the relationship between the Lord and mankind.

VI. TEXT

The Hebrew text of Ezra-Nehemiah has been fairly well transmitted. The Commentary refers to certain textual-critical difficulties, such as a few places where the text makes no sense and should be emended, and other instances in which the transmitted text can be maintained and explained from certain grammatical features in Biblical Hebrew or from the Northwest Semitic languages.

The LXX rendering of the canonical books Ezra-Nehemiah (titled 2 Esdras in the LXX) is represented by various manuscript traditions. An assessment of the recensions of the LXX is an entire study in its own right. However, the important variations between two of the most important codices, Vaticanus (LXX^B) and Alexandrinus (LXX^A), are to be noted. Furthermore, it is important to observe that the LXX is in some places shorter than the MT. Nevertheless, the value of the LXX for textual-critical problems in Ezra-Nehemiah should not be underestimated. The differences between the MT and the LXX are usually explained as a different interpretation of the MT by the LXX. With the discovery at Qumran of a Hebrew original of the strongly divergent LXX text of Jeremiah, Samuel, and Chronicles, this is no longer certain. The Qumran fragments of Ezra-Nehemiah, however, have not been studied sufficiently to warrant any conclusion.[1]

It is difficult to determine the value of 1 Esdras for studying the text of Ezra-Nehemiah. Quite possibly 1 Esdras is a translation from a Hebrew-Aramaic source. Interestingly, 1 Esdras was popular in the early Church until about the sixth century A.D., but was later regarded as noncanonical. Its early popularity must be ascribed to its presence in the LXX, which was generally venerated in the early Church.[2]

The apocryphal 2 Esdras (not to be confused with LXX 2 Esdras, which is the Greek text of Ezra-Nehemiah), also called IV Ezra or the Ezra Apocalypse, was probably written late in the first century A.D. It has no bearing on the canonical books.[3]

1 Esdras, the first book of the Apocrypha, starts with the Jewish history from the time of Josiah (cf. 2 Chr. 35:1ff.) and concludes in the time of Ezra. At the end of the canonical Chronicles the edict of Cyrus

1. For a discussion of the text of the writings cf. W. H. Brownlee, *The Meaning of the Qumrân Scrolls for the Bible* (New York: 1964), pp. 27ff.
2. For the importance of the LXX in the early Church see D. Y. Hadidian, "The Septuagint and its Place in Theological Education," *ExpT* 76 (1964/65), pp. 102–103 (= repr. in S. Jellicoe, ed., *Studies in the Septuagint* [New York: 1974], pp. 580–82).
3. See G. H. Box, "IV Ezra," in R. H. Charles, *The Apocrypha and Pseudepigrapha of the OT II: Pseudepigrapha* (Oxford: 1913), pp. 542–624.

is given and the canonical Ezra takes it up again, but 1 Esdras of the LXX smooths this out and directly connects it to the return under Sheshbazzar. This is followed, however, by a description of the correspondence of Persian high officials with Artaxerxes (*sic*) and of the interruption of building activities on the temple up to the time of Darius. This points to a mix-up of the historical situation in which Cyrus and Artaxerxes are interchanged. 1 Esdras then continues in recounting a story (without any historical value) of guardsmen in the time of Darius. This material does not occur in the canonical Ezra. After this story the history according to the canonical Ezra is again taken up, but the confusion of historical events is obvious. A second return under Zerubbabel is described that is connected to the list of returnees in the canonical Ezra 2 (cf. also Neh. 7). 1 Esdras then describes the completion of the building of the temple. The history is again taken up with the third return under Ezra and his measures against mixed marriages. The book concludes with a description of the reading of the law by Ezra, which occurs in Neh. 7:72–8:13.

It is obvious that we have here a mixture of phantasy and fact. It is of interest to note that only Ezra plays an important role in 1 Esdras; Nehemiah is completely omitted. It is also interesting that Josephus had a high regard for 1 Esdras and almost completely followed it in his description of this part of Jewish history.

VII. LANGUAGE

The grammar of Ezra-Nehemiah shows all the features present in postexilic Hebrew. It is a later development of Hebrew and should not be interpreted in the light of the grammar of preexilic Hebrew. Furthermore, influence from Aramaic can be detected in places. The Aramaic portions of Ezra reflect what is generally called Imperial Aramaic,[1] which is now well known from the Aramaic papyri from Egypt. Quite a few Persian loanwords have been employed (see Commentary), a reflection of the time in which the books originated. Some fourteen Persian words occur 41 times in Ezra-Nehemiah, only five of which are in the Hebrew sections. This disparity is to be expected, because the diplomatic vernacular of the Persian empire was Imperial Aramaic, which was thus more prone to accept loanwords than Biblical Hebrew.

The fourteen Persian loanwords are:

1. The name "Imperial Aramaic" (*Reichsaramäisch*) was coined in 1927 by J. Markwart; see H. H. Schaeder, *Iranische Beiträge* 1 (1930, repr. 1972), p. 2.

'aḏrazdā'	(Ezra 7:23)
'^{a}pars^{e}ḵāyē'	(Ezra 5:6)
'āsparnā'	(Ezra 5:8; 6:8, 12, 13; 7:17, 21, 26)
'eštaddûr	(Ezra 4:15, 19)
'uššarnā'	(Ezra 5:3, 9)
gizzaḇrayyā'	(Ezra 1:8; 7:21)
ginzayyā'	(Ezra 5:17; 6:1; 7:20)
dāṯā'	(Ezra 7:12, 25, 26)
hattiršāṯā'	(Ezra 2:63; Neh. 7:65)
zimnā'	(Ezra 5:3; Neh. 2:6)
ništ^{e}wān	(Ezra 4:7, 18, 23; 5:5; 7:11)
paršeg̱en	(Ezra 4:11, 23; 5:6; 7:11)
piṯgāmā'	(Ezra 4:17; 5:7, 11; 7:11)
š^{e}rōšiw	(Ezra 7:26)

For their meaning see the discussion of the relevant texts.

The Hebrew of Ezra-Nehemiah is clearly postexilic. It shares many features with the Hebrew of Chronicles. We want to draw attention to a few special features of the postexilic Hebrew of Ezra-Nehemiah.

First, we want to call attention to certain morphological deviations from preexilic and exilic Hebrew: Certain personal names have the Aramaic ending *-ā'* (cf., e.g., Ezra 2:48, 55; 10:23; Neh. 7:57). An interesting phenomenon is that a *waw*-consecutive first-person singular has an -â ending (e.g., Ezra 8:24 and Neh. 13:8).[2] There is also evidence that sometimes the intervocalic *hē* is retained, e.g., *y^{e}hôḏeh* (Neh. 11:17). Myers has pointed out that there is not nearly so much plene spelling as one might expect.[3] However, a form of the Hiphil *waw*-consecutive *wayyāḇî'* instead of *wayyāḇē'* (Neh. 8:2) is to be noted.

A new formation of late forms does also occur, e.g., *wā'ôṣ^{e}râ* in Neh. 13:13 and other examples ending on *-â* mentioned above.

Second, we want to draw attention to certain syntactical phenomena which can be classified as late. The distributive use of the preposition *b^e* is a fairly late usage, e.g., in Ezra 3:4 and Neh. 8:18. There are also examples of this usage in Chronicles.[4] The same is true of the usage of the preposition *'al* in connection with the indirect object (cf. Ezra 7:28 and Ezek. 1:19). Another important feature is the usage of the article as a relative before the perfect of the verb (cf. Ezra 8:25; 10:14, 17). This is

2. See H. Bauer and P. Leander, *Historische Grammatik der hebräischen Sprache des AT* (1922, repr. 1965), p. 333.
3. Myers, *Ezra. Nehemiah*, p. LXIII.
4. Cf. R. J. Williams, *Hebrew Syntax: An Outline* (Toronto: 1967), p. 49.

also fairly late. Another late feature is the usage of *'ayin* with the infinitive construct as gerundive (e.g., Ezra 9:15; 2 Chr. 20:6).[5] From these examples it is clear that various structural changes took place in Hebrew after the Exile.

A fair number of loanwords and new Hebrew formations occur in Ezra-Nehemiah. We have already referred to the Persian loanwords which occur especially in the Aramaic parts of Ezra. This is most significant, as we have pointed out. Quite a few Aramaic words are also present, as one may expect, e.g., *ribbō'* in Ezra 2:64 and Neh. 7:70. Further, the Jewish returnees came from Babylon where Babylonian was used. We have pointed out that the names Sheshbazzar and Zerubbabel are clearly Babylonian. Certain Babylonian loanwords also found their way into postexilic Hebrew, e.g., *peḥâ* and *middâ* (cf. Neh. 5:4). Thus Hebrew was influenced by Aramaic, Babylonian, and Persian. The influence of the Semitic languages, Aramaic and Babylonian, was much more pervasive than that of Persian. It is clear that Persian loanwords were taken over through Imperial Aramaic. This is to be expected because Imperial Aramaic became the *lingua franca* of the Persian empire and certain Persian technical terms became a necessity.

These examples, which are only a selection, show that various changes took place in the Hebrew of postexilic times. They also show that the influences of the times had their effect on the development of the language.

VIII. PERSONAL AND FAMILY NAMES

The study of personal names in the Bible is an intriguing subject. Various scholars have studied personal names in cuneiform tablets to discern the influence of a certain group of the population on a certain country, e.g., Amorite personal names have been studied to determine the influence of the Amorites on the ancient Near East.[1] The study of H. Huffmon concentrates on the grammatical structure of the names in an attempt to discover certain characteristics of Amorite grammar. J. J. Stamm has studied the most important Akkadian names to determine their composition.[2] Also important are the works of F. Gröndahl on Ugaritic names,[3] F. Benz on

5. *Ibid.*, pp. 69–70.
1. H. B. Huffmon, *Amorite Personal Names in the Mari Texts* (Baltimore: 1965).
2. J. J. Stamm, *Die Akkadische Namengebung* (1968).
3. F. Gröndahl, *Die Personennamen der Texte aus Ugarit* (Rome: 1967).

Phoenician-Punic names,[4] and M. Coogan on West Semitic names in some Neo-Babylonian texts.[5] From these studies it is clear that the forming of personal names was executed in the same way in the Semitic world and the principles involved remained the same for many centuries.

The study of Hebrew personal names has a long history. The first in modern times to tackle this subject was G. B. Gray.[6] This pioneer attempt still has its value. An exhaustive study was made by M. Noth in 1928.[7] It was followed by a shorter but useful study in Dutch by B. J. Oosterhoff.[8] The names in postexilic times are specially studied by L. H. Brockington[9] and M. Heltzer and M. Ohana.[10]

1. CERTAIN PROBLEMS

One of the important questions in the study of postexilic Hebrew personal names is whether the names still had meaning for the people of those times. Did people associate the name Jeremiah or its shortened form *yir-mᵉyâ* (Neh. 10:3 [Eng. 2]; 12:1, 34) with the meaning "may the Lord lift up"? It is very difficult to give a satisfactory reply to this question, because nowhere in our sources is there any indication whether the meaning of names still played a role. If names were used for many centuries, one must expect that they became fossilized and did not convey any wish or message to the people. We have various names in Ezra-Nehemiah that also occurred in earlier times, e.g., Hilkiah (Neh. 12), Jehonathan (Neh. 12), Baruch (Neh. 10), Zadok (Neh. 10), Hananiah (Neh. 12).

Another problem is the use of personal names and family names. It is not clear, especially in Ezra 2 and Neh. 7, whether personal names or family names are used. We must accept that a family name represents the personal name of a famous ancestor, the founder of a clan. In Neh. 11–12 a clear distinction is made between ancestors and people of later times (cf., e.g., the descendants of Judah's son Perez in Neh. 11:4). If we compare this with, e.g., Pahath-moab in Ezra 2 and Neh. 7, there is no

4. F. L. Benz, *Personal Names in the Phoenician and Punic Inscriptions* (Rome: 1972).

5. M. D. Coogan, *West Semitic Personal Names in the Murasu Documents* (Missoula: 1976).

6. G. B. Gray, *Studies in Hebrew Proper Names* (London: 1896).

7. M. Noth, *Die israelitischen Personennamen im Rahmen der gemeinsemitischen Namengebung*. BWANT III/10 (1928, repr. 1980).

8. B. J. Oosterhoff, *Israëlitische Persoonsnamen* (1953).

9. L. H. Brockington, *Ezra, Nehemiah and Esther*. NCB (1969, repr. 1977), pp. 40–45.

10. M. Heltzer and M. Ohana, *The Extrabiblical Tradition of Hebrew Personal Names* (1978), Excursus I (in Hebrew).

indication whether this is the name of a clan or that a person Pahath-moab with his family returned to Judah.

2. THE USE OF NAMES REFLECTS A CERTAIN TIME

Stamm has determined that the giving of new names never stopped, although the same principles of giving names were observed.[11] The same is true of Hebrew names. Although earlier names were used again, new names were also formed. By far the majority of names in Ezra and Nehemiah do not occur in earlier writings.

As we have already seen, certain personal names with an Aramaic form appear in Ezra-Nehemiah. It is interesting that these names are mainly those of people of a lower social stratification, among the Nethinim (Ezra 2:43ff.), e.g., *ṣîḥā'*, *ḥ^{a}śûpā'*, *sî'^{a}hā'*, *n^{e}qôḏā'*, *ḥ^{a}qûpā'*, *m^{e}ḥîḏā'*, *ḥar^{e}šā'*, and *ḥ^{a}ṭîpā'*. Among the servants of Solomon we have the same phenomenon (cf. Ezra 2:55ff.), e.g., *p^{e}rûḏā'*. This is exactly what one should expect. The lower social strata were particularly prone to outside influence.

On the other hand names like Sheshbazzar and Zerubbabel show some influence from Babylonia on groups of the higher social stratification. The presence of the name Zerubbabel is significant because he was of royal lineage. As we have seen, Jehoiachin, the father of Zerubbabel, was well treated at the Babylonian court and later even set free. The ex-king, his family, and the royal servants lived in close proximity to the Babylonian court and were thus influenced to some extent.

The great majority of names in Ezra-Nehemiah are Hebrew names formed according to certain old principles. Some of the names had a longer history of usage, as we have seen; others a shorter time, e.g., Jehohanan (Neh. 12:17). Other names occur for the first time in Ezra-Nehemiah. We must be cautious not to deduce too much from this phenomenon, because in Ezra-Nehemiah we have an especially large number of names in comparison with other books.

3. NAMES WITH THEOPHORIC ELEMENTS

Scholars have in the past drawn attention to the significance of theophoric elements in names for a better understanding of the religious history of a given time. It is to be noted that in the times which Ezra-Nehemiah describe only two elements were still in use, i.e., Yahweh and El, both of them referring to the God of Israel. The names are too numerous to discuss

11. Stamm, *op. cit.*, p. 4.

all of them and give their meanings, but a few examples will serve as illustrations.

One of the old principles in forming a theophoric personal name is to use an averbal or nominal clause which might be a statement or a question. A few examples may suffice:

Eliehoenai—To Yahweh are my eyes (Ezra 8:4)

Besodeiah—In the counsel of Yahweh (Neh. 3:8)

One example of a question as a nominal clause is:

Michael—Who is like God? (Ezra 8:8)

Another old principle is the combination of the theophoric element with the perfect of the verb. Note the following:

Jozabad—Yahweh has granted (Ezra 8:33; 10:23; Neh. 11:16)

Jonathan—Yahweh has given (Neh. 12:17)

Elnathan—God has given (Ezra 8:16)

Johanan—Yahweh is merciful (Neh. 12:22)

There are numerous examples of the combination of the theophoric element with the imperfect of the verb. The imperfect usually represents a pious wish:

Joiarib—May Yahweh defend the case (Neh. 12:5)

Eliashib—May God return (or restore) (Ezra 10:6)

Eliakim—May God establish (Neh. 12:41)

Only three examples occur of the theophoric element combined with the participle:

Meshezabel—God is one who delivers (Neh. 3:4)

Mehetabel—God is one who is beneficent (Neh. 6:10)

Mahalalel—God is one who gives light (Neh. 11:4)

Shortened forms occur occasionally, usually with the theophoric element omitted:

Bani—Yahweh has built (Ezra 10:34)

Bunni—Yahweh has built (Neh. 9:4)

Zabad—Yahweh has granted (Ezra 10:33)

We also have shortened forms with hypocoristic endings, like *-ai* and *-i*:

Shashai—The sixth part of. . . .(?) (Ezra 10:40)

Ahzai—Yahweh has grasped (Neh. 11:13)

Shimei—Listen, O Yahweh(?) (Ezra 10:38)

Zabdi—God (or Yahweh) has granted (Neh. 11:17)

It is to be noted that in these hypocoristic forms a theophoric element is not always necessary, as Noth has pointed out.[12]

12. Noth, *op. cit.*, p. 41.

4. NAMES DESCRIBING SOME CHARACTERISTICS OF A PERSON

As Stamm has point out for Akkadian names—and we must accept it also for Hebrew personal names—a name was given immediately after the birth of a child.[13] There also occurs, however, according to Stamm, a change of names when certain characteristics of a person become prominent.[14] We want to draw attention to certain examples:

Bakbuk—Flask (Ezra 2:51)—Squarely built(?)
Barzillai—Man of iron (Ezra 2:61)
Hagab—Locust (Ezra 2:46)
Hariph—The sharp one (Neh. 7:24; 10:20 [Eng. 19])
Hezir—Pig (Neh. 10:20 [Eng. 19])
Parosh—Flea (Ezra 2:3)

Sometimes a name refers to the kind of work somebody does:

Harsha—Engraver (Ezra 2:52)

Some other names refer to what happened to a person:

Kelita—The adopted (Ezra 10:23; Neh. 8:7; 10:11 [Eng. 10])

Some of these names are nicknames while others, like Kelita, could have been real names.

5. NAMES OF WOMEN

Although in Ezra-Nehemiah 367 personal names occur, only one is the name of a woman, i.e., Nodiah (or better Noadiah). This is the name of a prophetess who collaborated with Tobiah to frighten Nehemiah (Neh. 6:14). The name means "Yahweh has made himself known."[15] It is also interesting that in Ezra 8:33 a man has the same name.

IX. ANALYSIS OF CONTENTS

I. Return and Rebuilding of the Temple (Ezra 1:1–6:22)
- A. Cyrus's Decree; Response (1:1–11)
- B. Returnees to Jerusalem (2:1–70)
  1. Introduction (2:1–2a)
  2. Laity Identified by Family Relationship (2:2b–20)
  3. Laity Identified by Place Names (2:21–35)
  4. Priests (2:36–39)
  5. Levites, Singers, and Gatekeepers (2:40–42)

13. Stamm, *op. cit.*, pp. 8ff.
14. *Ibid.*, pp. 11ff.
15. Noth, *op. cit.*, p. 184.

6. Temple Servants (2:43–54)
7. Servants of Solomon (2:55–58)
8. Those Who Cannot Prove Ancestry (2:59–63)
9. Totals (2:64–67)
10. Voluntary Contributions to the Temple (2:68–69)
11. Location of the Returnees (2:70)

C. Institution of Sacrifices; Building of the Temple (3:1–6:22)
1. Institution of Sacrifices (3:1–6)
2. Laying of the Foundation of the Temple (3:7–13)
3. Suspension of Work on the Temple (4:1–23)
a. Samaritan tactics under Cyrus (4:1–5)
b. Samaritan tactics under Xerxes and Artaxerxes I (4:6–23)
4. Rebuilding of the Temple (4:24–6:22)
a. Suspension of work; resumption encouraged by Haggai and Zechariah (4:24–5:2)
b. Inquiries by Tattenai (5:3–5)
c. Tattenai's letter to Darius (5:6–17)
d. Discovery of Cyrus's edict (6:1–5)
e. Reply of Darius to Tattenai (6:6–12)
f. Completion of work on the temple (6:13–15)
g. Dedication of the temple (6:16–18)
h. First Passover in the new temple (6:19–22)

II. Ezra's Return and Reforms (7:1–10:44)

A. Ezra's Return (7:1–8:36)
1. Ezra's Mission (7:1–10)
2. Artaxerxes' Letter (7:11–26)
3. Ezra's Thanksgiving (7:27–28)
4. List of Family Heads Who Returned (8:1–14)
5. Enlistment of Temple Personnel (8:15–20)
6. Supplication to God for a Good Journey (8:21–23)
7. Treasure Bearers (8:24–30)
8. Return to Jerusalem (8:31–36)

B. Ezra's Reforms (9:1–10:44)
1. Marriage to Foreigners Reported; Ezra's Reaction (9:1–5)
2. Ezra's Prayer (9:6–15)
3. Covenant to Divorce the Foreign Women (10:1–6)
4. Assembly's Decision (10:7–17)
5. List of the Guilty (10:18–44)

III. Return of Nehemiah; Building of the Wall (Neh. 1:1–6:19)

A. Report from Jerusalem (1:1–4)
B. Nehemiah's Prayer (1:5–11)
C. Nehemiah's Mission (2:1–10)
D. Nehemiah's Inspection of Jerusalem; Reaction of the Officials (2:11–20)
E. Work on the Wall (3:1–32)
F. Samaritan Opposition (3:33–4:17 [Eng. 4:1–23])
1. Reaction of the Enemies (3:33–35 [Eng. 4:1–3])
2. Nehemiah's Prayer; Continuation of the Work (3:36–38 [Eng. 4:4–6])

VII. Reforms of Nehemiah's Second Administration (13:4–31)
- A. Action against Eliashib and Tobiah (13:4–9)
- B. Reorganization of the Levites (13:10–14)
- C. Restoration of the Sabbath (13:15–22)
- D. The Problem of Marriages to Foreigners (13:23–29)
- E. Summary of Nehemiah's Reforms (13:30–31)

X. SELECT BIBLIOGRAPHY

A. COMMENTARIES

L. W. Batten, *A Critical and Exegetical Commentary on the Books of Ezra and Nehemiah*. ICC (Edinburgh: 1913).
A. Bertholet, *Die Bücher Esra und Nehemia*. Kurzer Hand-Commentar zum AT (Tübingen: 1902).
R. A. Bowman, "The Book of Ezra" and "The Book of Nehemiah," *IB* III (Nashville: 1954).
L. H. Brockington, *Ezra, Nehemiah and Esther*. NCB (1969, repr. 1977).
H. Bückers, *Die Bücher Esdras, Nehemias, Tobias, Judith und Esther*. Herders Bibelkommentar (Freiburg: 1953).
R. J. Coggins, *The Books of Ezra and Nehemiah*. Cambridge Bible Commentary (New York: 1976).
J. de Fraine, *Esdras en Nehemias*. De boeken van het Oude Testament 5/2 (Roermand: 1961).
K. Galling, *Die Bücher der Chronik, Esra, Nehemia*. ATD 12 (Göttingen: 1954).
A. Gelin, *Le livre de Esdras et Néhémie*. La Sainte Bible de Jérusalem (Paris: ²1960).
H. H. Grosheide, *Ezra-Nehemia I: Ezra*. Commentaar op het Oude Testament (Kampen: 1963).
M. Haller, *Das Judentum*. SAT III (Göttingen: ²1925).
G. Hölscher, *Die Bücher Esra und Nehemia*. HSAT II (Bonn: ⁴1923).
W. Kessler, *Gottes Mitarbeiter am Wiederaufbau: die Propheten Esra und Nehemia*. Die Botschaft des AT (Stuttgart: 1971).
D. Kidner, *Ezra and Nehemiah*. Tyndale OT Commentary (Downers Grove: 1979).
A. Médebielle, *Esdras-Néhémie*. La Sainte Bible (Paris: 1952).
F. Michaeli, *Les livres des Chroniques, d'Esdras et de Néhémie*. Commentaire de l'AT 16 (Neuchâtel: 1967).
J. M. Myers, *Ezra. Nehemiah*. AB 14 (Garden City: 1965).
A. Noordtzij, *De boeken Ezra en Nehemia*. Korte Verklaring der Heilige Schrift (Kampen: 1951).
B. M. Pelaia, *Esdra e Neemia*. La Sacra Bibbia (Turin: 1960).
M. Rehm, *Esra-Nehemias*. Echter-bibel (Würzburg: 1956).
W. Rudolph, *Esra und Nehemia*. HAT 20 (Tübingen: 1949).
H. Schneider, *Die Bücher Esra und Nehemia*. HSAT 4/2 (Bonn: 1959).
A. van Selms, *Ezra en Nehemia*. Tekst en Uitleg (Gronigen: 1935).
J. J. Slotki, *Daniel, Ezra and Nehemiah*. Soncino (London: 1951).

B. BOOKS

G. C. Aalders, *Oud-Testamentische Kanoniek* (Kampen: 1952).
P. R. Ackroyd, *Exile and Restoration*. OTL (Philadelphia: 1968).
Idem, Israel under Babylon and Persia. New Clarendon Bible 4 (Oxford: 1970).
W. F. Albright, *The Biblical Period from Abraham to Ezra* (New York: 1963).
F. Altheim and R. Stiehl, *Die aramäische Sprache unter den Achaemeniden* I (Frankfort am Main: 1959–63).
A. J. Arberry, ed., *The Legacy of Persia* (Oxford: 1953).
K. Baltzer, *The Covenant Formulary* (E.T. 1971).
W. Bayer, *Die Memoiren des Statthalters Nehemia* (Speyer am Rhine: 1937).
J. A. Bewer, *Der Text des Buches Esra: Beiträge zu seiner Wiederherstellung*. FRLANT 31 (Göttingen: 1922).
J. Bright, *Covenant and Promise* (Philadelphia: 1976).
Idem, A History of Israel (Philadelphia: [2]1972).
B. S. Childs, *Introduction to the OT as Scripture* (Philadelphia: 1979).
R. J. Coggins, *Samaritans and Jews: The Origins of Samaritanism Reconsidered* (Atlanta: 1975).
G. R. Driver, *Aramaic Documents of the Fifth Century B.C.* (1957, repr. 1968).
O. Eissfeldt, *Die altorientalischen Reiche* III. Fischer Weltgeschichte (Frankfort am Main: 1967).
Idem, The OT: An Introduction (E.T. 1965).
R. N. Frye, *The Heritage of Persia* (New York: 1963).
K. Galling, *Studien zur Geschichte Israels im persischen Zeitalter* (Tübingen: 1964).
Idem, Syrien in der Politik der Achämeniden bis 448 vor Christus. AO 36 (1937).
S. Granild, *Ezrabogens litteraere Genesis undersoegt med saerlight Henblik paa et efterkronistik Indgreb* (Copenhagen: 1949).
H. H. Grosheide *De terugkeer uit de Ballingschap* (Hague: 1957).
R. Hanhart, *Text und Textgeschichte des 1. Ezrabuches* (Göttingen: 1974).
R. K. Harrison, *Introduction to the OT* (Grand Rapids: 1969).
S. Herrmann, *A History of Israel in OT Times* (E.T. 1975).
W. Th. In der Smitten, *Esra: Quellen, Überlieferung und Geschichte*. SSN 15 (Assen: 1973).
E. Janssen, *Juda in der Exilzeit*. FRLANT 69 (Göttingen: 1956).
E. Johannesen, *Studier over Esras og Nehemjas Historie* (Copenhagen: 1946).
O. Kaiser, *Introduction to the OT* (E.T. 1975).
A. S. Kapelrud, *The Question of Authorship in the Ezra-Narrative: A Lexical Investigation* (Oslo: 1944).
M. Kegel, *Die Kultusreformation des Esra* (Gütersloh: 1921).
U. Kellermann, *Nehemia: Quellen, Überlieferung und Geschichte*. BZAW 102 (Berlin: 1967).
K. Kenyon, *Jerusalem: Excavating 3000 Years of History* (New York: 1967).
F. K. Kienitz, *Die politische Geschichte Ägyptens vom 7. bis zum 4. Jahrhundert vor der Zeitwende* (Berlin: 1953).
H. G. Kippenberg, *Garizim und Synagoge: Traditionsgeschichtliche Untersuchungen zur samaritanischen Religion der aramäischen Periode*. Religionsgeschichtliche Versuche und Vorarbeiten 30 (New York: 1971).
R. Kittel, *Geschichte des Volkes Israel* III (Stuttgart: [3]1922–29).

O. Leuze, *Die Satrapieneinteilung in Syrien und im Zweistromlande vom 520 bis 320* (Halle: 1935).
E. Meyer, *Die Entstehung des Judentums* (1896, repr. 1965).
R. Mosis, *Untersuchungen zur Theologie des chronistischen Geschichtswerkes*. Freiburger theologische Studien 92 (Freiburg: 1973).
S. Mowinckel, *Ezra den Skriftlaerde* (Kristania: 1916).
Idem, Studien zu dem Buche Ezra-Nehemia I-III (Oslo: 1964–65).
M. Munk, "Ezra, der Schriftgelehrte nach Talmud und Midrasch" (diss., Würzburg, 1931).
J. M. Myers, *The World of the Restoration* (Englewood Cliffs: 1968).
M. Noth, *The History of Israel* (E.T. ²1960).
Idem, Überlieferungsgeschichtliche Studien (Tübingen: ³1957).
A. T. Olmstead, *History of the Persian Empire* (1948, repr. 1966).
R. H. Pfeiffer, *Introduction to the OT* (New York: ²1948).
J. V. Prášek, *Geschichte der Meder und Perser bis zur makedonischen Eroberung* (1906–1909, repr. 1968).
H. H. Schaeder, *Esra der Schreiber*. Beiträge zur historischen Theologie 5 (1930, repr. 1966).
Idem, Iranische Beiträge 1 (1930, repr. 1972).
M. A. Schmidt, *Prophet und Tempel* (Zurich: 1948).
E. Sellin, *Geschichte des israelitisch-jüdischen Volkes* II (Leipzig: 1932).
Idem, Serubbabel (Leipzig: 1898).
E. Sellin and G. Fohrer, *Introduction to the OT* (E.T. 1968).
M. Smith, *Palestinian Parties and Politics that Shaped the OT* (New York: 1971).
J. A. Soggin, *Introduction to the OT*. OTL (E.T. 1976).
C. C. Torrey, *The Chronicler's History of Israel* (New Haven: 1954).
Idem, The Composition and Historical Value of Ezra-Nehemiah (Giessen: 1896).
Idem, Ezra Studies (1910, repr. 1970).
R. de Vaux, *Ancient Israel*. 2 vols. (E.T. 1961).
H. C. M. Vogt, *Studien zur nachexilischen Gemeinde in Esra-Nehemia* (Werl: 1966).
T. C. Vriezen and A. S. van der Woude, *De Literatuur van Oud-Israël* (Wassenaar: ⁴1973).
A. C. Welch, *Post-Exilic Judaism* (Edinburgh: 1935).
G. Widengren, *Stand und Aufgaben der iranischen Religionsgeschichte* (Leiden: 1955).
J. S. Wright, *The Building of the Second Temple* (London: 1958).
Idem, The Date of Ezra's Coming to Jerusalem (London: 1958).
E. Würthwein, *Der 'amm ha'arez im AT*. BWANT IV, 17 (Stuttgart: 1936).
E. J. Young, *An Introduction to the OT* (Grand Rapids: ²1958).
R. C. Zaehner, *The Dawn and Twilight of Zoroastrianism* (London: 1961).

C. ARTICLES

P. R. Ackroyd, "The History of Israel in the Exilic and Post-exilic Periods," in G. W. Anderson, ed., *Tradition and Interpretation* (Oxford: 1979), pp. 320–350.
Idem, "Two OT Historical Problems of the Early Persian Period," *JNES* 17 (1958), pp. 13–27.
F. Ahlemann, "Zur Esra-Quelle," *ZAW* 59 (1942/43), pp. 77–98.

W. F. Albright, "The Date and Personality of the Chronicler," *JBL* 40 (1921), pp. 104–124.

Idem, "The Judicial Reform of Jehoshaphat," in S. Liebermann, ed., *Alexander Marx Jubilee Volume* (New York: 1950), pp. 61–82.

H. L. Allrick, "The Lists of Zerubbabel (Nehemiah 7 and Ezra 2) and the Hebrew Numeral Notation," *BASOR* 136 (1954), pp. 21–27.

A. Alt, "Judas Nachbarn zur Zeit Nehemias," *PJB* 27 (1931), pp. 66–74 (= *KS* II [Munich: 1953], pp. 338–345).

Idem, "Die Rolle Samarias bei der Entstehung des Judentums," in *Festschrift Otto Procksch* (Leipzig: 1934), pp. 5–28 (= *KS* II [Munich: 1953], pp. 316–337).

Idem, "Das Taltor von Jerusalem," *PJB* 24 (1928), pp. 74–98 (= *KS* III [Munich: 1959], pp. 326–347).

F. I. Andersen, "Who Built the Second Temple?", *ABR* 6 (1958), pp. 1–25.

D. K. Andrews, "Yahweh the God of the Heavens," in W. S. McCullough, ed., *The Seed of Wisdom*. Festschrift T. J. Meek (Toronto: 1964), pp. 45–57.

E. Auerbach, "Der Aufstieg der Priesterschaft zur Macht im alten Israel," *VTS* 9 (1962), pp. 236–249.

Idem, "Neujahrs- und Versöhnungsfest in den biblischen Quellen," *VT* 8 (1958), pp. 337–343.

M. Avi-Yonah, "The Walls of Nehemiah—a Minimalist View," *IEJ* 4 (1954), pp. 239–248.

A. Bentzen, "Priesterschaft und Laien in der jüdischen Gemeinde des fünften Jahrhunderts," *AfO* 6 (1931), pp. 280–86.

Idem, "Sirach, der Chronist und Nehemia," *ST* 3 (1949), pp. 158–161.

P.-R. Berger, "Zum Kyros II.—Zylinder VAB 3," *UF* 2 (1970), pp. 337–38.

Idem, "Zu den Namen *ššbṣr* und *šn'ṣr* (Esr. 1:8, 11; 5:14–16 bzw. I Chr 3:18)," *ZAW* 83 (1971), pp. 98–100.

E. J. Bickermann, "The Edict of Cyrus in Ezra 1," *JBL* 65 (1946), pp. 247–275.

F. M. Th. de Liagre Böhl, "Die babylonischen Prätendenten zur Anfangszeit des Darius (Dareios) I," *BiOr* 25 (1968), pp. 150–53.

J. Braslavi, "En-Tannin (Neh. 2:13)," *ErIs* 10 (1971), pp. 90–93. [Hebrew with English summary]

J. Bright, "The Date of Ezra's Mission to Jerusalem," in M. Haran, ed., *Yehezkel Kaufmann Jubilee Volume* (Jerusalem: 1960), pp. 70–87.

M. Burrows, "Nehemiah 3:1–32 as a Source for the Topography of Ancient Jerusalem," *AASOR* 14 (1934), pp. 115–140.

Idem, "Nehemiah's Tour of Inspection," *BASOR* 64 (1936), pp. 11–21.

Idem, "The Origin of Neh. 3:33–37," *AJSL* 52 (1935/36), pp. 235–244.

A. Causse, "La diaspora juive à l'époque perse," *RHPR* 8 (1928), pp. 32–65.

H. Cazelles, "La mission d'Esdras," *VT* 4 (1954), pp. 113–140.

R. J. Coggins, "The Interpretation of Ezra IV.4," *JTS* 16 (1965), pp. 124–27.

S. A. Cook, "The Age of Zerubbabel," in H. H. Rowley, ed., *Studies in OT Prophecy*. Festschrift T. H. Robinson (Edinburgh: 1950), pp. 19–36.

F. M. Cross, "Geshem the Arabian, Enemy of Nehemiah," *BA* 18 (1955), pp. 46–47.

Idem, "A Reconstruction of the Judean Restoration," *JBL* 94 (1975), pp. 4–18.

M. Delcor, "Hinweise auf das Samaritanische Schisma im AT," *ZAW* 74 (1962), pp. 281–291.

E. Dhorme, "Cyrus le Grand," *RB* 9 (1912), pp. 22–49 (= *Recueil Édouard Dhorme: Études bibliques et orientales* [Paris: 1951], pp. 351–382).

G. R. Driver, "Forgotten Hebrew Idioms," *ZAW* 78 (1966), pp. 1–7.

J. A. Emerton, "Did Ezra Go to Jerusalem in 428 B.C.?", *JTS* 17 (1966), pp. 1–19.

Z. W. Falk, "Ezra VII 26," *VT* 9 (1959), pp. 88–89.
F. C. Fensham, "Covenant, Promise and Expectation in the Bible," *ThZ* 23 (1967), pp. 305–322.
Idem, "Mědînâ in Ezra and Nehemiah," *VT* 25 (1975), pp. 795–97.
A. Fernández, "Epoca de la actividad de Esdras," *Bibl* 2 (1921), pp. 424–447.
Idem, "Esd. 9:9 y un texto de Josefo," *Bibl* 16 (1935), pp. 207–208.
Idem, "La voz *gāḏēr* en Esd. 9,9," *Bibl* 16 (1935), pp. 82–84.
R. Fruin, "Is Ezra een historisch persoon?", *NThT* 18 (1929), pp. 121–138.
K. Galling, "Zur Deutung des Ortnamens *ṭrpl* = Tripolis in Syrien," *VT* 4 (1954), pp. 418–422.
Idem, "Kronzeugen des Artaxerxes?", *ZAW* 63 (1951), pp. 66–74.
Idem, "Von Naboned zur Darius: Studien zur chaldäischen und persischen Geschichte," *ZDPV* 69 (1953), pp. 42–64; *ZDPV* 70 (1954), pp. 4–32.
Idem, "Nehemiabuch," *RGG* IV, pp. 1396–98.
Idem, "Serubbabel und der Wiederaufbau des Tempels in Jerusalem," in A. Kuschke, ed., *Verbannung und Heimkehr*. Festschrift W. Rudolph (Tübingen: 1961), pp. 67–96.
A. Gelston, "The Foundations of the Second Temple," *VT* 16 (1966), pp. 232–35.
H. L. Ginsberg, "Ezra 1:4," *JBL* 79 (1960), pp. 167–69.
R. Grafman, "Nehemiah's 'Broad Wall'," *IEJ* 24 (1974), pp. 50–51.
P. Grelot, "Études sur le 'Papyrus Pascal' d'Éléphantine," *VT* 4 (1954), pp. 349–384.
Idem, "Le Papyrus Pascal d'Éléphantine: essai de restauration," *VT* 17 (1967), pp. 201–207.
Idem, "Le Papyrus Pascal d'Éléphantine et le problème du Pentateuque," *VT* 5 (1955), pp. 250–265.
H. H. Grosheide, "Ezra, de Schriftgeleerde," *GTT* 56 (1956), pp. 84–88.
Idem, "Een geschrift van Tabeël?", *GTT* 50 (1950), pp. 71–79.
Idem, "Juda als onderdeel van het Perzische Rijk," *GTT* 54 (1954), pp. 65–76.
Idem, "Twee edicten van Cyrus ten gunste van de Joden (Ezra 1:2–4; 6:3–5)," *GTT* 54 (1954), pp. 1–12.
M. Haran, "The Gibeonites, the Nethinim and the Sons of Solomon's Servants," *VT* 11 (1961), pp. 159–169.
F. M. Heichelheim, "Ezra's Palestine and Periclean Athens," *ZRGG* 3 (1951), pp. 251–53.
J. Heller, "Die abgeschlagene Mauer," *CV* 11 (1968), pp. 175–78.
A. Ibánez Arana, "Sobre la colocazión original de Neh. 10," *EstBib* 10 (1951), pp. 379–402.
W. Th. In der Smitten, "Die Gründe für die Aufnahme der Nehemiaschrift in das chronistische Geschichtswerk," *BZ* N.F. 16 (1972), pp. 207–221.
Idem, "Historische Probleme zum Kyrosedikt und zum Jerusalemer Tempelbau von 515," *Persica* 6 (1974), pp. 167–178.
Idem, "Nehemias Parteigänger," *BiOr* 29 (1972), pp. 155–57.
Idem, "Der Tirschātā' in Esra-Nehemia," *VT* 21 (1971), pp. 618–620.
S. Japhet, "The Supposed Common Authorship of Chronicles and Ezra-Nehemiah Investigated Anew," *VT* 18 (1968), pp. 330–371.
A. Jepsen, "Nehemia 10," *ZAW* 66 (1954), pp. 87–106.
Idem, "Nehemia 10," *TLZ* 79 (1954), pp. 305–306.
Idem, "Pardes," *ZDPV* 74 (1958), pp. 65–68.
H. Kaupel, "Die Bedeutung von gāḏēr in Esr. 9:9," *BZ* 22 (1934), pp. 89–92.

U. Kellerman, "Erwägungen zum Problem der Esradatierung," *ZAW* 80 (1968), pp. 55–87.

Idem, "Die Listen in Nehemia 11 eine Dokumentation aus den letzten Jahren des Reiches Juda?", *ZDPV* 82 (1966), pp. 209–227.

R. Klein, "Ezra and Nehemiah in Recent Studies," in F. M. Cross *et al.*, eds., *Magnalia Dei: The Mighty Acts of God*. In memory of G. E. Wright (Garden City: 1976), pp. 361–376.

Idem, "Old Readings in I Esdras: The List of Returnees from Babylon (Ezra 2 // Nehemiah 7)," *HTR* 62 (1969), pp. 99–107.

A. Klostermann, "Esra und Nehemia," *RE* V (Leipzig: 1898), pp. 500–523.

K. Koch, "Ezra and the Origins of Judaism," *JSS* 19 (1974), pp. 173–197.

J. J. Koopmans, "Het eerste Aramese gedeelte in Ezra (4:7–6:19)," *GTT 55* (1955), pp. 142–160.

M. W. Leeseberg, "Ezra and Nehemiah: A Review of the Return and Reform," *CTM* 33 (1962), pp. 79–90.

M. R. Lehmann, "Biblical Oaths," *ZAW* 81 (1969), pp. 74–92.

B. A. Levine, "The Netînîm," *JBL* 82 (1963), pp. 207–212.

J. L. Liebreich, "The Impact of Nehemiah 9:5–37 on the Liturgy of the Synagogue," *HUCA* 32 (1961), pp. 227–237.

B.-Z. Luria, "W^{e}haṣṣōrîm yāš^{e}ḇû bāh m^{e}ḇî'îm dāg̱ w^{e}ḵol-meḵer," *Beth Mikra* 15 (1970), pp. 363–67.

Idem, "There have been mighty Kings also over Jerusalem," *Beth Mikra* 18 (1973), pp. 176–182.

W. S. McCullough, "Israel's Eschatology from Amos to Daniel," in J. W. Wevers and D. B. Redford, eds., *Studies on the Ancient Palestinian World* (Toronto: 1972), pp. 86–101.

H. E. del Medico, "Le cadre historique des fêtes de Hanukkah et de Purîm," *VT* 15 (1965), pp. 238–270.

F. Mezzacasa, "Esdras, Nehemias y el Año Sabático," *RevBib* 23 (1961), pp. 1–8, 82–96.

J. Morgenstern, "The Dates of Ezra and Nehemiah," *JSS* 7 (1962), pp. 1–11.

Idem, "Jerusalem—485 B.C.," *HUCA* 27 (1956), pp. 101–179; *HUCA* 28 (1957), pp. 15–47.

S. Mowinckel, "Erwägungen zum chronistischen Geschichtswerk," *TLZ* 85 (1960), pp. 1–8.

Idem, "'Ich' und 'Er' in der Ezrageschichte," in A. Kuschke, ed., *Verbannung und Heimkehr*. Festschrift W. Rudolph (Tübingen: 1961), pp. 211–233.

Idem, "'*Uššarnā*' Ezr. 5:3, 9," *ST* 19 (1965), pp. 130–35.

J. M. Myers, "The Kerugma of the Chronicler: History and Theology in the Service of Religion," *Int* 30 (1966), pp. 259–273.

E. Neufeld, "The Rate of Interest and the Text of Nehemiah 5.11," *JQR* 44 (1953/54), pp. 194–204.

E. W. Nicholson, "The Meaning of the Expression *'m h'rṣ* in the OT," *JSS* 10 (1965), pp. 59–66.

P. Nober, "'adrazdā' (Esdras 7:23)," *BZ* N.F. 2 (1958), pp. 134–38.

Idem, "Lexicalia irano-biblica," *VD* 36 (1957), pp. 102–105.

Idem, "De nuevo sobre el significado de *āsparnā* en Esdras," *EstBib* 19 (1960), pp. 111–12.

Idem, "El significado de la palabra aramea *'āsparnā* en Esdras," *EstBib* 16 (1957), pp. 394–401.

R. North, "Civil Authority in Ezra," in *Studi in onore di Edoardo Volterra* VI (Milan: 1971), pp. 377–404.
V. Pavlovský, "Ad chronologiam Esdras 7," *VD* 33 (1955), pp. 280–84.
Idem, "Die Chronologie der Tätigkeit Esdras: Versuch einer neuen Lösung," *Bibl* 38 (1957), pp. 275–305, 428–456.
J. R. Porter, "Son or Grandson (Ezra X.6)," *JTS* 17 (1966), pp. 54–67.
J. Prignaud, "Un sceau Hébreu de Jérusalem et un Ketib du livre d'Esdras," *RB* 71 (1964), pp. 372–383.
G. von Rad, "Die Nehemia-Denkschrift," *ZAW* 76 (1964), pp. 176–187.
A. F. Rainey, "The Satrapy 'Beyond the River'," *AJBA* 1 (1969), pp. 51–78.
M. Rehm, "Nehemia 9," *BZ* N.F. 1 (1957), pp. 59–69.
D. F. Robinson, "Was Ezra Nehemiah?", *ATR* 37 (1955), pp. 177–189.
L. Rost, "Erwägungen zum Kyroserlass," in A. Kuschke, ed., *Verbannung und Heimkehr.* Festschrift W. Rudolph (Tübingen: 1961), pp. 301–307.
H. H. Rowley, "The Chronological Order of Ezra and Nehemiah," in D. S. Löwinger and J. Somogyi, eds., *Ignace Goldziher Memorial Volume* I (Budapest: 1948), pp. 117–149 (= *The Servant of the Lord and Other Essays on the OT* [Oxford: ²1965], pp. 135–168).
Idem, "Nehemiah's Mission and Its Background," *BJRL* 37 (1954/55), pp. 528–561 (= *Men of God* [New York: 1963], pp. 211–245).
Idem, "The Samaritan Schism in Legend and History," in B. W. Anderson and W. Harrelson, eds., *Israel's Prophetic Heritage.* Festschrift J. Muilenburg (New York: 1962), pp. 208–222.
Idem, "Sanballat and the Samaritan Temple," *BJRL* 38 (1955/56), pp. 166–198 (= *Men of God* [New York: 1963], pp. 246–276).
F. Rundgren, "Zur Bedeutung von *ŠRŠW*—Esra VII 26," *VT* 7 (1957), pp. 400–404.
Idem, "Über einen juristischen Terminus bei Esra 6:6," *ZAW* 70 (1958), pp. 209–215.
R. Schiemann, "Covenanting with the Princes: Neh. VI 2," *VT* 17 (1967), pp. 367–69.
W. M. F. Scott, "Nehemiah—Ezra?", *ExpT* 58 (1946/47), pp. 263–67.
A. van Selms, "Weenen als aanvangsritus," *NTT* 24 (1935), pp. 119–127.
N. H. Snaith, "The Date of Ezra's Arrival in Jerusalem," *ZAW* 63 (1951), pp. 53–66.
Idem, "Nehemiah XII 36," *VT* 17 (1967), p. 243.
Idem, "A Note on Ezra viii.35," *JTS* 22 (1971), pp. 150–52.
L. A. Snijders, "Het 'volk des lands' in Juda," *NThT* 12 (1958), pp. 241–256.
E. A. Speiser, "Unrecognized Dedication," *IEJ* 13 (1963), pp. 69–73.
C. C. Torrey, "The Chronicler's History of the Return under Cyrus," *AJSL* 37 (1920/21), pp. 81–100.
Idem, "Sanballat 'the Horonite'," *JBL* 47 (1928), pp. 380–89.
C. G. Tuland, "Hanani—Hananiah," *JBL* 77 (1958), pp. 157–161.
Idem, "'Uššayyā' and 'Uššarnâ: A Classification of Terms, Date and Text," *JNES* 17 (1958), pp. 269–275.
Idem, "*'zb* in Nehemiah 3:8: A Reconsideration of Maximalist and Minimalist Views," *AUSS* 5 (1967), pp. 158–180.
A. Ungnad, "Keilinschriftliche Beiträge zum Buch Esra und Ester," *ZAW* 58 (1940/41), pp. 240–44.
A. Van Hoonacker, "Néhémie et Esdras: une nouvelle hypothèse sur la chronologie de l'époque de la restauration," *Le Muséon* 9 (1890), pp. 151–184, 317–351, 389–401.

Idem, "La succession chronologique Néhémie-Esdras," *RB* 32 (1923), pp. 481–494; *RB* 33 (1924), pp. 33–64.

R. de Vaux, "Les décrets de Cyrus et de Darius sur la reconstruction du Temple," *RB* 46 (1937), pp. 29–57 (= "The Decrees of Cyrus and Darius on the Rebuilding of the Temple," in *The Bible and the Ancient Near East* [E.T. 1971], pp. 63–96).

W. Vischer, "Nehemiah, der Sonderbeauftragte und Statthalter des Königs," in H. W. Wolff, ed., *Probleme biblischer Theologie*. Festschrift G. von Rad (Munich: 1971), pp. 603–610.

E. Vogt, "Das Wachstum des alten Stadtgebietes von Jerusalem," *Bibl* 48 (1967), pp. 337–358.

J. P. Weinberg, "*N^e^tînîm* und 'Söhne der Sklaven Salomos' im 6—4 Jh. v. u. Z.," *ZAW* 87 (1975), pp. 355–371.

A. C. Welch, "The Source of Nehemiah IX," *ZAW* 47 (1929), pp. 130–37.

C. F. Whitley, "The Term Seventy Years Captivity," *VT* 4 (1954), pp. 60–72.

G. Widengren, "The Persian Period," in J. H. Hayes and J. M. Miller, eds., *Israelite and Judaean History*. OTL (Philadelphia: 1977), pp. 489–538.

Idem, "The Persians," in D. J. Wiseman, ed., *Peoples of OT Times* (Oxford: 1973), pp. 312–357.

J. M. Wilkie, "Nabonidus and the later Jewish Exiles," *JTS* 2 (1951), pp. 36–44.

C. T. Wood, "Nehemiah-Ezra," *ExpT* 59 (1947/48), pp. 53ff.

The Book of EZRA

I. RETURN AND REBUILDING OF THE TEMPLE

(1:1–6:22)

A. CYRUS'S DECREE; RESPONSE (1:1–11)

1 *Now in the first year of Cyrus king of Persia, in order to fulfil the word of the Lord through Jeremiah, the Lord inspired Cyrus king of Persia, so that he issued a proclamation throughout all his kingdom, and also put it in writing, saying,*

2 *"Thus speaks Cyrus king of Persia: 'The Lord, the God of heaven, has given me all the kingdoms of the earth, and he has commanded me to build him a temple in Jerusalem, which is in Judah.*

3 *Whoever there is among you of all his people, may his God be with him. Let him go to Jerusalem in Judah, and rebuild the temple of the Lord, the God of Israel; he is the God who is in Jerusalem.*

4 *And every survivor, at whatever place he may live, let the people of that place support him with silver and gold, with goods and cattle, also with a voluntary offering for the temple of God in Jerusalem.'"*

5 *Then the heads of the families of Judah and Benjamin and the priests and the Levites prepared, even everyone whom God had inspired, to go and rebuild the temple of the Lord in Jerusalem.*

6 *And all their neighbors encouraged them with articles of silver, with gold, with goods, with cattle, and with valuables, aside from all that was given as a voluntary offering.*

7 *King Cyrus removed the articles of the house of the Lord that Nebuchadnezzar had carried away from Jerusalem and put them in the house of his gods;*

8 *and Cyrus king of Persia had them removed by Mithredath the treasurer, and he counted them out to Sheshbazzar the prince of Judah.*

9 *This was their number: 30 gold dishes, 1000 silver dishes, 29 duplicates.*

10 *30 gold bowls, 410 silver bowls of a second kind, and 1000 other articles.*
11 *All the articles of gold and silver numbered 5400. Sheshbazzar took them all with the exiles who went from Babylon to Jerusalem.*

1 *Now in the first year of Cyrus.* This book starts with a connecting *waw* exactly like 1 Kings. Some scholars are of the opinion that this *waw* proves that Chronicles and Ezra-Nehemiah were written by the same person.[1] Other scholars do not attach too much significance to this phenomenon.[2] It is not strange according to the Semitic style to start a book with a *waw,* especially when the author intended to write a continuation of the history of his people. He connects the history which he wants to write with the already-written history of his people by using the conjunction "and."

Cyrus (Persian *Kuruš*) became king of Anshan in 559 B.C. He was a vassal of King Astyages of the Medians, but later rebelled against him and succeeded in overwhelming his forces. After various victories over kings of the ancient Near East and Asia Minor, he took Sardis in 546 B.C.[3] He fought with great success against the Babylonians in 539 B.C. and his general, Ugbaru, conquered Babylon later in 539.[4] *The first year of Cyrus* obviously refers to the first year of the conquering of Babylon when he became king of Mesopotamia.[5] *King of Persia* is already mentioned in the Chronicle of Nabonidus.[6]

In order to fulfil the word of the Lord through Jeremiah. Cf. Jer. 29:10, a difficult passage to interpret. If we take the Exile as a starting point, only forty-eight years had elapsed between the fall of Jerusalem and the decree of Cyrus, not seventy. Some scholars are of the opinion that the seventy years were counted from the demolishing of the temple in 586 B.C. to its completion in 516 B.C. It was thus not in the mind of the author to describe the period of exile, but to show, by referring to the decree of Cyrus, that this decree was responsible for the restoration of the temple.[7]

1. E.g., W. Rudolph, *Esra und Nehemia.* HAT 20 (Tübingen: 1949), p. 2.
2. E.g., H. H. Grosheide, *Ezra,* p. 11.
3. Cf. R. N. Frye, *The Heritage of Persia* (New York: 1963), pp. 74ff.
4. For a discussion on the various sources in this connection cf. Galling, *Studien zur Geschichte Israels im persischen Zeitalter* (Tübingen: 1964), pp. 24ff.
5. Cf., e.g., F. Michaeli, *Les livres des Chroniques, d'Esdras et de Néhémie.* Commentaire de l'AT 16 (Neuchâtel: 1967), p. 252; L. H. Brockington, *Ezra, Nehemia and Esther.* New Century Bible (1969, repr. 1977), p. 48; R. A. Bowman, "The Book of Ezra," *IB* III (Nashville: 1954), p. 570.
6. Cf. Myers, *Ezra. Nehemiah,* p. 4.
7. Brockington, *op. cit.,* p. 48.

But it all depends on what Jeremiah intended by it. Modern scholars give various interpretations. Did Jeremiah refer to the period of the Exile or to a period of world domination by the Babylonians? The first possibility is problematic, because then we have to accept that "seventy" means either a round number or life span.[8] A close inspection of Jer. 29:10 shows, however, that the seventy years refers to Babylonian domination and might be counted either from 612 B.C. (the fall of Nineveh) to 539 B.C. or from 605 B.C. (Nebuchadnezzar's accession) to 539 B.C.[9] In either case it is approximately seventy years. In terms of a prophetic vision it is remarkably exact.

The Lord inspired Cyrus. Cf. Jer. 51:11; Hag. 1:14; 1 Chr. 5:26; 2 Chr. 21:16; 36:22. In typical OT fashion the author ascribes the political activities of Cyrus to the Lord. The Lord is not only the God of Israel or Judah, but of the whole world; it is he who inspired the tolerant decree of Cyrus. Cf. also Isa. 41:25; 43:14; 44:28; 45:1, 13ff.

A proclamation (qôl) . . . *in writing* (miḵtāḇ). In accordance with the spirit of the decree of Cyrus in which special attention was given to minority groups,[10] a proclamation by heralds was sent out to be communicated orally to the various Jewish communities. The official written document was then given to the communities as proof of the proclamation. It is quite probable that this document was written in Aramaic, the language of diplomacy in the Persian empire (cf. also 6:3–5).

2 *The Lord, the God of heaven, has given me all the kingdoms of the earth.* The official style of vv. 2ff. is to be noted, e.g., "God of heaven," "Jerusalem, which is in Judah." It is important to note also that the expression "God of heaven" occurs frequently in the Elephantine papyri.[11] It is thus acceptable to think that this decree was transmitted orally

8. Cf., e.g., P. R. Ackroyd, *Exile and Restoration.* OTL (Philadelphia: 1968), p. 240; C. F. Whitley, "The Term Seventy Years Captivity," *VT* 4 (1954), pp. 60–72; "The Seventy Years Desolation—A Rejoinder," *VT* 7 (1957), pp. 416–18; A. Orr, "The Seventy Years of Babylon," *VT* 6 (1956), pp. 304–306; P. R. Ackroyd, "Two OT Historical Problems of the Early Persian Period," *JNES* 17 (1958), pp. 23–27; K. Galling, *Studien zur Geschichte Israels,* p. 65; G. Larsson, "When Did the Babylonian Captivity Begin?", *JTS* 18 (1967), pp. 417–423; R. Borger, "An Additional Remark on P. R. Ackroyd, *JNES,* XVII, 23–27," *JNES* 18 (1959), p. 74.

9. Cf. J. Bright, *Jeremiah.* AB 21 (Garden City: 1965), p. 209.

10. Cf. for the decree *ANET,* p. 315.

11. Aram. *'lh šmy'*. Cf., e.g., *AP* 30:2, 27; 31:2; 32:3; 38:3, 5. Cf. also Myers, *Ezra. Nehemiah,* p. 4, and D. K. Andrews, "Yahweh, the God of the Heavens," in W. S. McCullough, ed., *The Seed of Wisdom.* Festschrift T. J. Meek (Toronto: 1964), pp. 45–57.

in Hebrew as it was remembered by the Jews.[12] It is also important to note that the Lord could have been acknowledged by Cyrus as being one of the many gods who assisted him in becoming a world monarch.[13]

3 *Temple of the Lord* (lit. "house of the Lord"). This is now attested in extrabiblical material in the Tell Arad ostraca.[14]

4 *And every survivor.* Two different interpretations are presented: Bickerman is of the opinion that *wᵉḵol-hanniš'ār* must be taken as the subject of the sentence and must refer to those Jews who stayed behind.[15] But this interpretation leaves us with a very complicated sentence construction, which could have been misinterpreted and which is strange for a royal proclamation. The more acceptable view is that this expression refers to the Jewish exiles in general, those who have escaped the sword of the Babylonians.[16]

The people of that place. This phrase is also differently interpreted. One view is that it refers to non-Israelite neighbors.[17] Another opinion is that this expression refers to those Jews who stayed behind.[18] It is difficult to determine what is meant by this phrase, but it seems preferable to regard the whole of v. 4 as referring to the Jews. It would have been indeed a strange situation if non-Jewish inhabitants of the Persian empire were called on to assist the Jews. *Goods* (Heb. *rᵉḵûš*) probably refers to goods in general, though the possibility must not be excluded that it could mean cattle[19] and goods.

It is probable that Cyrus was assisted by Jews in the drawing up of this decree; cf. v. 4, which is constructed with a good knowledge of current Jewish conceptions. This would also explain the undertones of the Exodus motif (also present in Isaiah).[20] It is understandable that the Jew or Jews who assisted the secretaries of Cyrus with the construction of the

12. Against, e.g., Rudolph, *Esra und Nehemia,* p. 3; R. de Vaux, *The Bible and the Ancient Near East* (E.T. 1971), pp. 80–96. But cf. also E. Bickermann, "The Edict of Cyrus in Ezra 1," *JBL* 65 (1946), pp. 249–275. F. I. Andersen, "Who Built the Second Temple?", *ABR* 6 (1958), pp. 1–35, argues for a more positive approach to the historical reliability of Chronicles. Cf. also Ackroyd, *Exile and Restoration,* p. 140.

13. Cf. Brockington, *op. cit.,* p. 49.

14. Cf. J. C. L. Gibson, *Textbook of Syrian Semitic Inscriptions* I (Oxford: 1971), p. 53 (C9–10).

15. Cf. Bickermann, *JBL* 65 (1946), pp. 258–260; Bowman, *IB* III, p. 572.

16. Cf., e.g., Brockington, *op. cit.,* p. 49; Grosheide, *Ezra,* p. 71.

17. Cf., e.g., Brockington, *op. cit.,* p. 49; Michaeli, *Les livres des Chroniques, d'Esdras et de Néhémie,* p. 252.

18. Cf., e.g., Grosheide, *Ezra,* p. 72.

19. Cf. also Brockington, *op. cit.,* p. 49.

20. Against the view held by Rudolph, *Esra und Nehemia,* pp. 3–7.

decree could have included their ideal of a new exodus in communications to their country.[21]

5–6 *Then the heads of the families of Judah and Benjamin and the priests and the Levites prepared.* This passage describes the return of certain Jews to rebuild the temple. In later Jewish history Benjamin was closely associated with Judah (e.g., in 1 Chr. 6:65; 12:16; 2 Chr. 11:1). Judah and Benjamin were taken into captivity by the Babylonians and these tribes were granted permission to return to the Holy Land. Consequently, however, only a small group returned and many pious and prosperous Jews remained in Babylon and vicinity.

And all their neighbors encouraged them with articles of silver. Verse 6 obviously refers back to v. 4 to show that the command of Cyrus was carried out. The Hebrew expression *biḵ^{e}lê-ḵesep̱* is awkward. Most scholars are inclined to follow the LXX, which reads *bakkōl bakkesep̱*,[22] thus placing silver and gold on the same footing, a much better arrangement. It is also better to read *lārōḇ* instead of *l^{e}ḇaḏ* with the LXX in 2:28 and to translate it "in abundance."[23]

7 *King Cyrus removed.* This verse refers to the vessels of the temple that Nebuchadnezzar took during his campaigns against Judah in 597 and 586 B.C. (2 K. 24:13; 25:13–16; 2 Chr. 36:10, 18; Jer. 52:17–19). *Hôṣî'* is used here in two different meanings: The first usage with Cyrus as subject means "set free" something that had been in captivity.[24] It refers to the release of the vessels from the temples of the gods in Babylon. The second *hôṣî'* with Nebuchadnezzar as subject refers to the forceful carrying away of the vessels from the temple of the Lord.

8 *And Cyrus king of Persia had them removed by Mithredath.* It is clear from this statement that Cyrus worked through official channels by commanding a high official of his kingdom, Mithredath, to release the vessels.[25] Quite probably this was written down as an official record, which was later used by the author of Ezra. All the particulars given by the author point to firsthand knowledge of a Persian document.[26] *Mith-*

21. The same ideal was also present many years later among the members of the Qumran sect. Cf. esp. F. M. Cross, *The Ancient Library of Qumran* (Garden City: ^{2}1961), p. 78.

22. E.g., Grosheide, *Ezra*, p. 77; Brockington, *op. cit.*, p. 49.

23. Rudolph, *Esra und Nehemia*, p. 4; Grosheide, *Ezra*, p. 77.

24. Cf. Ex. 3:10 and F. C. Fensham, *Exodus* (Nijkerk: 1970), p. 24. *Hôṣî'* is here used to denote the setting free from slavery. In Akkadian the causative is used *(ušēṣū)* to denote the manumission of a slave; cf. R. H. Pfeiffer and E. A. Speiser, "One Hundred New Selected Nuzi Texts," *AASOR* 16 (1936), p. 111.

25. Myers, *Ezra. Nehemiah*, p. 9.

26. Cf. Galling, *Studien zur Geschichte Israels*, pp. 78–88.

redath is a well-known Persian name, meaning "given to (the god) Mithra."[27] Mithra was worshipped as god from the earliest times of the Indo-Aryans.[28] *The treasurer* (Heb. *haggizbār*) occurs only here in the OT and is a loanword from Persian *ganzabara*. It probably refers to a high position among financial officials.[29]

And he counted them out to Sheshbazzar the prince of Judah. The name Sheshbazzar is commonly regarded as Babylonian, meaning either "Shamash [the sun-god] protects the son" (*šamaš-abla-uṣur*) or "Sin [the moon-god] protects the father" (*šin-ab-uṣur*).[30] Modern scholars are unanimous that Sheshbazzar was not the same person as Zerubbabel,[31] though early Jewish historians identified the two (cf. our discussion of 2:2). Sheshbazzar is a mysterious figure who is mentioned only a few times in Ezra (1:8, 11; 5:14, 16), and it is difficult to assess his precise role in the history of the Judean restoration. He was probably succeeded by Zerubbabel. *The prince (hannāśî')* means a person raised to a position of authority and nothing more.[32] It is not acceptable to identify Sheshbazzar with the Shenezzar of 1 Chr. 3:18.

9–11 *Gold dishes . . . gold bowls.* The meanings of the words *dishes ('ᵃgarṭᵉlîm)* and *bowls (kᵉpôrîm)* are uncertain.[33] There occurs no *l* in Old Persian, and the various attempts of modern scholars to explain *'ᵃgarṭᵉlîm* are still unsatisfactory.[34] Every attempt to explain *kᵉpôrîm* has failed.[35] The calculations in these verses are full of problems; they do not add up if we compare vv. 9 and 10 with 11. The problem is probably

27. Rudolph, *Esra und Nehemia*, p. 4.
28. For a discussion of Mithra in the Indo-Aryan pantheon cf. G. Widengren, *Stand und Aufgaben der iranischen Religionsgeschichte* (Leiden: 1955), pp. 22ff. An antiquated view is that Mithra became a god of the Persians only late in their history; cf. J. V. Prášek, *Geschichte der Meder und Perser bis zur makedonischen Eroberung* (Gotha: ²1906–1909; repr. Darmstadt: 1966), pp. 11, 127.
29. Galling, *Studien zur Geschichte Israels*, p. 81.
30. Cf. Rudolph, *Esra und Nehemia*, p. 4; Myers, *Ezra. Nehemiah*, p. 5; W. F. Albright, response to C. C. Torrey, "The Seal from the Reign of Ahaz Again," *BASOR* 82 (1941), p. 17.
31. E.g., cf. Myers, *op. cit.*, p. 9.
32. Cf. Grosheide, *Ezra*, p. 79; *idem*, "Juda als onderdeel van her Perzische Rijk," *GTT* 54 (1954), pp. 69ff.; Brockington, *Ezra, Nehemiah and Esther*, p. 50.
33. Galling, *Studien zur Geschichte Israels*, p. 82.
34. Cf. P. Humbert, "En marge du dictionnaire hebraïque," *ZAW* 62 (1950), pp. 199ff.; *KB*, p. 9; cf. also C. Rabin, "Hittite Words in Hebrew," *Or* 32 (1963), pp. 126–28; Galling, *Studien zur Geschichte Israels*, p. 82 n. 1.
35. Cf. esp. the attempt to connect Akkadian *kapru* with the Hebrew; cf. A. Ungnad, *Glossar zu den Neubabylonischen Rechts- und Verwaltungsurkunden* (Leipzig: 1937), p. 74; Galling, *Studien zur Geschichte Israels*, p. 82 n. 1.

due to textual corruption and appears to be insoluble.[36] In order to explain the textual corruption Galling proposes that this inventory was originally written in Aramaic and later used by the author of Ezra.[37] The transmission from Aramaic to Hebrew might have caused many of the problems in these verses.

B. RETURNEES TO JERUSALEM (2:1–70)

1. Introduction (2:1–2a)

1 *Now these are the people of the province who came up out of the captivity of the exiles, whom Nebuchadnezzar the king of Babylon had carried away to Babylon and returned to Jerusalem and Judah, each to his city.*
2a *These came with Zerubbabel, Jeshua, Nehemiah, Seraiah, Reelaiah, Mordecai, Bilshan, Mispar, Bigvai, Rehum, and Baanah.*

1 The connection between chs. 1 and 2 is not clear. In 1:5–11 the return of the cult vessels under the supervision of Sheshbazzar is described. In ch. 2 we have a description of the return to Judah of certain individuals and groups under the leadership of Zerubbabel. The precise chronological connection between the return of cult vessels and certain people under Sheshbazzar and the return of ch. 2 is unclear. One thing, however, is clear—this list of ch. 2 is introduced here in connection with ch. 3 (Zerubbabel and Jeshua are mentioned in 3:2).[1] The return under Zerubbabel can be placed sometime between 539 B.C. and 520 B.C., possibly at the same time as the return of Sheshbazzar in 538 B.C.[2]

The reason for this list is explained variously by modern scholars. K. Galling has argued that the list was drawn up to show that the persons and groups mentioned are legitimate Israelites in contrast to the Samaritans.[3] Although this proposal seems to be acceptable, the problem of identification by place and not by individual or family name weakens Galling's argument. A. Alt has maintained with some force that the list was drawn up to restore land rights which the Babylonians had confis-

36. Cf., e.g., Myers, *Ezra. Nehemiah,* p. 9.
37. Cf. K. Galling, "Von Naboned zur Darius," *ZDPV* 70 (1954), pp. 4ff.; *idem, Esra und Nehemia,* p. 187.
1. For a discussion of difficulties in connection with the continuation of chs. 1, 2, and 3 cf. Galling, *Studien zur Geschichte Israels,* pp. 89ff.; *idem,* "The 'Gōlā-List' according to Ezra 2 // Nehemiah 7," *JBL* 70 (1951), pp.149–158.
2. Against W. F. Albright, *The Biblical Period from Abraham to Ezra* (New York: 1963), p. 87, and Myers, *Ezra. Nehemiah,* p. 15.
3. Galling, *Studien zur Geschichte Israels,* pp. 89ff.

cated.[4] G. Hölscher has argued that it was a tax list, but that the main reason for its presence was to constitute a list of persons of pure Israelite blood.[5] Hölscher's view of pure Israelite blood can be questioned, because this is not borne out by the foreign names in the list; his view of a tax list is also unconvincing, because a Persian tax list should have included all the inhabitants of Judah and not only the Jews.[6] Rudolph has held that the list shows lack of systematization. This phenomenon points to successive later additions as the Jews arrived in Palestine.[7] The view that the list is fictitious is no longer accepted by scholars. It is uncertain whether this list has a concealed purpose for legitimizing Israelites or restoring land rights. It might only have been a list to show that certain leaders of families had returned to Palestine and that certain geographical places were occupied by the returnees.

The people of the province (b^enê hamm^{e}ḏînâ). Some exegetes, like Myers, are apt to put Judah in brackets after "province" to show that the Persian province of Judah is intended.[8] The omission of Judah might be important, because at the time of the return of Jews no Persian province of Judah existed.[9] It might only have designated a territorial area or the province from which the exiles returned, namely, the province of Babylonia. *Each to his own city* clearly designates that the places from which the Babylonians exiled the Jewish people were to be occupied by the Jews. This shows that after a period of c. fifty-three years the memory of the places from which families were taken was still very much alive.

2a This verse enumerates the names of certain important leaders. The comparable list in Neh. 7 differs in a few respects from this list, e.g., Neh. 7 has Azaraiah instead of Seraiah, Raamaiah instead of Reelaiah, Misperet instead of Mispar, Nehum instead of Rehum, and between Reelaiah (Raamaiah) and Mordecai the name Nahamani is inserted. A few of the differences can be explained as variations of the same name, but differences like Raamaiah for Reelaiah and Nehum for Rehum are not explained away easily.[10] The divergences in the lists of Ezra and Nehemiah

4. Cf. *KS* II, pp. 316–337, esp. pp. 334–35.

5. G. Hölscher, *Die Bücher Esra und Nehemia*. HSAT II (Bonn: ^{4}1923), pp. 303–304.

6. Cf. also Galling, *Studien zur Geschichte Israels*, p. 92; Rudolph, *Esra und Nehemia*, p. 15.

7. Cf. Rudolph, *Esra und Nehemia*, p. 17.

8. Cf. Myers, *Ezra. Nehemiah*, p. 15; F. C. Fensham, "Mĕdînâ in Ezra and Nehemiah," *VT* 25 (1975), pp. 795–97, argues against it.

9. Already stressed by Alt in *KS* II, p. 335 n. 1, and esp. Galling, *Studien zur Geschichte Israels*, p. 93.

10. For a clear comparison of Ezra 2 and Neh. 7 cf. Michaeli, *Les livres des Chroniques, d'Esdras et de Néhémie*, pp. 256–260.

occur mainly in proper names and in numerical information.[11] Such discrepancies might be due to textual corruption. H. L. Allrick has shown how the numerals in the Hebrew script could have been misinterpreted by later copyists.[12]

Some scholars have maintained that the list of Nehemiah is to be preferred to that of Ezra because the list of Ezra is a later addition to the book. This view presupposes that the author of Ezra had taken over the list from Neh. 7.[13] Others argue that the list belonged originally to Ezra.[14] It is difficult to make a clear-cut decision on this issue, but it is not improbable that the authors of Ezra and Nehemiah could have made use of another document or even of two different documents. In the case of Nehemiah it is mentioned that the list is drawn up from "the book of the genealogy" (Neh. 7:5). This document might have been the original for both authors.

Zerubbabel means "the seed of Babel" or "born in Babel." The relation between Zerubbabel and Sheshbazzar is not certain.[15] Sheshbazzar is only mentioned in Ezra (1:8, 11; 5:14, 16). Zerubbabel is mentioned in 1 Chr. 3:19; Ezra 2:2; 3:2, 8; 4:2, 3; 5:2; Neh. 7:7; 12:1, 47; Hag. 1:1, 12, 14; 2:3, 5, 24; Zech. 4:6, 7, 9, 10. Thus we are better informed about the work and role of Zerubbabel than we are about Sheshbazzar. It is also noteworthy that in Ezra, Nehemiah, Haggai, and Zechariah (cf. chs. 3 and 4) Zerubbabel is always somehow connected to Jeshua the high priest. Two explanations are given for the connection between Sheshbazzar and Zerubbabel. First, it is presumed that Sheshbazzar came to Jerusalem immediately after 539 B.C. and started on the foundations of the temple (Ezra 5:16). Later, c. 520 B.C., Zerubbabel and Jeshua arrived with another group of exiles and completed the temple. Second, it is held that Sheshbazzar was responsible to the Persian government and was regarded by the outside world as the person who had built the temple, while in fact Zerubbabel did it.[16] This theory supposes that they arrived at the same time. The latter possibility seems acceptable, because it eliminates most of the problems (cf. also at 3:8). It is obvious from the prophecies of Zechariah and Haggai (1:14) that work on the temple had somehow ceased and that

11. Cf. *ibid.*, p. 261.
12. H. L. Allrick, "The Lists of Zerubbabel (Nehemiah 7 and Ezra 2) and the Hebrew Numeral Notation," *BASOR*, 136 (1954), pp. 21–27.
13. E.g., Rudolph, *Esra und Nehemia*, pp. 14ff.; Galling, *Studien zur Geschichte Israels*, pp. 89–91.
14. Strongly propagated by H. H. Schaeder, *Esra der Schreiber*, pp. 20ff.
15. Cf. the discussion of Brockington, *Ezra, Nehemiah and Esther*, pp. 51–52.
16. Cf. F. I. Andersen, *ABR* 6 (1958), pp. 12ff.; Grosheide, *Ezra*, p. 79; Brockington, *op. cit.*, p. 52.

they tried to stir up the Jews to start building again. It is thus possible that soon after Sheshbazzar and Zerubbabel had finished the foundation, building activities diminished. In the time of Haggai and Zechariah (Ezra 5:1) Zerubbabel was again called upon to continue the work. It is probable that at this time Sheshbazzar was no longer in Palestine; he may have died.

Nehemiah. Some scholars think that his name is an anachronistic inclusion among the names of the companions of Zerubbabel and refers to Nehemiah the governor. It is clear, however, that the name Nehemiah could also have been given to somebody else, as in the case of Nehemiah of Beth-zur (Neh. 3:16; 7:7).[17]

2. *Laity Identified by Family Relationship (2:2b–20)*[1]

2b *The number of the men of the people of Israel:*
3 *the descendants of Parosh, 2172;*
4 *the descendants of Shephatiah, 372;*
5 *the descendants of Arah, 775;*
6 *the descendants of Pahath-moab, of the sons of Jeshua and Joab, 2812;*
7 *the descendants of Elam, 1254;*
8 *the descendants of Zattu, 945;*
9 *the descendants of Zaccai, 760;*
10 *the descendants of Bani, 642;*
11 *the descendants of Bebai, 623;*
12 *the descendants of Azgad, 1222;*
13 *the descendants of Adonikam, 666;*
14 *the descendants of Bigvai, 2056;*
15 *the descendants of Adin, 454;*
16 *the descendants of Ater and Hezekiah, 98;*
17 *the descendants of Bezai, 323;*
18 *the descendants of Jorah, 112;*
19 *the descendants of Hashum, 223;*
20 *the descendants of Gibbar, 95.*

The basis for the subdivision is that "the descendants of" (*b^{e}nê*) should denote family relationship, but we must add immediately that it is not clear in the case of Gibbar whether it is a place name or not (cf. Neh. 7). Neh. 7:25 has "the descendants of Gibeon." If we take "descendants of" as the clue for family relationship, Gibbar must be a personal name, and its inclusion in this subdivision is justified. But one cannot be too sure; note *b^{e}nê hamm^{e}ḏînâ* in 2:1 where *b^{e}nê* denotes the inhabitants of a region. *Gibbar.* Nehemiah has Gibeon, but according to Myers the town of Gibeon

17. Cf. Brockington, *op. cit.*, p. 52.
1. Cf. the subdivisions of Myers, *Ezra. Nehemiah*, pp. 17ff.

was at this stage part of the province of Trans-Euphrates (Neh. 3:7) and not of Judah. This interpretation is improbable, however. Cf. the discussion of Neh. 3:7.

We are referring here only to those names on which fresh light is thrown either by modern scholarly work or extrabiblical sources.

6 *Pahath-moab*. Mazar has regarded it as a tribal name and thinks that it refers to descendants of an ancestor exiled by Tiglath-pileser III.[2] This is difficult to prove, however.

7 *Zaccai* occurs on a stamp published by S. Moscati.[3]

12 *Azgad* occurs in the Aramaic papyri of Egypt.[4]

14 *Bigvai* is a Persian name. It occurs also in *AP*, p. 111 (30:1) and is conjectured in *AP*, p. 119 (31:1).

16 *Ater* occurs in *AP*, pp. 37 (13:3) and 39.

3. Laity Identified by Place Names (2:21–35)

21 *the men of Bethlehem, 123;*
22 *the men of Netophah, 56;*
23 *the men of Anathoth, 128;*
24 *the descendants of Azmaveth, 42;*
25 *the descendants of Kiriath-arim, Chephirah, and Beeroth, 743;*
26 *the descendants of Ramah and Geba, 621;*
27 *the men of Michmas, 122;*
28 *the men of Bethel and Ai, 223;*
29 *the descendants of Nebo, 52;*
30 *the descendants of Magbish, 156;*
31 *the descendants of the other Elam, 1254;*
32 *the descendants of Harim, 320;*
33 *the descendants of Lod, Hadid, and Ono, 725;*
34 *the men of Jericho, 345;*
35 *the descendants of Senaah, 3630.*

It is very difficult to tell whether all these names are place names. One cannot maintain that "the men of" refers to place names and "the sons of" refers to personal names; see, e.g., "the sons of" before well-known place names like Kiriath-arim, Chephirah, Beeroth, Lod, Hadid, etc. Cf. also our discussion above in reference to *b^{e}nê hamm^{e}ḏînâ*. The two ways of expressing the inhabitants of localities are a stylistic device and nothing more. There might be some doubt whether all the names in vv. 21–35

2. B. Mazar, *IEJ* 7 (1957), p. 232; Myers, *op. cit.*, pp. 12–13.
3. Cf. S. Moscati, *L'epigrafia ebraica antica* (Rome: 1951), p. 75; Myers, *op. cit.*, p. 13.
4. See *AP*, p. 193 (81:31).

refer to localities; cf., e.g., the reference to "the other Elam" in v. 31 with the first Elam, a personal name, in v. 7. It is thus implied that Elam in both instances must be a personal name. But we cannot be certain, because ancient writers were not always logical in their approach to these matters.

It is obvious from the place names that a certain geographical order is followed. It starts in the south with Bethlehem and Netophah, moves to the north with Anathoth and Azmaveth, then to the northwest to the old Gibeonite confederacy with Kiriath-arim, Chephirah, and Beeroth,[1] to the far north of Judah with Michmas, Bethel, and Ai, to the southwest with Nebo, Magbish, Elam, and Harim, then to the vicinity of Joppa with Lod, Hadid, and Ono, and finally to the northwest with Jericho and Senaah.[2]

4. Priests (2:36–39)

36 *The priests: the descendants of Jedaiah of the house of Jeshua, 973;*
37 *the descendants of Immer, 1052;*
38 *the descendants of Pashhur, 1246;*
39 *the descendants of Harim, 1017.*

This is a carefully transmitted list as is proved by a comparison of Ezra 2, Neh. 7, and Ezra 10. The names are to be connected to the priestly orders enumerated in 1 Chr. 24. It is also interesting to note that the priests formed about a tenth of the total of returnees.[1] The mention of the house of Jeshua shows that the preexilic important family of the high priests is connected to the postexilic first high priest, Jeshua. The name Pashhur is quite probably of Egyptian origin.[2]

5. Levites, Singers, and Gatekeepers (2:40–42)

40 *The Levites: the descendants of Jeshua and Kadmiel, of the descendants of Hodaviah, 74.*
41 *The singers: the descendants of Asaph, 128.*
42 *The descendants of the gatekeepers: the descendants of Shallum, the descendants of Ater, the descendants of Talmon, the descendants of Akkub, the descendants of Hatita, the descendants of Shobai, in all 139.*

A small minority of Levites returned in comparison with the priests. The small number is quite possibly due to the Levites' lowly kind of work, to

1. Cf. the remarks of J. Blenkinsopp, *Gibeon and Israel,* p. 98.
2. Cf. Myers, *Ezra. Nehemiah,* pp. 17–18; see also the discussion in F.-M. Abel, *Géographie de la Palestine* II (Paris: ²1938), pp. 120–21.
1. Grosheide, *Ezra,* pp. 90–91; Myers, *Ezra. Nehemiah,* p. 18.
2. Cf. M. Noth, *Die israelitischen Personennamen,* p. 63; cf. the discussion of M. Heltzer, *Šntwn lmqr' wlḥqr hmzrḥ hqdwm* (1977), pp. 56–57.

which they were not eager to return. The problem of the small number of Levites is also reflected in Ezra 8:15ff., where it is stated that Ezra could muster only thirty-eight after his call.[1]

The Chronicler associated the singers with the Levites (e.g., 1 Chr. 6:16). It is not always clear what the precise relation was between Levites and singers. In our list they are separated from one another, while in Neh. 11–12 they are identified with each other. Modern scholarship becomes more and more vague about the early origin of the temple singers. Albright held that David organized the first religious music in Israel.[2] As we now know through the discoveries at Ras Shamra, singing formed an important part of Canaanite cultic practices.[3] It is therefore not surprising to find early traces of organized religious music in Israel.

The service rendered by the gatekeepers was to lock and unlock the doors of the temple and to watch over the treasury (1 Chr. 9:17–29). It was a fairly large number (139, and according to Neh. 7:45, 138) of gatekeepers who returned.

6. *Temple Servants (2:43–54)*

43 *The temple servants: the descendants of Ziha, the descendants of Hasupha, the descendants of Tabbaoth,*

44 *the descendants of Keros, the descendants of Siaha, the descendants of Padon,*

45 *the descendants of Lebanah, the descendants of Hagabah, the descendants of Akkub,*

46 *the descendants of Hagab, the descendants of Shalmai, the descendants of Hanan,*

47 *the descendants of Giddel, the descendants of Gahar, the descendants of Reaiah,*

48 *the descendants of Rezin, the descendants of Nekoda, the descendants of Gazzam,*

49 *the descendants of Uzza, the descendants of Raseah, the descendants of Besai,*

50 *the descendants of Asnah, the descendants of Meunim, the descendants of Nephisim,*

51 *the descendants of Bakbuk, the descendants of Hakupha, the descendants of Harhur,*

52 *the descendants of Bazluth, the descendants of Mehida, the descendants of Harsha,*

1. Cf. R. de Vaux, *Ancient Israel* II (E.T. 1961), pp. 388–390.
2. W. F. Albright, *Archaeology and the Religion of Israel* (Baltimore: ^{5}1969), pp. 121–25.
3. Cf. A. Kapelrud, *The Ras Shamra Discoveries and the OT* (E.T. 1965), pp. 67ff.

53 *the descendants of Barkos, the descendants of Sisera, the descendants of Temah,*
54 *the descendants of Neziah, the descendants of Hatipha.*

This is the lowest class of temple personnel. The precise origin of the temple slaves *(n^e^ṯînîm)* is not yet clear. Because of the close link between the *n^e^ṯînîm* and the Gibeonites in Chronicles, where the *n^e^ṯînîm* are associated with the Levites and the genealogy of the Gibeonites is repeated in 1 Chr. 9, Jewish tradition and certain modern scholars hold that the *n^e^ṯînîm* must be regarded as Gibeonites (cf. 1 Chr. 8 and 9);[1] the connection is not convincingly clear, however. The Jewish tradition has obviously been based on Josh 9:23 and must be regarded as secondary. We have indications in the OT that war captives were presented to serve in the sanctuary (e.g., Num. 31:25–47). The *n^e^ṯînîm* might be their descendants.[2] E. A. Speiser is correct with his surmise that the *n^e^ṯînîm* formed a class of religious servitors distinct from and subordinate to the priests and the Levites.[3] This kind of religious service was not unknown in the Canaanite world, as is shown by an Ugaritic text with the term *ytnm*.[4]

Ezra's list has three names more than Neh. 7. A few interesting points on the names in this pericope must be noted: Ziha is an Egyptian name occurring in the Elephantine Papyri;[5] Hagab occurs in the Lachish Letters;[6] Asnah is another well-known Egyptian name.

7. *Servants of Solomon (2:55–58)*

55 *The descendants of Solomon's servants: the descendants of Sotai, the descendants of Hassophereth, the descendants of Peruda,*
56 *the descendants of Jaalah, the descendants of Darkon, the descendants of Giddel,*
57 *the descendants of Shephatiah, the descendants of Hattil, the descendants of Pocheret-hazzebaim, the descendants of Ami.*
58 *All the temple servants, and the descendants of Solomon's servants, were 392.*

1. Cf. Blenkinsopp, *Gibeon and Israel,* pp. 106–108, and the review of D. Lys, *Études théologiques et religieuses,* 48 (1973), p. 379.
2. Cf. I. Mendelsohn, *Slavery in the Ancient Near East* (New York: 1949), pp. 101ff.; Myers, *Ezra. Nehemiah,* p. 19.
3. E. A. Speiser, "Unrecognized Dedication," *IEJ* 13 (1963), p. 71. He also draws attention to a similar practice in Neo-Babylonian times of the *širku,* from *šarāku,* "to grant."
4. Cf. C. H. Gordon, *Ugaritic Textbook* (Rome: 1965), p. 416; B. A. Levine, "The Netînîm," *JBL* 82 (1963), pp. 207–212.
5. Written as *ṣḥ'* and not *ṣyḥ* as here. Cf. *AP,* p. 307, and esp. p. 47 (15:2).
6. Cf. H. Torczyner, *Lachish* I (London: 1938).

The origin of these servants is uncertain. Their forebears might have been taken into captivity by Solomon,[1] although Solomon is not known in the Bible as a king of military action. Sennacherib once took forty-one persons captive and gave them to the service of the god Zababa.[2] This may point to a common practice in those days. This group is also mentioned in Neh. 7:60 and 11:3, but these texts bring us no nearer to solving the riddle of their origin. Two of the names, viz., Hassophereth and Pocheret-hazzebaim, are feminine and may point to a certain guild or may denote a particular office, e.g., Hassophereth may denote the guild or office of scribes.

8. Those Who Cannot Prove Ancestry (2:59–63)

59 *Now these are those who came up from Tel-melah, Tel-harsha, Cherub, Addan, and Immer, but they were not able to give evidence of their father's genealogies, and their descendants, whether they were of Israel:*

60 *the descendants of Delaiah, the descendants of Tobiah, the descendants of Nekoda, 652.*

61 *And of the descendants of the priests: the descendants of Habaiah, the descendants of Hakkoz, the descendants of Barzillai, who took a wife from the daughters of Barzillai the Gileadite and was called by their name.*

62 *These searched for their registration in the genealogies, but they could not be located; therefore they were considered unclean and were excluded from the priesthood.*

63 *The governor said to them that they should not eat from the most holy things until a priest stood up with the Urim and Thummim.*

We have here two separate cases: one referring to laymen (vv. 59–60) and the other to priests (vv. 61–63). We may infer from this pericope as it is clearly stated in 1 Chr. 5:17 and Neh. 7:5 that Jewish families kept genealogies to prove their Jewish descent, and to ascertain that mixture with foreign groups was somehow excluded. A pure line had religious significance, because foreign elements could bring apostasy in the Jewish community. The laymen who were unable to prove their Jewish lineage may have been from families who had lost their genealogical records because of the Exile. It seems as if they had presented a great problem to the authorities. The real problem arose with the priests. They must be cultically clean and of true Jewish descent. As long as they could not prove

1. Cf. Brockington, *Ezra, Nehemiah and Esther*, p. 60.
2. Mendelsohn, *Slavery in the Ancient Near East*, pp. 96–99; cf. also Myers, *Ezra. Nehemiah*, p. 19.

their Jewish descent they were regarded as unclean and outside the priesthood. The governor, or Persian high official *(tiršāṯā')*, a title also used for Nehemiah (Neh. 8:9; 10:1), was quite probably Zerubbabel.[1] He took action to prohibit these unfortunate priests from eating any of the most holy things (cf. Lev. 2:3; 7:21–36). *The most holy things (qōḏēš haqqᵒḏāšîm)* refer here to the food that priests had as their perquisites after cultic services. The prohibition was made to prevent a cultic sin that was widespread in the ancient Near East. The Urim and Thummim should be used to prove whether they were Jewish, or whether they should be regarded as priests. Some scholars propose to read "high priest" instead of "priest,"[2] with some Greek manuscripts.[3] The former reading would mean that the temple was operating fully, and that the list was of a later date than commonly accepted. If "priest" is read, it could imply either that the priests had to wait until the temple was finished, or that Jeshua already had the Urim and Thummim with him.[4] The Urim and Thummim are one of the thorny problems of the OT. From 1 Sam. 14:41 it is clear that they were used to discover the will of God, but by a process of elimination.[5]

Of interest is the case of Barzillai ("iron-man"), who took his name from his father-in-law and thus started a matriarchal lineage. It is the only example of this kind of custom in the OT, and it is stated here as an extraordinary example of people who were proud of their patriarchal lineage.

Who came up ('ōlîm). The same word as in v. 1. Its use here suggests that the places mentioned must be situated where they were in exile, namely, Babylonia. Not one of these places is known from any other source, although two Babylonian place names are known to be formed with *tel*, e.g., Tel-abib (Ezek. 3:15) and Tel-assar (2 K. 18:12).

9. *Totals (2:64–67)*

64 *The whole assembly numbered 42,360,*
65 *besides their male and female servants, who numbered 7337; and they had 200 male and female singers.*
66 *Their horses were 736; their mules, 245;*
67 *their camels, 435; their donkeys, 6720.*

The total in v. 64 leaves us with an insoluble problem. If we add up the figures for the different families, we arrive at a total of 29,818. Some have

1. Cf. W. Th. In der Smitten, "Der Tirschātā' in Esra-Nehemiah," *VT* 21 (1971), pp. 618–620.
2. E.g., Brockington, *Ezra, Nehemiah and Esther*, pp. 61–62.
3. Cf. *BHK*.
4. Grosheide, *Ezra*, p. 100.
5. For a discussion cf. K. Galling, "Urim und Tummim," *RGG* VI, pp. 1193–94.

proposed that women and children are left out in the totals of the families, but this leaves us with 12,542 women and children, much too low a figure.[1] This total of 42,360, however, occurs also in Neh. 7 and must be regarded as correct. Somehow, through textual corruption[2] or by the omission of certain families, this discrepancy happened.

Assembly (qāhāl) must be taken as referring to the cultic community.[3] It is definitely not a crowd as Rost has maintained,[4] but included all the Jews, women as well as servants.[5]

10. Voluntary Contributions to the Temple (2:68–69)

68 *And some of the heads of fathers' households, when they arrived at the house of the Lord which is in Jerusalem, offered willingly for the house of God to restore it on its foundation.*

69 *According to their ability they gave to the treasury for the work 61,000 gold drachmas, and 5000 silver minas, and 100 priestly garments.*

There are discrepancies between this description and that of Neh. 7. It is clear that the author uses round numbers.[1] *Gold drachmas (darkᵉmōnîm)* are either the Persian daric or the Greek drachma. At this time the Greek drachma was in general use and it is quite probably meant here. The Babylonian mina was probably generally used as a unit for silver.[2] The money is meant to pay for the building activities of the temple (cf. 3:7). This action was quite probably inspired by the example of the Israelites during the exodus period who donated various precious objects to build the tabernacle (Exod. 25:4–7; 35:2–9).[3]

11. Location of the Returnees (2:70)

70 *Now the priests and the Levites, some of the people, the singers, the gatekeepers, and the temple servants lived in their cities, and all Israel in their cities.*

1. Cf. Brockington, *Ezra, Nehemiah and Esther,* p. 62; Myers, *Ezra. Nehemiah,* pp. 20–21; Grosheide, *Ezra,* p. 102.
2. Allrick, *BASOR* 136 (1954), pp. 21–27.
3. Grosheide, *Ezra,* pp. 101–102.
4. Cf. L. Rost, *Die Vorstufen von Kirche und Synagoge im AT.* BWANT IV/24 (Stuttgart: 1938), p. 24.
5. Galling, *Studien zur Geschichte Israels,* p. 100 n. 2.

1. Cf. Galling, *Studien zur Geschichte Israels,* pp. 101ff.
2. Cf. Brockington, *Ezra, Nehemiah and Esther,* p. 62.
3. Cf. Myers, *Ezra. Nehemiah,* p. 21.

Some scholars hold that this verse is textually corrupt and that with the LXX "in Jerusalem" must be inserted after "the people."[1] This sensible suggestion means that the priests, Levites, and some of the people lived in Jerusalem or vicinity and the others in their different cities. *Some of the people (ûmin-hā'ām)* refers, according to Speiser, to the natives of the country and thus not to the returnees.[2] Grosheide holds that this expression refers to the heads of families.[3] A better approach is to regard "some of the people" as laymen in contrast to the priests and Levites previously mentioned. It would be strange that in the list of returnees with their location, "natives" would be inserted who did not return from the Exile.

C. INSTITUTION OF SACRIFICES; BUILDING OF THE TEMPLE (3:1–6:22)

1. Institution of Sacrifices (3:1–6)

1 *With the coming of the seventh month, while the Israelites were in the towns, they gathered as one man in Jerusalem.*

2 *Jeshua the son of Jozadak, with his companions the priests, and Zerubbabel the son of Shealtiel, with his companions, started to rebuild the altar of the God of Israel in order to offer sacrifices according to what is written in the law of Moses, the man of God.*

3 *The erected the altar on its original place in spite of the fear they had for the people of the country around them, and on it they offered sacrifices to the Lord, sacrifices in the morning and evening.*

4 *They celebrated the Feast of Tabernacles, as it is written, and as many sacrifices daily as are prescribed,*

5 *and besides the daily sacrifices, they also offered on the New Moon feasts and on all the other holy festivals of the Lord as well as the voluntary sacrifices to the Lord.*

6 *From the first of the seventh month they started to offer sacrifices to the Lord, but the foundations of the temple of the Lord had not yet been laid.*

1 The connection between chs. 2 and 3 is obvious. The previous chapter described the return of the Jews. This chapter pictures the beginning of a legitimate worship. The seventh month, when all the Israelites were gathered, is the month Tishri (September-October). It is of interest that in Neh. 7:73, where the meeting of Ezra at the Water Gate is described, the

1. Cf., e.g., Grosheide, *Ezra*, p. 108.
2. Speiser, *IEJ* 13 (1963), p. 70.
3. Grosheide, *Ezra*, p. 107.

seventh month is also mentioned. There is a remarkable similarity between the two descriptions.[1] But it is obvious that both Ezra 3:4 and Neh. 8:14 mention the Feast of Tabernacles. This is the point of connection between the two descriptions. But when did this happen? There is no reference to any year. Most scholars agree that it is the seventh month of the first year of return, c. 537 B.C.[2]

While the Israelites were in the towns. It is impossible to read with various manuscripts *b^{e}'ārêhem* instead of *be'ārîm*. The translation would then be "in their own towns" (cf. JB).[3] This expression refers to the fact that the Israelites had arrived in the Holy Land and were already settled. *k^{e}'îš 'eḥāḏ*—as one man, with common purpose.[4] It may also refer to the fact that every Israelite had to attend the three major festivals of the Lord (cf., e.g., Exod. 23:17; 34:23; Deut. 16:16).

2 On Jeshua and Zerubbabel see the discussions of 2:2 and 3:8. Some scholars, referring to Jer. 41:5, hold that at that stage an altar must have already existed.[5] This can be admitted readily. It is quite probable that a temporary altar was erected, but that this altar was not regarded as being built in accordance with the description of the law of Moses. Thus it was felt necessary to build a new altar.[6]

3 This altar was constructed on the place of the foundations of the altar of the temple of Solomon. We must accept that the altar which is referred to in Jer. 41:5 was also built on the same place. The returnees demolished the old altar to build a new one in its place. It is to be expected that such an act would kindle hostility among the old inhabitants of the land. If we approach the problematic expression *kî b^{e}'êmâ '^{a}lēhem mē'-ammê hā'^{a}rāṣôṯ* from this angle, it is unnecessary to regard it as a gloss as Rudolph does.[7] The Hebrew of this expression is difficult to explain, however. The *kî* must be taken as causal[8] and the *b^{e}* in the meaning "out of."[9] *The people of the country around them* refers to all the old inhabitants

1. Brockington, *Ezra, Nehemiah and Esther*, p. 63; Myers, *Ezra. Nehemiah*, p. 26.
2. Cf., e.g., B. M. Pelaia, *Esdra e Neemia*. La Sacra Bibbia (Turin: 1960), p. 54; Rudolph, *Esra und Nehemia*, p. 29; Grosheide, *Ezra*, p. 112.
3. Grosheide, *Ezra*, p. 111. Cf. also Neh. 7:72.
4. L. W. Batten, *A Critical and Exegetical Commentary on the Books of Ezra and Nehemiah*. ICC (Edinburgh: 1913), p. 107.
5. Cf. esp. E. Janssen, *Juda in der Exilzeit*. FRLANT 69 (Göttingen: 1956), pp. 94–104.
6. Grosheide, *Ezra*, p. 114; Myers, *op. cit.*, p. 27; Brockington, *op. cit.*, pp. 63–64.
7. Rudolph, *Esra und Nehemia*, p. 28.
8. Grosheide, *Ezra*, p. 115.
9. This meaning for *b^{e}* is strongly attested in Hebrew as well as in Ugaritic; cf. F. C. Fensham, "Ugaritic and the Translation of the OT," *BT* 18 (1967), pp. 71–74.

of the country.[10] They may be Jewish or Samaritan. Clearly at this stage a rift had been created between the returnees and the older inhabitants of the country. The author shows that the regular sacrifices as they are described in the law of Moses were instituted. In v. 3b the Tamid or morning and evening sacrifices are mentioned.

4 The Feast of Tabernacles was held. Since this feast was usually celebrated on the fifteenth of the seventh month, its mention here corroborates the seventh month of the year mentioned in v. 1 (on this feast see Exod. 23:16; 34:22; Lev. 23:33–36, 39–43; Deut. 16:13–15; Num. 29:12–38).

5 In this verse the other sacrifices are mentioned. *The voluntary sacrifices* refer to any sacrifice which can be offered at any day when an Israelite feels obliged to do so. If we compare the mentioning of sacrifices by the Chronicler (1 Chr. 33:31; 2 Chr. 2:4; 8:13; 31:3) with what we have here, the omission of the sabbath sacrifice is strange, but we have no textual support for adding it.[11]

6 The first part of this verse clearly refers to the fact that all the sacrifices, except those connected with the Feast of Tabernacles, were instituted on the first of the seventh month. According to the law of Moses the Feast of Tabernacles must be celebrated on the fifteenth of the seventh month.

The last part of this verse states that the foundations of the temple had not been laid. We might take the *waw* as either "and" or "but." If we take it as "and," it stands in a loose connection with the previous expression. It is then a transitional expression which is strongly connected to what follows. It seems, however, that the author wanted to draw attention to the fact that the altar was built before the foundation of the temple had been laid. Thus the translation "but" is better.[12]

2. Laying of the Foundation of the Temple (3:7–13)

7 *So money was given to the masons and workmen and food, drink, and oil to the Sidonians and Tyrians to bring cedar wood from Lebanon by sea to Jafo; permission for this was granted by Cyrus king of Persia.*

8 *In the second month of the second year after they had come to the temple of God in Jerusalem, Zerubbabel the son of Shealtiel and*

10. Cf. Grosheide, *GTT* 54 (1954), pp. 73ff. Cf. also L. A. Snijders, "Het 'volk des lands' in Juda," *NThT* 12 (1958), pp. 241–256.

11. Against Rudolph, *Esra und Nehemia*, p. 28; Galling, *Die Bücher der Chronik, Esra, Nehemia*. ATD 12 (Göttingen: 1954), p. 192; Myers, *Ezra. Nehemiah*, p. 25.

12. K. Galling, *Die Bücher der Chronik, Esra, Nehemia*, p. 192; against Grosheide, *Ezra*, p. 118.

Jeshua the son of Jozadak, with the rest of their companions, the priests, the Levites, and all who had returned to Jerusalem from captivity, began the work. They appointed the Levites from twenty years upward to superintend the work on the temple of the Lord.

9 *Jeshua, his sons and companions, and Kadmiel, his sons, sons of Judah, were all willing to superintend the work on the temple of the Lord, and also the sons of Henadad, their sons and companions, the Levites.*

10 *When the builders had laid the foundations of the temple of the Lord, the priests with their vestments came with trumpets and the Levites, sons of Asaph, with cymbals to praise the Lord according to the directions of David king of Israel,*

11 *and they sang in praise and thanksgiving to the Lord as follows: He is good, his covenant love is for ever over Israel. All the people shouted also aloud in praise of the Lord, because the foundation of the temple of the Lord had been laid.*

12 *But many of the old priests, Levites, and heads of families who had seen with their own eyes the first temple on its foundation wept aloud, though many others shouted loudly with joy.*

13 *It was impossible for the people to distinguish the loud shouts of joy from the weeping of the people, because they shouted so loudly that the noise could be heard from afar.*

One of the most important problems of this passage is to harmonize it with what is written in Haggai. In Hag. 2:15–18 the laying of foundations is mentioned, but the exegesis of this pericope is full of problems. Is Haggai referring here to the laying of the foundation for the first time in 537 B.C. or to the laying of the foundation in the time of Darius? The harmonizing of Hag. 1:14; 2:3; and 2:18 is indeed difficult, and various proposals have been made to solve the problem.[1] Some scholars even hold that the whole description in Ezra 3 is to be regarded as the fiction of the Chronicler.[2] This would then solve certain problems in Haggai. But if we take seriously the arguments of F. I. Andersen that *ysd* has a wide meaning and that it refers not to a point in time, but to a period in time, many problems created by Haggai disappear.[3] It is quite possible that the foundation had been laid in 537 B.C. and that in the time of Haggai work had started on the foundation again by removing the rubble and strengthening the weak

1. For a discussion of the various views see J. L. Koole, *Haggai*. Commentaar op het Oude Testament (Kampen: 1967), pp. 92ff.
2. Cf. the discussion of Michaeli, *Les livres des Chroniques, d'Esdras et de Néhémie*, p. 266.
3. F. I. Andersen, *ABR* 6 (1958), pp. 1ff.; cf. also Koole, *Haggai*, p. 92.

spots in the foundation laid in 537 B.C.[4] In the wider semantic sphere of the meaning of *ysd,* as demonstrated by Andersen, this is a possible solution.

7 *So money was given.* The third person plural of the verb can sometimes be translated by the passive. *The masons* (Heb. *ḥōṣᵉḇîm*). The Hebrew term refers to quarrying. Heb. *ḥārāšîm* may mean workmen, perhaps including carpenters as well as bricklayers.

The following points are of interest in connection with the mentioning of the Sidonians and Tyrians. Sidon and Tyre were the two famous cities of the Phoenicians nearest to Judah. Some want to point out that by placing the Sidonians first the author wants to stress the importance of Sidon over Tyre. But the mentioning of both may only point to Phoenicia as a whole without reference to any priority.[5] Scholars have pointed out that some similarity existed between this description and the ones in Chronicles dealing with the building of David's palace (1 Chr. 22:2; 22:15; and esp. 22:4, where the Sidonians and Tyrians are mentioned).[6] It is clear that roughly in the period of the Chronicler, in the later postexilic times, this kind of terminology was used.

It is also of interest that the payment in kind, namely, food (grain), drink (wine), and oil for cedar wood, is mentioned in 2 Chr. 2:9 in connection with the building of the temple of Solomon. It shows that at this time, as in the times of David and Solomon, cedar wood was procured from Lebanon. Because of the lack of arable land in Phoenicia, commodities like grain, wine, and oil were supplied in exchange for cedar wood.

Permission for this was granted by Cyrus king of Persia (Heb. *kᵉrišyôn kôreš meleḵ-pāras ʿᵃlêhem*). This expression is interpreted in two different ways. First, it is regarded as a loose expression referring to the whole venture of the building of the temple. It is then interpreted as if this expression refers back to the edict of Cyrus in which the rebuilding of his subjects' demolished sanctuaries is allowed.[7] The problem with this view is the awkward position of this expression immediately following the sentence in which reference is made to the bringing of the cedar wood to Jafo. Second, the grammatically sounder view is that this expression refers to the sentence immediately preceding. The author wants to point out that the delivery of cedar wood for the temple was approved by Cyrus. We must keep in mind that we have here a transaction between two different

4. Koole, *op. cit.,* p. 95.
5. Grosheide, *Ezra,* p. 18.
6. Myers, *Ezra. Nehemiah,* p. 27.
7. Rudolph, *Esra und Nehemia,* p. 31; Grosheide, *Ezra,* p. 119.

provinces in the Persian empire, and permission for it had to be granted by the satrap of the Trans-Euphrates in the name of the king.[8]

Rišyôn is a hapax legomenon in the OT that may be connected to the Aram. *ršy,* meaning "have the right," e.g., to sell a house.[9] Here in Ezra it means "according to the right or permission granted by Cyrus. . . ."

8–9 *In the second month of the second year.* It is also stated that the building of the temple under Solomon started in the second month (1 K. 6:1; 2 Chr. 3:2). This is the month Iyyar (April-May).[10] That both 1 K. 6:1 and this verse refer to the second month should be expected, because it is then the beginning of the dry season after the major harvest is gathered in and the important festivals are already held.[11] It is thus the right time to start building operations.

Zerubbabel . . . Jeshua. It is important to note that Ezra 5:6 states that Sheshbazzar was responsible for the beginning of building activities on the temple. Here the names of Zerubbabel and Jeshua are mentioned, representing the Davidic and the priestly lineage. Some scholars have advanced the view that the Chronicler has identified Zerubbabel with Sheshbazzar.[12] Myers even suggests that the Chronicler may have deliberately substituted Zerubbabel for Sheshbazzar, because the attempts of Sheshbazzar to build the temple failed and those of Zerubbabel succeeded at a later stage.[13] This leaves the mentioning of Sheshbazzar in 5:6 unexplained.[14] As we have seen already, the whole question of the relationship between Sheshbazzar and Zerubbabel is unclear. It is possible that Sheshbazzar as an old man played a minor role in the building of the foundation in 537 B.C., but that the younger Zerubbabel from the Davidic lineage played the important role. It is also possible that Sheshbazzar died before the second, successful attempt to build the temple.[15] Although this is to be regarded as a solution of most of the problems, the whole situation is not at all clear. The enumeration of all the groups which began the work shows that the laity (Zerubbabel and his companions), priests (Jeshua and his companions), and Levites are clearly distinguished.

Twenty years upwards was regarded as an age to take responsibility

8. Cf. R. N. Frye, *The Heritage of Persia,* p. 103.
9. Cf. *DISO,* p. 284.
10. Pelaia, *Esdra e Neemia,* p. 58.
11. Grosheide, *Ezra,* p. 120.
12. Rudolph, *Esra und Nehemia,* p. 31; Brockington, *Ezra, Nehemiah and Esther,* p. 64. Cf. for a discussion K.-M. Beyse, *Serubbabel und die Königserwartungen der Propheten Haggai und Sacharja* (Stuttgart: 1972).
13. Myers, *Ezra, Nehemiah,* p. 28, gives this as one possible explanation.
14. For a discussion of the whole problem cf. Michaeli, *Les livres des Chroniques, d'Esdras et de Néhémie,* pp. 265ff.
15. Grosheide, *Ezra,* p. 120; Myers, *op. cit.,* p. 28.

(cf. 1 Chr. 23:27; 2 Chr. 31:17). In Num. 8:24 it is twenty-five and in Num. 4:3, 23, 30 it is thirty. The superintending of the Levites and the priests was to assure that the work was ritually correct.

10–11 In these verses the celebrations are described after the foundation had been laid.[16] The leading role was played by the priests and the Levites. The priests were clad in their typical vestments (cf. Exod. 28; 2 Chr. 5:12; 20:21) and they blew the trumpets. The Levites played on the cymbals (cf. Ps. 150:5) which consisted of two metal plates with which they gave the beat (cf. 1 Chr. 15:16, 19; 16:5; 25:1–6; 2 Chr. 7:6). According to the author this was done as David prescribed. He was at this stage regarded as the most important figure who had initiated music in the cult.

The music accompanied the singing. Two types of songs were sung, namely, songs of praise and thanksgiving songs. As an example the *introitus* of a song is given which was popular in the time of the author. *Ḥeseḏ* as part of this song is indeed a difficult word to translate. In some parts of the OT it is closely connected to the covenant idea and may mean covenant solidarity or covenant love.[17] The meaning "covenant love" seems appropriate here. The music and singing were accompanied by loud shouting of the laity in praise of the Lord.

12–13 The following Hebrew expression is difficult to interpret: *'^{a}šer rā'û 'eṯ-habbayiṯ hāri'šôn b^{e}yās^{e}ḏô zeh habbayiṯ b^{e}'ênêhem bōḵîm b^{e}qôl gāḏôl*. It is uncertain whether *b^{e}yās^{e}ḏô* must be taken with the preceding expression or the expression that follows. In our translation we have taken it with the preceding phrase. If so, *zeh habbayiṯ* remains unexplained. It might be a parenthetic clause which can be translated "it is now this house," this poor house (temple). Then the first temple would stand in contrast to this newly built temple. But the Hebrew is awkward and to a certain extent unintelligible. What is clear is that the older people who had seen the temple of Solomon wept in disappointment. It is not quite certain what created the disappointment. The contrast between the smaller stones used here and the huge blocks used in Solomon's temple might have been

16. The use of the prefix conjugation (imperfect) of *ysd* here is regarded as strange. However, this is to be taken as a past tense in the form of the prefix conjugation, or else as a *waw* consecutive prefix conjugation which was erroneously punctuated by the Masoretes.

17. Cf. F. C. Fensham, "Ps 21—A Covenant Song?", *ZAW* 77 (1965), pp. 193–202. For the semantic field of *ḥeseḏ* see N. Glueck, Ḥesed *in the Bible* (E.T. 1967); K. D. Sakenfeld, *The Meaning of Hesed in the Hebrew Bible* (Missoula: 1978); H. J. Stoebe, "Die Bedeutung des Wortes *ḥäsäd* im AT," *VT* 2 (1952), pp. 244–254; *idem, THAT* I, pp. 600–621.

too much for the older people.[18] Even today the smaller Turkish stones of the Western Wall of the platform stand in glaring contrast to the huge stones used in Herod's time. The author points out that the older people wept, but that the enthusiasm of the rest of the people was so overwhelming that outsiders could not distinguish between the weeping and the shouts of joy. The disappointment of the older people is also mentioned in Hag. 2:3, but this happened with the second attempt to rebuild the temple. Some scholars presume that Ezra 3:12–13 is built on Haggai and could therefore be unhistorical.[19] But nothing contradicts the fact that at two separate occasions the disappointment of the older people was demonstrated. It is noteworthy that in Haggai weeping is not mentioned. Another explanation for the weeping is given by Van Selms and Coggins, namely, that it is a ritual weeping that has nothing to do with emotions.[20] This is unacceptable, however, because in such a case the reference to the first temple would be left unexplained.[21]

Some take the description of 3:7–13 as a fiction in which the Chronicler created the impression that the foundation of the temple had been laid immediately after the return of the first group of Jews in the days of Cyrus.[22] The basis on which this assumption is built is indeed slender, as we have seen in our discussion. The so-called similarities between the descriptions of the building of David's palace and the Solomonic temple compared with the description here are not so clear-cut as has been presumed. The contrast between Haggai and this chapter is also overemphasized. It is not easy to compare prophetical pronouncements with historical facts, because the historical allusions of the prophets are not organized in a chronological order. There is nothing in this chapter which cannot be counted as historical.

3. Suspension of Work on the Temple (4:1–23)

a. Samaritan tactics under Cyrus (4:1–5)

1 *When the enemies of Judah and Benjamin learned that the exiles were building a temple for the Lord, the God of Israel,*
2 *they approached Zerubbabel and the heads of the families with the request: "We want to build with you, because we seek your God, as*

18. Cf. also Myers, *op. cit.*, p. 29.
19. Rudolph, *Esra und Nehemia*, p. 32 and Myers, *op. cit.*, p. 29.
20. Cf. A. van Selms, "Weenen als aanvangsritus," *NTT* 24 (1935), pp. 119–127; R. J. Coggins, *The Books of Ezra and Nehemiah*. Cambridge Bible Commentary (Cambridge: 1976), p. 25.
21. Grosheide, *Ezra*, pp. 124–25.
22. Cf. the discussion of Pelaia, *Esdra e Neemia*, p. 60.

you do, and we have sacrificed to him from the time of Esarhaddon king of Assyria who brought us here."

3 *Zerubbabel, Jeshua, and the other heads of the Israelite families said: "You have no right to build a temple for our God, but we have. We alone shall build for the Lord, the God of Israel, because Cyrus king of Persia commanded us to do so."*

4 *Then the people of the land were disheartening the people of Judah and frightened them from building,*

5 *and they hired counsellors against them to break up their plans. This lasted from the time of Cyrus king of Persia to the reign of Darius king of Persia.*

1–2 In ch. 3 the beginning of the building activities is sketched, but the temple is not completed till twenty years later in the reign of Darius. In 4:1–5 the reason for this delay is given. *The enemies of Judah and Benjamin.* Some scholars argue that "the people of the land" was originally used here, but was later changed by the Chronicler into "the enemies," because in his time, though not in the time of Cyrus, the Samaritans were enemies of the Jews. But the antagonism had already started with the building of the altar (cf. our discussion at 3:3), and it is thus not farfetched to call the people of the land "enemies." Their altar in Jerusalem had been destroyed and now they wanted to have a hand in the building of the temple. It is also clear from their request that they desired to be regarded as an independent group, because they served God like the exiles. Although there were two independent groups, they had the same religious purpose, namely, to serve God.

The term *lō'* is difficult. The negative makes no sense here; we should expect it directly before the verb. It is possible to take it as the asseverative *lû,* "indeed," well known in Ugaritic and also in Hebrew.[1] We follow the Qere, *lô,* "to him," which also eliminates the difficulty.

From the time of Esarhaddon. Esarhaddon ruled from 681 B.C. to 669 B.C. Nowhere in the Bible is it explicitly stated that Esarhaddon deported people from Samaria and brought other people back, although Isa. 7:8 might refer to such an act.[2] We are not well informed in the OT about the time of Esarhaddon. We know, however, from a cylinder of Esarhaddon that he conquered Sidon during one of his campaigns,[3] and it is most likely that Northern Israel (Samaria) was also involved in the

1. Cf. W. Gesenius and F. Buhl, *Hebräisches und Aramäisches Handwörterbuch über das AT* (Berlin: 1949), p. 380; in Ugaritic C. H. Gordon, *Ugaritic Textbook,* p. 425.
2. Cf. Alt, *KS* II, p. 321 n. 4; Myers, *Ezra. Nehemiah,* p. 35.
3. Cf. D. J. Wiseman, "An Esarhaddon Cylinder from Nimrud," *Iraq* 14 (1952), pp. 54–60; Myers, *Ezra. Nehemiah,* p. 35; Alt, *op. cit.*

rebellion against the Assyrians. With such a rebellion the deportation could have taken place as the fulfillment of a curse of a vassal treaty.[4]

3 This verse supplies us with the dividing line between the returnees and the Samaritans, the beginning of hostility between these two groups. The latest research on the Samaritans tries to show that the rift appeared much later, only developing gradually.[5] It may be granted that the hostility was not as vehement in the beginning as it was later. The differences were of a political and religious nature, and these differences had already developed during the existence of the two monarchies, viz., Northern Israel and Judah. The religious differences are clearly visible in the final redactor's editing of 1 and 2 Kings. From the political viewpoint it is to be noticed that after the Assyrians made Northern Israel into an Assyrian province in the time of Sargon, the position remained the same under the Neo-Babylonians.[6] The Persians took over the provinces of the Neo-Babylonians and did not change the legal principles on which they were administered. So the old hostility between Samaria and Jerusalem simply continued. From the religious viewpoint it is important to note that strong opposition to the religion of the north was demonstrated in Judah. This religious contempt for the cultic practices of the north became a dominant factor.[7] The returnees as exiles from Judah did not want the people of the north to aid them with the building of the temple, and their reply to the Samaritans stated so diplomatically. It is a no, built on legal grounds. The Persian king granted the right to rebuild the temple only to the returnees, not to any other people. But as a background we have the old political and religious differences.

4–5 *Disheartening the people of Judah* (Heb. *m^e^rappîm y^e^ḏê ʿam-y^e^hûḏâ,* lit. "weakening the hands of the people of Judah"; cf. Jer. 38:4 and Lachish Letter 6:6–7). The people were somehow discouraged from continuing the work. The phrase *ûm^e^ḇal^a^hîm* is difficult. The verb is a

4. We have a vassal treaty between Baal of Tyre and Esarhaddon in which the deportation of people is mentioned as a curse, cf. R. Borger, *Die Inschriften Asarhaddons, Königs von Assyrien* (1956), § 69; *idem, ZA* 54 (1957), pp. 183ff. Cf. also E. Reiner in *ANET,* pp. 97–98. For other vassal treaties of Esarhaddon see D. J. Wiseman, "The Vassal-Treaties of Esarhaddon," *Iraq* 20 (1958), *passim.*

5. Cf. F. M. Cross, "Papyri of the Fourth Century B.C. from Dâliyeh," in D. N. Freedman and J. C. Greenfield, eds., *New Directions in Biblical Archaeology* (Garden City: 1969), pp. 45–69; R. J. Coggins, *Samaritans and Jews: The Origins of Samaritanism Reconsidered* (Atlanta: 1975); H. J. Kippenberg, *Garizim und Synagoge: Traditiongeschichtlich Untersuchungen zur Samaritanisch Religion der aramäischen Periode.* Religiongeschichtliche Versuche und Vorarbeiten 30 (New York: 1971), esp. p. 57.

6. Cf. Alt, *KS* II, pp. 317ff.

7. Cf. the discussion of Widengren, *Israelite and Judaean History,* p. 512.

hapax legomenon from *blh.* The noun *ballāhâ* means "fright." But the Qere reads *m^{e}ḇah^{a}lîm* from *bhl,* "to frighten." In such a case we must accept that metathesis occurred in *m^{e}ḇal^{a}hîm*.

It is not expressly stated what had disheartened and frightened the people of Judah. If we take *counsellors* as referring to the Persian governors, the whole issue becomes clear. The Persian officials were bribed to frustrate the plans of the returnees. Bribery as a practice was well known in Persian times.[8] *This lasted from . . . Darius king of the Persians.* This phrase shows that the author had a correct view of the historical sequel. Through the reign of Cambyses up to the time of Darius the enemies of Judah[9] succeeded in stopping the building operations.

b. Samaritan tactics under Xerxes and Artaxerxes I (4:6–23)

6 *In the beginning of the reign of Xerxes (Ahasuerus) they made a complaint against the inhabitants of Judah and Jerusalem.*

7 *Then in the time of Artaxerxes, Bishlam, Mithredath, Tabeel, and the rest of their companions wrote a letter to Artaxerxes king of Persia. The contents of the letter were written in Aramaic and translated in Aramaic.*

8 *Then Rehum the high official and Shimshai the secretary wrote yet another letter against Jerusalem to Artaxerxes the king.*

9 *Then Rehum the high official, Shimshai the secretary, the rest of their companions, the judges, the legates, the consuls, the officials, the Arkewites, the Babylonians, those of Susa—that is the Elamites—*

10 *and the other people whom the honorable Osnapar the great deported and settled in the towns of Samaria and the rest of the Trans-Euphrates—*

11 *this is the copy of the letter which they sent to him: "To Artaxerxes the king, your servants, the men of the Trans-Euphrates:*

12 *The king must know that the Jews who have come from you to us and arrived in Jerusalem are rebuilding the rebellious and evil city; they are restoring the wall and are laying the foundations.*

13 *Now the king must know that if that city is rebuilt and the wall is restored, they will not pay tribute, tax, or duty, and the treasury of the king will suffer loss.*

14 *Now, because we are subservient to the king and we do not want to see the king put to shame, we send this letter to inform the king*

8. Frye, *The Heritage of Persia,* p. 110. Cf. also Josephus *Ant.* xi.2.1.

9. Cf. the opinion of R. J. Coggins, "The Interpretation of Ezra IV.4," *JTS* 16 (1965), pp. 124–27, that the enemies could not be regarded as Samaritans, but as Jewish nationalistic groups who were against the building of the temple. This is unacceptable.

15 *that inquiry must be made in the archives of your predecessors, and you will discover in the archives and learn that that city was rebellious, damaging to kings and provinces, that revolts were stirred up from ancient times; that is why that city was destroyed.*
16 *We let the king know that if that city is rebuilt and the wall restored, then soon you will have nothing left in the Trans-Euphrates."*
17 *The king sent the following message to Rehum the high official, Shimshai the secretary, and their companions who lived in Samaria and the rest of the Trans-Euphrates: "Peace,*
18 *the document which you sent to us is interpreted and read before me,*
19 *and I ordered a search and discovered that that city has indeed risen from ancient times against kings and that rebellion and revolt have been contrived in it.*
20 *Powerful kings were over Jerusalem, ruling over everything of the Trans-Euphrates, and receiving tribute, tax, and duty.*
21 *Now, you must order the work of those men to stop. That city is not to be rebuilt until I give further orders.*
22 *Beware of negligence concerning this matter. Why should damage increase and harm be done to the interests of the king?"*
23 *Then, after a copy of the document of Artaxerxes the king was read to Rehum, Shimshai the secretary, and their companions, they went at once to Jerusalem to the Jews and stopped them by force of arms.*

Ezra 4:5b states that the contriving of the enemies of Judah to stop the building of the temple lasted from the time of Cyrus to that of Darius. This includes the time of Cyrus (536–530 B.C.), Cambyses (530–522 B.C.), Pseudo-Smerdes (523 B.C.), and Darius (from 522 B.C. onward). In 4:6, however, Xerxes (486–465 B.C.) is mentioned and in 4:7 Artaxerxes I (465–425 B.C.). Earlier interpreters identified Ahasuerus with Cambyses and Artachshashta with Pseudo-Smerdes (Gaumata),[1] but this view is no longer held, because the identification of Ahasuerus with Xerxes and Artachshashta with Artaxerxes can on grammatical grounds no longer be doubted.[2] It is thus obvious that we have a chronological line from 4:5b to 4:6 and 7. Only Cambyses is not mentioned. In spite of this, Rudolph presumes that the Chronicler had no idea of the historical sequence of the Persian kings and mentioned typical names which are accidentally correct chronologically.[3] Rudolph arrives at this conclusion because of the sudden switch to Darius in 4:24 (see our discussion there). Thus it is understandable that modern scholars, reasoning from their own logic, should regard

1. Cf. the discussion of Rudolph, *Esra und Nehemia,* p. 35.
2. Cf. H. H. Schaeder, *Iranische Beiträge* 1, pp. 269–270 for Xerxes, and p. 268 for Artaxerxes.
3. Rudolph, *Esra und Nehemia,* p. 37.

the historical reliability of this chapter with suspicion. But there is another kind of perfectly legitimate logic to the reasoning of the author of this chapter: he is referring in this chapter in chronological order to the hindrances placed in the way of the Jews to rebuild the temple and the wall of Jerusalem.[4] When he discussed the problems of the building of the temple in 4:1–5, it reminded him of later similar troubles with the rebuilding of the wall of Jerusalem, and so 4:6–23 has been inserted, almost parenthetically, before the argument of the building of the temple has again been taken up in 4:24ff. (already noted by C. F. Keil in the last century).

6 In this verse we have a cryptic reference to a complaint made in the time of Xerxes. Nothing is known about this complaint and what happened to it.[5] *In the beginning of the reign of Xerxes* is an Aramaic technical term translated into Hebrew. It refers to the time of the actual assumption of power and not the year in which the king ascended the throne. The latter year is usually counted as the last year of the previous king.[6] The beginning of Xerxes' reign refers therefore to 485 B.C. According to Galling the complaint had not been heeded because Xerxes had to put down a revolt in Egypt.[7] Morgenstern proposes that with the accession of Xerxes a revolt broke out in Egypt and Palestine, and it is to this rebellion of the Jews that Ezra 4:6 refers. The neighboring nations of the Jews who remained loyal to the Persians overran Judah and destroyed the temple in Jerusalem.[8] This view has found partial support from archeological results which show that major disturbances took place at about this time in sites like Shechem, Bethel, Gibeon, and Tell el-Ful.[9] But it is just these widespread disturbances which make this view questionable. Why also Shechem? The author of this chapter clearly refers to hostile activities of the Samaritans. Why is Shechem, in the heartland of the Samaritans, destroyed? There is also nothing to support Morgenstern's view in the OT.[10]

7 This verse is as cryptic as the previous one. It states only that a letter is written; nothing is said about the contents. If vv. 6–8 form a

4. Pelaia, *Esdra e Neemia,* p. 65; Brockington, *Ezra, Nehemiah and Esther,* p. 68; Coggins, *The Books of Ezra and Nehemiah,* p. 30; Grosheide, *Ezra,* pp. 132ff.
5. Widengren, *Israelite and Judaean History,* p. 525.
6. Rudolph, *Esra und Nehemia,* p. 41; Myers, *Ezra. Nehemiah,* p. 32.
7. Galling, *Studien zur Geschichte Israels,* p. 155.
8. J. Morgenstern, "Jerusalem—485 B.C.," *HUCA* 27 (1956), pp. 101–179; continued in *HUCA* 28 (1957), pp. 15–47.
9. Y. Aharoni, *Land of the Bible* (E.T. 1967), p. 358; G. E. Wright, *Shechem: The Biography of a Biblical City* (New York: 1965), p. 164; cf. also Widengren, *Israelite and Judaean History,* p. 526.
10. Cf. the apt criticism of Widengren, *op. cit.,* p. 526; Galling, *Studien zur Geschichte Israels,* p. 133 n. 1; F. M. Th. de Liagre Böhl, *HTS* 16 (1961), p. 273.

kind of sequel, this letter must also be regarded as a complaint against the Jews by their enemies. The name Tabeel in this verse has given rise to another theory, first proposed by Klostermann and later fully worked out by Schaeder and followed by various scholars.[11] It has been built on the supposition that the Chronicler made use of a source, 4:8–6:18, which was written as an apology by a certain Jew, Tabeel, to Artaxerxes after the letter of Rehum and Shimshai had been written (vv. 9ff.) and the reply of Artaxerxes had been received. The purpose of Tabeel's apology was to bring about a revision of the verdict of Artaxerxes. Tabeel gave a verbal quotation of the letter of Rehum and Shimshai and the reply. This quotation was used as the starting point of his arguments. It was then followed by a retrospective survey of the whole history of hostility between the Samaritans and the Jews. He wrote an exhaustive survey of events in the time of Darius. He also referred to a complaint against the Jews in the time of Xerxes. The Chronicler had at his disposal a copy of Tabeel's letter and made use of it as he saw fit. Some of the material was rewritten by the Chronicler, as possibly with the history before Darius. He omitted something after 4:23 and wrote v. 24 as a transition to what Tabeel had written about Darius. The Chronicler also summarized what Tabeel had written about the time of Xerxes.

This is, indeed, a neatly worked-out hypothesis, but it rests too much on supposition.[12] It is doubtful that one could derive so much from 4:7. Nothing is mentioned in 4:7 about the contents of the letter and nowhere else is the name Tabeel connected to such an apology. It is also disturbing that the moment the hypothesis is in jeopardy, the loophole of the editing of the Chronicler is used (e.g., with v. 24). It is much safer to accept that the author of this chapter enumerated the different hostile actions against the Jews and that the action of Tabeel and his associates is one of them. *Bishlam.* There is a difference of opinion about this term. Some take it as equivalent to Heb. *biš*ᵉ*lôm,* meaning "in agreement with"; thus Tabeel wrote his letter in agreement with Mithredath.[13] Another view is that this term is an abbreviation for *biḏ*ᵉ*ḇar y*ᵉ*rûšālaim,* "in the matter

11. Klostermann, *RE* 5 (1898), pp. 516ff.; Schaeder, *Iranische Beiträge* 1, pp. 212–225; A. van Selms, *Ezra en Nehemia.* Het Oude Testament (Gronigen: 1935); A. Noordtzij, *De boeken Ezra en Nehemia.* Korte Verklaring der Heilige Schrift (Kampen: 1951); cf. Grosheide, *Ezra,* p. 22.
12. Cf. the criticism of Rudolph, *Esra und Nehemia,* pp. 37ff. and J. J. Koopmans, "Die eerste Aramese deel van het Boek Ezra, 4:7–6:19," *GTT* 55 (1955), pp. 142–160.
13. Cf. the discussion of Brockington, *Ezra, Nehemiah and Esther,* p. 67; Grosheide, *Ezra,* p. 135.

of Jerusalem."[14] A third view—and the more acceptable one—is to take it as a proper name. *Mithredath* occurs also in the Egyptian Aramaic papyri and is probably a Persian name.[15] *Tabeel* means "God is good."

The first Aramaic section of Ezra begins in v. 8.

8–10 These three verses describe another attempt to stop the work of the Jews. From the contents of the letter it is clear that work on the wall of Jerusalem and in the city itself is meant. Some time before Nehemiah had succeeded with his request, the Jews started rebuilding the wall and the ruins of Jerusalem. Rehum and his associates thwarted this effort. Some are of the opinion that the Jews were aroused by the preaching of a prophet (Malachi?) to start the work.[16] *Rehum* was a well-known Semitic name of those times.[17] The *high official* or chancellor presided quite probably over a group of minor officials[18] and was chiefly responsible for his conduct to the satrap, or, if he was a satrap, to the Persian king. *Shimshai,* a good Semitic name, is derived from *šmš,* "sun." *Secretary* (*sāprā'*) has been studied from various angles. According to Schaeder the Persians took over the categories of the Babylonian officials, and the term secretary must be connected to the Babylonian *šāpiru,* a high official.[19] The latest tendency is to emphasize the Northwest Semitic development of the term in the meaning "writer" or "secretary."[20] But we must keep in mind that *sāprā'* here refers to an official in the service of the Persian king and must be interpreted accordingly. In such a case the view of Schaeder still holds good.

In v. 9 all the friends of Rehum and Shimshai are enumerated. It is indeed a difficult list. It seems as if the beginning of the list refers to certain officials and the latter part to certain principalities.[21] *The judges.* Probably the royal judges who were concerned with judgment of cases in connection with the safety of the state.[22] *Legates ('ᵃparsaṯkāyē')* may be

14. Brockington, *op. cit.,* p. 67. Cf. Rudolph, *Esra und Nehemia,* p. 34 for "against Jerusalem." Cf. also Myers, *Ezra. Nehemiah,* p. 32.
15. Cf. *AP,* pp. 89 (26:2 and 7), 190 (80:7); *BMAP,* p. 156 (3:23b).
16. Myers, *op. cit.,* p. 38.
17. Cf. *BMAP,* pp. 250 (10:19), 260 (11:14), 272 (12:34). Cf. also Ezra 2:2; Neh. 3:17; 10:26 (Eng. 25); 12:3.
18. Cf. *BMAP,* p. 33; Schaeder, *Iranische Beiträge* 1, p. 265.
19. H. H. Schaeder, *Esra der Schreiber,* pp. 46ff. Cf. also Eilers, *OLZ* 34 (1931), pp. 930ff.; E. Ebeling, *RLA* I, pp. 445, 456.
20. Cf. T. N. D. Mettinger, *Solomonic State Officials* (Lund: 1971), pp. 18, 42–45. Cf. also J. Kühlewein, *THAT* II, p. 163.
21. Cf. the discussion of K. Galling, "Kronzeugen des Artaxerxes?", *ZAW* 63 (1951), pp. 66–74; *idem,* "Zur Deutung des Ortnamens *ṭrpl* = Tripolis in Syrien," *VT* 4 (1954), pp. 418–422.
22. Frye, *The Heritage of Persia,* p. 100.

connected to the Persian *apara-saraka*. *The consuls (ṭarpᵉlāyē')* are taken by some as referring to the people of Tripolis, but this is not certain. *The Arkewites* are the people of the Mesopotamian Erech.[23] *Those of Susa* are the inhabitants of one of the principal cities of Elam that was conquered by the Persians. *Osnapar* refers to Ashurbanipal (669–626 B.C.), the last successful king of Assyria. Nowhere in the extant sources is this deportation mentioned. We know, however, of his conquering twenty-two kings of the West and also of his continuing policy of deportation practiced by earlier Assyrian kings.[24] The *Trans-Euphrates* was a large Persian province to the west of the Euphrates that also included Palestine.

11–12 Various groups of Jews had migrated to Palestine. Bright is of the opinion that the Jewish population had grown gradually during the first half of the fifth century B.C.[25] The reference to a migration in v. 12 probably refers to a return of certain Jews before Nehemiah.[26] They arrived in a city without city walls and consequently they were easy game for marauders. It is thus understandable that they decided to rebuild the wall to protect themselves and their property. But for this they had not received permission from the Persian government.

The Aramaic of v. 12 is difficult to interpret. The problem of v. 12a is that it is not the intention of the author to focus the attention of Artaxerxes on the return of the Jews, but on the rebuilding of the city. Verse 12a is therefore not to be taken as an independent clause, but as an introductory clause to v. 12b.[27] *Rebellious and evil city* shows both the contempt of the officials for Jerusalem and their diplomatic contrivance with which they want to persuade the Persian king. Especially the choice of the word *rebellious* is important, because the Persian empire was plagued with rebellions during the fifth century, e.g., the one of the satrap Megabyzus of the Trans-Euphrates. With this in mind the effect of the complaint of the Persian officials can be understood.[28]

The latter part of v. 12 is also difficult to explain. The suffix conjugation *'šaḵᵉlîlû* might be interpreted as an expression of confidence.

23. Brockington, *Ezra, Nehemiah and Esther*, p. 68; Torrey, *Ezra Studies*, p. 170.
24. Cf. D. D. Luckenbill, *Ancient Records of Babylonia and Assyria* II (Chicago: 1927), p. 340. Cf. also Myers, *Ezra. Nehemiah*, p. 33.
25. Cf. J. Bright, *A History of Israel* (Philadelphia: ²1972), pp. 377–78.
26. Cf. S. Herrmann, *A History of Israel in OT Times* (E.T. 1975), p. 308; Widengren, *Israelite and Judaean History*, p. 527.
27. Grosheide, *Ezra*, p. 146.
28. Herrmann, *op. cit.*, p. 308. There is not enough evidence to follow Josephus— again taken up by W. S. McCullough — that the Jews were involved in the Phoenician rebellion of 451 B.C. Cf. McCullough, "Israel's Eschatology from Amos to Daniel," in J. W. Wevers and D. B. Redford, eds., *Studies on the Ancient Palestinian World* (Toronto: 1972), p. 90.

It is thus expected that in the future the wall will be restored. The verb *yaḥîṭû* is difficult. It might be derived from Aram. *ḥṭṭ,* "dig," and thus mean: "They are digging for the foundations."[29] But this meaning is difficult in the light of the restoring of the wall in the previous phrase. The best guess would be "lay the foundations." The term *'uššayyā'* is a cognate of Akk. *uššū*, "lower part" or "foundation."[30]

13–16 In these verses the consequences of the building activities of the Jews are sketched for the king. The first consequence was that if the city were strengthened, the Jews would not be willing to pay tax. Taxation was regarded as very important in the Persian empire.[31] Any cessation of payment was regarded as rebellion. The three different words for types of taxation mentioned here are probably to be derived from Babylonian terminology, e.g., *mindâ* from Babylonian *mandattu,* a monetary tax, *b^elô* from Babylonian *biltu,* a payment in kind, and *h^alāḵ,* whose derivation is uncertain, is probably a kind of duty tax.[32] The loss suffered with the suspension of these taxes would harm the financial position of the king. After the expensive wars of Darius and Xerxes, especially with the Greeks, the royal treasury was depleted. Further damage to the treasury had to be avoided. The term *treasury ('app^eṯōm)* is difficult to explain. Our translation is derived from the Avestan term *pathma,* "storehouse."[33] *The king.* In the Aramaic text the word is *māl^eḵîm.* It is a Hebrew word in the plural. If taken as plural it might refer to the descendants of Artaxerxes. A better explanation is to take the plural as a *pluralis majestatis* referring to Artaxerxes.[34]

The second consequence, couched in a metaphor, refers to the fact that such a rebellion will put the king to shame. In v. 14 the close relationship between the officials and the king is expressed by a metaphor, "we eat the salt of the palace" or "we salted with the salt of the palace."[35] *The king put to shame.* In Aramaic, "we do not want to see the shame of the king." Verse 14 shows that the Samaritans were also interested in their own future. There is a strong egoistic tendency in what they wrote. Did they believe in what they wrote? It was a typical lie, clad in the clothes

29. Cf. *DISO,* p. 85. KB, p. 1074, suggests *ḥwṭ,* meaning "repair" or "inspect."
30. Noted by Myers, *op. cit.,* p. 33. See KB, p. 1054; S. Kaufman, *The Akkadian Influences on Aramaic* (Chicago: 1974), pp. 37, 110.
31. Frye, *The Heritage of Persia,* p. 109.
32. Rudolph, *Esra und Nehemia,* p. 38; Myers, *op. cit.,* pp. 33–34. Cf. S. Kaufman, *op. cit.,* p. 44.
33. See Albright, *JBL* 40 (1921), pp. 114f.
34. In such a case the proposal to connect the final *m* with the next word is unnecessary. Cf. Rudolph, *Esra und Nehemia,* p. 39.
35. Grosheide, *Ezra,* p. 149.

of "genuine" anxiety for the case of the king—a method of approach not unknown in our own time.

In v. 15 the king is requested to search in the archives for the history of Jerusalem. This must refer to the Babylonian and possibly to the Assyrian records.[36] In those records the king could learn about the rebellions of Hezekiah, Zedekiah, etc. Morgenstern holds that this verse refers to the rebellion against Xerxes in 485 B.C., because it would be strange that a Persian king should possess the records of Babylonian kings.[37] But we must never underestimate the ability of ancient kings to preserve the documents of their predecessors, even if they were of a different nation (cf. the preservation of ancient documents by Ashurbanipal).[38]

In v. 16 a typical example of the exaggeration of the Samaritans occurs. They wanted the king to believe that the rebuilding of the wall of Jerusalem would create such a dangerous position in the province of the Trans-Euphrates that at the end nothing would be left for the king. This could only happen if a rebellion in Jerusalem could spread over the whole province. It is obviously an exaggeration of the real circumstances.

17–22 This pericope gives the reply of Artaxerxes. The complaint of his officials in the province Samaria is taken seriously. This is to be expected because of the exaggerated language they have used. The king was alarmed. *Message* in v. 17 is in Aramaic *piṯgāmā'* and is a Persian loanword *paiti-gāma,* meaning "which is due to."[39] According to a common practice in those days the letter of the Samaritan officials was written in Aramaic, the chancellory language of the Persian empire, and was read for the king. Because he did not understand Aramaic, the letter was interpreted *(mᵉpāraš)* for him. This means that it was translated into Persian to make it intelligible for him.[40] The term *ništᵉwānā'* is to be derived from a Persian word meaning "document."[41]

The contents of v. 20 are unclear. There are two possible interpretations. *Powerful kings* can refer to kings in Jerusalem, thus Israelite and Judean kings. In such a case the phrase *ruling over everything of the Trans-Euphrates* is difficult to interpret. Even in the times of David and Solomon they had not ruled over such a large area. It is also questionable whether a Persian king should have in his archives particulars involving the Israelite

36. Brockington, *Ezra, Nehemiah and Esther,* p. 69; Grosheide, *Ezra,* pp. 149–150; Pelaia, *Esdra e Neemia,* p. 70.
37. Morgenstern, *HUCA* 27 (1958), pp. 101–179; *idem, HUCA* 28 (1959), pp. 15–47.
38. Cf. W. von Soden, *Herrscher im Alten Orient* (Springer: 1954), pp. 131ff.
39. Rudolph, *Esra und Nehemia,* p. 42.
40. The discussion of Schaeder, *Iranische Beiträge* 1, pp. 204ff., is still valid.
41. *Ibid.,* p. 265.

and Judean kings, e.g., about their internal affairs. Otherwise we must accept that the references to Israelite and Judean kings in the annals of the Assyrian and Babylonian kings are meant.[42] Even in such a case the phrase "everything of the Trans-Euphrates" is an exaggeration. Grosheide, to avoid this problem, refers to the possibility that the enemies of the Jews in the service of the king might be responsible for this exaggeration.[43] This can only be regarded as a vague possibility. Galling is of the opinion that this verse refers to the Assyrian, Babylonian, and Persian kings.[44] The only objection to this view is that it falls outside the scope of a reply to the letter of the Samaritans. But one must accept that the king in his reply could add something to the arguments of the Samaritans. His direct reply ends with v. 19, and in v. 20 he gives a further particular which became clear with the investigation in the archives, namely, that Jerusalem was for centuries subservient to foreign kings who received tax from them. The view of Galling is thus to be preferred.

In the light of the complaint and the confirmation thereof in the archives Artaxerxes gave an order *(ṭᵉʿēm)* that the building activities of the Jews must stop. Commentators often overlook that the king had never given the Jews the right to rebuild the wall. Their work on it without his permission made him suspicious. Some scholars regard v. 21b as a later addition to the letter of the king, because it does not occur in 3 Esd. 2:24.[45] According to this theory the addition was written by the Chronicler to leave the option open for the return of Nehemiah and his rebuilding of the wall. On the other hand, Artaxerxes could have been cautious in not ordering the stoppage of the work forever. He left the option open to make another decision in the light of new circumstances. Because of the long distance the king made sure that his order would be executed.

23 After the Samaritan officials received the letter of the king, they hurried to Jerusalem to stop building activities. *By force of arms* quite probably refers to a contingent of soldiers they took with them. This was a day of great shame to the Jewish population because their honest endeavor was thwarted by their archenemies, the Samaritans, and it was forced on them by Samaritan soldiers.

42. Cf. the discussion of Pelaia, *Esdra e Neemia*, pp. 70–71; B.-Z. Luria, "There have been mighty Kings also over Jerusalem," *Beth Mikra* 18 (1973), pp. 176–182.
43. Grosheide, *Ezra*, p. 152.
44. Galling, *Die Bücher der Chronik, Esra, Nehemia*, p. 198; *idem*, *ZAW* 63 (1951), p. 69.
45. Rudolph, *Esra und Nehemia*, p. 43; Galling, *ZAW* 63 (1951), p. 74.

4. *Rebuilding of the Temple (4:24–6:22)*

a. Suspension of work; resumption encouraged by Haggai and Zechariah (4:24–5:2)

24 *Thus the work on the temple of God in Jerusalem ceased, and it remained so until the second year of the reign of Darius the king of Persia.*

1 *At this stage the prophets Haggai and Zechariah the son of Iddo prophesied to the Jews of Judah and Jerusalem in the name of the God of Israel who was over them.*
2 *Then Zerubbabel the son of Shealtiel and Jeshua the son of Jozadak started again to rebuild the temple of God in Jerusalem. The prophets of God were with them, assisting them.*

24 This verse begins with the Aramaic conjunction *bē'ḏayin*. Usually this conjunction refers back to the immediately preceding phrase.[1] In this case it would then refer to the stoppage of work on the wall of Jerusalem by Rehum and Shimshai. But this could not be the case here, for the activities of Rehum and his friends were in the time of Artaxerxes, while v. 24 refers explicitly to the reign of Darius, many years earlier. We have already taken notice of the composition of Ezra 4 and have reached the conclusion that Ezra 4:6–23 must be regarded as parenthetical. In such a case *bē'ḏayin* of v. 24 refers back to 4:5, which states that the work on the temple was stopped from the time of Cyrus to the time of Darius—and in v. 24 the work is taken up again. If we accept this solution, it is not necessary to connect *bē'ḏayin* to 4:23, but to 4:5. Thus ch. 4 is not meant to be in chronological sequence; rather it supplies us with a logical thought pattern wherein the most important actions of the Samaritans against the Jews are enumerated. In v. 24 the author comes back to his chronological sequence, interrupted by 4:6–23.

Darius I Hystaspes (522–486 B.C.)[2] was one of Cambyses' officers in the army he took to Egypt. With the death of King Cambyses in Syria and the news that Pseudo-Smerdes (Gaumata) had usurped the Persian throne, Darius went hastily to Persia and conquered the Persian throne by overthrowing Pseudo-Smerdes. However, all over the Persian empire revolts broke out and Darius had to put them down. It was thus a time of uncertainty, and all kinds of rumors were spread. Soon after he had quelled the rebellions, he stabilized the empire and built it up in a brilliant fashion.

1. Cf. F. Rosenthal, *A Grammar of Biblical Aramaic* (Wiesbaden: 1961), p. 40.
2. Cf. Bright, *A History of Israel*, p. 375.

He must be regarded as one of the most successful kings of the Persian empire, although at the end of his reign he was not able to conquer Greece—his forces lost the battle of Marathon in 490 B.C.

1–2 These verses set the scene in the second year of Darius, viz., the beginning of 519 B.C. At this time everything was still uncertain. From a political viewpoint this would have been the right time to restart building activities on the temple.[3] Strict supervision in the Persian provinces was not possible. Nobody was certain who would be the next king. Accompanied by the political insight in the situation was the religious zeal of the prophets Haggai and Zechariah (Hag. 1:2, 12; 2:1ff.; Zech. 3:1, 6). From their prophecies it is clear that the rebuilding of the temple was regarded as the only priority for the Jews. Haggai castigated the Jews for living in well-built houses and pursuing prosperous economic and agricultural activities while the temple was still in ruins (Hag. 1:2ff.).

It is interesting that the same two persons mentioned in 4:4, Zerubbabel and Jeshua, were taking the initiative with the rebuilding. It is clear from Haggai (1:1, 14; 2:2, 21) that Zerubbabel was the most important person in Judah.[4] That Haggai called him the governor *(peḥâ)* of Judah shows that he was a Persian official, appointed over Judah.[5] In the light of political instability certain scholars, notably R. Kittel, have held that the messianic expectations of Haggai and Zechariah influenced Zerubbabel and a revolt or revolution broke out against the Persians.[6] As a result of this revolt Zerubbabel was removed. Kittel assumes that the absence of Zerubbabel at the inauguration of the temple is thus to be explained. Morgenstern, while building on the same view, is of the opinion that Zerubbabel, probably against his wish, became involved in a revolt and was removed.[7] It is true that Zerubbabel disappears in a strange way from our sources. This is particularly curious since he was so highly regarded by both Haggai and Zechariah. Clear messianic overtones in connection with Zerubbabel and Jeshua appear in Zechariah (Zech. 4; 6:12).[8] One problem with the view of Kittel and Morgenstern is that it is built on an *argumentum e silentio*. Any guess is as good as another. All that we can say is that Zerubbabel disappeared. He could have died of natural

3. Myers, *Ezra. Nehemiah,* p. 44. Against Grosheide, *Ezra,* pp. 158ff., who wants to minimize the political consequences.

4. Grosheide, *Ezra,* pp. 159–160.

5. F. C. Fensham, "*Peḥâ* in the OT and the Ancient Near East," *OTWSA* 19 (1976), pp. 44–52.

6. Cf. R. Kittel, *Geschichte des Volkes Israel* III (Stuttgart: [3]1929), pp. 461ff.

7. Morgenstern, *HUCA* 27 (1957), p. 159.

8. Cf. the discussion in Bright, *A History of Israel,* pp. 371–72; Widengren, *Israelite and Judaean History,* p. 521.

causes. Also, Haggai's clear reference to Zerubbabel as governor of Judah, i.e., as a high official of the Persian empire and not as king (as we would expect if he was regarded as the Son of David, the Messiah), testifies against the surmise of Kittel. The messianic fervor of Haggai and especially Zechariah is not to be denied. This fervor is understandable in the light of the instability of the Persian empire at that time, but the idea of a political revolt or revolution has no support in our sources. These prophets made no direct pronouncement against the Persian authorities. Their prophecies are mainly of a religious nature, emphasizing a change of heart in the Jewish community (cf. Zech. 1:3–6).

Zechariah the son of Iddo. In Zech. 1:1 we have "Zechariah the son of Berechiah, the son of Iddo"; in other words "the son of Berechiah" is left out here. Some scholars have taken pains to explain this,[9] but "son of . . ." does occasionally in the OT refer not to a direct son, but to a descendant.[10] *Who was over them* (*ʿalêhôn*) is not so clear. We take this word as referring back to the immediately preceding phrase (cf. also JB),[11] while Grosheide wants to connect it to "name" (*šum*) in the sense that the name of God was pronounced over the Jews.[12] *Assisting them* means quite probably assisting them by the fervor of their pronouncements.

b. Inquiries by Tattenai (5:3–5)

3 *At that time Tattenai the governor of Trans-Euphrates, Shethar-bozenai, and their companions came to them and asked: "Who gave you permission to build this temple and to erect this structure?"*

4 *Then they also asked them: "What are the names of the men who are building this building?"*

5 *But God took care of the Jewish leaders because they were not stopped while a report was dispatched to Darius and then an official document awaited.*

3–5 This passage describes a visit of Tattenai and Shethar-bozenai to Jerusalem. Although not stated, it is possible that the Samaritans again made a complaint against the Jews. Tattenai is called *governor of Trans-Euphrates,* although we know that at this time Ushtani was the satrap of the Trans-Euphrates.[1] The interpretation of this phrase depends on what one understands by *peḥâ*. This individual could be a high official directly responsible to the king and thus a satrap, or he could be a high official responsible to the satrap.[2] The latter possibility must be accepted for

9. Rudolph, *Esra und Nehemia,* p. 46.
10. Grosheide, *Ezra,* p. 157; Brockington, *Ezra, Nehemiah and Esther,* p. 70.
11. Myers, *Ezra. Nehemiah,* p. 40.
12. Grosheide, *Ezra,* p. 158; it is left out in the translation of Coggins, *The Books of Ezra and Nehemiah,* p. 32.
1. Cf. K. Galling, *ZDPV* 70 (1954), pp. 18–22.
2. F. C. Fensham, *OTWSA* 19 (1976), pp. 44–52.

Tattenai in this case. Later in the reign of Darius, Tattenai was appointed as satrap, according to a Babylonian document.[3] Tattenai may be a shortened form of a Babylonian name *Nabu-tattanu-uṣur,* "Nabu protects him you gave."[4] *Shethar-bozenai,* who might have been the secretary,[5] has a Persian name in a distorted form, from *štrzn,* which occurs in the Aramaic papyri of Elephantine.[6] *To erect this structure.* The meaning of the term for "structure," *'uššarnā',* is uncertain. It appears in the Aramaic papyri, but there also the meaning is unclear.[7] Kraeling thinks of "lumber" as a possible rendering.[8] If it has the meaning "wooden structure," Rudolph is of the opinion that the building activities had proceeded far enough to call for the attention of Tattenai.[9]

Tattenai arrived in Jerusalem and did two things expected of an able official: first, he asked the Jews who gave them permission for the rebuilding of the temple, and second, he took down the names of those responsible for it. The word *'ᵃmarnā',* "we said," is quite possibly a scribal error for *'ᵃmārû,* "they said." The first person form makes no sense here.

In v. 5 the outcome of Tattenai's visit, namely, that the building operations were not stopped, is interpreted by the author in terms of special care taken by the Lord on behalf of his people. Literally it is said: "and the eye of their God was on the elders of the Jews." A good eye turned on someone means that special care is taken of a person or persons.[10] *A report was dispatched.* The term for report, *ṭa'mā',* means full particulars on what was happening.[11] The Jews were allowed to continue their work until an official document was received from the Persian king. This may be due to Tattenai's uncertainty as to what to expect of the new Persian king.

3. Cf. A. Ungnad, "Keilinschriftliche Beiträge zum Esra und Ester," *ZAW* 58 (1940–41), pp. 240–43; A. T. Olmstead, "Tattenai, Governor of 'Across the River'," *JNES* 3 (1944), p. 46; Myers, *Ezra. Nehemiah,* p. 44.
4. Brockington, *Ezra, Nehemiah and Esther,* pp. 70–71.
5. Rudolph, *Esra und Nehemia,* p. 51.
6. *AP,* p. 11 (5:16); Grosheide, *Ezra,* p. 162; Brockington, *op. cit.,* p. 71.
7. Cf. *AP,* p. 93 (26:5).
8. *BMAP,* p. 163 (3:23), and p. 102. Cf. also C. G. Tuland, "'Uššayā' and 'Uššarnâ: A Classification of Terms, Date and Text," *JNES* 17 (1958), pp. 269–275; S. Mowinckel, "*'Uššarnā'* Ezr. 5:3, 9," *ST* 19 (1965), pp. 130–35.
9. Rudolph, *Esra und Nehemia,* p. 51.
10. Cf. F. C. Fensham, "The Good and Evil Eye in the Sermon on the Mount," *Neotest* (1967), pp. 51–57.
11. This word occurs in the Hermopolis papyri (c. 500 B.C.) where a request is made that a report *(ṭ'm)* must be written on all that has been happening in a household. Cf. J. C. L. Gibson, *Textbook of Syrian Semitic Inscriptions* II (Oxford: 1975), pp. 130, 132. In Ezra 5:5 and in this papyrus *ṭ'm* has a meaning different from its usual one, "command."

c. Tattenai's letter to Darius (5:6–17)

6 *Copy of the letter which Tattenai the governor of Trans-Euphrates, Shethar-bozenai, and their companions the officials of Trans-Euphrates sent to Darius the king.*

7 *The message they sent to him was written as follows: "To Darius the king, all peace.*

8 *The king must know that we went to the province of Judah, to the temple of the great God that is being built with large stones, and wooden beams have been placed in the walls. That work is being done energetically and prospers under their hands.*

9 *Then we asked these leaders: 'Who gave you permission to build this temple and to complete this wooden structure?'*

10 *We also asked their names to inform you. We have written the names down of the men who are at their head.*

11 *They gave us the following message in reply: 'We are the servants of the God of heaven and earth. We are rebuilding a temple which was built earlier, many years ago. A great king of Israel built and completed it.*

12 *But because our ancestors angered the God of heaven, he gave them into the power of Nebuchadnezzar the king of Babylon of the Chaldeans. He destroyed it and took the people in exile to Babylon.*

13 *In the first year of Cyrus the king of Babylon, Cyrus the king gave permission to rebuild this temple of God.*

14 *Furthermore, the golden and silver vessels of the temple of God that Nebuchadnezzar had removed from the temple in Jerusalem and had brought to the temple of Babylon Cyrus the king removed from the temple of Babylon and gave them to a man named Sheshbazzar, whom he appointed as governor.*

15 *He said to him: "Take these vessels, go and place them in the temple of Jerusalem, namely, the temple of God which is to be rebuilt on its original site."*

16 *Then this Sheshbazzar came and laid the foundation of the temple of God in Jerusalem. From then till now it is being built, but not completed.'*

17 *If it pleases the king, let a search be made in the treasuries of the king in Babylon to see if it is true that Cyrus the king gave permission to rebuild the temple of God in Jerusalem. Let the king's decision concerning this matter be sent to us."*

6–7 These two verses are a sequel to vv. 3–4. In v. 6 the singular suffix is added to *companions*, literally "his companions." Some scholars are of the opinion that the singular suffix refers back to Shethar-bozenai and shows that Shethar-bozenai and the other officials are clearly distinguished from the governor Tattenai.[1] But in v. 3 we have the plural suffix. The

1. Grosheide, *Ezra*, p. 164.

singular suffix can also refer back to plural nouns. *The officials*. This term might be connected to the *'zdkry'* of the Elephantine papyri, and might mean "informers."[2] In such a case it would be another form of the term used in 4:9.

8–10 Tattenai as high official went to Jerusalem to investigate the complaint against the Jews and made a few careful observations which he transmitted as an able official to the king. In the Persian province of Judah the Jews were rebuilding the temple of their God. *The temple of the great God* can also be translated "the great temple of God." Some interpreters think that it is impossible for a Persian official to call the God of the Jews "the great God," but it may have been a token of reverence for the God of this territory.[3] *Large stones* can be interpreted in different ways. As we have taken it, the term *large (g^elāl)* is connected to the root *gll,* which means "roll." In such a case the stones were so large that they were rolled to the building site.[4] Another possibility is to connect *g^elāl* to Akk. *galālu,* a small stone or pebble.[5] This would then refer to small stones which were used for the rebuilding. The latter possibility is tempting, because the Jews who knew the temple of Solomon were so disappointed with the new edifice that they cried. But it is important to note that Tattenai stressed that careful work had been done. The use of the term "pebbles" would thus stand in glaring contrast to what he was actually saying. *Wooden beams have been placed in the walls*. This phrase is not clear. It might mean either that the walls were panelled[6] or that beams were built in the wall to strengthen it. "Energetically" *('osparnā')* is a loanword from Persian *usprna.*[7]

Tattenai the governor immediately inquired who gave them permission to rebuild the temple. It is possible that with the verb "ask" or "inquire" the author wants to draw the reader's attention to a legal suit which developed between the governor and the Jews.[8] With this question Tattenai laid a charge against them, and in 5:11ff. they gave their defense against the accusation. Tattenai had written down their names, but these names were not included in this letter, although the word *to inform you*

2. *AP,* pp. 53–54 (17:5). W. Eilers, *Iranische Beamtennamen in der keilinschriftlichen Überlieferung* I (1940), thinks of a meaning "investigator." Cf. Myers, *Ezra. Nehemiah,* p. 42.
3. Brockington, *Ezra, Nehemiah and Esther,* p. 71.
4. *Ibid.;* Grosheide, *Ezra,* p. 165.
5. Cf. *AHW* I, p. 273.
6. Rudolph, *Esra und Nehemia,* p. 50.
7. *Ibid.*
8. Cf. F. Rundgren, "Über einen juristischen Terminus bei Esra 6 6," *ZAW* 70 (1958), pp. 209–215.

(l^ehôḏā'ûṯāḵ) creates the impression that the names were included in the letter. Some scholars think that the list of Ezra 2 and Neh. 7 supplies us with these names, but this is uncertain and unlikely. It is possible that the author left out the names or that Tattenai kept the names back until he had heard from the king. *Who are at their head.* The b^e before *rā'š^ehōm* is to be regarded as a *b essentiae*.[9]

11 In spite of his accusation Tattenai wanted to be fair to the Jews and gave their justification of their act in full detail to the Persian king. Besides, it would have been wrong for a Persian official to go contrary to a command of a Persian king. The plea of the Jews contains a clear reference to the religious situation and to the cultic center where they wanted to serve their God. It is evident that this reference points to the edict of Cyrus. *The God of heaven* is probably an attempt by the Jews to create sympathy for their cause in the Persian court, because Ahuramazda, the Persian god, was also regarded as "god of the heaven,"[10] and was known as the creator of heaven and earth.[11] The Jews referred to the previous temple which was built by *a great king of Israel,* Solomon. In the edict of Cyrus permission is given to rebuild sanctuaries on their original sites. *Himmô* is here used as a copula, and the third person suffix to *'aḇ^eḏôhî* is used proleptically.

12 It is clear that the Jews argued from religious as well as historical grounds. According to the history, it was Nebuchadnezzar, the Babylonian king of the Aramaic tribe of the Chaldeans, who destroyed the temple of the Lord and exiled the Jewish people. This is a reference to the events of 597 B.C. and especially 586 B.C. In 586 B.C. Jerusalem was conquered and the temple destroyed (2 K. 25:9 and 2 Chr. 36:19). However, it is important to note that the destruction of the temple is here described as an act of God through Nebuchadnezzar. Because the sins of the Jewish ancestors angered God, he gave them into the power of Nebuchadnezzar. *Into the power of* is literally "in the hand of." Because this verse is strongly colored with Jewish religious conceptions, some, notably C. C. Torrey, have held that this part is unhistorical. But we must keep in mind that Tattenai gave a faithful reproduction of what the Jews had said or perhaps written.[12]

13 In this verse the most important argument of the Jews is used. They had received permission from Cyrus to rebuild the temple (cf. our

9. Grosheide, *Ezra,* p. 165. See GKC, § 119i.
10. Myers, *Ezra. Nehemiah,* p. 45; Widengren, *Israelite and Judaean History,* pp. 497–98. Cf. also Widengren, *Iranische Geisteswelt von den Anfängen bis zum Islam* (Baden-Baden: 1961), p. 113, for the heaven as a dress of Ahuramazda.
11. Cf. J. Duchesne-Guillemin, *La religion de l'Iran ancien* (Paris: 1962), p. 145.
12. Grosheide, *Ezra,* pp. 166–67.

discussion of Ezra 1). Cyrus is here called *the king of Babylon.* Quite obviously Cyrus, after he conquered Babylon, took over the terminology used by the Babylonian kings. In his edict or decree it is stated: "I am Cyrus, king of the world, great king, legitimate king, king of Babylon, king of Sumer and Akkad, king of the four rims (of the earth)."[13] This is anachronistic—in the time of Cyrus Akkad did not even exist. The reference to Cyrus as king of Babylon was made in order to connect him to his predecessor Nebuchadnezzar, who destroyed the temple, whereas Cyrus commanded the rebuilding of it.

14–15 The removal of the sacred vessels of the temple of God was regarded as a major catastrophe (cf. our discussion of Ezra 1:7). That these vessels were placed in the temple of another god, in Babylon, was regarded as a great shame to the Jews. Throughout the religious history of Israel and especially in postexilic times the radical separation between the God of Israel and the gods of other nations was propagated with great fervor. It is understandable that the presence of cultic vessels from the temple of God in the temple of Nabu or Marduk was regarded as shameful. The edict of Cyrus that commanded that these vessels must be restored to the Jews aroused among the Jews a feeling of thanksgiving and joy. For *Sheshbazzar* cf. 1:8 and 4:3. Sheshbazzar is called here a governor *(peḥâ).* We have already referred to the difficulties of interpreting *peḥâ.* There are hints from cuneiform material that a *peḥâ* could also be appointed for a specific task.[14] In this case Sheshbazzar was appointed for the specific task of rebuilding the temple and placing the sacred vessels back into it. Sheshbazzar never fulfilled this task. What happened to the vessels in the meantime is nowhere mentioned.

The last phrase of v. 15, *namely, the temple of God which is to be rebuilt on its original site,* has given rise to various explanations and alterations of the text. According to Batten, who translates this phrase "and the house of God shall be built upon its place," it stands in direct contradiction to the preceding phrase, where it is stated that the vessels must be placed in the temple.[15] If we take the *waw* before *bêṯ* as explicative, this problem of contradiction disappears. It is also possible that the Persian king was so certain of the execution of his command that he envisaged the

13. Cf. *ANET,* p. 316. In the Babylonian court this title was fictitiously used.
14. Cf. Galling, *Studien zur Geschichte Israels,* pp. 81–82; O. Leuze, *Die Satrapieneinteilung in Syrien und im Zweistromlande von 520 bis 320* (Haale: 1935), pp. 18ff.; and Fensham, *OTWSA* 19 (1976), p. 47.
15. Batten, *A Critical and Exegetical Commentary on the Books of Ezra and Nehemiah,* p. 137.

temple as already built. *On its original site* means where the temple of Solomon stood.[16]

16 Cf. our discussion of Ezra 3:8–10 and 4:3. Sheshbazzar received the special commission from Cyrus to rebuild the temple. We would expect that Zerubbabel, as governor of Judah, also partook in the work. *From then till now it is being built* is difficult to explain. There is no reference to the activities of the Samaritans (4:1–5). Nothing is said of the lax conduct of the Jews (Hag. 1), perhaps to avoid alarming Tattenai and Darius unnecessarily. From Ezra 4:1–5 and Haggai it is clear that the work was stopped, but here the impression is created that the work continued from the time of Sheshbazzar. Or do we understand the Aramaic incorrectly? Is it not possible that these words refer to the beginning of the rebuilding *(min-'ᵉḏayin)* and the resumption of the work in the time of Darius that had progressed satisfactorily *(wᵉ'aḏ-kᵉ'an)*? If not, it is possible that the Jews wanted to create the impression that they had continued the work as commanded by Cyrus and that his decree had not become void by default.[17]

17 In this verse the able official Tattenai requested that Darius search the treasuries or archives in Babylon for the edict of Cyrus to see if permission had been granted for the rebuilding of the temple. It is quite natural that a copy of the edict concerning the Jews should be kept in Babylon, because they came from Babylon to Palestine.[18] The Cyrus Cylinder, with its toleration toward other religions and its concessions to the rebuilding of destroyed sanctuaries, was discovered by Rassam in Babylon. It is obvious that the Jews could not supply Tattenai with a copy of this edict, or else this letter would have been unnecessary. It is doubtful that Cyrus had given a copy of his edict to the Jews; in such a case they could have used it with great effect against the Samaritans (4:1–5). Thus the Jews went to Jerusalem under the edict, but did not carry a written copy with them. Tattenai was eagerly awaiting the outcome of his letter and the decision of the king.

d. Discovery of Cyrus's edict (6:1–5)

1 *Then Darius the king commanded a search in the archives of the treasuries in Babylon where it was kept,*
2 *and in Ecbatana, in a fortress of the province Media, a scroll was found on which the following memorandum was written:*

16. In the Elephantine papyri it is stated that the sanctuary of the God of heaven at Elephantine shall be built on its original site. Cf. *AP,* p. 123 (32:8); also Galling, *Studien zur Geschichte Israels,* p. 130 n. 6.
17. Brockington, *Ezra, Nehemiah and Esther,* p. 72.
18. Myers, *Ezra. Nehemiah,* p. 46.

3 *In the first year of Cyrus the king, Cyrus the king commanded: "About the temple of God in Jerusalem. The temple must be rebuilt at a place where sacrifices are offered and burnt offerings are brought. Its height must be sixty cubits, its width also sixty cubits,*
4 *with three courses of large stones and one course of wood. The cost must be paid from the royal treasury.*
5 *The golden and silver vessels of the temple of God are also to be restored; these vessels which Nebuchadnezzar removed from the temple in Jerusalem and brought to Babylon must be given back to the temple in Jerusalem, everything in its place. You must put them in the temple of God."*

1–2 These two verses state that Darius carried out the request of Tattenai. A search was made in the archives for a decree by Cyrus. *Archives of the treasuries.* The sequence of the terms is regarded as awkward by some scholars.[1] It is probable, however, that the documents of the Persian kings were kept at the treasuries (cf. also 5:17). *In Babylon.* Various scholars hold that Babylon is here a broad term, referring to the province and not to the city.[2] According to Xenophon's *Cyropaedia* (viii.6.22), however, in the winter Cyrus lived in Babylon, in the spring in Susa, and in the summer in Ecbatana. It is thus probable that Darius started his search in the city of Babylon. Later on the edict was discovered in Ecbatana. *Ecbatana* is the Greek form of the Persian *Hagmatana,* which is *'aḥmeṯā'* in Aramaic. It was the headquarters of the Medes and became, after Cyrus's victory over the Medes in c. 550 B.C., part of the Persian empire. The discovery of the edict here shows probably that it was promulgated during the summer of 538 B.C. *In a fortress (bebîrtā').* The *be* might be dittography, although the repetition of *be* is not grammatically impossible. *Bîrtā'* is a loanword from Akk. *birtum,* "fortress."[3] It was a fortress city in the province of Media. Some scholars think that *scroll (megillâ)* is a reference to a cuneiform tablet. If so, the choice of the word *megillâ* is indeed awkward. It is more likely that a whole scroll with particulars about various sanctuaries is meant here[4] (cf. below). *Memorandum (dikerônâ)* also occurs in the Elephantine papyri as *zkrn,* meaning "record."[5] De Vaux gives the meaning here as "memorandum" or "protocol."[6]

1. Rudolph, *Esra und Nehemia,* p. 54.
2. Cf. R. de Vaux, "The Decrees of Cyrus and Darius on the Rebuilding of the Temple," in *The Bible and the Ancient Near East* (E.T. 1967), p. 89; Myers, *Ezra. Nehemiah,* p. 51.
3. *AHW* I, p. 129. Cf. also *AP,* p. 119 (31:5).
4. Cf. K. Galling, "Syrien in der Politik der Achaemeniden bis 448 v. Chr.," *AO* 36/3–4 (1937), pp. 30ff.
5. *AP,* p. 123 (32:1).
6. De Vaux, *op. cit.,* p. 93. His reference to Cowley 31 must be 32.

3–5 It is possible that the author of these verses gives a summary of the decree of Cyrus. Ezra 1:2ff. emphasizes certain aspects of the return of the Jews and not so much the building of the temple. The pericope here emphasizes the aspects of the building activities. Cyrus commanded the rebuilding of the temple and also prescribed the way in which it should be done. Even the measures of the temple are given to ensure that the costs of the building are staying within limits.[7] *About the temple of God in Jerusalem.* Scholars agree that these words are a superscription, covering what follows. As Galling has proved, this superscription quite probably indicates that the decree of Cyrus covered different sanctuaries in various countries of which the temple in Jerusalem was just one. That is why the term scroll *(m^e^gillâ)* is used in v. 2.[8] One would expect a preposition before *bêṯ* in this superscription. The preposition probably would be *b^e^*, which was left out before the *bêṯ* of the next word—a common phenomenon in Hebrew and Aramaic. *And burnt offerings are brought.* This is uncertain. Literally the Aramaic has "and its foundations must be supported." There are a few problems with this reading, however. First, the word *m^e^sôḇ^e^lîn* would then be derived from the root *sbl,* "support." But what does it mean to support foundations? Second, the sequence of sacrifices offered and burnt offerings brought is more logical. It requires only a change of vowels, reading *'eššōhî* instead of *'uššôhî.*[9] The suffix of *'eššōhî* refers back to *bay^e^ṯā'*.

Its height must be sixty cubits, its width also sixty cubits. This expression is full of problems, because the length measure is lacking and because of its peculiar architecture. According to 1 K. 6:2 the measurements of the temple of Solomon were sixty by twenty by thirty cubits. It is clear from various pronouncements in Ezra that Cyrus commanded that the temple must be built on the very spot where the temple of Solomon stood, i.e., it must be built on the place where the foundation of the previous temple existed. We should thus expect a temple on the same scale as the one of Solomon. According to our text this was not the case. It is possible that something went wrong with the text and that the second *sixty (šittîn)* was erroneously read as a result of a skipping of the eye back to the first sixty.[10] Another problem posed by scholars is that if the new temple was of the same measurement as the one of Solomon, or even a larger building, why should the older people have cried in disappointment

7. Grosheide, *Ezra,* p. 174; Brockington, *Ezra, Nehemiah and Esther,* pp. 72–73.
8. Cf. n. 4.
9. Cf. *BHK*.
10. Cf. Grosheide, *Ezra,* pp. 173–74; Brockington, *op. cit.,* p. 73.

(Ezra 3:12–13)? However, it is nowhere mentioned that they cried over the measurements of the temple; it might have been over the smaller masonry.

The king also gave a prescription for the way in which the temple should be built, that is to say, *three courses of large stones and one course of wood*. It is usually understood that the wooden course must have been in the inside as a kind of panelling on the wall.[11] The Aramaic reads *ḥaḏaṯ*, "new," instead of *ḥaḏ*, "one." But "new wood" would make no sense. It is thus better to accept the small textual alteration from *ḥaḏaṯ* to *ḥaḏ*.[12] *Royal treasury*. The costs must come from taxation in the particular province in which the temple was to be rebuilt (cf. v. 8), but must first be paid into the king's treasury, which was also his private treasury,[13] and then paid over for the specific task. For v. 5 cf. our discussion of 5:14–15.

e. Reply of Darius to Tattenai (6:6–12)

6 *Therefore, Tattenai governor of Trans-Euphrates, Shethar-bozenai, and your companions the officials of Trans-Euphrates, withdraw from there.*

7 *Let the work on this temple of God alone. Let the governor of the Jews and the leaders of the Jews rebuild this temple of God on its original site.*

8 *Herewith a command is issued how you can assist the work of these Jewish leaders to rebuild this temple: The cost from taxation in Trans-Euphrates must immediately be paid from the royal treasury to these men, without delay.*

9 *What is required for sacrifices to the God of heaven, namely, bulls, rams, and lambs as well as wheat, salt, wine, and oil is to be supplied to them without fail as requested by the priests of Jerusalem,*

10 *that they may offer acceptable sacrifices to the God of heaven and pray for the lives of the king and his sons.*

11 *Herewith a command is issued that if anyone changes this edict, a beam must be pulled out of his house and he must be impaled on it and his house be turned into a dunghill on account of this.*

12 *May the God who lives there overturn any king or people who dares to change this and to destroy this temple of God in Jerusalem. I Darius command this. Let it be carried out with diligence.*

In this pericope an extract from a letter of Darius is given. The edict of Cyrus was discovered and Darius honored it. He ordered that the work of the Jews should not be obstructed.[1] Darius had a high opinion of his

11. Cf. R. de Vaux, *Ancient Israel* II, pp. 316, 323–24.

12. With LXX^{B}; cf. *BHS*.

13. On taxation cf. Frye, *The Heritage of Persia*, pp. 109ff.

1. Widengren, *Israelite and Judaean History*, p. 522; Myers, *Ezra. Nehemiah*, p. 51.

predecessor Cyrus; for example, at Pasargadai he undertook extensive rebuilding work and had inscriptions concerning Cyrus erected.[2] On the other hand, it is clear that with this legal act Darius showed a sense of righteousness. From a political view his decision was also expedient. His reign had just begun and the unrest after his succession to the throne had just been quelled. It would have been imprudent to create new unrest by an unjust verdict.[3]

6–7 *Withdraw from there (raḥîqîn h^a wô min-tammâ)* is to be taken with Rundgren as a technical legal term meaning "the accusation is rejected."[4] This kind of legal principle occurs also in the Elephantine papyri.[5] Interesting is a deed of conveyance in which a Jewish father gave property to his daughter as dowry with full powers over it. The measurements of this property are given (cf. Ezra 6:3). A certain Dargman had laid claim to this property, but his claim was rejected and he gave the Jewish father a deed of renunciation *(spr mrḥq).*[6] The pronouncement of Darius meant that the Persian officials had to stay away from the temple, the Jewish property, and that they had no right to interfere with the Jews' activities.

The governor of the Jews refers here to Zerubbabel. In the request of Tattenai and his companions he is not mentioned (5:9), but because he was probably appointed by Cyrus as governor, his appointment is again confirmed by Darius. There is no necessity to regard this phrase as a later addition.[7] *The leader of the Jews.* The Aramaic has here a difficult *l^e* before *śāḇê.* It could not be an indication of the accusative, because "the leaders" are the subject of the sentence. It must then be taken as the *lamedh emphaticum. On its original site.* The emphasis on this expression from the beginning of Ezra is understandable in the light of the general ancient Near Eastern practice of rebuilding a sanctuary precisely on the site where the previous building stood.[8]

8–10 These verses picture Darius as a generous king. This is in conformity with what we know about him from other sources. He had a special interest in restoring specific cults in his empire and contributed to

2. Cf. R. Borger and W. Hinz, "Eine Dareois-Inschrift aus Pasargadae," *ZDMG,* 109 (1959), p. 127; Frye, *The Heritage of Persia,* p. 71.
3. Galling, *Studien zur Geschichte Israels,* p. 155.
4. F. Rundgren, *ZAW* 70 (1958), p. 213.
5. *AP,* pp. 16, 18 (6:22) in the form *mrḥq.*
6. *AP,* pp. 22–23 (cf. 8:25). Cf. also the discussion of R. Yaron, *Introduction to the Law of the Aramaic Papyri* (Oxford: 1961), pp. 103ff., for a possible origin of this legal principle. His view that it is of Greek origin is uncertain, however.
7. Grosheide, *Ezra,* p. 176.
8. Cf. K. Galling, "Serubbabel und der Wiederaufbau des Tempels in Jerusalem," in A. Kuschke, ed., *Verbannung und Heimkehr.* Festschrift W. Rudolph (Tübingen: 1961), pp. 67–96.

the restoration liberally. We know of these activities from the West among the Greeks, and even in Egypt (e.g., the cult of Neith).[9] He had an interest in particulars about the cultic practices and prescribed minute detail,[10] perhaps because of the ancient Near Eastern belief that the correct procedure had to be followed in order not to anger a specific god. In the light of this situation his generosity can be understood, as also the careful description of the sacrifices. The use of bulls, rams, and so forth is in accordance with prescribed Israelite practices (cf. Exod. 29:38ff.; Num. 28:1ff.; Lev. 2:1). He was quite probably informed by Jews close to his court about these cultic practices. It is also notable that these prescriptions covered only the daily sacrifices, and not the special ones associated with great festivals. In exchange for his liberal supply of sacrificial material he asked for prayers for him and his sons. Jeremiah asked the exiles to pray for the place to which they were exiled (Jer. 29:7). Cyrus requested prayers for the welfare of himself and his son.[11] That it was a common practice in those days to pray for the king and higher officials in a temple is attested by the Elephantine papyri.[12] The situation there was the same as in Judah: the temple of Yahu was demolished and the Jews wanted to rebuild it. They were writing to the governor of Judah, Bagohi (Bagoas), a Persian, assuring him that if the temple should be rebuilt, they would pray for him at all times.[13] Although Darius revered Ahuramazda especially, it is understandable that in a world of polytheism he would want to make sure that he was in the favor of every god in his empire.

The cost from taxation. Cf. 6:4. *Bulls, rams, and lambs.* The term *bᵉnê* before "bulls" does not imply that they are *young* bulls, as various exegetes and translators have taken it. *Bēn* in Hebrew and *bar* in Aramaic refer occasionally to kind or type, and not necessarily to the age of the animal.[14]

11–12 A curse is pronounced upon anyone who changes the decree of Darius. Verse 11 has no curse formula, but does state that the punishment for the transgression would be impalement after a beam is pulled out of the house of the guilty and planted in the ground. Impalement was a well-known kind of punishment in the ancient Near East for grave

9. See de Vaux, *The Bible and the Ancient Near East,* pp. 76–77. For Neith cf. A. H. Gardiner, *Egypt of the Pharaohs* (Oxford: 1961), pp. 366–68.
10. De Vaux, *op. cit.,* pp. 91–92; Myers, *Ezra. Nehemiah,* p. 52.
11. Cf. *ANET,* p. 316.
12. *AP,* pp. 111–14 (30).
13. *AP,* pp. 113–14 (30:26).
14. Cf. F. C. Fensham, "The son of a handmaid in Northwest-Semitic," *VT* 19 (1969), pp. 312–321.

offences.[15] One side of a beam was sharpened and the other side planted in the ground. The sharp point was inserted under the chest of a person and pushed through his esophagus and lungs. He was then left to hang until he died. *Dunghill.* The meaning of this word is uncertain. Brockington wants to derive it from the Arab. *wly,* which has *inter alia* the meaning "the right to succession to property." It may mean then "confiscate,"[16] but this is uncertain.

In v. 12 we have a curse formula. The curse formula was used throughout ancient Near Eastern history to protect what was regarded as precious, e.g., the sarcophagus of a king.[17] It was also used to protect a treaty. The overturning of a king meant the overturning of his throne, as we know from the curse formula.[18] In the Bagistan Inscription Darius invoked the hostility of Ahuramazda against anyone who would destroy the inscription.[19] Scholars refer to the Deuteronomistic language of v. 12 (lit. "May the God whose name lives there . . .") as proof that this could not have been used by Darius.[20] As we have already seen, the sacrificial terminology used by Darius might have been inspired by the Jews. It is possible that we have here the same phenomenon. In the last part of v. 12 the seriousness of the command of Darius is again underlined. It must be carried out immediately.

f. Completion of work on the temple (6:13–15)

13 *Then Tattenai the governor of Trans-Euphrates, Shethar-bozenai, and their companions carried out diligently the order that Darius the king had sent.*

14 *The Jewish leaders built with success under influence of the prophecies of Haggai the prophet and Zechariah the son of Iddo. They finished the building in accordance with the order of the God of Israel and the order of Cyrus, Darius, and Artaxerxes the king of Persia.*

15. In the British Museum a relief of Sennacherib's attack on Lachish shows how certain Israelites were impaled. See *ANEP,* no. 373; cf. nos. 362, 368.
16. Brockington, *Ezra, Nehemiah and Esther,* p. 74.
17. E.g., in the Ahiram Inscription, *KAI* I, p. 1; II, pp. 2, 4; in the Eshmunazar Inscription, *KAI* I, p. 3; II, pp. 19ff. Cf. also the curses pronounced by Yaḫdun-Lim with the dedication of the temple of Shamash at Mari. Cf. G. Dossin, "L'inscription de fondation de Iaḫdun-Lim, roi de Mari," *Syria* 32 (1955), pp. 1–28.
18. In Phoenician from the root *hphk;* cf. Ahiram, *thtphk ks' mlkh, KAI* I, p. 1. Aramaic *mgr* has the meaning "overturn." Cf. *AP,* pp. 112–13 (30:14); *DISO,* p. 142.
19. F. W. Koenig, *Relief und Inschrift des Königs Darius I. am Felsen von Bagistan* (Leiden: 1938), p. 56.
20. Grosheide, *Ezra,* p. 381. Cf. also Brockington, *op. cit.,* p. 74.

15 *This temple was finished on the third of the month Adar. It was the sixth year of the reign of Darius the king.*

13–15 The command of Darius is carried out to the letter by the Persian officials. In one of his inscriptions Darius exhorted his followers to believe what he had written and not to disobey his laws.[1] As we may expect, after the order of Darius the work on the temple was tackled with eagerness. The prophets Haggai and Zechariah were still there to inspire the workers with their prophecies. We know that the prophecies of Haggai written in the biblical book of Haggai were delivered not later than the beginning of 519 B.C. Those of Zechariah could not have been pronounced later than 518 B.C. For some scholars this is a problem.[2] How could they have inspired the completion of the temple, if their prophecies had stopped three or four years earlier? It is probable, however, that they pronounced prophecies which were not taken up in the canonical books of the Bible. We must accept that not every pronouncement of a prophet has been transmitted to us.

It is of importance that in v. 14 only the Jewish leaders are mentioned and Zerubbabel is not. This might point to the fact that he died during the building activities. In v. 14b we have a piece of pure Jewish theology. According to this verse, the work was finished by the order or command of God and the Persian kings. God commanded it through his prophets and the Persian kings were instruments of God in commanding the completion of the work. This verse thus shows that God works through history and historical processes. It is therefore of importance to note that the name of God had been given priority in the list of names.

And Artaxerxes the king of Persia is exceedingly difficult. The logic of the names Cyrus and Darius is obvious in the light of the preceding description. But why Artaxerxes? Nowhere in any source extant is it mentioned that Artaxerxes had anything to do with the rebuilding of the temple. By and large, the temple was completed in 516 B.C., in the days of Darius, long before Artaxerxes. It is now generally accepted by scholars that the reference to Artaxerxes must be regarded as an early gloss,[3] because it also appears in the LXX. This is a possible explanation. On the other hand, we must keep in mind that our twentieth-century logic is not the same as that of the Jews in the days of Ezra. Artaxerxes could have been added because the author gave a list of Persian kings who were special instruments in the hand of God to favor the Jews. Up to Darius the sentence refers to the completion of the temple, but with Artaxerxes the other

1. Frye, *The Heritage of Persia,* p. 100.
2. Rudolph, *Esra und Nehemia,* p. 60.
3. *Ibid.;* Grosheide, *Ezra,* pp. 183–84; Brockington, *op. cit.,* p. 74.

thought pattern predominates, viz., the divine process in which Persian kings were used in the service of God (cf. also Isa. 45:1).

The third of the month Adar. 3 Esdras 7:6 reads the twenty-third day. Josephus (*Ant.* xi.4–7) has the same, although Josephus got his information from 3 Esdras. Kugler calculates that the third of Adar fell on March 12, 515 and that this was a sabbath.[4] Thus he prefers the twenty-third. It is possible that the numeral *twenty* fell out by haplography. The calculations are not so certain as they seem to be, because of our ignorance of many facets of Jewish chronology. This new temple would stand many years more than that of Solomon. Solomon's temple existed for just under 400 years, while this one lasted for 585 years until it was destroyed by Titus in A.D. 70 while still in process of expansion. Herod was responsible for its majestic, renovated form.[5]

g. Dedication of the temple (6:16–18)

16 *The Israelites, namely the priests, Levites, and the remainder of the exiles, celebrated the dedication of this temple of God with joy.*
17 *For the dedication of this temple of God they offered one hundred bulls, two hundred rams, four hundred lambs, and twelve he-goats as a sin offering for the whole of Israel, according to the number of the tribes of Israel.*
18 *And they appointed the priests in their divisions and the Levites in their positions for the service of God in Jerusalem, as it is written in the book of Moses.*

16–18 We have reached the point in the description where the final consummation of the expectations of the exiles was experienced. Handicapped by the hostility of the Samaritans, they waited for a long time to reach this ideal, namely, the rebuilding of the temple and the reinstitution of temple worship. Twenty-one years after the laying of the foundations, the temple was completed. Since the temple of Solomon had been destroyed in 586 B.C., the Jewish religious community could not have functioned satisfactorily, because during the almost four hundred years of its existence, the temple of Solomon had such a firm hold on the cultic and liturgical practices that religion without it seemed unthinkable. Now all these religious practices could be exercised again. No wonder that the dedication of the temple was received *with joy.*

In v. 16 a few important points are stressed. The participants of the dedication are described as Israelites and not Jews (lit. "sons of Israel,"

4. Rudolph, *Esra und Nehemia,* p. 59. This calculation of Morgenstern, *HUCA* 27 (1956), pp. 45ff. is unacceptable.
5. Rudolph, *op. cit.,* p. 60.

the technical term in the OT for the covenant people). This points to a broad approach, although idealistically conceived. It is the temple of the whole Israel and not only of the two tribes of Judah and Benjamin. This statement might also have been made to contradict the claims of the Samaritans on the temple. We can derive this purpose from the careful description of the three different categories of Israelites, namely, the priests, the Levites, and the remainder of the exiles, the laity. In the description there is no place for Samaritans, or for the Jews who were not exiled. We must also keep in mind that it is the exiles who received permission to rebuild the temple, and not other groups. So only the exiles had the right to celebrate.

Verse 17 describes the festival. In comparison with the exuberant dedication ceremony in the time of Solomon (1 K. 8; 2 Chr. 7:3ff.), this festival reflected the poverty of the Jewish community.[6] *Twelve he-goats as a sin offering.* It is interesting that this kind of offering was performed with a dedication, for example, in the time of Hezekiah when the temple was dedicated anew (2 Chr. 29:24).[7] It was done to dedicate to God something made by men, a changeover from the profane to the divine. It must also be kept in mind that from 586 B.C. to 516 B.C. no sin offering could have been made. In the meantime the sins of Israel grew immensely and something had to be done to eradicate their sins. For the ceremony of the he-goat, cf. Lev. 3:23ff. and especially Num. 7. In accordance with the term "Israelites" in v. 16, the sin offering was performed for every one of the twelve tribes of Israel. In Num. 7 this procedure is described; for example, the tribe of Judah (7:16) brought to Moses a he-goat for a sin offering, as also the tribe of Issachar (7:22). It is uncertain, however, where representatives of every tribe among the exiles could have come from. But no explanation is given by the author.

In v. 18 the institution of the priests and Levites is mentioned. The new temple needed temple personnel. According to the Chronicler, David organized the priestly and Levitical orders (1 Chr. 23–24), but here it is stated that it was done according to *the book of Moses.* It is difficult to ascertain what is meant by the book of Moses, but it quite probably refers to the legal prescriptions in the Pentateuch (Exod. 29; Lev. 8; Num. 3:5ff.;

6. In ancient times dedication ceremonies were accompanied by excessive feasting. Cf., e.g., the ceremony of Ashurnaṣirpal II with the dedication of his palace. D. J. Wiseman, "A New Stela of Assur-naṣir-pal II," *Iraq* 14 (1952), pp. 24–44; A. K. Grayson, *Assyrian Royal Inscriptions* II (Wiesbaden: 1976), pp. 175ff.

7. Grosheide, *Ezra,* p. 186.

8:5ff.). That the author mentions the book of Moses testifies against the surmise that the Chronicler wrote 6:16–18.[8]

This is the end of the first Aramaic part of Ezra.

h. First Passover in the new temple (6:19–22)

19 *The exiles celebrated the Passover on the fourteenth of the first month.*

20 *The priests and Levites purified themselves as one man. All of them were pure, so they slaughtered the Passover (lamb) for all the exiles, for the priests, and for themselves.*

21 *The Israelites who had returned from the Exile ate it, as well as everyone who had separated himself from the impurity of the people of the land to seek the Lord, the God of Israel.*

22 *They also held the Feast of Unleavened Bread with joy, for the Lord gave them joy because he turned the goodwill of the king of Assyria in their favor by assisting them with the work on the temple of God, the God of Israel.*

19–21 This passage describes the first Passover festival in the new temple. This is the Passover of 516 B.C., in the second half of April, according to our calendar. With this description the author wants to stress that the religious activities at the temple were normal again. *The fourteenth of the first month* is 14 Nisan. *The Passover* festival is described in Exod. 12:6; Lev. 23:5–6; Num. 9:11. With the dedication of the temple of Solomon the Passover was not celebrated, because it was not at that time of the year. With the rededication of the temple in the days of Hezekiah and Josiah, however, the Passover was celebrated, according to the Chronicler (2 Chr. 30:13ff.; 2 Chr. 35:1ff.).[1] It is not clear from our text in v. 20 who slaughtered the Passover lamb. It could have been both the priests and the Levites, or the Levites alone. If we consider the descriptions in 2 Chr. 30 and 35, it becomes evident that the Levites were responsible for this rite. Originally the ceremony was performed by the father of a household. In the time of Hezekiah the Levites were only used in a case of emergency when the father of a household was not pure (2 Chr. 30:17). But in the time of Josiah apparently the Levites performed the rite for all the people (2 Chr. 35:2). In this case, however, all the people, after the sins they had committed, might have been regarded as impure. The same might have been true of the situation described in Ezra 6:20. The exiles and proselytes could

8. Cf. esp. Myers, *Ezra. Nehemiah,* p. 53. Cf. also the general discussion on the dedication ceremony by H. E. del Medico, "Le cadre historique des fêtes de Hanukkah et de Purîm," *VT* 15 (1965), pp. 238–270.

1. Myers, *Ezra. Nehemiah,* p. 54; Rudolph, *Esra und Nehemia,* p. 61.

have been regarded as so contaminated with sins that the rite could only be performed by the Levites.

As well as everyone who had separated. There is some difference of opinion about the people described in this phrase. They might have been Israelites of the former northern kingdom[2] or Jews who were not exiled, or proselytes (cf. Exod. 12:44, 48).[3] The last possibility seems best. The Passover was intended for a wider group of people, according to Exod. 12. The stern exclusiveness of the dedication ceremony was set aside to meet the requirements of the law in connection with the Passover. It is clear, however, that nobody who was not regarded as pure was allowed to attend the festival. The Samaritans would definitely have been excluded.

22 *The Feast of Unleavened Bread* was usually celebrated as part of the Passover (Exod. 12:15–20; Lev. 23:6–8; Num. 28:17)[4] on the day immediately following the Passover feast. It is noteworthy that in 2 Chr. 30:21, where the Feast of Unleavened Bread is described with the rededication of the temple in Hezekiah's time, the motif of joy is emphasized strongly. The same emphasis is made in this verse in Ezra.

The king of Assyria has given occasion to various interpretations. It is held that the author has committed here a *lapsus calami,* because Darius was king of Persia and not of Assyria. Some even surmise that the author followed the common practice of speaking of the king of Assyria because of the frequent occurrence of this expression in the OT.[5] Others regard it as anachronistic because the Chronicler, living in the time of the Seleucids, thought of the kings of his own time.[6] On the other hand, the title "king of Assyria" might be not so farfetched as some scholars believe. We have evidence from the ancient Near East that new rulers or foreign rulers were incorporated in the king lists of a particular country. This is the case with a king list of Babylon, which starts with the Assyrian Kandalanu, mentions the Chaldeans Nabopolassar and Nebuchadnezzar, refers to Cyrus, Cambyses, and Darius, and ends with the names of Seleucid kings.[7] Because Darius was also the sovereign of Assyria, he could easily have been called king of Assyria. The choice of this title might seem awkward. It is possible that the author wanted to refer here to a title which

2. Cf. J. S. Wright, *The Building of the Second Temple* (London: 1952), p. 20; S. Talmon, "Divergences in calendar reckoning in Ephraim and Judah," *VT* 8 (1958), p. 69.

3. Kittel, *Geschichte des Volkes Israel* III, p. 381; J. D. W. Kritzinger, *Qehal Jahwe* (Kampen: 1957), p. 91. Cf. also Grosheide, *Ezra*, p. 190.

4. Brockington, *Ezra, Nehemiah and Esther,* p. 75.

5. Cf. *ibid.*, p. 76.

6. M. Noth, *Überlieferungsgeschichte Studien* I (Tübingen: [3]1957), p. 145.

7. Cf. *ANET,* p. 566.

had for a long time in history inspired fear in the hearts of the Jews. The Assyrian kings were used by the Lord to chastise his people (cf. Neh. 9:32). But now the Lord had used the Assyrian king (Darius) to grant favor to the Jews, a great change in the historical situation.[8] In this verse we have again a religious approach, well known in the OT. The Lord is supreme and even the mightiest king is in his power. God is the Lord of history. Through the historical process his will becomes clear to his followers.

II. EZRA'S RETURN AND REFORMS (7:1–10:44)

A. EZRA'S RETURN (7:1–8:36)

1. Ezra's Mission (7:1–10)

1 *After this, during the reign of Artaxerxes the king of Persia, Ezra the son of Seraiah, the son of Azariah, the son of Hilkiah,*
2 *the son of Shallum, the son of Zadok, the son of Ahitub,*
3 *the son of Amariah, the son of Azariah, the son of Meraioth,*
4 *the son of Zerahiah, the son of Uzzi, the son of Bukki,*
5 *the son of Abishua, the son of Phinehas, the son of Eleazar, the son of the high priest Aaron,*
6 *this man Ezra came from Babylon. He was a secretary, versed in the law of Moses which the Lord, the God of Israel, had given. Because of the favor of the Lord his God, the king gave him everything he requested.*
7 *Some of the Israelites, priests, Levites, singers, and gatekeepers, as well as temple servants, went to Jerusalem in the seventh year of Artaxerxes the king.*
8 *He arrived in Jerusalem in the fifth month. It was the seventh year of the king.*
9 *For it was determined for him to go from Babylon on the first of the first month, and on the first of the fifth month he arrived in Jerusalem, for the favor of his God was with him.*
10 *For Ezra had set his heart on the study of the law of the Lord, to practice it and to teach Israel statutes and customary law.*

Chapter 6 described the completion of the temple. Chapter 7 brings us to the date 458 B.C., the seventh year of Artaxerxes I (cf. the Introduction). There is a lapse of time of approximately fifty-seven years between Ezra

8. Cf. W. Th. In der Smitten, *Esra: Quellen, Überlieferung und Geschichte*. SSN 15 (Assen: 1973), pp. 8–9.

6 and 7. We know almost nothing of what happened to the returnees in this period. The only reference we have is from Ezra 4:6–23, where the hostility of the Samaritans is described. We may deduce from this that the poor Jewish community in Judah was subjected to occasional acts of hostility by neighboring enemies. This kind of life was not conducive to religious purity. The Jews had to live with their neighbors, and some of them even became apostate in order to live in peace with them.

1–6 These verses provide a chronological connection with the time of Artaxerxes, as well as the genealogy and certain characteristics of Ezra. Scholars have two problems with the genealogy of these verses. First, the genealogy stands in an awkward position between the name of Ezra as subject in v. 1 and the verb of the sentence ("came") in v. 6. Thus some scholars have proposed that the genealogy is secondary and must be deleted.[1] But the arguments that the author inserted this genealogy here are not cogent.[2] It is clear from *this man Ezra* in v. 6, where the subject of v. 1 is repeated, that the author was well aware of the distance between subject and verb and with the repetition solved the problem. Second, the genealogy occurs in a shortened form. If we compare it with the Aaronite-Zadokite genealogy in 1 Chr. 6, it is clear that this genealogy in Ezra follows the one in 1 Chronicles up to Meraioth.[3] From there onward certain names are left out, and at the end names are added to come up to the time of Ezra. This genealogy of Ezra begins with Ezra and works back in history to the time of Aaron, the first high priest. The omission of names in a genealogy is not an uncommon phenomenon. As we have already seen, "the son of . . ." does not necessarily refer to a direct descendant; sometimes many generations are passed over.[4] The point which the author wants to make is that Ezra is a direct descendant of Aaron and thus has the right to act as a priest and to introduce certain reforms.

From Babylon. Ezra came from Babylon and Nehemiah from Susa. Ezra lived, therefore, in Babylon where the great majority of nonrepatriated Jewish exiles were still living. That Ezra was entrusted with such an important mission indicates that the Jews prospered in Babylon and were well educated.

1. Noth, *Überlieferungsgeschichtliche Studien,* pp. 145ff.; A. S. Kapelrud, *The Question of Authorship in the Ezra-Narrative: A Lexical Investigation* (Oslo: 1944), pp. 19–20; Galling, *Die Bücher der Chronik, Esra, Nehemia,* p. 204; Batten, *A Critical and Exegetical Commentary on the Books of Ezra and Nehemiah,* p. 303.
2. Cf. also the discussion of In der Smitten, *Esra,* p. 8; cf. Rudolph, *Esra und Nehemia,* pp. 71–72.
3. Myers, *Ezra. Nehemiah,* p. 60.
4. Cf. W. F. Albright, *New Horizons in Biblical Research* (New York: 1966), p. 11 n. 1.

Ezra is a shortened form of Azariah, meaning "the Lord has helped."[5] *Zadok.* The precise role played by this priest is enigmatic.[6] *Azariah.* This name is well attested in extrabiblical material, e.g., on seal impressions[7] and also on jar handles from Gibeon,[8] from early preexilic to postexilic times. *Amariah.* It has now for the first time been discovered in extrabiblical sources on jar handles at Gibeon.[9]

He was a secretary, versed in the law of Moses. On *secretary* cf. 4:8. The title "secretary" for Ezra might have a double meaning.[10] In the first place it refers to a Persian office. Ezra was appointed by Artaxerxes for the specific task of acting as secretary in Judah on behalf of the religious institutions.[11] He was also a priest, however, who had made a special study of the law of Moses, the legal parts of the Pentateuch. He was thus able to interpret the law for the Jewish community. Some scholars hold that Ezra as a scribe and learned man in the law was the compiler and final editor of the law.[12] But there is in Ezra and Nehemiah nothing to prove this surmise. It is much better, and true to these books, to accept that Ezra must be regarded as the founder of Jewish exegesis on the method of the *midrash halakha.*[13] He was thus an interpreter par excellence.

Secretary, versed. This may also be translated "skilled secretary" or "scribe." Ahiqar calls himself "a wise and skilled scribe" *(spr ḥkym wmhyr).*[14] Cowley translates this by "a wise and ready scribe."[15] In the Elephantine papyri the following expressions appear: *spry 'wsr'* and *spry mdynt'*,[16] which can be translated, respectively, "the secretaries of the treasury" and "the secretaries of the province." In the Aramaic papyri from the Persian period published by G. R. Driver the term *spr'* also means

5. Brockington, *Ezra, Nehemiah and Esther,* p. 76. Cf. also Noth, *Die israelitischen Personennamen,* p. 154.
6. Cf. H. H. Rowley, "Melchizedek and Zadok," in W. Baumgartner, *et al.*, eds., *Festschrift für Alfred Bertholet* (Tübingen: 1950), pp. 461–472; M. D. Rehm, *IDBS*, pp. 976–77.
7. E.g., D. Diringer, *Le iscrizioni antico-ebraiche Palestinesi* (Florence: 1934), pp. 184 (24), 199 (40).
8. Cf. J. B. Pritchard, *Hebrew Inscriptions and Stamps from Gibeon* (Philadelphia: 1959), pp. 7–8, 10.
9. Cf. *ibid.*, pp. 8, 10–11.
10. Cf. the arguments of H. H. Schaeder, *Esra der Schreiber,* pp. 39ff.
11. Cf. *ibid.;* opposed by Galling, *Studien zur Geschichte Israels,* p. 166. Cf. also Widengren, *Israelite and Judaean History,* p. 535.
12. Cf. the discussion of Grosheide, *Ezra*, p. 196.
13. Cf. S. Talmon, *IDBS*, p. 317.
14. *AP,* p. 212 (Ahiqar 1:1).
15. *AP,* p. 220.
16. *AP,* pp. 4 (2:12, 14), 53 (17:1, 6).

"scribe" or "clerk."[17] From all these examples it is clear that *spr* had a variety of meanings. In the case of Ezra, who was sent by the Persian king, this term should have something to do with an official errand.

The word *versed* or "skilled" *(māhîr)* is interesting. It is evident from the above-mentioned usage in Ahiqar that the combination of "wise" and "skilled" refers to a scribe of the highest efficiency, a professional of the highest order.[18] Here the term "skilled" is definitely connected to "scribe," but in Ezra 7:6 it is probable that the efficiency of Ezra is connected to his knowledge of the law of Moses.

Which the Lord, the God of Israel, had given. The legal stipulations were not regarded as the product of an important person in the history of Israel, e.g., Moses, but were venerated as coming directly from God. Their origin is placed in the divine sphere. Customary law is sanctioned by the Lord. This approach to the legal material of the OT is already prevalent in the Pentateuch and developed at an early stage.[19]

Because of the favor of the Lord (lit. "as the hand of the Lord is on him"). This expression was popular in the time of Ezra (cf. Ezra 7:28; 8:18; Neh. 2:8, 18). "The hand of the Lord on someone" indicated that the Lord had given his favor to that person. The author wants to show that in this important matter it was the Lord, the God of history, who influenced the Persian king to react sympathetically to the overtures of Ezra. *The king gave him everything he requested.* Nothing is said of what he asked. We may presume that Ezra asked for the things mentioned in the letter of Artaxerxes (7:11ff.).

7–9 These verses state that a group of Jews accompanied Ezra to Jerusalem (for a list cf. Ezra 8). The dates of his departure from Babylon and his arrival at Jerusalem are given; it took the caravan about three-and-a-half months to reach their destination. A direct route from Babylon to Jerusalem is about 500 miles, but they probably took the route through northern Syria to avoid the desert.[20] In those days such a journey was dangerous. At that time a rebellion had broken out in Egypt and the highways were to a certain extent unsafe. No wonder that the author regarded the safe arrival of Ezra as a special favor of the Lord (the same expression is used here as in 7:6).

The seventh year of Artaxerxes. Some scholars hold that the numeral thirty fell out by haplography so that we should read "the thirty-seventh

17. Cf. G. R. Driver, *Aramaic Documents of the Fifth Century B.C.* (1957, repr. 1968), pp. 25 (4:4), 28 (6:6), 29 (7:10), 31 (8:6), 32 (9:3), and 33 (10:5).
18. Cf. *DISO*, p. 144.
19. Cf. F. C. Fensham, "The rôle of the Lord in the legal sections of the Covenant Code." *VT* 26 (1976), pp. 262–274.
20. Brockington, *Ezra, Nehemiah and Esther*, p. 79.

year of Artaxerxes."[21] But this theory is without any textual evidence. The seventh year of Artaxerxes is, as we have seen, 458 B.C.

It was the seventh year of the king is regarded with suspicion because it is a mere repetition of what is said in the previous verse.[22] But is it a mere repetition? The author obviously wants to stress that Ezra arrived in Jerusalem in the same year as his departure from Babylon.[23]

For it was determined. The vocalization of the Hebrew is *y^{e}sud̲*, "that was the foundation of." With a change in the vowels we may read *yussad̲*, "it was determined."

The first of the first month is the first of Nisan (April 8). *The first of the fifth month* is the first of Ab (August 4). Thus they began the trip in the spring and they arrived in midsummer. This time of the year is another reason why they should have avoided the desert.

10 The conjunction *kî* connects this verse to the immediately preceding phrase, "for the favor of his God was with him." The favor of God was with him because he set his heart on the study of the law, etc. *Ezra has set his heart on the study.* The word "heart" *(lēḇāḇ)* connotes the whole of one's being.[24] Ezra thus concentrated his whole life on the study of the law. But it is not only a question of study—he also practiced the law. It was not a dead letter, but a living reality to him (cf. also Jas. 1:22). *To teach Israel.* This phrase refers to the fulfilling of his mission. He taught the Jews the law in Babylon and now he had come to Judah to do likewise. Myers is of the opinion that the expression "to practice . . . to teach" might be a hendiadys and should be translated "to teach effectively."[25] This would mean that the emphasis is not laid on the practicing of the law, but on the teaching. Although the proposal of Myers is not grammatically impossible, it is important to note that the LXX, the earliest interpretation of these terms, has separated them, and that in the MT punctuation, an *athnach* is placed under *la'^{a}śōṯ* to separate it clearly from the next verb, *ûl^{e}lammēd̲*.

Ezra's actions in the rest of the book must be interpreted in the light of this verse.

2. *Artaxerxes' Letter (7:11–26)*

11 *This is the copy of the letter which the king gave to Ezra the priest and secretary, learned in the commandments of the Lord and his statutes for Israel.*

21. Rudolph, *Esra und Nehemia,* p. 70.
22. *Ibid.*, p 67.
23. Grosheide, *Ezra,* p. 202. Cf. also In der Smitten, *Esra,* p. 10.
24. Cf. F. Stolz, *THAT* I, p. 863; W. H. Schmidt, "Anthropoligische Begriffe im AT," *EvTh* 24 (1964), pp. 383ff.
25. Myers, *Ezra. Nehemiah,* p. 58.

12 *Artaxerxes, king of kings, to Ezra the priest, the scribe of the law of the God of heaven. Its total contents are as follows:*

13 *"Herewith is my command that anyone in my kingdom of the Israelites, priests, and Levites who is willing to go to Jerusalem may go with you.*

14 *For you are sent by the king and his seven counsellors to make an inspection of Judah and Jerusalem in accordance with the law of your God, which you have with you,*

15 *and also to carry with you the silver and gold which the king and his counsellors have contributed voluntarily to the God of Israel who stays in Jerusalem,*

16 *and also all the silver and gold which you find in the whole of the province of Babylon, together with the voluntary gifts given by the people and priests for the temple of their God in Jerusalem.*

17 *Furthermore, you must buy diligently with this money bulls, rams, and lambs, as well as the meal and drink offerings, and offer them upon the altar of the temple of your God in Jerusalem.*

18 *What is left over of the silver and gold you can spend as you like, in accordance with the will of your God.*

19 *You must deliver the vessels that have been given to you for the service of the temple of your God before the God of Jerusalem.*

20 *For anything else which is required for the temple of your God and which you want to provide, you may draw from the royal treasury.*

21 *Herewith I, Artaxerxes the king, command all the treasurers of Trans-Euphrates that whatever Ezra the priest and scribe of the law of the God of the heavens may ask you must be done diligently.*

22 *This is up to a hundred talents of silver, a hundred kors of wheat, a hundred baths of wine, a hundred baths of oil, and the amount of salt is not prescribed.*

23 *Everything demanded by the God of heaven must be provided carefully for the temple of the God of the heavens. Why should anger come on the kingdom of the king and his sons?*

24 *You must know that no tribute, tax, or duties must be imposed on any of the priests, Levites, singers, gatekeepers, temple servants, or anyone else who serves in this temple of God.*

25 *You, Ezra, must appoint magistrates and judges for all the people of Trans-Euphrates, according to the wisdom of your God that you possess, that is, for all who have knowledge of the laws of your God, and you must teach it to all who have not.*

26 *Everyone who does not comply with the law of your God—it is also the law of the king—let judgment be diligently meted out to him: death, corporal punishment, confiscation, or imprisonment."*

For various reasons the authenticity of this letter or parts of it has been rejected,[1] although certain modern scholars do accept its authenticity.[2] The main objection against this letter is the clear Jewish influence and terminology. It is not deemed possible for a Persian king in the fifth century B.C. to have written such a letter. Some are of the opinion that a grain of truth might lie in it, but that it has been strongly edited by a Jewish redactor and certain things added. Objections are made against a pure OT term like *miṯnaddaḇ* in a letter of a Persian king,[3] against an expression like "the whole province of Babylon," and against the fact that Ezra was invested with extensive powers, far more extensive than one would expect.[4]

E. Meyer already in 1896 had proposed a solution for most of these problems by accepting that Ezra himself was probably responsible for a draft of this letter that was later on sanctioned by the king.[5] It is also important to note that certain clear Persian expressions are used, e.g., "king of kings" and "seven counsellors," which reflect an intimate knowledge of the Persian court. Objections against the availability of revenue for the temple are not acceptable in the light of certain texts from Persian times that show that the Persian kings were indeed interested in the restoration of sanctuaries and cultic services. From these texts it is also clear that revenue was given to accomplish this task.[6] Furthermore, it is interesting to note that special powers were granted to a certain person to throw people out of a sanctuary, e.g., Udjeharresne in the time of Cambyses in connection with the sanctuary of Neith in Egypt.[7] This physician wrote in his autobiography that he was a companion and director of the king. This shows that the Persian kings had used certain persons from the local population to instruct them about the customs of their people. In the light of

1. Cf., e.g., S. Mowinckel, *Ezra den Skriftlaerde* (Kristania: 1916), pp. 19–23; F. Ahlemann, "Die Esra-Quelle, eine literarkritische Untersuchung" (dissertation, 1941), pp. 20ff.; A. S. Kapelrud, *The Question of Authorship in the Ezra-Narrative*; S. Granild, *Ezrabogens litteraere Genesis undersoegt med saerligt henblik paa et efterkronistish Indgreb* (Copenhagen: 1949), pp. 28–95. Against the authenticity of 7:20–24 is In der Smitten, *Esra,* p. 19.

2. Cf., e.g., Myers, *Ezra. Nehemiah,* p. 63; Brockington, *Ezra, Nehemiah and Esther,* pp. 79–80; Grosheide, *Ezra,* pp. 216–17; H. Cazelles, "La mission d'Esdras," *VT* 4 (1954), pp. 122–26.

3. Kapelrud, *op. cit.,* p. 29.

4. Cf. the discussion by In der Smitten, *Esra,* pp. 14–19.

5. E. Meyer, *Die Entstehung des Judenthums* (1896, repr. 1965), p. 65.

6. Cf. A. H. Gardiner, *Egypt of the Pharaohs,* pp. 366–67, for the text. It runs as follows: "And His Majesty commanded that the revenues should be given to Nēith the great."

7. *Ibid.* Cf. also In der Smitten, *Esra,* pp. 17–18, for the Gadatas Inscription.

this evidence nothing extraordinary is to be found in the letter of Artaxerxes.[8] Another important fact is that in view of the trouble in Egypt, Artaxerxes wanted to consolidate his subjects in Palestine and to make them satisfied. He invested Ezra with special powers to accomplish this task.

11 This verse is written in Hebrew while the letter of Artaxerxes (7:12–26) is written in Aramaic. Verse 11 is to be regarded as an introduction, stating to whom the letter was given. The term used for *letter* can also mean "a diplomatic note."[9] This is not an ordinary letter, but a letter with certain remarks on the official function of Ezra as well as commands to be carried out. *The priest and secretary.* The first title is to be derived from the priestly genealogical account in 7:1–5. It refers to his office among the Jews. For *secretary* cf. 7:6. *Learned in the commandments (sōp̄ēr* is used here for "learned"). This phrase shows that the author of this verse combined the Persian office of secretary with that of a Jewish scholar of the law of God.

12–13 After the formal announcement of the sender of the letter, it is stated to whom it is given. *King of kings* is typical Persian chancellery terminology.[10] *The scribe of the law of the God.* We have decided to translate *sāp̄ar* here by "scribe," because "secretary" would make no sense. *Law (dāṯā')* is a loanword from the Persian *dāta*.[11] This word is connected with the customary law of the Persians,[12] but later on it developed a much wider meaning, as in this case. The Persians had respect for the laws of other nations as long as they did not conflict with their own.

Its total contents are as follows. This clause is difficult. Some scholars, following the LXX, think that the word *šᵉlam* has dropped out; such a corruption is not impossible.[13] The Aram. *gᵉmîr* is not clear. We derive its meaning from later Aram. *gmryn* in the sense "total, complete."[14]

In v. 13 permission is given to the three categories of Jews, viz., laity, priests, and Levites, who are willing to return to Judah, to go back. The Jews were already scattered over the Persian empire. We know from the Elephantine papyri that a whole colony of Jews lived in the south of Egypt. The greatest concentration of Jews, however, was in Babylon and

8. Against Kapelrud, *op. cit.*, p. 42.
9. Cf. W. Th. In der Smitten, "Eine aramäische Inschrift in Pakistan aus dem 3. Jh. v. Chr.," *BiOr* 28 (1971), 309–311; *idem, Esra*, p. 11.
10. In der Smitten, *Esra*, p. 12.
11. Cf. W. Brandenstein and M. Meyrhofer, *Handbuch des Altpersischen* (Wiesbaden: 1964), p. 115.
12. Cf. Frye, *The Heritage of Persia*, p. 100.
13. Myers, *Ezra. Nehemiah*, p. 58; In der Smitten, *Esra*, pp. 12–13.
14. *DISO*, p. 51 under the second root.

vicinity. And it is clear from 7:7–9 that the Jews who had returned with Ezra came from Babylon; otherwise 7:7–9 would make no sense.

14–16 In these verses Ezra is commanded by the king and his counsellors to go to Judah and see if the Jews there are living in accordance with the law of God, that is, the law which Ezra had at his disposal—we may presume the Pentateuch. No reason is given for this order. Is it possible that Ezra had heard of certain malpractices in Judah? From this account it is not clear. It seems as if Ezra was sent to make an inspection to see if the law of God was still being kept. For the Persian king, in the circumstances described above, it was a necessity that peace should prevail in Judah, a territory which was always easily influenced by Egypt. Such a mission would have been fruitless without the necessary means. Silver and gold were granted by the king and his counsellors for the temple service: even the silver and gold which could be collected among the people of the province of Babylon might be used.

His seven counsellors. Cf. Esth. 1:14. We know that Cyrus had seven counsellors who advised him (Xenophon *Anabasis* i.6.4–5).[15] This phrase points to a purely Persian background. *The God of Israel who stays in Jerusalem* is regarded by Kapelrud as "an ordinary everyday expression used by the Jews in exile, to indicate that it is in Jerusalem [where] the real House of God is situated."[16] It is of interest, however, that this kind of terminology is used in a much wider sphere of meaning, e.g., "the god Khnub *(ḥnwb)* who is in Yeb, the fortress,"[17] or even "Yahu, the God who is in Yeb, the fortress."[18] *Which you find* means all the silver and gold which are offered voluntarily for this purpose. It does not mean that Ezra had a free hand to demand what he wanted,[19] but that the Jews and other inhabitants of this province were free to give as they pleased (cf. also 8:25).

17–20 When all the silver and gold had been acquired from the different sources, it was to be spent on the cultic services of the temple, just as in the time of Darius (6:9). There is one important difference, namely, the specification of the meal and drink offerings (cf. Lev. 2; Num. 15:1–10).[20] *What is left over of the silver and gold* is regarded with suspicion by scholars, because the regular service of the temple would demand a constant supply of money. But this view is reading too much into the

15. Myers, *op. cit.*, p. 58.
16. Kapelrud, *op. cit.*, p. 33.
17. *AP*, p. 112 (30:5).
18. *BMAP*, pp. 142, 145 (2:2). Cf. also S. Segert, "Aramäische Studien," *ArOr* 24 (1956), p. 403.
19. Grosheide, *Ezra*, pp. 207–208; against Kapelrud, *op. cit.*, pp. 32–33.
20. Kapelrud, *op. cit.*, p. 34.

text. Quite probably it was expected that Ezra and the returnees would present a major offering on their arrival, and would also offer on behalf of the king and his counsellors. What was left over after this offering could be spent according to the will of God, according to what was commanded in his law. We must keep in mind that Ezra and the returnees had no occasion in Babylon to make sacrificial offerings for their sins. With their arrival one would expect a major attempt to present offerings for the pardoning of their sins. *The vessels.* These could not have been the vessels removed by Nebuchadnezzar, because they had been restored long ago. It might have been vessels provided by the king and the Jews in exile (cf. 8:25–27). If anything more was required, Ezra had the right to draw on the royal treasury. This could not mean that he had a free hand, but that his needs should be met. It is also notable that this money had to come from the province Trans-Euphrates, because local public works were financed by local taxes (cf. 6:8).[21]

21–24 In these verses the treasurers of Trans-Euphrates are addressed. Certain modern scholars hold that the commandments here issued are so unreasonable that the authenticity of these verses must be rejected.[22] It is quite possible that the requirements of Ezra were not meant only for the temple, but also for food for the exiles on their way to Jerusalem. Ezra thus received what might be described as a letter of introduction to the treasurers of Trans-Euphrates to aid him on his journey. Some are of the opinion that a special letter was sent by the king to the treasurers and that a summary of this letter was inserted here. On the other hand, it is quite probable that along with the instructions to Ezra certain orders to the treasurers were incorporated.[23] Ezra had these orders with his commission ready at hand to persuade the Persian officials en route to supply necessities. It is obvious from v. 22 that these supplies were kept within certain limits. The quantities are calculated by Myers as follows: *a hundred talents of silver* are just more than 3¾ tons; *a hundred kors of wheat* are approximately 650 bushels; and *a hundred baths* of wine and oil are 607 gallons each.[24] It is unclear whether these requirements were meant for the temple or for the returnees on their journey, or for both.

It is of interest that wine is mentioned. In the OT we have only a few references to wine as an offering, e.g., Exod. 29:40 and Hos. 9:4.[25]

21. Frye, *The Heritage of Persia,* p. 110.
22. Cf. the discussion of In der Smitten, *Esra,* pp. 14, 19.
23. Grosheide, *Ezra,* p. 210.
24. Myers, *op. cit.,* p. 59. For slightly different equivalencies cf. Brockington, *Ezra, Nehemiah and Esther,* pp. 80–81.
25. Cf. W. Rudolph, *Hosea.* KAT 13/1 (Gütersloh: 1966), p. 176; H. W. Wolff, *Hosea.* Hermeneia (E.T. 1974), *in loc.*

In the latter text Hosea prophesies a time of exile for the Israelites in which they will not be able to bring an offering of wine. For salt, a relatively cheap commodity, no limits were set. *Carefully ('aḏrazdā')* is a loanword from Persian *drazdā,* meaning "to do something carefully and faithfully."[26] *Why should anger come?* It was typical of a Near Eastern potentate to be afraid that the anger of God might fall on his person, his empire, and his sons if God was not served according to his instructions. It was thus in the king's own interest that the cultic activities should continue in proper order.[27] *Anger* (*q*ᵉ*ṣap* in Aramaic and *qeṣep* in Hebrew) is used only for the anger of the Lord in the OT (Num. 1:53; 18:5; Josh. 9:20; 22:20; etc.).

Verse 24 states that no taxation should be imposed on the clerics. This situation is paralleled by the Gadatas Inscription of Darius in which exemption of taxation for the priests of Apollo is prescribed.[28] It shows that this practice was not unknown in the Persian empire. It is most unlikely that the letter of Artaxerxes can be regarded as fictitious, because the author had an intimate knowledge of the temple personnel.[29] As we have already seen, this kind of detail could have been communicated by Ezra. He made his request (7:6) and it was granted by the king accordingly.

25–26 Where the king had given orders to his treasurers in vv. 21–24, he returns to Ezra in vv. 25–26. The Aramaic is clear about who is addressed. Verse 21 states that the king commands the treasurers. Verse 25 starts with "You, Ezra, must appoint." *Magistrates and judges (šāp*ᵉ*ṭîn w*ᵉ*ḏayyānîn)* might be regarded as tautological. On the other hand, it is of interest that in the Achaemenian empire two kinds of tribunals existed, namely, a kind of social tribunal for cases of customary law, and royal tribunals for cases in which the state was interested.[30] It is thus probable that the two kinds of judicial offices described in this verse might refer to two kinds of legal activities as known in the Persian empire. Ezra was entrusted with an important mission, not only to take care of the customary law of the Jews, but also to ensure loyalty to the king.

All the people of Trans-Euphrates. This is a much larger area than the province of Babylon mentioned in v. 16.[31] Scholars agree that this is a reference to the Jews who lived in Trans-Euphrates. The Jewish population is singled out, and they must be instructed by Ezra in the law of God. The Persian king is thus satisfied that the law of God will not clash with the laws of his empire. Because of the religious sphere in which this

26. Cf. P. Nober, "'adrazdā' (Esdras 7:23)," *BZ* N.F. 2 (1958), pp. 134–38.
27. Kapelrud, *op. cit.*, p. 38.
28. In der Smitten, *Esra*, p. 17; Myers, *op. cit.*, p. 63.
29. Kapelrud, *op. cit.*, p. 40.
30. Frye, *The Heritage of Persia*, p. 100.
31. In der Smitten, *Esra*, p. 16.

law operated, Artaxerxes on the one hand wanted to appease the God of the heavens, and on the other hand wanted to satisfy the desires of his Jewish subjects who were living mainly in Trans-Euphrates. Some scholars think that this order of Artaxerxes was impossible to fulfil, because Ezra would simply not be able to organize the Jews in such a large area. But we do not have any knowledge of where the Jews were mainly concentrated. It might have been only in Babylon and vicinity and in Judah. In such a case the execution of this order was not impossible.

Two groups of Jews are distinguished in v. 25b: those that have knowledge and those that do not. This comes out clearly in the rest of Ezra where the ignorance of certain Jews is demonstrated. Ezra's mission was to teach them afresh the law of God and to discipline them to live according to it.

According to the wisdom of your God which you possess. The word for "wisdom" *(ḥoḵmâ)* has a variety of meanings. It might refere here to skill in applying the law. Ahiqar is called a wise (skilled) scribe.[32] In the case of Ezra, God gave him the skill to interpret and apply the law for his people.

In v. 26 Artaxerxes identifies his law with the law of God. The king had sanctioned the application of the law of God to the Jews, and by this sanctioning it became his law. This law was not to be disobeyed. As we have seen already, Darius exhorted his followers to believe what he had written and not to disobey the laws.[33] The Persian kings were anxious to see that their laws were enforced. Artaxerxes even prescribed the punishment if the law was not kept, namely, the death sentence, corporal punishment, confiscation, and imprisonment. *Corporal punishment (šᵉrōšô)* is usually interpreted as banishment, from a Hebrew root *šrš*, "uproot."[34] However, this word is to be derived from the Persian word *sraušyā*, meaning "corporal or physical punishment," which was well known in the Persian empire.[35] The punishments were not derived from the law of God, although some of them are mentioned in the Pentateuch (Lev. 24:12; Num. 15:34); rather, they are of Persian origin and are thus state penalties. Extraordinary powers were granted to Ezra, but this was not foreign to practices in the Persian empire (see above, p. 107). To hold that this verse is fictitious because Ezra had not used his right to punish (although cf. 10:8) is most surprising. Just because one has the right to inflict certain

32. *AP,* pp. 212, 200.
33. Frye, *op. cit.,* p. 100.
34. E.g., Brockington, *op. cit.,* p. 81.
35. Cf. F. Rundgren, "Zur Bedeutung von *ŠRŠW*—Esra VII 26," *VT* 7 (1957), pp. 400–404. Cf. also Z. W. Falk, "Ezra VII 26," *VT* 9 (1959), pp. 88–89.

punishments does not mean that he is forced to do so. It might depend on what kind of transgressions have been committed.

Here in v. 26 the second Aramaic part of Ezra ends.

3. Ezra's Thanksgiving (7:27–28)

27 *Blessed be the Lord, the God of our forefathers, who influenced the king about this matter to adorn the temple of the Lord in Jerusalem,*
28 *who extended to me (his) love before the king, his counsellors, and all the powerful officials of the king. I took courage, because the Lord my God favored me, and I gathered from Israel the leaders to accompany me.*

27–28 These verses start the Hebrew version which runs through to the end of ch. 10. These verses also start with the first person and are thus part of the memoirs of Ezra[1] (cf. the Introduction). Some scholars are of the opinion that the I-parts are fabrications of the Chronicler and have nothing to do with the memoirs of Ezra.[2] It is certain, however, that the "I" from here to 9:15 is Ezra; otherwise the whole passage would make no sense.

In these two verses the historical approach to the religion of Israel is again clearly discernible. As God from ancient times has influenced foreign kings to do his will, he now influences the Persian king to grant favorable conditions for the adornment of the temple. *To adorn (lᵉp̄ā'ēr)* is used in the latter part of Isaiah (55:5; 60:7, 9, 13) as well as in Ps. 149:4. In all these cases the Lord is the subject of the verb. The objects in these sentences are the temple (Isa. 60:7, 13), the people of God (Isa. 55:5; 60:9), and the meek (Ps. 149:4). In Isaiah the term has some definite eschatological overtones. The references in Isaiah to the temple are of interest. Is it possible that Ezra, by using the same terminology, wanted to show that the pronouncements of Isaiah were fulfilled?

Although the king was instrumental in the adornment of the temple, it was actually God who did it. He is the real subject of the verb "adorn." It is not clear what is meant by *adorn.* Does it refer to the offerings in the temple, or to the renovation of the temple? One may be tempted to think of the latter possibility in the light of Isa. 60:13, where the wood of the Lebanon is mentioned, but the letter of Artaxerxes mentions nothing of such a venture. Or must we accept that not all the orders of Artaxerxes were given in his quoted letter? At the same time we must keep in mind

1. Brockington, *Ezra, Nehemiah and Esther,* p. 81. Cf. esp. Schaeder, *Esra der Schreiber,* pp. 6ff.
2. Cf. lately In der Smitten, *Esra,* pp. 19–20.

that in Isa. 60:7 the adornment of the temple is associated with offerings.[3] We are thus not able to reach any definite conclusion in the light of Isaiah. Because both possibilities are open, it is better to accept that the adornment must be connected with the offerings, as also in the light of the letter of Artaxerxes.

Some take v. 28b from *I took courage* as part of the next chapter.[4]

4. List of Family Heads Who Returned (8:1–14)

1 *These are the heads of families and the genealogies of those who went with me from Babylon during the reign of Artaxerxes the king:*
2 *From the descendants of Phinehas: Gershom; from the descendants of Ithamar: Daniel; from the descendants of David: Hattush*
3 *of the descendants of Shecaniah; of the descendants of Parosh: Zechariah, with whom a hundred and fifty men were registered;*
4 *from the descendants of Pahath-moab: Eliehoenai, the son of Zerahiah, and with him two hundred men;*
5 *from the descendants of Zattu: Shecaniah, the son of Jahaziel, and with him three hundred men;*
6 *from the descendants of Adin: Ebed, the son of Jonathan, and with him fifty men;*
7 *from the descendants of Elam: Jeshaiah, the son of Athaliah, and with him seventy men;*
8 *from the descendants of Shephatiah: Zebadiah, the son of Michael, and with him eighty men;*
9 *from the descendants of Joab: Obadiah, the son of Jehiel, and with him two hundred and eighteen men;*
10 *from the descendants of Bani: Shelomith, the son of Josiphiah, and with him a hundred and sixty men;*
11 *from the descendants of Bebai: Zechariah, the son of Bebai, and with him twenty-eight men;*
12 *from the descendants of Azgad: Johanan, the son of Hakkatan, and with him a hundred and ten men;*
13 *from the descendants of Adonikam, those who are last, with the names: Elipheleth, Jeiel, and Shemaiah, and with them sixty men;*
14 *from the descendants of Bigvai: Uthai and Zabbud, and with him seventy men.*

Some scholars doubt the authenticity of this list.[1] This doubt is connected with the fact that only twelve families are mentioned, probably contrived in this way to represent the twelve tribes of Israel. A second argument

3. Cf. W. Kessler, *Gott geht es um das Ganze; Jesaja 56–66 und Jesaja 24–27.* Die botschaft des AT 19 (Stuttgart: 1960), pp. 56ff.
4. Grosheide, *Ezra,* p. 219; cf. NEB.
1. Kapelrud, *The Question of Authorship in the Ezra-Narrative,* pp. 45–46.

against the authenticity is that most of the names which occur in this list are also found in other parts of Ezra, Nehemiah, and Chronicles. Against these arguments it can be urged that nowhere in our list is it said that the twelve families represent the twelve tribes. We know that the Israelites were especially fond of certain numbers, such as seven, twelve, forty, and seventy. Sometimes these numbers have symbolic value, such as an indication of completeness.[2] Ezra's choice of twelve families might be attributed to his belief that such a complete number would invest blessing for his journey to Jerusalem. Also, it is wrong to argue that most of the names appear elsewhere in Ezra, Nehemiah, and Chronicles and must therefore be fictitious. On the contrary, their occurrence in late literature testifies to their authenticity, because at that stage this nomenclature was in general use. There is thus nothing in this list to cast doubt on its authenticity.[3]

1–14 In this list of names the heads of two priestly families are mentioned first. In Ezra 2 it is just the reverse, for there the priestly families are mentioned last. A few other differences between the list in ch. 2 and this list are important. The priests here followed the Aaronite lineage, while in Ezra 2 they followed the Zadokite lineage.[4] In Ezra 2:6 the Joab lineage is regarded as part of the Pahath-moab family, while here it is independent (compare v. 4 with v. 9). From these differences we may deduce that this list was not copied from the list in ch. 2. Another important fact is the inclusion of the descendants of King David in this list. The head of the family is Hattush, who, according to 1 Chr. 3:22, is a grandson of Shecaniah. In 1 Chr. 3:17ff. we have the list: Jehoiachin, Pedaiah, Zerubbabel, Hananiah, Shecaniah, Shemaiah, Hattush.[5] Thus Hattush is the fourth generation after Zerubbabel. If Zerubbabel was born c. 560 B.C. and if we reckon approximately twenty-five years for a generation, the date for Hattush comes close to 458 B.C.

Another interesting feature of the list is that in the case of the two priestly families and the one of David, the number of the men who accompanied the heads of the families is left out. It is impossible to say why. Some of the numbers are probably round numbers. The two priestly families represent two houses, namely, Phinehas-Gershom and Ithamar-Daniel. Phinehas was the son of Aaron's third son Eleazar (Exod. 6:23–25) and Ithamar Aaron's fourth son (Exod. 6:23).[6] We have inserted two names, with almost all modern scholars, on the basis of the reading of

2. Cf. F. C. Fensham, *PEQ* 109 (1977), pp. 113–15.
3. Cf. lately In der Smitten, *Esra*, pp. 20–21.
4. Myers, *Ezra. Nehemiah*, p. 69.
5. *Ibid.*, p. 70.
6. Brockington, *Ezra, Nehemiah and Esther*, p. 82.

LXX^{B}:[7] Zattu in v. 5 and Bani in v. 10. It is obvious that these names fell out by haplography.

Another problem is posed in v. 14, where we have two names of heads of families in the line of Bigvai, namely Uthai and Zabbud (or with Qere, Zakkur), while the suffix in the next phrase *('immô)* is singular. It is conceivable that something went wrong in the transmission of the text, but it is impossible to make a convincing emendation. It is of interest that R. du Mesnil du Buisson derives the name Bebai (v. 11) from the divine name Babi,[8] though this derivation is rather improbable.

The phrase *those who are last* in v. 13 is problematic and has been variously interpreted. Some scholars regard it as a later intrusion in the text and want to delete it, but the textual evidence in its favor is too strong. Others interpret it as referring to the younger sons of Adonikam,[9] but this would be an extraordinary expression for younger sons. The best explanation is to understand this phrase as referring to the last three heads of the family of Adonikam who had returned to Judah. Thus it means that the whole family of Adonikam had migrated to Judah.[10]

5. *Enlistment of Temple Personnel (8:15–20)*

15 *I assembled them at the stream that runs to the Ahava River and we camped there for three days. When I reviewed the people and priests, I discovered that there were no Levites.*

16 *Then I sent for Eliezer, Ariel, Shemaiah, Elnathan, Jarib, Elnathan, Nathan, Zechariah, and Meshullam as leaders, and for Joiarib and Elnathan as interpreters (of the law).*

17 *I sent them to Iddo, the head of the place Casiphia, and I told them what to say to Iddo and his brothers and the temple servants at Casiphia to provide us with servants for the temple of our God.*

18 *They provided us through the favor of our God with an able man from the descendants of Mahli, the son of Levi, the son of Israel: Sherebiah with his sons and kinsmen: eighteen men,*

19 *as well as Hashabiah and with him Jeshaiah from the descendants of Merari, their kinsmen and sons: twenty (men),*

20 *and from the temple slaves, whom David and his officials had appointed to serve the Levites, two hundred and twenty. All of them were designated by name.*

15 Ezra 7:6–8 mentions briefly Ezra's departure from Babylon, giving the date as the first of the first month in the seventh year of Artaxerxes.

7. Cf. *BHS*.

8. Cf. R. du Mesnil du Buisson, *Nouvelles études sur les dieux et les mythes de Canaan* (Leiden: 1973), pp. 232–33.

9. Cf., e.g., JB.

10. Myers, *Ezra. Nehemiah,* pp. 69–70; Grosheide, *Ezra,* p. 223.

Here in the memoirs of Ezra more particulars are given. He assembled the returnees at the Ahava River. It is quite probable that the Ahava was one of the canals of the Euphrates that derived its name from a place name. But we know nothing more of this place or river. The returnees camped there for three days. *Three days* for an encampment is quite reasonable and should not be regarded with suspicion because Nehemiah had waited for three days after his arrival at Jerusalem (Neh. 2:11).[1] *When I reviewed the people*. Ezra had now for the first time the opportunity to inspect the returnees. He discovered that there were no Levites. It is possible that the Levites were not particularly numerous in Babylon at that time (see above on 2:40). The Levites were important for the temple service, and because Ezra wanted to celebrate a big festival in Jerusalem, it was necessary for him to have them in his company.

16–17 *Then I sent for*. The grammatical construction with verb plus *l*ᵉ before the proper names can be interpreted in two ways. *L*ᵉ may be taken as a preposition, and the phrase would mean that Ezra had sent for Eliezer and the others. Ezra made use of a person to go and call all these individuals and then they were sent. Or, the *l*ᵉ may be regarded as an indication of the accusative, as in Aramaic and late Hebrew. It is difficult to make a choice, because either is possible, and in the context it makes no difference.

We have nine names of heads and two names of interpreters, eleven names altogether. There are some problems with this list of names. The repetition of certain names, e.g., Elnathan thrice and Jarib (Joiarib) twice, is regarded as a sign that some confusion occurred in the transmission of this list. But the repetition of names does not necessarily indicate that the same person is meant. Grosheide is of the opinion that if different persons were meant identification through the mention of the father's name should have been made.[2] But is this necessary? It is also not clear what is meant by *leaders*. Are they heads of families or are they leaders? It seems better to regard them as leaders among the returnees who could use their influence to get the Levites.[3]

The last two persons of the list are designated as *interpreters (mᵉḇînîm)*. The term *mᵉḇînîm* is difficult to understand. It might mean "men with insight" or "teachers." In the postexilic period this word apparently expressed the effectiveness of a teacher.[4] In Neh. 8:8–9 it refers clearly to the interpretation or teaching of the law, and this is probably the meaning

1. Against Kapelrud, *The Question of Authorship in the Ezra-Narrative*, p. 46.
2. Grosheide, *Ezra*, p. 226.
3. Cf., e.g., Myers, *Ezra. Nehemiah*, p. 70.
4. Brockington, *Ezra, Nehemiah and Esther*, p. 86; H. H. Schmid, *THAT* I, p. 306; H. Ringgren, *TDOT* II, p. 103.

here. By using the law the interpreters of the law were also sent to persuade the Levites to accompany Ezra to Jerusalem.

The head of the place Casiphia. Head here may refer to Iddo's role as teacher or head of the school. We know nothing about the site Casiphia, although some refer to the possibility that it might have been Ktesiphon on the Tigris.[5] The term *ksp'* appears in the Elephantine papyri, but there it refers to a profession, "silversmith" or the like.[6] The question is, Why is Casiphia called a *place (hammāqôm)*? For some scholars *hammāqôm* is a clear reference to a sanctuary in the neighborhood of Babylon, in the same manner as the sanctuary of Yahu which existed at Yeb (Elephantine).[7] They also refer to Deut. 12:5; Jer. 7:3, 6, 7, where *māqôm* is used for a sanctuary[8] (cf. also Deut. 12:11; 14:23; 1 K. 8:29).[9] Another interpretation is to regard Casiphia as a place where a major concentration of the Jewish population of Babylon lived.[10] Or it could have been to distinguish it from another Casiphia which is not a place name. The usage of *māqôm* in the later OT literature, however, points to a sanctuary, possibly a kind of synagogue where pupils were instructed in the law.

I told them what to say. Literally "I placed in their mouths the words to say." *Iddo and his brothers and the temple servants.* We have read *'eḥāyw* instead of MT *'eḥîw.* C. C. Torrey proposes another solution by reading *'āḥî* ("my brother") and taking the *waw* with the next word: *w^e-hann^eṯînîm.*[11] Ezra thus refers to Iddo as his brother. The word brothers in the case of the reading *'eḥāyw* is not to be taken literally, but refers to kinsmen. The text is not clear that Iddo and his brothers must be regarded as temple servants. In our translation we have inserted a *waw* before temple servants that might have been left out as a result of haplography. If we accept the MT as it stands, Iddo and his brothers must be regarded as temple servants. This is doubtful, however. From vv. 17 and 18 it is clear that Iddo must be considered an important person. It is thus unlikely that he could have been a temple servant.[12] It is important to note that the name Iddo of Zechariah's ancestor is differently spelled in Hebrew (*'iddô'*, 5:1) from this name Iddo *('iddô).*

5. Brockington, *op. cit.*, p. 86.
6. Cf. the discussion of Kraeling, *BMAP,* p. 158.
7. Michaeli, *Les livres des Chroniques, d'Esdras et de Néhémie,* p. 298; Brockington, *op. cit.*, p. 86; B. Oded, "Judah and the Exile," in *Israelite and Judaean History,* p. 483.
8. E.g., Brockington, *op. cit.*, p. 86.
9. Cf. J. Bright, *Jeremiah,* p. 55.
10. Pelaia, *Esdra e Neemia,* p. 101. Cf. also Grosheide, *Ezra,* p. 227; de Vaux, *Ancient Israel* II, p. 339.
11. C. C. Torrey, *Ezra Studies,* p. 265.
12. Grosheide, *Ezra,* p. 227.

18–20 Ezra's overtures to Iddo were successful. He succeeded in procuring the services of two independent Levitical families. The one group under Sherebiah traced its lineage back to Mahli and the other group under Hashabiah and Jeshaiah to Merari. *With an able man.* Some scholars hold that a proper name fell out before this expression. The LXX takes *able man ('îš śēḵel)* as a proper name, perhaps because it seemed too far removed from *Sherebiah,* which it apparently determines, but such distance between a modifier and the word it modifies is not grammatically impossible. One should interpret the *waw* before Sherebiah as a *waw explicativum,* viz., ". . . with an able man . . . namely, Sherebiah." What does "able" mean? It quite probably refers to his capable service as a Levite. *Through the favor of our God.* For this expression cf. 7:6. In 7:6 the Lord moved the Persian king. In this case the Lord moved the leaders of the Levites. Again we may observe that the will of the Lord was responsible for the willingness of the Levites to accompany Ezra. The author accepts that without the will of the Lord this would not have been possible.

In v. 19 a few problems occur, e.g., *and with him Jeshaiah—with him (w^{e}'ittô)* is read by the LXX as *w^{e}'eṯ* and thus as *nota accusativi,* which also precedes Hashabiah. The expression of the MT, however, refers to a close relationship between Hashabiah and Jeshaiah. Another problem is the reading *'eḥāyw ûḇ^{e}nêhem* with a singular suffix in the former and a plural suffix in the latter word. Although it is possible that the antecedent of the former is either Hashabiah or Jeshaiah (cf. RSV, NEB, AV), it is better to accept here a scribal error for *'aḥêhem.*[13] In all, thirty-eight Levites joined the trek to Jerusalem. This small number of Levites might indicate that not many Levites were living in Babylon.

Verse 20 mentions that two hundred and twenty temple servants were enrolled. According to vv. 15–17 Ezra asked only for Levites, and now the enrollment of temple servants is also mentioned. Myers may be correct "that the decision of such a large number of temple slaves to accompany Ezra was a factor in persuading the Levites to go."[14] The temple servants were there to aid the Levites in their task. The phrase *whom David and his officials* is regarded as a secondary addition by most scholars.[15] In the time of David, according to a biblical tradition accepted by the Chronicler, the cult was organized in an elaborate fashion.[16] From v. 20b it is clear that Ezra also had the credentials of the temple servants, but they were so numerous that a list of their names was not supplied. It is obvious

13. So NAB; see Grosheide, *Ezra,* p. 230. *BHS* and JB suggest a slight emendation and transposition, reading "Hashabiah . . . and his brother [Heb. *'āḥîw*] Jeshaiah."
14. Myers, *Ezra. Nehemiah,* p. 70.
15. E.g., Grosheide, *Ezra,* p. 231.
16. Brockington, *op. cit.,* p. 87; cf. also Pelaia, *op. cit.,* p. 102.

that Ezra had with him a list of all the names of the returnees. This list fulfilled a double duty: he had it ready at hand to check that he had all the returnees with him on his long and laborious journey, and, since the list included the names of their ancestors, Ezra could ascertain whether they were of pure Jewish ancestry.

6. *Supplication to God for a Good Journey (8:21–23)*

21 *I proclaimed a fast there at the Ahava River to humble ourselves before our God, to seek from him a successful journey for us, the weak, and all our belongings.*
22 *For I was ashamed to ask from the king a group of soldiers and horsemen to protect us against an enemy on the way, because we had told the king: "The hand of our God is a blessing for all who seek him and his powerful wrath is on all who forsake him."*
23 *So we fasted and sought out God about this matter, and he answered us.*

21–23 Here Ezra describes his preparation for the journey. This passage has strong religious orientation, as we may expect from Ezra, who lived according to the requirements of the law. He proclaimed a fast at the Ahava River, quite probably immediately after the arrival of the Levites and temple servants. Fasting was accompanied by prayer (cf. 2 Chr. 20:3ff.; Esth. 4:16). The prayer here was a humble supplication to God to assist them on their journey, especially since whole families were returning. *The weak* (Heb. *ṭap̱*) literally means "small children," but this term has also a wider scope of meaning, and scholars hold that it refers here to all the weak returnees, like women, children, and the aged.[1] *All our belongings.* As we shall see in the next pericope these belongings include also all the silver and gold they have collected. In those days banditry on the roads was a common phenomenon. It was thus dangerous to travel with valuables. As believers in the power of the Lord they prayed to him for his protection and for a safe and successful journey. *Successful journey (dereḵ y^e^šārâ)* is literally "a straight road" (cf. also Isa. 40:3–4). Faith in God and his power over the Jews' enemies clearly radiates from these verses. Faith in God is an adventure. It is clearly wrong to argue, like Pavlovský, that Ezra was aware that the road to Jerusalem was safe and therefore he had not requested an escort from the king.[2] In these verses it is obvious that Ezra was sensitive to the imminent danger which confronted him.

1. Cf. Myers, *Ezra. Nehemiah,* p. 67; and esp. Grosheide, *Ezra,* p. 232.
2. Cf. V. Pavlovský, "Die Chronologie der Tätigkeit Esdras: Versuche einer neuen Lösung," *Bibl* 38 (1957), pp. 275–305, 428–456.

Ezra acted in faith and relied totally on the Lord for the outcome of his journey.

In v. 22 Ezra underlined one of the motives of his supplication to God. While negotiating with the king about the cult of his God in Jerusalem he stressed the power of his God, and it would have defeated his purpose if he had asked the king for a military escort. He told the king that God protects the supplicant and his powerful wrath rejects those that forsake him. *Powerful wrath* is literally "his power and his wrath," which we have taken as a hendiadys.[3] The supplication to the Lord is answered by him—they had a safe journey. Some scholars want to see in these verses an apologetic tendency against Nehemiah, because he travelled with a military escort (Neh. 2:9). It is then regarded as a subtle hint of the superiority of Ezra over Nehemiah.[4] But we can explain this difference of approach as follows. Ezra the priest went to Jerusalem on a religious mission. In such a case a military escort would have seemed strange, because the religious group would then have shown no faith in their God. Nehemiah went as a political official, a governor, to Jerusalem. In such a case, the king would protect his official with a military escort.

7. *Treasure Bearers (8:24–30)*

24 *I chose from the leaders of the priests twelve men, as well as Sherebiah and Hashabiah and with them from their kinsmen, ten men.*
25 *I weighed out to them the silver, the gold, and the vessels as contribution to the temple of our God that the king, his counsellors, his officials, and all the people present had made.*
26 *I weighed out and gave to them six hundred and fifty talents of silver, one hundred silver vessels of two talents, one hundred talents of gold,*
27 *twenty golden bowls of a thousand darics, and two vessels of fine bright copper as precious as gold.*
28 *I said to them: "You are holy to the Lord and the vessels are consecrated. The silver and gold are a voluntary offering to the Lord, the God of your ancestors.*
29 *Keep them carefully until you weigh them before the leaders of the priests, the Levites, and the heads of the families of Israel in Jerusalem in the chambers of the temple of the Lord."*
30 *Then the priests and the Levites picked up the weight of the silver, the gold, and the vessels and carried them to Jerusalem, to the temple of our God.*

24 *As well as Sherebiah and Hashabiah.* With almost all modern scholars we are reading here a conjunction *waw* instead of *l^e*. It is clear from

3. Grosheide, *Ezra*, p. 233; Myers, *op. cit.*, p. 67.
4. Cf. Myers, *op. cit.*, p. 71.

8:18–19 that Sherebiah and Hashabiah were Levites. Thus we have here twelve priests and twelve Levites. Since the priests and the Levites represented only two tribes of Israel, it is unacceptable to think that twelve refers here to the twelve tribes of Israel.[1] It is obvious that the author was especially fond of the number twelve. From Num. 3:8, 31; 4:5ff. it is clear that the priests had to handle the sacred objects and the Levites had to carry them.[2] Ezra as a student of the law was well aware of this custom, and to carry the legal prescription out he made sure that the ritual procedures were done correctly.

25–27 From these verses it is clear that Ezra as an official of the Persian king who was entrusted with a large amount of valuables accepted his task in all seriousness. The king, his counsellors, and his officials had contributed to the venture, and an official like Ezra must have made doubly sure that none of the valuables became lost. He weighed carefully the silver, gold, and vessels. Myers estimates the weight of these valuables as follows: six hundred and fifty talents are approximately twenty-four-and-a-half tons, and a hundred talents are about three-and-three-quarter tons.[3] *One hundred silver vessels of two talents* is problematic, because in Hebrew only the plural of talent appears *(kikkārîm)*. This problem is solved in one of two ways. First, some think that a number fell out by haplography, but it is difficult to tell what number.[4] Second, changing only the vowels, not the consonants, one could read the dual of talent (*kikkārāyim;* see *BHS*). This is the solution for which we have opted. *Two vessels of fine bright copper as precious as gold.* This translation is an attempt to explain the difficult Hebrew, especially the hapax legomenon *muṣhāḇ*. If we take all the weights of the silver and gold into account, it was a tremendous amount of precious material. Some doubt the authenticity of this account.[5] We must keep in mind that the court as well as the ordinary people had contributed, and the Persian kings were well known for their incomparable riches.[6] Even the ordinary people were well off; for example, the banking business of the Jewish Murashu family was flourishing c. 455–403 B.C.[7] People like these could have contributed a substantial gift for the temple in Jerusalem. We must not underestimate the means of the Jews in Babylon and vicinity.

28–29 Ezra was not only a Persian official, but also a priest of

1. Against Myers, *Ezra. Nehemiah,* p. 71.
2. Pointed out, e.g., by Brockington, *Ezra, Nehemiah and Esther,* p. 87; Myers, *op. cit.,* p. 71.
3. Myers, *op. cit.,* pp. 67–68.
4. Cf. *ibid.,* p. 66; Myers leaves a space open where the number should be.
5. Cf. the discussion of Grosheide, *Ezra,* p. 237.
6. Frye, *The Heritage of Persia,* p. 110.
7. *Ibid.,* p. 109.

the Lord. His important mission was religious, to teach the law and to glorify the Lord; hence the importance of the religious connotation in this historical text. Ezra made his choice of twelve priests and twelve Levites to carry the valuables of the Lord to Jerusalem, according to the law, correct ritually. The gifts now belonged to the Lord and were thus changed from the profane to the divine sphere. For their task as keepers of the valuables the priests and Levites became holy, consecrated to the Lord.

Keep them carefully—literally: "Be awake and keep." We have taken this expression as a hendiadys. The priests and Levites must keep the vessels carefully, probably to safeguard them against theft. Theft could occur from outside, by bandits on the way, or from inside, from dishonest Jews who were in the caravan. *The heads of the families of Israel.* Some scholars are of the opinion that this phrase is a later addition, because these people are not mentioned in v. 33,[8] which does mention the names of certain priests in Jerusalem who were witnesses of the correct weight of the valuables. Nobody else is mentioned. It is probable that v. 33 mentions only the priestly leaders who were responsible for the keeping of the sacred objects of the temple. Other witnesses were simply left out, because they were already mentioned in v. 29.

30 This verse states that the priests and Levites obeyed the command of Ezra, accepted the responsibility, and carried the valuables to the temple. *The weight* might also be translated "the weighed silver, etc." (JB) or "the consignment" (Myers). GNB has left it untranslated.

8. Return to Jerusalem (8:31–36)

31 *We left the Ahava River for Jerusalem on the twelfth of the first month. The favor of our God was with us and he protected us against enemies and bandits on the way.*

32 *We reached Jerusalem and remained there for three days.*

33 *On the fourth day we weighed the silver, the gold, and the vessels in the temple of our God and handed them over to Meremoth the priest, the son of Uriah, and with him was Eleazar the son of Phinehas, as well as Jozabad the son of Jeshua, and Noadiah the son of Binnui, the Levites.*

34 *According to the number and weight all were there. Every weight was recorded at that time.*

35 *Those that returned from captivity, the exiles, offered burnt offerings to the God of Israel: twelve bulls for the whole of Israel, ninety-six rams, seventy-seven lambs, and twelve he-goats as a sin offering—all this was a burnt offering for the Lord.*

8. E.g., Rudolph, *Esra und Nehemia,* p. 82.

36 *They also gave the king's instructions to the satraps of the king and the governors of Trans-Euphrates, and they aided the people and the temple of God.*

31 The chronological sequence of events becomes clear in this verse. On the first of the first month the exiles were assembled at the Ahava River. They stayed there for three days before Ezra discovered that no Levites were present (8:15). A search for Levites was made, and they arrived at the Ahava River after a time. Only on the twelfth of the first month was the caravan ready to start its journey to Jerusalem.[1] For the Semitic mind there was nothing wrong with the calculation of the departure on the first of the first month. The exiles left their houses in Babylon and assembled at the Ahava River. These actions are then regarded as the first stage of departure. *He protected us against enemies and bandits. Protected* (from the Hebrew root *nṣl*) may also mean "save." If we translate it "save," the meaning is that enemies and bandits had attacked the caravan, but that it was saved by the Lord. From the broader context of its usage here, however, it is clear that the term must mean "protect" and that the Lord protected them from being attacked.[2]

32–34 Of the adventures on the long and tedious journey of approximately nine hundred miles from Babylon to Jerusalem nothing is said. (Straight through the desert it is five hundred miles, but they took the road through the Fertile Crescent.) The next we hear of them is that they have arrived safely in Jerusalem. *For three days*—cf. the discussion of 8:15. Quite naturally one would expect that the returnees would need some rest after such a long and tedious trek. The *three days* before the consignment of valuables is delivered to the authorities in Jerusalem must be understood in this light. Other scholars have another explanation, namely, that if the Jubilee calendar was in force,[3] the exiles' arrival would have been on a Friday, which was so close to the sabbath that they naturally waited until after the sabbath for the weighing of the valuables.[4] The three days' wait might have a ritualistic significance, but this is uncertain and it is better to accept that they were resting.

In v. 33 various names of priests and Levites are mentioned. Some are well-known names from this period, and it is not an easy task to connect them with the same names which occur in other places of Ezra and Nehemiah. Brockington is of the opinion that the Meremoth son of

1. Myers, *Ezra. Nehemiah,* p. 71.
2. Cf., e.g., U. Bergmann, *THAT* II, pp. 96–99, where the meaning "protect" is not given to the term *nṣl*.
3. Cf. A. Jaubert, "Le calendrier des Jubilés et de la secte de Qumrân. Ses origines bibliques," *VT* 3 (1953), p. 261.
4. Cf. F. Nötscher, "Zur Auferstehung nach drei Tagen," *Bibl* 35 (1954), pp. 313–19; Myers, *op. cit.,* p. 72.

Uriah mentioned in Neh. 3:4 and 21 is the same person as the one mentioned here.[5] That he is called "the son of Uriah" makes this certain. Avigad holds that the name *'wryw* discovered on a seal at Jericho[6] is the name Uriah, and that he was the father of Meremoth.[7] This is quite uncertain, however, because this seal is dated to the second quarter of the fifth century B.C. Because Meremoth is called in Neh. 3:21 "the son of Uriah, the son of Hakkoz," and Hakkoz is mentioned in Ezra 2:61 as a family which still had to prove its priestly genealogy, Meremoth is regarded as part of this family. If it is so, as seems likely, the family of Meremoth had succeeded in proving its identity because Meremoth is pictured in v. 33 in a leading position as priest.

And handed them over. Literally the Hebrew has "we weighed . . . on the hand of Meremoth."[8] It is quite probable that the valuables were handed over to Meremoth, but that the other persons mentioned were present as witnesses. This, then, explains the extraordinary Hebrew construction *wᵉ'immô . . . wᵉ'immāhem* (and with him . . . and with them). Ezra as an official of the Persian king recorded the number of vessels and the weight carefully so as to make certain that nothing disappeared. Everything was in order. *At that time* has given occasion to various presumptions. Some want to connect it to the next verse, because v. 35 begins with an asyndeton. But it is not impossible that a Hebrew sentence could begin like this.[9] Other scholars want to read *haqqāhāl,* "the community," instead of *hammišqal,* "the weight."[10] They argue that Ezra made a list of people at that time. This emendation is without any textual support, however.

35–36 For the beginning of v. 35 cf. the discussion of v. 34. It is important to note that these verses are written in the third person, while the whole of the previous part is written in the first person. Scholars accept that these two verses were written by the Chronicler.[11] Brockington regards these verses as an editorial note,[12] while Grosheide holds that they are an editorial note built on the Ezra memoir.[13] It is difficult to ascertain which

5. Brockington, *Ezra, Nehemiah and Esther,* p. 88.
6. Cf. P. C. Hammond, "A Note on Two Seal Impressions from Tell es-Sulṭan," *PEQ* 89 (1957), pp. 68–69.
7. Cf. N. Avigad, *IEJ* 7 (1957), pp. 146ff.
8. Cf. the translation of Rudolph, *Esra und Nehemia,* p. 84. For a discussion of the name Meremoth in preexilic times cf. M. Heltzer, *Šntwn lmqr' wlḥqr hmzrḥ hqdwm* (1977), p. 56.
9. Grosheide, *Ezra,* pp. 242–43.
10. Schaeder, *Esra der Schreiber,* pp. 21ff.
11. Cf., e.g., Myers, *op. cit.,* p. 72.
12. Brockington, *op. cit.,* p. 89.
13. Grosheide, *Ezra,* p. 243.

proposal is correct. The verses seem to be an editorial note to make the whole picture complete. In 7:17 Artaxerxes commanded that certain offerings had to be made. In 8:35 his command was carried out (cf. also the offerings with the inauguration of the temple in 6:17). Cf. our discussion of 7:17.

It is noteworthy that the numbers in v. 35 are twelve or can be divided by twelve, except one, that is, seventy-seven. In 1 Esdras 8:66 the number seventy-two is given and this is also adopted by Josephus.[14] Seventy-two can also be divided by twelve. The Hebrew word for "seven" is then regarded as a scribal error for "two." Other textual evidence stands firmly in favor of the MT. In such a case the more problematic reading, seventy-seven, is to be preferred. Esdras has obviously reasoned in the same way as some modern scholars, and wanted to connect the seventy-two with the twelve tribes of Israel.[15] We know, for example, from the Ugaritic literature that seventy and seventy-seven were used as a literary device to denote a fairly large number (for seventy-seven cf. *UT,* 75:II:49).[16] There is obvious merit, therefore, in the view of some scholars that seventy-seven must be regarded as symbolic and should not be changed.[17]

N. Snaith has pointed out the problem of the last part of v. 35, namely, *all this was a burnt offering for the Lord.* For the burnt offering the animal was burnt in its entirety, while in a sin offering only part of the animal was burnt; the other part was for the priests (cf. Lev. 4:22ff.).[18] It seems as if in v. 35b the phrase refers back to the burnt offerings, because they were the largest part of the offering.

Verse 36 states that Ezra gave the instructions of Artaxerxes to the satraps and governors (cf. 7:20, 21–24, 25–26). The word for *satraps* (*'ᵃḥašdarpᵉnîm*) is a Persian loanword which usually means satrap but could also mean another high official.[19] The problem here is the use of the plural. Trans-Euphrates was only one satrapy. What does the plural then mean? It is not unlikely that the satraps of Trans-Euphrates and Egypt are meant here. Palestine is near enough to Egypt, which had a substantial Jewish population, to include the Egyptian satrap. It is nowhere stated that only one province, Trans-Euphrates, should assist the Jews. It could have covered that part of the Persian empire in which the Jews were living. It

14. Cf., e.g., Rudolph, *Esra und Nehemia,* p. 84; Pelaia, *Esdra e Neemia,* p. 106.
15. Myers, *op. cit.,* p. 68.
16. F. C. Fensham, "The Numeral Seventy in the OT, and the Family of Jerubbaal, Ahab, Panammuwa, and Athirat," *PEQ* 109 (1977), pp. 113–14.
17. Kapelrud, *The Question of Authorship in the Ezra-Narrative,* p. 58.
18. N. Snaith, "A Note on Ezra viii.35," *JTS* 22 (1971), pp. 150–52; Grosheide, *Ezra,* p. 243.
19. Cf. Leuze, *Die Satrapieneinteilung in Syrien,* pp. 19ff.

is also interesting that this verse mentions *satraps of the king*, but *governors of Trans-Euphrates*. The satraps were thus not only of Trans-Euphrates.

B. EZRA'S REFORMS (9:1–10:44)

1. Marriage to Foreigners Reported; Ezra's Reaction (9:1–5)

1 *After the conclusion of these events the leaders approached me and said: "The people of Israel, the priests, and the Levites did not separate themselves from the people of the land with their abominations—from the Canaanites, Hittites, Perizzites, Jebusites, Ammonites, Moabites, Egyptians, and Amorites—*

2 *but they and their sons have married some of their daughters. The holy people have intermingled with the people of the land—the leaders and chiefs were prominent in this treachery."*

3 *When I heard this, I tore my garment and my mantle and I pulled out some of the hair of my head and my beard. I sat down dumbfounded.*

4 *All those who were trembling at the words of the God of Israel about the treachery of the exiles gathered around me. I sat dumbfounded until the evening sacrifice.*

5 *At the evening sacrifice I rose from my humbled state and with my torn garment and mantle I went on my knees and spread out my hands to the Lord, my God.*

1 *After the conclusion of these events.* These words may refer back to the preceding chapter, either to the weighing of the valuables (8:33–34) or to the sacrifices (8:35). Another possibility is that they refer back to 8:36 and that Ezra needed some time to deliver the orders of Artaxerxes to the satraps and governors. According to 10:9 the assembly of the exiles gathered on the twentieth day of the ninth month. Between Ezra's arrival on the first of the fifth month (8:33) and the twentieth of the ninth month we have more than four-and-a-half months. This long period between the arrival and discovery of the marriages to foreigners poses a problem. Was he not aware of this fact? If he stayed for more than four months in Jerusalem, one would expect that he would have become acquainted with this phenomenon. One explanation is that he was so busy with his instruction of the law of God, of which nothing is mentioned here in Ezra, that this grievous sin had escaped his attention. Some scholars are of the opinion that the events of Neh. 8:1–18 had happened in the meantime. A better place for Neh. 8:1–18 would then be immediately after Ezra 8:36.[1] But

1. See Brockington, *Ezra, Nehemiah and Esther,* p. 89; Myers, *Ezra. Nehemiah,* p. 76; and the discussion of Grosheide, *Ezra,* p. 246.

if we accept this solution, we must accept that Ezra's actions described in 9:3 are only a dramatic act, without any sincerity.[2] Some scholars hold that Ezra could not have been ignorant of this situation and must have been aware of it even before his arrival.[3] But in Ezra nothing of this is reported. Ezra 9:1 creates the impression that it suddenly dawned on him when the leaders informed him about it.

A second solution is that Ezra had travelled extensively after his arrival to bring his credentials from the Persian king to the attention of the high officials of the Persian empire who lived close to Judah. Then the above-mentioned phrase of 9:1a can be interpreted as referring to 8:36. This is a more acceptable solution, but at the same time we must confess that the situation is not at all clear.

The leaders (śārîm). This term is indeed opaque. It probably refers to the leaders from three different categories of Jews also mentioned in this verse, namely, the laity, the priests, and the Levites. *Did not separate themselves.* The prohibition of marriages between foreigners and Israelites was not always kept in Israelite history (cf. Num. 12; Ruth 1; and the Israelite kings' marriages to foreign princesses as part of a diplomatic action). In an early stage of Israelite history the marriages between Israelites and certain foreign nations were prohibited (cf. esp. Exod. 34:16). Later on the prohibition was repeated occasionally (cf., e.g., Deut. 7:1–4).[4] The reason for this attitude had nothing to do with racism, but with a concern for the purity of the religion of the Lord. Marriages with foreigners, especially when those foreigners were in an important position as in the time of Ezra,[5] were fraught with problems for the Jews. The influence of a foreign mother, with her connection to another religion, on her children would ruin the pure religion of the Lord and would create a syncretistic religion running contrary to everything in the Jewish faith. In the end it was a question of the preservation of their identity,[6] their religious identity. *The Canaanites, Hittites . . . Amorites.* This list is very similar to the conventional list which occurs occasionally in the OT (Exod. 3:8, 17; 33:2; Deut. 7:1; etc.). The only differences are that this list excluded the Hivites and added three nations, viz., Ammonites, Moabites, and Egyptians, probably to bring the list up to date. Such a list was only an indication that no marriages would be allowed with any of the neighboring nations. It is thus wrong to presume that certain nations were left out by mistake, e.g., the Edomites or the Samaritans. It is also wrong to accept

2. Cf. the discussion of R. Kittel, *Geschichte des Volkes Israel* III, pp. 595ff.
3. J. Bright, *A History of Israel,* p. 388.
4. Myers, *op. cit.,* p. 76.
5. *Ibid.,* p. 77.
6. Herrmann, *A History of Israel in OT Times,* pp. 307–308.

that the mention of nations which did not exist anymore, like the Hittites, Perizzites, Jebusites, and Amorites, shows that these names are to be regarded as a gloss.[7] The reasoning of the author might have been that in ancient times the Israelites were not allowed to marry members of the Canaanites, Hittites, etc., but in his time the Israelites were not allowed to marry into the following nations: Ammonites, Moabites, etc.

2 *Have married some of their daughters.* This is contrary to the law (Exod. 34:16; Deut. 7:1). Cf. our discussion of v. 1. *The holy people*—literally: "the holy seed" (cf. 6:13; Neh. 9:2). The term "holy" shows that the term "seed" has nothing to do with racial prejudice. It is the people whom God had elected as his people (Exod. 19:6) to carry his revelation, to be a light to the nations (Isa. 42:6). It was a question of the living relation between the Lord and his people, and not of who one's ancestors might be. When the living relation is broken, they are no longer the people of God (Hos. 1:9). By intermingling with foreign nations and being contaminated with their idol worship, the true religion was in danger of losing its pure character. The most disturbing factor in this digression from the pure religion was that the leaders were prominent in such a movement. *The leaders and chiefs (haśśārîm wᵉhassᵉḡānîm).* It is very difficult to distinguish between these two appellations. *The leaders* is the same term as in v. 1, but there they were complaining to Ezra. We must accept that in v. 1 some of the leaders approached Ezra and that here in v. 2 some of the leaders were accused of the transgression. The term *chief (sāgān)* is a loanword from Akk. *šaknu,* meaning "official,"[8] in about the same meaning as *bēl pīḫāti* or *peḥâ,* "governor." In Nehemiah, however, this term is used in the sense of chief. They might have formed a kind of council which were elected by the Jewish assembly.[9] *Treachery* might also be translated "unfaithfulness."

3–5 These verses describe the effect which the news of the infidelity of Jews had on Ezra. *I tore my garment.* This action showed his distress (2 Sam. 13:19). A great sin had been committed, a sin which ran contrary to the law of God. Ezra identified himself with this sin, although he and the exiles who had returned with him did not commit it. In a certain sense Ezra accepted his solidarity with his people. He became a mediator for them as Moses did after the golden bull was worshipped at Sinai (cf. Exod. 32:33ff.). In a time like today in which individuality is emphasized, people cannot always understand this attitude. For the Israelites, and later for the Jews, the Lord contracted a covenant with all the people and not

7. Cf. Bowman, *IB* III, p. 644.
8. Cf. E. Ebeling, *RLA* I, pp. 454–55. Cf. also *BMAP,* p. 243; *AHW* II, p. 1141.
9. Cf. Widengren, *Israelite and Judaean History,* p. 523.

only with individuals. All the people were responsible for the acts of every individual or group (cf. also Judg. 19–21). *I pulled out some of the hair.* This is a gesture of grief. In Isa. 50:6 and Neh. 13:25 it is an act of violence.[10] It was an emotional act of Ezra to draw the people's attention to his inner feeling of distress. *Dumbfounded* (Heb. *m*^{e}*šômēm*)—without saying anything. *M*^{e}*šômēm* can also be translated "overcome" or "appalled."

In v. 4 the people who were aware of the demands of the words or the law of God stood trembling around Ezra. They had the same feeling of solidarity with their brothers who had sinned against the Lord. Ezra quite probably sat down at a prominent place where the people could see him. *The exiles* could not have been the exiles who had returned with Ezra. They must be the exiles who had returned previously. Various groups of exiles returned from 538 B.C. up to the time of Ezra. Some of the earlier returnees were the culprits. *The evening sacrifice.* Some scholars point out that in earlier times the evening offering was not a burnt offering, but a food offering.[11] In this case, however, a sacrifice is clearly mentioned. The whole question as to whether this sacrifice should be regarded as an ancient custom is difficult to solve because of the lack of clear evidence.

During the evening sacrifice Ezra, with the people around him, went on his knees to pray to the Lord. The spreading out of hands is a typical gesture in prayer (Exod. 9:29; 1 K. 8:22; Isa. 1:15; etc.). *With my torn garment.* Some think that Ezra had torn his clothes for a second time. The Hebrew has literally: "in my tearing of my garment. . . ." It is better to take it as "with my torn garment. . . ."[12]

2. *Ezra's Prayer (9:6–15)*

6 *And I said: "O my God, I am very much ashamed to lift my face to you, my God, because our iniquities have increased until they are higher than our heads and our guilt has risen as high as the heavens.*
7 *From the times of our ancestors until today our guilt is great. On account of our iniquities we, our kings, and our priests were delivered into the power of the kings of the lands, to the sword, to captivity, to pillage, and to shame—it is still the case today.*
8 *But now, for a short time, the Lord our God granted us the favor to have a remnant and to give us a foothold in his holy place. Our God gave us fresh courage and a little bit of reviving in our servitude.*
9 *For we are slaves; our God has never left us alone in our servitude and he demonstrated his love to us before the Persian kings; he has*

10. Brockington, *op. cit.*, p. 90.

11. Kapelrud, *The Question of Authorship in the Ezra-Narrative*, p. 63. Cf. the discussion of Pelaia, *Esdra e Neemia*, p. 109.

12. Michaeli, *Les livres des Chroniques, d'Esdras et de Néhémie*, p. 301.

revived us so that we could build the temple of our God and restore its ruins; he has provided for us protection in Judah and Jerusalem.

10 *But now, what shall we say, our God, after what happened. We have abandoned your commandments*

11 *which you have given through your servants the prophets as follows: 'The land you are going to possess is unclean, polluted by the people of the lands. Their abominations filled the land from end to end with their uncleanness.*

12 *But now, you must not let your sons marry their daughters and your daughters their sons. You must never further their welfare and prosperity, so that you may become strong and enjoy the prosperity of the country and let your sons inherit it for ever.'*

13 *After all that happened to us on account of our evil deeds and our great guilt, you, our God, have punished us less than our iniquities deserve and have given us such an escape as this.*

14 *Shall we again break your commandments by marrying these people who commit such abominations? You would become so angry with us that you would destroy us, so that there would be no remnant or no one that escapes.*

15 *O Lord, God of Israel, you are righteous, for we have a remnant who have escaped up to this very day. Now we are in front of you with our guilt and we are not able to survive in your presence with it."*

Some are of the opinion that these verses are the work of the Chronicler.[1] Arguments in favor of this view are, for example, the Chronicler's preference for prayers; the style of the Chronicler in its liveliest form occurs here;[2] the typical vocabulary of the Chronicler is present.[3] Clearly, if one accepts that 9:1–5 was written by the Chronicler, one is forced to conclude that 9:6–15 was also written by him. The logical sequence between 9:1–5 and 9:6–15 is obvious. But some of the arguments above in favor of the authorship of the Chronicler are not cogent. Any author could have written down a prayer when it was necessary in the text, as in this case. Although Kapelrud is convinced of the Chronicler's role in this part, there is also an uneasiness to be detected in his reasoning, as for example his reference to archaizing and to similarities with prophetic pronouncements. It is not always clear how scholars can distinguish between typical late Hebrew terminology and structure and the specific terminology and stylistic devices of the Chronicler. One could ask legitimately: Was it not the common

1. Cf. M. Noth, *Überlieferungsgeschichtliche Studien*, pp. 160ff.; Kapelrud, *The Question of Authorship in the Ezra-Narrative*, pp. 70–71; In der Smitten, *Esra*, pp. 25–28; Coggins, *The Books of Ezra and Nehemiah*, p. 58.
2. Torrey, *Ezra Studies*, p. 270.
3. Kapelrud, *op. cit.*, p. 70.

usage and style of those days? Because this prayer like 9:1–5 was written in the first person, we accept that it came from Ezra's memoirs.[4]

The structure of this prayer is as follows: It starts with a confession of sin (vv. 6–7a); proceeds to the punishment on the sins (7b); to the favor of the Lord and his influence on the Persian kings on behalf of the exiles (8–9); to another confession of sin and a reference to the marriage with foreigners (10–14); and it concludes with a doxology to God (15).[5] Confession of sin stands in the center of the whole prayer.

6–7 In these verses we have Ezra's striking confession of sin, pictured with strong metaphors. The two metaphors concern the iniquities which increased until they were higher than their heads and the guilt that had risen as high as the heavens. The sudden change in v. 6 from the first person singular to the plural is interesting. The prayer begins with *I am very much ashamed* (lit. "I am ashamed and blush"). In these words Ezra describes his feeling of disappointment in the religious conduct of his people. Suddenly he changes the singular into a plural and speaks of "our iniquities" and "our guilt." As we have seen in our discussion of 9:3–5, Ezra wants to express his solidarity with his people. He not only intercedes for his people, but also identifies himself with them.[6] The iniquities which have mounted up since ancient times, but especially since the last days of the kings of Judah, and which have caused the Exile, are also the responsibility of the later generations. It is as if Ezra has realized that immediately in front of him are all the cumulative iniquities which have heaped up through history. What an extraordinary view of sin! But it shows that the Jews have explained their predicament in history as slaves of other people in terms of the consequences of their sins. It is a specific sense of guilt. The burden of their guilt was heavy and was still increasing by the sin of intermarriage. They were punished for their sins, but the lesson was not taken to heart. They were still sinning. In Ezek. 18, especially, another approach to the responsibility of sin occurs, namely, that everybody was responsible only for his own sin.[7] But a careful reading of Ezek. 18 shows that the prophet is interested in those who are living strictly according to the commandments of the Lord (vv. 5–9). They will not die for the sins of their fathers.[8] They have returned to the Lord. As mediator between

4. Scholars in favor of the authorship of Ezra are, e.g., Rudolph, *Esra und Nehemia,* pp. 90ff.; Pelaia, *Esdra e Neemia,* p. 109; Brockington, *Ezra, Nehemiah and Esther,* p. 91; Myers, *Ezra. Nehemiah,* pp. xxxix ff.; Grosheide, *Ezra,* pp. 253ff.

5. In der Smitten, *Esra,* pp. 25–26.

6. Myers, *op. cit.,* p. 78.

7. Rudolph, *op. cit.,* p. 91.

8. Cf. the discussion of W. Zimmerli, *Ezekiel* I. Hermeneia (E.T. 1979), pp. 378ff.

God and his people, Ezra wanted the guilty to return to their God. Before their return, all the Jews were responsible for their sins. *The kings of the lands.* Myers refers to the Murashu documents in which the Persian kings are called by this title.[9] It is important, however, to note that in the prayer of Nehemiah, with almost similar contents (Neh. 9:32), the Assyrian kings are mentioned.[10] It is thus probable that this expression refers to any foreign king who held Israel in servitude.

8–9 In these verses Ezra comes back to the situation under the Persian kings. During the reign of the Babylonian kings the exiles had no hope of returning to their country. Under the Persian kings with the favor of God the situation had changed drastically. *For a short time* (cf. Isa. 26:20). This refers to the first return from the Exile (538 B.C.) and the subsequent returns until the time of Ezra. In this short period of eighty years the favor of the Lord became visible. It is indeed a short period in comparison with the long history of Israel. Galling interprets these terms as meaning "a sudden change,"[11] but this is rather doubtful.[12] *A remnant.* This term is a combination of the verb *šā'ar,* "remain," with *p^elēṭâ,* "escape"; it can also be translated "an escaped remnant."[13] The escaped remnant are those who had returned by permission of the Persian kings.[14] The conclusion we may draw from this is that the exiles in Babylon or elsewhere were not regarded as the remnant. A remnant could exist only in Judah and Jerusalem. It is not clear what the meaning of "escaped" is. Are they the Jews who had escaped the ordeal of God and who were taken into captivity? This seems not to be the case. It probably refers to the exiles who had returned and who escaped from exile. It is a purified group of the real Israel who came back to form the eschatological community.[15]

A foothold (lit. "a tent peg"). This is language from nomadic life, and it refers to a place reached after a long journey where a tent may be pitched. It may have certain legal overtones. The nomad can pitch his tent

9. Myers, *op. cit.*, p. 75. Cf. A. T. Clay, *Business Documents of the Murashû Sons of Nippur Dated in the Reign of Darius II (424–404 B.C.)* (Philadelphia: 1904), p. 28.
10. Brockington, *op. cit.*, p. 91.
11. Galling, *Studien zur Geschichte Israels*, pp. 61–62, esp. p. 62 n. 1. On *rega'* cf. also L. Kopf, "Arabische Etymologien und Parallelen zum Bibelwörterbuch," *VT* 8 (1958), pp. 161–215; L. Delekat, "Zum hebräischen Wörterbuch," *VT* 14 (1964), pp. 7–66.
12. In der Smitten, *Esra*, p. 28 n. 83.
13. Myers, *op. cit.*, pp. 75–76. Cf. his reference to the Qumran literature.
14. In der Smitten, *Esra*, p. 26.
15. Cf. also *ibid.*, p. 27.

only where he has the right to do so.[16] The reading *yeṯer* ("remnant") instead of *yāṯēḏ* ("tent peg") in one manuscript is clearly a later correction of the more difficult word.[17] *Our God gave us fresh courage*—literally "Our God makes our eyes shine." It might also mean to receive fresh joy from the Lord. *Reviving*. The author obviously regarded his people as dead while they were in exile (cf. Ezek. 37:1–14), but after their return they received new life. But this reviving had not yet come in its fullness; it was only *a little bit* of it *(mᵉʻaṭ)*, i.e., only a portion of the Jews had returned. Many of them still lived in Mesopotamia and Egypt. Their situation in these countries is described as servitude. They were slaves of their overlord; they were not anchored to their country. Only by living in their country and having the right to serve their Lord properly were they free. In their servitude in the foreign countries the Lord never abandoned them. Through his love for his people he influenced the Persian kings to let them return. *He demonstrated his love*—literally "He has extended love before the Persian kings." Some want to translate "He has shown us kindness in the eyes of the kings of Persia" (JB) or "You made the emperors of Persia favor us" (GNB). It is uncertain whether "love" (or "kindness") should be related to God or to the Persian kings. It is possible to translate the Hebrew either way, but the tendency to connect "love" or "covenant love" *(ḥeseḏ)* to the Lord favors the first possibility.

So that we could build the temple of our God and restore its ruins. The whole hypothesis of Morgenstern discussed above,[18] namely, that the temple was destroyed in the time of Xerxes and was rebuilt in the time of Ezra, hinges on this text. It all depends on how we interpret the "we" (first person plural). As we have seen, Ezra had proclaimed his solidarity with his people, not only with the people of his own time, but also with the people of the past. In such a case he refers here to the rebuilding of the temple in the times of Cyrus and Darius. *He has provided for us protection in Judah and Jerusalem*. The term "protection" (lit. "fence"—*gāḏēr*) has given occasion to the interpretation that when Ezra arrived in Jerusalem there was already a wall around the city, in other words, that Ezra arrived after Nehemiah had built the wall.[19] The terms is not used

16. In modern Bedouin society there is a constant struggle for possession of certain areas to pitch tents and to live there. Cf. A. Musil, *The Manners and Customs of the Rwala Bedouin* (New York: 1928), pp. 52ff.

17. Cf. *BHS*.

18. Cf. J. Morgenstern, "The Dates of Ezra and Nehemiah," *JSS* 7 (1962), pp. 1–11, esp. p. 3; cf. also the criticism of Widengren, *Israelite and Judaean History*, p. 526.

19. Cf. H. Kaupel, "Die Bedeutung von Gādēr in Esr. 9:9," *BZ* 22 (1934), pp. 89–92; *idem*, "Zu *gāḏēr* in Esr. 9,9," *Bibl* 16 (1935), pp. 213–14; lately Widengren, *op. cit.*, p. 504.

for a city wall, however, but for an enclosure of a vineyard and the like (cf. Isa. 5:1–7; Ps. 80:13 [Eng. 12]). It is thus a stone fence which forms the border between the properties of owners. This meaning is now also clear from inscribed jar handles from Gibeon.[20] It has the meaning of a protected area and has nothing to do with a city wall. The expression *in Judah and Jerusalem* also testifies against it; obviously, no wall could be built around Judah!

10–12 Ezra prayed to the Lord before spectators who had gathered around him. This might have influenced his choice of words. He wanted them to hear certain important arguments. The prayer was also intended for them, and as such was a form of sermon prayer.[21] Verses 10–12 are understandable in this light. All the catastrophes which had befallen the Jews happened on account of their disobedience to the commandments of God. Ezra proceeds to connect these commandments to the prophets. It is obvious that the meaning of "prophet" is here taken in its widest sense, just as Moses is called a prophet in Hos. 12:14; Deut. 18:15; 34:10. The citations in vv. 11–12 are a conglomeration of expressions borrowed from various parts of Scripture, e.g., Deut. 4:5ff. for *the land you are going to possess; unclean* or "polluted" in Lev. 18:25ff.; 20:22ff. and Lam. 1:17; *their abominations* in Deut. 18:9; 2 K. 16:3; 21:2; 2 Chr. 28:3; 33:2; *filled the land from end to end* in 2 K. 21:16; *your daughters their sons* in Deut. 7:3; *further their welfare and prosperity* in Deut. 23:7; *become strong* in Deut. 11:8; *enjoy the prosperity of the country* in Gen. 45:18; Isa. 1:19; and *inherit it for ever* in Ezek. 37:25. The texts are not literally cited, but the essentials of the thought pattern are there. It is also interesting to note that most of the citations come from Deuteronomistic literature;[22] Ezra was obviously strongly influenced by it. *You must never further their welfare and prosperity* is literally "You must not seek their peace and the good for them for ever." *Enjoy the prosperity of the country* is literally "eat the good of the land."

13–15 The Jews were punished to a certain extent for their sins. They were exiled and nearly wiped out. In the times of the Persian kings, however, the Lord saved a remnant, who returned to the Holy Land. They were there as a token of his love and grace. And now, if these exiles committed evil deeds and heaped guilt on themselves, the remnant came into danger of being destroyed—and then nothing would be left. It is this

20. Cf. J. B. Pritchard, *Hebrew Inscriptions and Stamps from Gibeon* (Philadelphia: 1959), pp. 9–10. Cf. also Myers, *op. cit.*, p. 75.
21. In der Smitten, *Esra*, p. 26; but cf. already Noth, *Uberlieferungsgeschichtliche Studien*, p. 160; U. Kellermann, *Nehemia: Quellen, Überlieferung und Geschichte*. BZAW 102 (Berlin: 1967), p. 66.
22. Myers, *op. cit.*, p. 79.

kind of reasoning which we have in these verses. But there is still hope. If the exiles confess their sins, the Lord will grant forgiveness through his love.

You, our God, have punished us less than our iniquities deserved. This sentence is taken by most scholars as elliptical, a sentence which is inserted between vv. 13a and 14.[23] This is a possibility. The aim of this sentence would then be to draw attention again to what is said in vv. 8 and 9. A more likely possibility is to take *kî* as the interjection "behold" and to connect 13b with 13a as we have done. It would mean then that many things happened to the Jews on account of their sins, but these things that happened were only a partial punishment, because a remnant remained. *Less than . . . deserve.* This phrase is difficult. Heb. *l^emaṭṭâ* is used in the sense of "below," as in "You have punished us below (the extent of) our iniquities." Ezra saw the iniquities heaped up as high as the heads of men (9:6), but the punishment was less than the iniquities merited. Some want to read *l^emaṭṭê,* "to the rod," and translate: "You, O our God, have kept from the rod some of our iniquities."[24] The usage of *l^emaṭṭâ* as "less than" makes good sense, however.

In v. 14 we have two questions which are both rhetorical. The answer to the first question (14a) is no. The second question (with *h^alō'*)[25] we have translated positively. *You are righteous (ṣaddîq 'attâ).* Scholars have long since recognized that the root *ṣdq* in its different usages does not always refer to a legal situation, but that especially in postexilic times the meaning of grace is also included. It points in the direction of a meaning "beneficial."[26] This expression means that the Lord was friendlily disposed to them. He was so friendlily disposed that in spite of their sins they were granted a remnant. The remnant was in danger, because with the sin of intermarriage the guilt of the remnant grew immensely. The only way out was to confess this sin and to hope for the grace of God.

3. Covenant to Divorce the Foreign Women (10:1–6)

1 *While Ezra was praying and confessing, he wept prostrated before the temple of God. A very large crowd of men, women, and children from Israel assembled around him and the people wept bitterly.*

23. Grosheide, *Ezra,* p. 262.
24. Myers, *op. cit.,* p. 75. Cf. already P. A. H. de Boer, *De voorbede in het Oude Testament. OTS* 3 (1943), p. 117.
25. For *h^alō'* see A. van Selms, "*H^alō'* in the Courtier's Language in Ancient Israel," *Fourth World Congress of Jewish Studies,* Papers, I (1967), pp. 137–140.
26. Cf. K. Koch, *THAT* II, pp. 507–530. Cf. also N. H. Snaith, *The Distinctive Ideas of the OT* (New York: 1950), pp. 70–74.

2 *Then Shecaniah the son of Jehiel from the descendants of Elam said to Ezra: "We have betrayed our God while marrying foreign wives from the people of the land, but there is still hope for Israel concerning this matter.*

3 *Now, let us make a covenant with our God to send away all the wives and those born from them according to the counsel of my Lord and those that tremble at the commandment of our God. Let it be done according to the law.*

4 *Get up! This is a case for you to handle. We shall assist you. Take courage and act!"*

5 *Then Ezra stood up and made the leaders of the priests, the Levites, and all Israel take an oath to do what had been said. And the oath was taken.*

5 *Ezra left from before the temple of God and went to the room of Jehohanan the son of Eliashib. He went there without eating food or drinking water because he was mourning over the treachery of the exiles.*

The sequence between Ezra 9 and 10 is obvious. Ezra 10:1 brings us back to the situation described in 9:3–5 and tells us what happened there at the temple after the prayer of Ezra. It is of importance that Ezra 10 speaks of Ezra in the third person, while in Ezra 9 the first person is used. On account of this shift certain scholars accept a different source for ch. 10, maintaining that it could not be part of the memoir of Ezra.[1] Others are of the opinion that this chapter was written by the Chronicler while making use of Ezra's memoir.[2]

1 Ezra was kneeling before the temple while interceding for the sins of his people. In 9:4 it is said that those who trembled at the words of God assembled around him. In the meantime Ezra had said the prayer of 9:6–15. This gave opportunity for more and more people to assemble until, according to our text, they were a very large crowd.[3] Those who made up the crowd are also specified here, namely, men, women, and children. It is to be expected that this strange behavior of an important person like Ezra, an official of the Persian king, should have attracted the attention of the passersby. The emotional situation in which Ezra was supplicating and weeping on behalf of his people proved infectious for the assembled crowd. They wept bitterly. This is typical of the Orientals—they could easily be moved by the emotions of another—but it is also typical of all mankind. Thus we have here a true description of human

1. Cf., e.g., O. Eissfeldt, *The OT: An Introduction,* p. 544.
2. Rudolph, *Esra und Nehemia,* p. 93.
3. The Heb. *qāhāl* has here the ordinary meaning of "crowd"; cf. Kritzinger, *Q^{e}hal Jahwe,* p. 45.

conduct in such circumstances. *While Ezra was praying . . . he wept prostrated.* Another possibility is to take all these verbs as part of a subordinate clause. *And the people wept bitterly* (Heb. *kî-ḇāḵû hā'ām harbēh-ḇeḵeh*). The Hebrew of this expression is not very clear. It all depends on how *kî* is interpreted. If we take *kî* as a conjunction with the meaning "because" or "for," it does not make sense. The crowd could not have assembled because they wept bitterly. We are taking *kî* here in a sense which is more and more attested in Hebrew and which is fairly common in Ugaritic, namely, as an interjection drawing attention to what follows, e.g., "behold," "indeed," or "truly."[4] It can be translated by these words, or left untranslated as we have done.

2–4 *Shecaniah,* probably a leader of his people and one who agreed with Ezra over the problem of intermarriage, took action. He confessed their sin of intermarriage. All is not lost; there is still hope for Israel. The logical outcome from the prayer of Ezra is that if the iniquity is removed, there would be forgiveness for their sin. God is righteous; he is a God of grace. Thus, there must be hope. It is difficult to identify this Shecaniah with any other individual of the same name in Ezra-Nehemiah. There were probably six different men with this name.[5] The same is true of his father's name, Jehiel. Shecaniah was of the family of Elam that is mentioned in 2:7; 8:7; 10:26. *Foreign wives (nāšîm noḵrîyôṯ)* clearly refers to a woman from another ethnic group.[6] At that time ethnic traditions overlapped with a specific religious belief. In the case of the Jews it was their faith in the Lord. It must be granted that the Samaritans also believed in the Lord. Their religion, however, was not acknowledged as legitimate by the Jewish purists.

Now, let us make a covenant with our God. K. Baltzer points out convincingly that in Ezra 9–10 a covenant renewal is reflected.[7] The covenant was broken by the sin of intermarriage, but also by all the sins committed by the Jews before the destruction of Jerusalem and the temple. In the situation sketched here the immediate recognition of the sin regarding intermarriage was the most important. There was also an admission of guilt. In v. 3 Shecaniah proposes the renewal of the covenant with God.[8] It is not just a question of renewal, since something must also be done to remove the evil from among the exiles. *To send away (lᵉhôṣî)*—cf. Deut. 24:2, where the root *yṣ'* is also used in connection with divorce. We must,

4. Cf., e.g., M. Dahood, *Psalms III.* AB 17A (Garden City: 1970), p. 473.
5. Brockington, *Ezra, Nehemiah and Esther,* p. 92.
6. Cf. P. Humbert in *Opuscules d'un hébraïsant* (Neuchâtel: 1958), p. 115.
7. Cf. K. Baltzer, *The Covenant Formulary* (E.T. 1971), pp. 47–48.
8. Cf. Myers, *Ezra. Nehemiah,* p. 83, where this covenant is called a typical suzerainty covenant.

however, keep the differences between Deut. 24 and Ezra 10:3 in mind. In Deut. 24 the element of the foreign woman is not present. There the legal grounds for divorce are mentioned in normal circumstances. Here in Ezra we have a totally different situation. Foreign women were married contrary to the law of God. The marriages were illegal from the outset. The sending away of the women is to guard the exiles against the continuation of an illegal act. With their foreign wives they lived in sin. It is thus clear from v. 4 that there is a strong legal background against which Shecaniah has formulated his proposal. The dividing line between the permissible and impermissible is strongly emphasized. Even the children born from the illegal marriages must be sent away. This proposal is harsh in the light of modern Christian conceptions. Why should innocent children be punished? We must remember that the religious influence of the mothers on their children was regarded as the stumbling block. To keep the religion of the Lord pure was the one and only aim of Ezra and the returned exiles. As a small minority group, the repatriates lived in the Holy Land among a large population of influential people who were followers of various polytheistic religions. Against such larger numbers they had to defend themselves and their religious identity. Thus the drastic measures are understandable.[9]

My lord. The Hebrew has "the Lord" *('ᵃḏōnāy)* referring to God. This is impossible in the context, however. It must refer to Ezra. With a minor change of vowels (*'ᵃḏōnî*) we can arrive at "my lord." This shows that Shecaniah held Ezra in high esteem. Ezra came as a Persian official, but also as a priest and someone with a special knowledge of the law. From Ezra 7 on he is depicted as an able man, for which he received due respect. While standing before the supplicating Ezra who was dumbfounded with grief Shecaniah encouraged Ezra. Shecaniah as a man of action wanted Ezra to execute his proposal, namely, to send away the foreign wives. They had to act immediately to exterminate the grave sin from their midst. They had to renew the covenant with God in great haste. The sense of urgency comes out clearly in the imperatives of v. 4.

5–6 In v. 5 the last ritual of the covenant renewal is described. The leaders of the three different groups of Jews took an oath to execute the command of Shecaniah to send the foreign women away. They were now bound by oath. The action must follow (Ezra 10:7ff.). *And went to. . . . He went there.* The repetition of *went* is regarded by almost all scholars with suspicion.[10] With the LXX of 1 Esdras 9:2 they want to read

9. Grosheide, *Ezra,* pp. 268–69; Myers, *op. cit.,* p. 85.
10. Cf., e.g., RSV; Brockington, *op. cit.,* p. 93; Myers, *op. cit.,* p. 80; Grosheide, *Ezra,* p. 270.

wayyālen, "and he spent the night." The second *went (wayyēleḵ)* is considered a scribal error in which the *k* is mistakenly read for *n.* This is possible. On the other hand, the reading of the LXX might be an intentional change to remove the awkwardness of the two "wents" so close to one another. The second "went" makes good sense and to our mind should be maintained. *The room.* In the temple were different rooms occupied by various people, especially the priests. Ezra went to one of these rooms and fasted because of the sin of his people. He was still interceding for his people. *Jehohanan the son of Eliashib.* Jehohanan was a fairly common name. The one here was probably of a priestly family if we accept that the Eliashib of Neh. 3:1 is the same as the father or grandfather of Jehohanan. This particular situation has been interpreted by scholars as proof that Ezra arrived after Nehemiah.[11] Reference is made to Neh. 12:22, where the names occur in the following sequence: Eliashib, Joiada, Johanan, and Jaddua. This sequence shows that Johanan was the grandson of Eliashib.[12] It is clear that Johanan as a grandson of Eliashib could not have invited Ezra to his room in 458 B.C., but only much later. Another argument in favor of this view is that, according to the Elephantine papyri,[13] Johanan was high priest in the time of Darius II (424–405 B.C.). It would then be impossible for Johanan to have had a room in the temple as far back as 458 B.C.[14] These seem to be weighty arguments in favor of a later date for Ezra. Much remains unexplained, however. Why should the Jehohanan of v. 6 necessarily be the same person as the grandson of Eliashib? In the light of the common usage of the name Johanan the Jehohanan of v. 6 might be another son of Eliashib and a brother of Joiada. We are not even certain that the Eliashib of v. 6 is the same as the Eliashib of Neh. 12:22–23—this name was also not uncommon (cf. Neh. 13:4). The proper name Johanan in those days is somewhat like Smith in our times. A Smith under President Grant could not be the same person as a Smith under President Carter. The general occurrence of the name Johanan in the time of Ezra and Nehemiah and later is one of the weak points in the reasoning of modern scholars. The burden of proof still rests on the scholarly world to demonstrate convincingly that the Johanan of v. 6 is the grandson of Eliashib. If we accept that Eliashib was the high priest, he could have had a son Johanan (the one in v. 6) and also a grandson Johanan (the one mentioned in Neh. 12:22–23).

11. Cf. W. F. Albright, *JBL* 40 (1921), pp. 121ff.
12. Brockington, *op. cit.,* p. 93. For the name Eliashib in the Arad ostraca cf. Gibson, *Textbook of Syrian Semitic Inscriptions* I, pp. 51–54 (Arad B1; C1–2; D2).
13. *AP,* pp. 112 (30:18), 120 (31:17).
14. Myers, *op. cit.,* pp. 85–86.

4. Assembly's Decision (10:7–17)

7 *So a message was sent through Judah and Jerusalem to all the exiles to gather in Jerusalem.*
8 *"Anyone who does not come within three days, according to the demand of the chiefs and leaders, will have all his property confiscated and he will be excluded from the community of the exiles."*
9 *So all the men of Judah and Benjamin assembled in Jerusalem after three days—that was on the twentieth of the ninth month—and all the people sat in the square of the temple of God; they were trembling on account of this matter and on account of the heavy rain.*
10 *Then Ezra the priest stood up and said: "You have committed treason by marrying foreign women and have added to the guilt of Israel.*
11 *But now, thank the Lord, the God of your ancestors, and do his will. Separate yourselves from the people of the land and from the foreign wives."*
12 *The whole congregation responded with a loud voice: "Yes! We shall do as you say!*
13 *But the people are many, besides it is the time of heavy rains; we are not able to remain in the open, nor is it a work for a day or two because many have transgressed in this respect.*
14 *Let our chiefs stand in for the whole congregation. Let all who are in the towns and who have taken foreign wives come on appointed times and with them their leaders and judges of every city so that we can avert God's anger from us about this matter."*
15 *Only Jonathan the son of Asahel and Jahzeiah the son of Tikvah opposed this, but Meshullam and Shabbethai the Levite supported the proposal.*
16 *And so it was done by the exiles. Ezra the priest selected men as heads of families according to the house of their ancestors, and all were registered by name. The representatives set aside the first of the tenth month to investigate the matter.*
17 *On the first of the first month they concluded their investigation into all the men who had married foreign women.*

7–8 It is obvious that Ezra stayed in the background, because here the initiative was taken by the leaders. Ezra's reticence might have been for diplomatic reasons. He was a Persian official and should not act overtly lest he create a feeling against Persian authority. We have here a kind of democratic instrument,[1] which Ezra used effectively. *A message was sent.* Some want to give the "message" more emphasis and translate "proclamation."[2] The message was carried by messengers to all the exiles in Judah. Such a message was proclaimed loudly in the streets of the smaller towns

1. Myers, *Ezra. Nehemiah,* p. 86.
2. *Ibid.*

and also in the streets of Jerusalem. *The exiles.* As we have seen already (cf. our discussion of 9:3–5), the exiles were only those who had returned. All the men were called on to appear in Jerusalem for an investigation. If anyone disobeyed this message, his property would be confiscated and he would be banned out of the community of exiles. Ezra received from the Persian king the right to take drastic measures (7:25–26). In spite of this, he still stayed in the background, because the demand was made by the leaders. But if anyone doubted the validity of this demand, the authority that Ezra received from the Persian king was still there to make it perfectly legal.

Will have all his property confiscated. The term for "confiscated" (from the Hebrew root *ḥrm*) has a long history in Hebrew literature. In earlier times this term was used for the holy ban. All the property was demolished and the people and animals killed (cf., e.g., Josh. 6:21). In later times the term received the meaning of confiscation of movable property and its delivery to the priests (cf. Ezek. 44:29).[3] *He will be excluded from the community.* The culprits will be removed from the community, viz., they would not be allowed at the service of the temple, and it might also mean that they would forfeit their rights as citizens. These were for Jews severe measures indeed. They were then not allowed to partake in the daily sacrifices for the removing of their sins. They were totally cut off from other members of the community and could expect no help in times of distress. They were regarded as foreigners without any claim on the religious communion of the exiles. *Within three days*—or "at the end of three days." The aim of this expression is clear: All the men must be in Jerusalem at a given time and that is after three days. Judah constituted a comparatively small area and Jerusalem could be reached easily within three days' time.

9 After three days the men from Judah and Benjamin were there. *Judah and Benjamin* might be a reference to a geographical area (cf. also 1:5). In the open in the square of the temple they gathered. The square must have been fairly large to accommodate all the men. A considerable number of exiles had returned in different groups since the first return in the time of Cyrus. They had fairly large families, and the sons of the exiles who had returned at the second half of the sixth century were already grown up and therefore partook in this investigation. *On the twentieth of the ninth month*—that is, the month Kislev and thus in midwinter. The date was given intentionally to show that the gathering of the people was not without some personal sacrifice. It is also there to support the last

3. Cf. C. Brekelmans, *THAT* I, p. 635, and esp. p. 637. Cf. also Brockington, *Ezra, Nehemiah and Esther,* p. 93.

expression of this verse, namely, the heavy rain. *They were trembling on account of this matter and on account of the heavy rain.* In the English translation the important difference between the two prepositions does not come out, viz., *'al* before "this matter" and *min* before "heavy rains." The preposition *'al* has here a kind of emotional value.[4] *min* means "as a result of." The difference between the two causes of the trembling is clearly emphasized. It is an inward emotional experience and an outward physical experience on account of the heavy rain and the cold weather.[5] The emotional experience might have come from different dispositions, namely, fear for the consequences of the grave sin, or fear of being subjected to a demand to send away the foreign wife and children. It is but human to have developed love for wife and children. The demand to expel them must have created a crisis in the inner self of many a husband present. The physical experience is also understandable, because in the heavy winter rains *(gešem)* of that cold time of the year trembling would be all too natural.

10–11 Ezra, the leader par excellence appointed by the Persian king, addressed the crowd. The bad weather prohibited a long speech. In a few sentences the whole position was summarized. It is amazing how well these few sentences were formulated to bring out the guilt of the people, and to show them what to do to be saved from a religious catastrophe. They had committed treason, not against the state, but against God. They had violated the prescriptions of his law and with it his covenant. With this violation they had increased the guilt of Israel (cf. also 9:6). These words were motivated religiously. The relationship with God had been broken and had to be restored somehow. *Thank the Lord.* Some scholars think that this phrase is closely connected to the confession of sins.[6] It may mean that the Lord was willing to forgive their sins and for that he had to be thanked. *Do his will* ("will" is Heb. *rāṣôn*) might mean "to do his pleasure,"[7] "to do that which pleases him." In later literature, as here, the meaning of "will" for *rāṣôn* predominates.[8] The doing of the will of God is always closely connected with the keeping of his law. This is substantiated by v. 11b where the doing of his will is connected with separation from the people of the land and from foreign wives. Only by this separation could the people atone for their sins.

4. Kapelrud, *The Question of Authorship in the Ezra-Narrative,* p. 76.
5. Grosheide, *Ezra,* pp. 278–79.
6. Cf. F. Horst, "Die Doxologien im Amosbuch," *ZAW* 47 (1929), pp. 50ff. and H. Grimme, "Der Begriffe von hebräischen *hwdh* und *twdh,*" *ZAW* 58 (1940/41), pp. 234–240.
7. Cf. Myers, *op. cit.,* p. 81.
8. Cf. G. Gerleman, *THAT* II, pp. 811–12.

12–14 These verses describe the reaction of the congregation. They agreed with Ezra. Their assent was given loudly, probably the way it was done in those days.[9] *Yes, we shall do as you say*—literally "Yes, as your words [or word] to us to do." We must accept that these words were said by the congregation. The reasoning of vv. 13–14 cannot have come from the congregation, but presumably from certain leaders, since it would have been impossible for a crowd to shout their arguments to Ezra. The role of the leaders is fully recognized in Ezra, and here on behalf of their people they produced three arguments why on that very day the investigation into the marriages with foreign women should not proceed. First, the people gathered there were a large crowd, and it would take a long time to organize the crowd. Second, it was raining and they were standing in the open without any protection. The situation was not favorable for a calm investigation; tempers could flare up easily. It would not be easy to decide on such a personal matter and nothing should stand in the way of a calm investigation in favorable circumstances. Third, a great number of cases had to be decided. Some of them might be problematical. It was thus unwise to draw hasty conclusions and to commit an injustice to people. In the situation there in the open, with a large crowd assembled, the reasonableness of these arguments was beyond cavil. But they also had a solution for the problem. This shows that their arguments were not an escape from the problem of intermarriage. They proposed that the chiefs must substitute for the congregation. They must organize the whole investigation. On appointed times those that had married foreign wives had to come to Jerusalem for the investigation. But they should not come on their own. Their local leaders and judges who knew their circumstances were to accompany them. This last proposal is very important. The people wanted a fair investigation in which every case would be carefully scrutinized with the aid of leaders who had an intimate knowledge of the circumstances.

The proposals were concluded with a religiously motivated clause, namely, the important aspect that the anger of God must be averted. The prayer of Ezra had made a lasting impression on them. Because of the marriages to foreign women the whole congregation was contaminated. Now they must purify themselves. *Judges* refers probably to the local judges in towns and not to state judges.[10] *About this matter.* The Hebrew preposition is the difficult *'aḏ,* which does not make sense. It might have

9. In Greece, e.g., in Sparta, leaders were elected by acclamation of the assembled citizens; cf. V. Ehrenberg, *From Solon to Socrates* (London: 1969), p. 45.
10. Frye, *The Heritage of Persia,* p. 100.

been a scribal error on account of the preceding *'aḏ*. We are reading with most modern scholars *'al* instead of *'aḏ*.[11]

15 This is one of the most difficult verses in the whole book of Ezra. We have four names used in grammatical constructions which are indeed problematical to understand. First, the Hebrew expression *'āmaḏ 'al* should mean here "opposed to."[12] But opposed to what? The Hebrew has the cryptic *zō't*, "this." Does *this* refer to the preceding, namely, the proposals of the representatives of the congregation? This interpretation seems best. Jonathan and Jahzeiah did not want to waste time; they wanted immediate action. They were supporting zealously the cause of Ezra. But what about Meshullam and Shabbethai? Again the Hebrew is not clear. What does *'ᵃzârum* mean?[13] Does it mean that these two persons assisted Jonathan and Jahzeiah in their protest? Or does it mean that Meshullam and Shabbethai supported the proposals of the congregation? The problem is the plural suffix to *'zr*. We prefer the interpretation in which the plural suffix refers back to the congregation. We take the *waw* before Meshullam as adversative. On this interpretation Meshullam and Shabbethai expressed themselves in favor of the proposals in vv. 13–14. We must admit that this is but one possibility.

The whole issue is obscure. One could with persuasion argue for the interpretation that Jonathan and Jahzeiah had opposed the plans of Ezra, and that they were against the drastic measures, possibly because they had foreign wives themselves. They were then opposed by Meshullam and Shabbethai. The latter had won the day and Ezra could continue with his measures. Both possibilities can be defended from the Hebrew.[14] It is quite probable that while Shabbethai is called a Levite and the other not, they were both from the laity.[15]

16–17 At the beginning of v. 16 it is stated that the exiles accepted the proposals of vv. 13–14 and acted accordingly. Ezra was in the background, maintaining a low profile, but the moment the decision was made by the exiles, he started to execute their plans. Ezra was a good diplomat and did not enforce his opinions on the exiles. He gave his views and waited for them to decide. We have here the traces of a form of democracy. As an able administrator he registered carefully the council he had selected. We may presume that he was advised about his choice.

11. Two mss. and the versions also read *'al;* cf. *BHS*.

12. Pelaia, *Esdra e Neemia,* p. 119.

13. *'zr* might be from root II, "to liberate" or "to rescue." Thus, "Meshullam and Shabbethai rescued them (from it)"(?). For root II see B. Q. Baisas, "Ugaritic *'ḏr* and Hebrew *'zr* I," *UF* 5 (1973), p. 41.

14. Grosheide, *Ezra,* pp. 283–84.

15. Cf. H. Cazelles, *VT* 4 (1954), p. 130.

Leaders who were guilty of the transgression could not have been taken up in the council. The registration of the names and the determination of their genealogy shows that Ezra wanted to make sure that only the exiles of pure Jewish origin were taken up. It seems strange that no list of these leaders is supplied, because the author was very fond of lists of names. The council worked about seventy-five days on this project; this figure gives us, if we compare it with the list from 10:18ff., not two cases a day. It is thus possible that certain cases were investigated in which the accused were not found guilty, or else not all the cases were registered in 10:18ff.[16] The first possibility seems likely. It is to be expected that difficult situations were investigated that took a long time to decide. That only one hundred ten cases in seventy-five days were investigated reflects the care with which the whole difficult position was managed. We read in v. 16 *lid̮rôš* ("select") instead of *l*^{e}*d̮ar*^{e}*yôš* ("to Darius"), a slight and obvious change. The article is probably left out before *'*^{a}*nāšîm* in v. 17 by haplography.

5. *List of the Guilty (10:18–44)*

18 *Among the priests the following were found to have married foreign wives: from the descendants of Jeshua the son of Jozadak and his brothers: Maaseiah, Eliezer, Jarib, and Gedaliah.*

19 *They pledged to send their wives away and they offered as guilt offering a ram from the flock.*

20 *From the descendants of Immer: Hanani and Zebadiah;*

21 *from the descendants of Harim: Maaseiah, Elijah, Shemaiah, Jehiel, and Uzziah;*

22 *from the descendants of Pashhur: Elioenai, Maaseiah, Ishmael, Nethanel, Jozabad, and Elasah;*

23 *from the Levites: Jozabad, Shimei, Kelaiah—that is, Kelita—Pethahiah, Judah, and Eliezer;*

24 *from the singers: Eliashib; from the gatekeepers: Shallum, Telem, and Uri;*

25 *from Israel, from the descendants of Parosh: Ramiah, Izziah, Malchijah, Mijamin, Eleazar, Malchijah, and Benaiah;*

26 *from the descendants of Elam: Mattaniah, Zechariah, Jehiel, Abdi, Jeremoth, and Elijah;*

27 *from the descendants of Zattu: Eliashib, Mattaniah, Jeremoth, Zabad, and Aziza;*

28 *from the descendants of Bebai: Jehohanan, Hananiah, Zabbai, and Athlai;*

29 *from the descendants of Bani: Meshullam, Malluch, Adaiah, Jashub, Sheal, and Jeremoth;*

16. Rudolph, *Esra und Nehemia*, p. 97.

30 *From the descendants of Pahath-moab: Adna, Chelal, Benaiah, Maaseiah, Mattaniah, Bezalel, Binnui, and Manasseh;*
31 *from the descendants of Harim: Eliezer, Isshijah, Malchijah, Shemaiah, Shimeon,*
32 *Benjamin, Malluch, and Shemariah;*
33 *from the descendants of Hashum: Mattenai, Mattattah, Zabad, Eliphelet, Jeremai, Manasseh, and Shimei;*
34 *from the descendants of Bani: Maadai, Amram, Uel,*
35 *Benaiah, Bediah, Cheluhi,*
36 *Vaniah, Meremoth, Eliashib,*
37 *Mattaniah, Mattenai, and Jaasu;*
38 *from the descendants of Binnui: Shimei,*
39 *Shelemiah, Nathan, Adiah;*
40 *from the descendants of Zaccai: Shashai, Sharai,*
41 *Azarel, Shelemaiah, Shemariah,*
42 *Shallum, Amariah, and Joseph;*
43 *from the descendants of Nebo: Jeiel, Mattithiah, Zabad, Zebina, Jaddai, Joel, and Benaiah.*
44 *All these had married foreign wives, and they sent the wives and children away.*

18–24 The list of priests who married foreign women is given first. This is probably to demonstrate that even they, the important religious leaders, had committed the sin. The high-priestly family is mentioned right at the beginning to emphasize how deeply the exiles were involved in this matter. *They pledged* — literally "and they gave their hands" (cf. 2 K. 10:15; 1 Chr. 29:24; 2 Chr. 30:8; Ezek. 17:18). It might mean that they took an oath. *And they offered as guilt offering*—literally it may mean "their guilt offering. . . ." The guilt offering is described in Lev. 5:14–26. It usually refers to an unintentional transgression. If it should have the same meaning here, the marriages were regarded as an unintentional act. This is not impossible, because although the law in general was known to the exiles, the finer distinctions and the interpretation of certain stipulations could have escaped them. Ezra was sent to teach them these distinctions and to interpret the law for them (7:10). It is this lesson they had to learn in order to realize that their marriages to foreign women were wrong.

Another problem is that the pledge and the guilt offering are mentioned only in connection with the priests. Was it also expected of the other groups mentioned from v. 20 on? Some are of the opinion that it is given here as a general rule for all the other groups. The author does not repeat it. It then stands in an awkward position. It creates the impression that it is meant only for the priests. This is not impossible. As the religious leaders the priests should set an example, and thus it was they who were expected to bring a guilt offering.

It is also of interest that among the temple personnel the temple servants are not mentioned. They were of a lower social class and one might expect that intermarriage would play among them a far greater role than among the higher classes. However, we are not well informed about the social stratification in those days, particularly about the social stratification among the people of the land. The impression one has is that the people of the land were better off than the exiles. In such a case the temptation for intermarriage would have been greater among the upper classes of the exiles.

25–43 *From Israel* means that the names of the laity are now given. The term *Israel* is thus used in Ezra with two different meanings. It may refer to the whole Israel with the priests included (6:17), or it may denote the laity of the exiles with the priests and Levites excluded (e.g., 6:20; 10:25). Eleven or twelve families of the laity are mentioned, while in Ezra 2 seventeen are found. Four of the eleven or twelve do not occur in Ezra 2.[1] The name Shemariah (v. 32) is also attested in the Arad ostraca.[2]

In this list are a few difficult textual problems and some other problems. In v. 38 the MT has: "Bani, Binnui, Shimei." With virtually all scholars we read with a minor adjustment of the text and a change of vowels: *from the descendants of Binnui (mibb^{e}nê binnûy* instead of *ûḇānî ûḇinnûy)*. This reading is supported by 1 Esdras 9:34. Another problem is in v. 40 where the cryptic Machnadebai appears; it is difficult to explain as a Hebrew name. In 1 Esdras 9:34 the reading is "from the descendants of Ezora." Ezora is also difficult. This might point in the direction of a corruption of Zaccai (2:9).[3] Another problem is the repetition of names, but this could be explained by the fact that these names were generally used in those days. The same name in the same family tree, e.g., Malchijah in the family of Parosh (v. 25), might have been descendants from different fathers. It is also surprising that two families have the same name, viz., Bani (cf. vv. 29, 34).

44 We must accept that at the end of this chapter some corruption of the text has crept in. Does it mean that we have with the last sentence only part of the conclusion of the chapter? We shall never know. Verse 44 says literally: "All these had married foreign women and there was from them women and they put children." The Greek text of 1 Esdras 9:36 has "and they sent them and the children away," but the LXX text (2 Esdras 10:44) follows the MT. We have followed the text of 1 Esdras, but the whole position is indeed problematic.

1. Brockington, *Ezra, Nehemiah and Esther,* pp. 94–95.
2. Cf. Gibson, *Textbook of Syrian Semitic Inscriptions* I, p. 53 (C 4).
3. Grosheide, *Ezra,* p. 290; Brockington, *op. cit.,* p. 99.

Rudolph refers to the fact, as he sees it, that this list is not complete. According to him, a complete list would be embarrassing for the Chronicler, because he would not have admitted that his idealized community of exiles could have sinned in such a large number.[4] This presumption of Rudolph is unacceptable, because from Ezra 9:1ff. it is flatly stated that the exiles had sinned by marrying foreign wives. In this list even people as important as the family of the high priest are mentioned. We have no support from Ezra to presume that names were willfully omitted. The author clearly emphasized the gravity of the sin which was committed.[5] The law of God must be kept, and any transgression of this law was regarded as serious.

4. Rudolph, *Esra und Nehemia,* p. 97.
5. Myers, *Ezra. Nehemiah,* p. 88.

The Book
of
NEHEMIAH

III. RETURN OF NEHEMIAH; BUILDING OF THE WALL (1:1–6:19)

A. REPORT FROM JERUSALEM (1:1–4)

1 *The words of Nehemiah, the son of Hacaliah. In the month Kislev in the twentieth year I was in the citadel Susa,*
2 *and Hanani, one of my brothers, arrived with other men of Judah. I inquired about the Jews, those who had escaped and who were left over from captivity, and about Jerusalem.*
3 *They replied to me: "Those who are left over from captivity are there in the province; they are in great trouble and shame. The wall of Jerusalem is broken down and its gates burnt down."*
4 *When I heard these words I sat down, wept, and mourned for days. I fasted and prayed to the God of the heaven.*

Nehemiah held an important position in the Persian court (cf. our discussion of 1:11). It is not very clear what the historical position was in Judah at the time of Nehemiah's return. If we accept that he had returned in the twentieth year of Artaxerxes I, it would have been in 445 B.C. Artaxerxes had serious problems when he ascended to the throne. There was a revolt of his brother, Hystaspes, in Bactria at the beginning of his reign. In Egypt a nationalistic revolt under Inarus broke out in 460 B.C. This uprising was supported by the Athenians, but it was put down in 455 B.C. In 448 B.C. Megabyzus, the satrap of Trans-Euphrates, rebelled. He was reconciled later to the Persian king.[1] This historical process of revolts shows the instability of the Persian empire at that time, and especially its instability in the neighborhood of Egypt. Judah and Jerusalem formed part of the

1. Cf. Widengren, *Israelite and Judaean History,* p. 528; W. Vischer, "Nehemia, der Sonderbeauftragte und Statthalter des Königs," in H. W. Wolff, ed., *Probleme biblischer Theologie*. Festschrift G. von Rad (Munich: 1971), p. 604.

province Trans-Euphrates. Judah was situated close to Egypt and was therefore an important buffer state. From a political viewpoint it is clear that friendly relations between the Persian king and the Jews were expedient. In the light of this political situation the attitude of Artaxerxes toward Nehemiah must be understood.

1–3 *The words of Nehemiah.* It is uncertain whether this superscription is to be regarded as the work of the final editor. One thing is clear, however—this superscription describes carefully that which follows. This book is concerned mainly with Nehemiah. The superscription could also be the caption of Nehemiah's memoir that was taken over by the editor.

The proper name *Nehemiah* means "the Lord comforts." Two other persons in Ezra-Nehemiah have the same name (cf. Ezra 2:2; Neh. 3:16; 7:7). The building of a personal name with *nḥm* is well known in extrabiblical literature.[2] Sir. 48:13 mentions Nehemiah as an important person, and 2 Macc. 1:18–36 refers to him as playing an important role in the ceremony of the Feast of Tabernacles and in founding a library.[3] Nehemiah thus became a legendary figure in later Jewish literature. The origin and meaning of *Hacaliah* are unknown.

In the month Kislev in the twentieth year. It is not clear to what the twentieth year refers. Two possibilities are open. It might refer to the twentieth year of Nehemiah's presence in Susa. This can be derived from the Hebrew as it stands. But this possibility is rather improbable, because it would be strange for the cupbearer of the king to stay only in one place, since the Persian kings shifted their dwelling place with the change of seasons (Xenophon *Cyropaedia* viii.6.22). The second possibility is that the name of Artaxerxes was left out by haplography, and that the twentieth year refers to the twentieth year of his reign. In the light of Neh. 2:1 this is the best solution to the problem. But Rudolph points out another problem if this solution is accepted.[4] In Neh. 2:1 the month Nisan is mentioned in connection with the twentieth year of Artaxerxes. If the calendar is calculated from the spring, the month Kislev should fall in the nineteenth year of Artaxerxes. Rudolph wants to emend the text to fit this view. But the Jews also calculated another calendar from autumn. In such a case both Kislev and Nisan would fall in the twentieth year of Artaxerxes.[5] This seems to be an acceptable solution.[6]

2. Diringer, *Le iscrizioni antico-ebraiche palistinesi,* p. 190; H. Huffmon, *Amorite Personal Names in the Mari Texts,* pp. 237–39.
3. Brockington, *Ezra, Nehemiah and Esther,* p. 104; Myers, *Ezra. Nehemiah,* p. 93.
4. Rudolph, *Esra und Nehemia,* p. 102.
5. For these calculations see E. R. Thiele, *The Mysterious Numbers of the Hebrew Kings* (Grand Rapids: [2]1965), pp. 30, 161.
6. Myers, *op. cit.,* p. 92.

And Hanani, one of my brothers, arrived. Hanani probably was a real brother of Nehemiah, although "brother" may be used in the sense of "kinsman."[7] The text states only that Hanani and several other Jews arrived. The question is, What was the purpose of their visit? Some want to discover in this visit a special mission. These scholars accept that Judah was at that time part of the province of Samaria. Hanani and his companions were on a diplomatic mission bypassing the officials of Samaria due to the hostility between the Jews and the Samaritans. They contacted Nehemiah because of his important position at the court and told him about their precarious position in Judah.[8] There is one problem with this solution: The impression from the text is that Nehemiah made a casual inquiry about the whereabouts of his compatriots in Judah. He spoke first and then the position was explained to him. The visit might have been on business, or his brother Hanani may have come from Judah to visit him concerning family affairs.[9] From the text it is difficult to discern which one of these possibilities is most likely.

Verses 2 and 3 describe Nehemiah's inquiry about the situation of the exiles and the condition in Jerusalem, and the reply of the visiting Jews to the question. The impression one has of Nehemiah's inquiry (cf. our discussion above) is that he was interested to know in what conditions his fellow Jews were living. Such an inquiry would be very natural for somebody who lived far removed from his people. His family members were also living in Judah and it is to be expected that he would have an interest in the circumstances under which they were living.

Those who had escaped and who were left over from captivity. These words can be interpreted in two different ways. They may refer to the Jews who were not taken into captivity by the Babylonians.[10] This interpretation is rather improbable in the light of the terms used in v. 2 that we have already discussed in Ezra 8:35 and especially Ezra 9:8. It is more likely that these words refer to the returned exiles. Thus *those who had escaped* (Heb. *happ^e^lêṭâ*) refers to the exiles who had returned and escaped further captivity. Exile was regarded as a great shame for the Jewish people. If they returned to the Holy Land, it was interpreted as an escape from shame (cf. Ezra 9:13–14). *Who were left over from captivity* (cf. the Hebrew root *š'r*). This refers to the remnant, to those who had returned from captivity. It is thus clear that Nehemiah inquired about his brethren in Judah who were in exile and who had returned.[11]

Verse 3 is probably only a short summary of the Jews' reply, stress-

7. Cf. Brockington, *op. cit.*, p. 104.
8. Cf. the discussion of Myers, *op. cit.*, p. 94.
9. Pelaia, *Esdra e Neemia*, p. 127; Brockington, *op. cit.*, p. 105.
10. Myers, *op. cit.*, p. 93.
11. Rudolph, *Esra und Nehemia*, p. 104.

ing the most important points. *There in the province*—which province is meant here? There are different approaches to this question. Some postulate that Judah was at this time still part of the Persian province of Samaria, and the Samaritans were not about to repair the defenses of Jerusalem.[12] Further evidence for this explanation is that nowhere in the negotiations between Artaxerxes and Nehemiah is it mentioned that the latter was appointed governor *(peḥa)*. Only later on, after Nehemiah's work had progressed, was he called a governor. Others hold that Judah was instituted as a province in the time of Cyrus or Darius. In the days of Nehemiah it had been for a long time a province of the Persian empire. Proponents of this view refer to the fact that Zerubbabel is called a governor by Haggai (Hag. 1:1, 14; 2:2, 21). Aharoni and others propose that *province* here refers to the province of Trans-Euphrates.[13] That the name of the province is not given and is thus presumed as being obvious to Nehemiah indicates that the large, well-known province of Trans-Euphrates, of which Judah formed a part, was intended.

The wall of Jerusalem is broken down and its gates burnt down. This expression is also not clear. It may be taken as a recent disaster which struck Jerusalem, perhaps action taken against the Jews when they rebuilt the wall illegally in the early years of Artaxerxes (Ezra 4:8ff.).[14] The problem with this view is that the description in Ezra 4:8ff. nowhere creates the impression that the wall was broken down. It only states that the work was stopped by force of arms. We must then presume that the part of the wall which was already built—if it was built, because nothing is said of it—was broken down by the enemies of the Jews. So if we follow this view, it is necessary to make a few assumptions. Another view is that this phrase refers to the destroying of Jerusalem in the time of Nebuchadnezzar. From that time onward the wall and the gates were in ruins. The one and only attempt to restore it in the early years of Artaxerxes was thwarted. Jerusalem was still a city without defenses. The temple of Jerusalem could be destroyed easily by the enemies, because no proper stand could be made against enemies without a defense wall. After a hundred and forty years Jerusalem and its inhabitants, the Jews, were still easy game for any enemy who wanted to attack them. The latter view seems to be the more acceptable.

4 This report was bad news to Nehemiah. The ideal circumstances in which he had pictured the Jews in Judah were unrealistic; the

12. Myers, *op. cit.*, p. 95. Cf. also Alt, *KS* II, p. 346.
13. Cf. Y. Aharoni, *The Land of the Bible*, p. 357. Cf. also F. C. Fensham, "Mĕdînâ in Ezra and Nehemiah," *VT* 25 (1975), 795–797.
14. Rudolph, *op. cit.*, p. 103; Brockington, *op. cit.*, p. 105.

citizens were in danger and with them their religion. This verse depicts Nehemiah as a devoted Jew, dedicated to the religion of his ancestors in spite of the fact that the formal Persian term for his God is used, namely, *God of heaven* (see below on v. 5). As Ezra did when he heard about the sin of the exiles, Nehemiah sat down and wept, fasted, and prayed. The religious devotion of this practical man cannot be denied. It comes out occasionally in the following chapters.

B. NEHEMIAH'S PRAYER (1:5–11)

5 *I said: "O Lord, God of heaven, great and terrible God who keeps the covenant and covenant love with those that love him and those that keep his commandments.*

6 *Listen attentively and keep your eyes open for the prayer of your servant that I pray day and night on behalf of the Israelites your servants. I am confessing the sins of the Israelites that they have committed against you. I and my father's family have also sinned.*

7 *We have acted perversely against you and did not keep the commandments, the statutes, and legal prescriptions which you commanded Moses your servant.*

8 *Remember the warning you gave to Moses your servant: 'If you act treacherously, I shall scatter you among the nations,*

9 *but if you return to me and keep my commandments and practice them, even if you should be dispersed to the sky's end, I shall gather them from there and bring them to the place which I have chosen for my name to dwell.'*

10 *These are your servants and your people whom you have redeemed with your mighty power and arm of strength.*

11 *O Lord, listen attentively to the prayer of your servant and the prayer of your servants who have a delight in the fear of your name. Let your servant have success today and receive mercy from this man." Then I was cupbearer to the king.*

This prayer is in the style of the lamentations of the people.[1] The characteristics of this prayer are, first, Nehemiah's feeling of solidarity with his people. As in the intercessions of Moses and Ezra, Nehemiah identified himself and his family totally with the Jews. This comes out clearly from the first person plural he is using. Second, it is clear that Nehemiah was steeped in the literature of the OT, especially the Deuteronomistic part of it. He was a student of Scripture, or else he could not have used the OT so liberally. Third, Nehemiah, in accordance with the views of his time,

1. H. Gunkel and J. Begrich, *Einleitung in die Psalmen*. HAT (Göttingen: 1933), pp. 121ff.

had a special reverence for the legal parts of the Bible. The Pentateuch had played a dominant role in his life. His conception of religion, like that of Ezra, was closely linked with the law. If one could keep the law, the highest ideal of his religious life would be reached.

This prayer has a simple structure. It starts with an invocation of God, proceeds to a confession of sins, then a request to the Lord to remember his people, and concludes with a request for success.

Some scholars regard this prayer as a pure fabrication of the Chronicler.[2] Others hold the opinion that it was expanded by the Chronicler.[3] The similarities between this prayer and those composed by the Chronicler can be explained as contemporary usage.[4] The Deuteronomistic language used in the prayer indicates that Nehemiah was well versed in it, probably like all his contemporaries. To ascribe this to the Chronicler is a one-sided approach which does not take into account the probability that Deuteronomistic terminology could have had a pervasive influence on the Jews in the time of Ezra and Nehemiah.[5] There is nothing in this prayer that testifies against its authenticity.

5 In this invocation Nehemiah uses the proper name of the *Lord* and the name *God of heaven,* which was well known in the Persian empire. It is impossible that *God of heaven* could have been used as diplomatic language to impress the Persian authorities, since the proper name, *Lord* (Heb. *yhwh*), was used. Thus in Nehemiah's time *God of heaven* had become part of the religious language of the Jews. *Terrible God* (Heb. *hannôrā'*). This term can be translated "awe-inspiring" (Myers) or "stand in fear" (GNB). It is that which is wonderful, which is astonishing, but which inspires awe.[6] While this root is not used in Ezra, it occurs fourteen times in Nehemiah. *The covenant and covenant love (habbᵉrîṯ wāḥeseḏ).* In this case the covenant *(bᵉrîṯ)* is closely connected to *ḥeseḏ,*[7] which expresses here solidarity between covenant partners and can be translated "covenant love."[8] The Lord keeps his covenant and covenant love with those who love him (Deut. 5:10; 7:9; etc.). This shows clearly that the covenant and its maintenance is bound by love, the love of God's people for God. A second condition for the keeping of the covenant is that God's

2. E.g., Batten, *A Critical and Exegetical Commentary on the Books of Ezra and Nehemiah,* p. 188.
3. Cf. Bowman, *IB* III, p. 666.
4. Myers, *Ezra. Nehemiah,* p. 95.
5. Cf. also the discussion of Rudolph, *Esra und Nehemia,* pp. 105–106.
6. Cf. H. P. Stähli, *THAT* I, pp. 768–69; S. Plath, *Furcht Gottes. Der Begriff yr' im AT* (Stuttgart: 1963), p. 23; J. Becker, *Gottesfurcht im AT* (Rome: 1965), p. 47.
7. H. J. Stoebe, *THAT* I, p. 602.
8. See N. Glueck, Ḥesed *in the Bible* (E.T. 1967).

people must keep his commandments, the stipulations of the covenant. Love and keeping of the law are thus the two pillars on which the covenant rests.

6–7 Verse 6 begins with another invocation. Nehemiah asks for the Lord's attention. He is praying day and night for the Israelites. *Day and night*—literally "today [or now] day and night." It must not be taken literally or else Nehemiah would not have had time to serve the king, but it is a hyperbole generally used in ordinary language.[9] In vv. 6b and 7 the confession of sins is given. In v. 6b it is stated in plain and simple language that the Israelites have sinned against the Lord. Of interest is the fact that Nehemiah combined this confession with his own and that of his family. Ezra stood outside the circle of sinners, but identified himself with them. Nehemiah confessed his involvement in the sinning. This gives his prayer a clear ring of an honest confession of a sinner. All have sinned, even the supplicant and his family. In v. 7 the sin which has been committed is described. The commandments of the Lord were not kept. The threefold designation *commandments, statutes, and legal prescriptions* is a comprehensive description of the law of God. It refers definitely to the Pentateuch, as the words *which you commanded Moses* show. The stipulations of the covenant were broken and thus the covenant also. In such a case the Jews were not entitled to the covenant love of God. This is the reason why they had to live in such precarious circumstances in the Holy Land. *Legal prescriptions* (Heb. *hammišpāṭîm*) are the customary laws which through the decisions of judges became generally acknowledged. That part of the customary law which is taken up in the Pentateuch, and hence sanctioned by the Lord, is meant here.

8–9 After the confession of sins and the effect it had regarding the breaking of the covenant, Nehemiah sketches the result of the sin (v. 8). The result is that the sinners will be scattered among the nations, that they will go into exile. *Act treacherously* (from the Hebrew root *m'l*) is also used by Ezra in his prayer (9:6). Here in Nehemiah the curse on the treason is balanced by two significant verbs in v. 9, viz., *return* and *keep.* Covenantal language is used. In the covenant, as also in ancient Near Eastern treaties, the curses were balanced by blessings. If one transgressed the stipulations, the curse would come into operation, but if one kept the stipulations, the blessing would be bestowed. It was an either/or choice.

At the beginning of v. 8 it is said that a warning was given to Moses, and then the either/or sentence is given. It is clear that Nehemiah is citing from the Pentateuch, actually conflating Deut. 30:1–4. Parts of it are a free citation and part quoted verbatim (e.g., *dispersed to the sky's*

9. See S. J. DeVries, *Yesterday, Today and Tomorrow* (Grand Rapids: 1975), pp. 250–51.

end from Deut. 30:4).[10] In its shortened form it is a true reflection of what is said in Deuteronomy. It is of interest that Deut. 30:1 clearly states that it is a choice between curse and blessing. It is obvious that Nehemiah in his conflation prefers that part which refers to the return from captivity. He was thinking of the returnees in the Holy Land.

10–11a After confessing the sins of Israel and referring to the alternative of curse and blessing, Nehemiah reminds the Lord that these people with their sins and their inclination to move away from God are his servants and his people. They are his possession (Exod. 19:5–6). Proof of this is that he has redeemed them. *Redeemed* (from the Hebrew root *pdh*) refers occasionally in the OT to the payment of a price to redeem one from slavery.[11] In cultic terminology it is used to denote the redeeming of the firstborn with an animal. In religious usage with God as subject of the verb, the legal connotation is pushed into the background and the meaning "to save" becomes predominant.[12] We must keep in mind, however, that the redeeming of Israel from the Egyptian slavery always remains an underlying feature.

The terminology *your mighty power and arm of strength* is used in connection with the redeeming of Israel from Egypt (cf. Exod. 6:1; 9:16; and esp. 32:11), but here it probably refers to the redeeming from exile. By using this terminology Nehemiah compares the return of the exiles to the Holy Land and their redemption from captivity to the events of the Exodus. In later chapters of Isaiah the same notion is emphasized strongly, while the Exodus also plays an important role in sections of Ezekiel.[13] In Judaism a fresh return to the Holy Land was interpreted as a new Exodus, e.g., later by the sect of Qumran.[14]

In v. 11a we have another invocation. Nehemiah asks again for the Lord's attention. This time only the expression *listen attentively* is used; *keep your eyes open* is left out (cf. v. 6). Another difference between vv. 6 and 11 is the addition of *the prayer of your servants*. What does it mean? It could mean that other Jews were praying with him; it might be Hanani and his men. This is unlikely, however, in the light of vv. 4–5, which state

10. Rudolph, *op. cit.*, p. 105; Myers, *op. cit.*, pp. 95–96.
11. Cf. J. J. Stamm, *THAT* II, p. 391.
12. *Ibid.*, pp. 396ff.
13. Cf., e.g., W. Zimmerli, "Le nouvel 'exode' dans le message des deux grands prophètes de l'exil," in *Hommage a Wilhelm Vischer* (Montpellier: 1960), pp. 216–227; *idem,* "Der 'Neue Exodus' in der Verkündigung der Beiden Grossen Exilspropheten," in *Gottes Offenbarung* (Munich: 1963), pp. 192–204. Cf. also G. Gerleman, *Esther. BKAT* 21 (Neukirchen: 1973), pp. 11ff. for the exodus motif in Esther.
14. Cf. F. M. Cross, *The Ancient Library of Qumran* (Garden City: ²1961), p. 78.

that Nehemiah sat down, wept, mourned, fasted, and prayed. Nothing is mentioned of other Jews. Another possibility is that this expression reflects Nehemiah's attitude as an intercessor, his feeling of solidarity with his people. As he was praying, many of his people who served God were also praying for the cause of the Jews in the Holy Land. The latter interpretation seems to be the best.

The prayer of Nehemiah concludes with a personal note. He wanted to approach the Persian king on account of the situation in Jerusalem. He knew of the fickleness of the Persian kings and their sudden changes of mood (cf. the book of Esther), but also of their tolerant attitude toward subjects.[15] With the expression *this man* at the end of the prayer Nehemiah shows the big difference between his reverence for his God and his conception of his master, the Persian king. In the eyes of the world Artaxerxes was an important person, a man with influence, who could decide on life or death. In the eyes of Nehemiah, with his religious approach, Artaxerxes was just a man like any other man. The Lord of history makes the decisions, not Artaxerxes.[16]

11b The last sentence of this verse orients us to the position held by Nehemiah. He was a cupbearer of the king. Recent studies have shown the importance of this position. In the ancient Near Eastern court the cupbearer, with his direct access to the king, was regarded as important and influential.[17] In Tobit it is said that Esarhaddon's cupbearer was second only to him in his kingdom (Tobit 1:22).[18] In the *History* of Herodotus (iii.34) it is stated that Cambyses did one of his friends a favor by appointing his son as cupbearer.[19] For Nehemiah to have reached this position was an important achievement. It shows what influential positions some of the Jews of the Exile had reached. Another important point is that Nehemiah as cupbearer quite probably had been a eunuch.[20] Men in the service of the king who came in contact with the king's harem were usually eunuchs. Thus Nehemiah was not only from the Jewish laity, but he was also a eunuch. In comparison with Ezra, who was a priest and secretary, Nehemiah's position among his own people must have been difficult. The odds were against him, but in spite of this, by will power, a strong personality, and a deep-rooted devotion to the Lord he was destined to play

15. Cf. J. H. Iliffe, "Persia and the Ancient World," in A. J. Arberry, ed., *Legacy of Persia* (Oxford: 1953), p. 8.
16. Cf. Vischer, *op. cit.*, p. 603.
17. Cf. E. F. Weidner, "Hof- und Haremserlasse assyrischer Könige aus dem Jahrtausend vor Chr.," *AfO* 17 (1956), pp. 264ff.
18. Myers, *op. cit.*, p. 96.
19. Vischer, *op. cit.*, p. 603.
20. Rudolph, *Esra und Nehemia*, p. 103; Myers, *op. cit.*, p. 96.

an important role in the history of his people and in the history of the revelation of God.

C. NEHEMIAH'S MISSION (2:1–10)

1 *In the month Nisan, in the twentieth year of Artaxerxes the king, wine was placed before him. I took up the wine and gave it to the king. I had never been depressed before this.*
2 *The king said to me: "Why are you so depressed? Are you unwell? If not, it seems that you are sad of heart." A terrible fear came over me.*
3 *I said to the king: "May you be king for ever! Why should I not be depressed while the city where my ancestors' graves are lies in ruins and its gates are destroyed by fire?"*
4 *The king said to me: "What do you want of me?" I prayed to the God of heaven*
5 *and said to the king: "If it pleases the king and if your servant is in your favor, send me to Judah, to the city with the graves of my ancestors, so that I can rebuild it."*
6 *The king asked me, while the queen sat at his side: "How long will your journey take? When will you be back?" So the king agreed to send me after I had given him an appointed time.*
7 *Then I said to the king: "If it pleases the king, let letters be given to me for the governors of Trans-Euphrates that they may allow me to pass through until I reach Judah,*
8 *also a letter to Asaph, keeper of the park of the king, to provide me with timber for beams of the gates of the fortress which is close to the temple, and for the wall of the city and for the house I am to occupy." The king gave his permission because the favor of my God was with me.*
9 *So I came to the governors of Trans-Euphrates and gave them the letters of the king. The king also sent with me an escort of officers and cavalry.*
10 *When Sanballat the Horonite and Tobiah the Ammonite official heard of it, they were very much displeased that someone had come to promote the welfare of the Israelites.*

1 On *Nisan* and *the twentieth year of Artaxerxes* cf. the discussion of 1:1. The description in v. 1 creates the impression that a festival was held. The Persian kings were famous for their drinking parties (cf. Esth. 1:3ff.),[1] which were an ancient custom in the Near East.[2] *Wine was placed before*

1. Cf. G. Gerleman, *Esther,* pp. 56ff.
2. Cf. H. Bardtke, *Der Prediger. Das Buch Esther.* KAT XVII/5 (Gütersloh: ²1963), p. 279.

him—literally "wine was before him." Certain manuscripts of old translations have "wine was before me."[3] It might also be freely translated "I was in charge of the wine." The Hebrew may, however, denote that the wine was placed before the king. The work of the cupbearer was then to take the wine up and to give it to the king. Thus the cupbearer was close to the king, so close to him that the king could immediately see when something was wrong with his servant. *I had never been depressed before this*—literally "and I had not been bad [Heb. *ra'*] before him." Three possible approaches to this expression have been taken. First, some want to read the asseverative *lû* instead of *lō'*.[4] It can be translated "Verily, I was depressed in his presence." It is not impossible to interpret it this way. The problem is that we do not have much textual support for it. Second, *lō'* can be retained, but then *l^epānîm*, "before," instead of *l^epānāyw*, "before him," can be read.[5] Third, one may retain the MT and take the third person suffix as not referring to the king, but to an impersonal "it" or "this," i.e., as referring to the disturbing report from Jerusalem.

In the month Kislev Nehemiah had heard of the unfavorable position of his people in Judah. Four months later, in the month Nisan, his opportunity arrived to put his case to the king. In the four-month interval, we may presume that Nehemiah had fasted, mourned, and prayed. This had an effect on his personality, making him become gloomy and dissatisfied. We must also presume that now for the first time since the month Kislev the king held a festival. What had happened in the meantime we do not know. It is clear from the last words of this verse that this was the first time that Nehemiah had served the king with a gloomy countenance.

2–3 The king had noticed Nehemiah's change of appearance and asked Nehemiah a few questions about it. It was important to him that his cupbearer should not move around at the festival with a gloomy face. All the people were enjoying the party. Why should his cupbearer spoil the party? *Why are you so depressed?* Literally "Why is your face so bad?" The word translated *depressed* (plural of *ra'*, which was used in v. 1) has a great variety of meanings. It is always associated with something unpleasant, bad, or wicked.[6] In this case the inner feeling of Nehemiah was reflected in his outward appearance. The term *depressed* is the best translation of this phenomenon. The next question, *Are you unwell?* shows the concern of the king for his servant, who, though perhaps ill, was still willing to perform his duty. The last expression speaks of *sad of heart* (Heb. *rōa'*

3. Cf. *BHS*.
4. Myers, *Ezra. Nehemiah,* p. 98.
5. Rudolph, *Esra und Nehemia,* p. 106.
6. Cf. H. J. Stoebe, *THAT* II, pp. 794–803.

lēḇ). The term *rōa'* (from the same root as *ra'*) has a fairly large semantic field, including "bad, evil, ugly, sad," and so on. The combination with heart *(lēḇ)* occurs also in 1 Sam. 17:28, where it can be translated "evil of heart,"[7] but this is not the meaning here in v. 2. In Eccl. 7:3 *rōa'* is used with *pānîm,* "face," meaning "sad of face." Similarly, then, it seems that here in v. 2 this expression means "sad of heart." The king has made a threefold inquiry about Nehemiah's health, namely, an inner experience which is reflected in the outward appearance; illness of his body; and sadness of heart; in other words, unhappiness about something. It shows that Artaxerxes was a keen observer. It also indicates that the king took an interest in the disposition of his servant, a reflection of his humane character.

A terrible fear came over me. The reason for this fear is not given. It might be ascribed to two reasons. First, Nehemiah's sad countenance in festive circumstances might have angered the king. Second, the great moment had arrived for Nehemiah on which he had set his heart for the preceding four months. He knew of the failure to rebuild the wall of Jerusalem at the beginning of the reign of Artaxerxes (Ezra 4:23).[8] The king even demanded that all building activities must be stopped. Would the king react favorably to his overtures in such circumstances? It was a moment of great anxiety for Nehemiah. How was the king going to react if he heard of Jerusalem, the rebellious city?

In v. 3 Nehemiah states the cause of his depression: The city with the graves of his ancestors was in ruins and its gates destroyed. This remark may have had a double duty. For Nehemiah such a state of affairs was unacceptable and a shame for his people. For the Persian king a city without defense walls was useless. But it is of interest that nowhere in Nehemiah's conversation with the king is the word *Jerusalem* used. Some scholars regard this as a masterstroke of diplomacy. The name Jerusalem could have reminded the king of his earlier inquiry into the history of that city (Ezra 4:8–23).[9] But it must be asked, Was the king not aware that Nehemiah referred to Jerusalem? It would have been indeed strange that the king would send his cupbearer to rebuild an unknown city in an unknown country. But at the beginning of Nehemiah's negotiations it would obviously have been expedient not to mention the name of the city.

Where my ancestors' graves are. The mentioning of this fact to a Persian king might seem strange. We have evidence that the Persians did not bury their dead, but exposed them to be eaten by wild animals. They

7. Cf. the discussion of H. J. Stoebe, *Das erste Buch Samuelis.* KAT VIII/1 (Gütersloh: ²1973), p. 324.
8. Brockington, *Ezra, Nehemiah and Esther,* p. 106; Myers, *op. cit.,* p. 99.
9. Myers, *op. cit.,* p. 99; Brockington, *op. cit.,* p. 106.

had intricate rituals for the soul of the dead, however, and even a special festival for the dead.[10] But their approach was in no way uniform. We have evidence that the Achaemenian kings were buried and not exposed.[11] The Jews had high reverence for the graves of their forefathers.[12] It is possible that Artaxerxes as an Achaemenian king had the same reverence, in which case the words of Nehemiah drove home an important point.

4–5 It was clear to the king that Nehemiah wanted to make a request. He was willing to listen. This is yet another proof of the tolerant attitude of Artaxerxes. Nehemiah prayed to God in order to make his request correctly, so that it would be acceptable to the king. This demonstrates again the devotion and piety of Nehemiah. He was fully convinced that in every step he was taking the Lord guided his way. The mighty Persian king was also subjected to the will of God. Nehemiah's request was that the king send him to Judah to rebuild the city. Jerusalem is again not expressly mentioned, but Judah. Would the king have been so ignorant of his provinces that he did not know that Jerusalem was the most important city of Judah? This seems rather unlikely. The avoiding of the name might have been deliberate so as not to draw too much attention to Jerusalem.

6 The king was probably fond of his cupbearer. He did not want to lose him for ever. He wanted to send him only for an appointed time. He did not fix the time himself, but left it to Nehemiah to decide. The two questions of Artaxerxes were interpreted by Nehemiah as a positive reply to his request. By asking him how long his journey and return would take, Artaxerxes tacitly granted his request. It was only a question of negotiation concerning the time of his leave. The appointed time of Nehemiah's absence is not given here, but in 5:14 twelve years are mentioned.[13]

While the queen sat at his side. Queen (šēgal) is used here and in Ps. 45:10 (Eng. 11) to denote a queen; in Biblical Aramaic *šegal* denotes a concubine (Dnl. 5:2–3, 23).[14] Damaspia was the wife of Artaxerxes. Why is this particular given? It might have been to show that a witness

10. Cf. J. Duchesne-Guillemin, *La religion de l'Iran Ancien*, pp. 103ff.; and for the festival pp. 118–120.

11. Cf. R. C. Zaehner, *The Dawn and Twilight of Zoroastrianism* (London: 1961), p. 162.

12. Rudolph, *op. cit.*, p. 107. For the situation of the old cemetery see B. Mazar, "Jerusalem in the Biblical Period," in Y. Yadin, ed., *Jerusalem Revealed* (New Haven: 1976), p. 8.

13. Brockington, *op. cit.*, p. 106.

14. For the origin of *šgl* cf. A. R. Millard, "[F]Ša Ekalli—ŠGL—[D]sagale," *UF* 4 (1972), pp. 161–62; E. Lipiński, *Studies in Aramaic Inscriptions and Onomastics* (1975), p. 99; and contra Millard, S. Kaufman, *The Akkadian Influences on Aramaic*, p. 97.

was present, or that Nehemiah was in her favor.[15] We know that the influence of women was strong during the reign of Artaxerxes.[16] Another possibility is that the party of Artaxerxes is described in vv. 1–5, but later on, while the king and queen were together and served by Nehemiah, the final answer to his request was given (v. 6).

7–8 Further petitions of Nehemiah are given in these verses. First, he requested letters of introduction to *the governors of Trans-Euphrates* for a safe passage. Nehemiah travelled on a different mission from Ezra's, his mission being a political one. In such a case he might have expected hostility from the Persian officials en route. To protect him against this he wanted to carry letters for safe conduct.

The term for *governors* is the plural of *peḥa*. This can refer to either a satrap or a governor of a smaller province of Trans-Euphrates. We must keep in mind that the governor of Samaria was one of those that he would encounter on his journey. Without the permission of the Persian king, Sanballat would never have let him through.

Second, he asked for a letter of introduction to Asaph, the chief forester of the king, to provide him with timber for his building activities. It is clear that Nehemiah had formed his plans well in advance. His knowledge of the circumstances and what was needed must have been received from Hanani and his friends. This is another proof that not all of the conversation between Nehemiah and Hanani is given in 1:2–3. *Asaph* is a Jewish name, but this does not mean that he lived in Judah and that the king had a park here. *The park* (Heb. *pardēs* from the Persian *paridaida*)[17] was probably the forests of the Lebanon. In the time of Darius, timber was supplied from the Lebanon for the building of the temple (Ezra 3:7).[18] The timber was requested for three different projects, namely, the gates of the fortress, the wall of the city, and his own house.

The gates of the fortress which is close to the temple. This clause is not clear. Does it mean that a special fortress existed that protected the temple? Or does it mean a fortress, *the* fortress, which protected the city and also the temple? Some think that it was a fortress to the north of the temple.[19] It might have been the tower or fortress of Hananel mentioned in 3:1.[20] Nehemiah thus gave to the king an example of what he thought should be restored immediately. This structure is one of the first towers

15. Widengren, *Israelite and Judaean History,* p. 528.
16. Myers, *op. cit.,* p. 98; Rudolph, *op. cit.,* p. 107.
17. Cf. W. Brandenstein and M. Mayrhofer, *Handbuch des Altpersischen* (1964), p. 137; A. Jepsen, "Pardes," *ZDPV* 74 (1958), pp. 65–68.
18. Myers, *op. cit.,* p. 100.
19. *Ibid.,* p. 98.
20. Brockington, *op. cit.,* p. 107.

mentioned by Nehemiah in his famous list of the rebuilding operations. *For the wall of the city.* Timber for the wall of the city might seem strange, but wood was used extensively in walls in the ancient Near East as is shown by the study of the architect Rudolf Naumann in connection with Hittite buildings.[21] The same phenomenon occurs in the Holy Land.[22] *For the house I am to occupy* — literally "and for a house in which I could enter." Nehemiah already had a house in mind, perhaps suggested by Hanani. *Because of the favor.* Cf. the discussion of Ezra 7:6.

9 It is not clear how much time had elapsed between the king's permission and Nehemiah's departure. Josephus (*Ant.* xi.5) mentions a timespan of five years, but this is rather improbable. One could not imagine that Nehemiah, after his anxious request, could have waited that long. The letters of introduction were delivered to the governors and no problems occurred. *An escort of officers and cavalry*—literally "officers of the army and cavalry." Nehemiah was ensured a safe journey in the company of a contingent of soldiers. How he had acquired them is not told. We may presume that Artaxerxes was anxious for a safe journey for his cupbearer. He was on his way to fulfil an important mission. At that time he was already appointed as governor of Judah. His political role as governor in an unstable part of the Persian empire was important. His safe conduct was intended to ensure that his mission would be fulfilled. For the difference between the missions of Ezra and Nehemiah cf. the discussion of Ezra 8:22.

10 Nehemiah's arrival created immediate problems with the neighboring nations. Since the building of the temple the rift between these people and the Jews had grown wider. Earlier in the reign of Artaxerxes their accusations against the Jews were upheld. Now a Jew arrived, appointed governor of Judah with the clear permission to rebuild the defenses of the city. To them it was a major catastrophe. *Sanballat the Horonite* was governor of Samaria. This is substantiated by the Elephantine papyri, where his name is mentioned and also the names of his two sons.[23] He must have been an old man in 408 B.C. when this letter was written. With the discovery of the papyri at Wadi Daliyeh the sequence of the governors of Samaria became much clearer, namely, Sanballat I, Delaiah, Sanballat II, Hananiah, and Sanballat III.[24] In this case Sanballat I is meant. The names of his sons are formed with the theophoric element Yahu, which

21. Cf. R. Naumann, *Architektur Kleinasiens* (1955), pp. 51–52.

22. Cf., e.g., G. E. Wright, *Shechem*, p. 70.

23. *AP*, p. 113 (30:19). Sanballat is called governor *(pḥh)* of Samaria

24. Cf. F. M. Cross, "The Discovery of the Samaria Papyri," *BA* 26 (1963), p. 120 (repr. in E. F. Campbell and D. N. Freedman, eds., *The Biblical Archaeologist Reader 3* [1970], p. 237).

shows that he served the Lord, but in terms of a kind of religion that was unacceptable to pure Judaism. *Horonite* might mean that he came from one of the towns with the element Horon in it, but this is uncertain. *Tobiah the Ammonite official.* The term *official* is literally "servant," but this is problematic.[25] "Servant" refers here to his position in the Persian empire, namely, that of an official. *Ammonite* could refer to his role as official among the Ammonites,[26] or perhaps only to his ancestry. The arguments of Rudolph that Tobiah must have been an official in Samaria and that Ammonite refers to his ancestry are unacceptable. He is of the opinion that the officials mentioned in this verse were some of the governors of territories through which Nehemiah travelled to Judah. Nehemiah could not have passed through Ammon, however; hence Tobiah could not have been an Ammonite official.[27] This is reading too much into v. 10. Nowhere in this verse is it said that the two persons mentioned were governors of territories along Nehemiah's route. It is stated plainly that they had heard of his mission. It is probable, however, that Nehemiah travelled through the province of Samaria and gave his letter of introduction to Sanballat. From Sanballat the news travelled to Tobiah, and so within a short time the purpose of Nehemiah's mission was known.

D. NEHEMIAH'S INSPECTION OF JERUSALEM; REACTION OF THE OFFICIALS (2:11–20)

11 *After I arrived in Jerusalem and was there three days,*

12 *I arose in the night and a few men were with me, and I told no one what my God made clear to me to do for Jerusalem. There was no other animal with me except the one on which I rode.*

13 *In the dark I went out through Valley Gate to Jackal's Well and to Dung Gate. I inspected the walls of Jerusalem that were broken down and its gates that had been destroyed by fire.*

14 *Then I crossed over to Fountain Gate and King's Pool, and there was no place for my animal to pass.*

15 *In the dark I went along the valley and inspected the wall. I returned through Valley Gate and was back.*

16 *The officials did not know where I went and what I did. At that time I said nothing about the work to the Jews, the priests, the citizens, the officials, or anyone else.*

17 *Then I said to them: "You can see for yourselves the trouble we are*

25. Cf. C. C. McCown, "The 'Araq el-Emir and the Tobiads," *BA* 20 (1957), pp. 71–72.

26. Myers, *op. cit.*, p. 99; W. F. Albright, "Dedan," in *Geschichte und AT. Festschrift A. Alt* (Tübingen: 1953), p. 4.

27. Rudolph, *op. cit.*, p. 109.

in while Jerusalem lies in ruins and its gates burned. Come, let us rebuild the wall of Jerusalem and let us no longer be in disgrace."
18 *I told them that the favor of God was on me and also the words which the king had said to me. They said: "Come, let us rebuild!" So they encouraged themselves for the good cause.*
19 *When Sanballat the Horonite, Tobiah the Ammonite official, and Geshem the Arab heard about it, they scorned and despised us saying: "What are you busy doing? Are you rebelling against the king?"*
20 *I replied to them: "The God of heaven will grant us success. We, his servants, are going to build. You have no legal share or right nor a cultic memorial in Jerusalem."*

11–12 On the *three days* cf. the discussion of Ezra 8:15, 32. It refers here to three days of rest and obtaining information about the situation of Jerusalem. Nehemiah did his inspection secretly at night, accompanied by a few men whose names are not given. He used only one animal to ride on; more animals would have drawn the attention of the inhabitants of Jerusalem. His *animal* (*b^ehēmâ*) might have been an ass or horse, probably an ass,[1] because a snorting horse at night could have attracted attention. In the night while the whole of Jerusalem was soundly asleep, Nehemiah and his small escort sneaked out. The men with him might have been residents of Jerusalem who knew the city well and could direct Nehemiah on his way.

Why the secret mission? Guided by God, Nehemiah had already made plans, but he wanted to keep his thoughts to himself until he had inspected the position to see if his plans could be executed. Thus the people of Jerusalem had not been unduly informed, especially since some of his own people had contacts with the neighboring nations. If they knew about his plans, they could have sold his secret. He wanted to keep his enemies in the dark as long as possible concerning what he intended to do. They must not know what he was planning or else, as in the beginning of the reign of Artaxerxes, they might try to thwart his efforts. Thus Nehemiah was a clever and able man who knew his own people and his enemies.

13–15 Here we have one of the best topographical descriptions of Jerusalem. At the same time we must concede that it is very difficult to locate the places named in this description. All the attempts to locate the places that were made prior to the excavations of K. Kenyon can be left aside because it was erroneously presumed that the walls of the pre-

1. So Myers, *Ezra. Nehemiah,* p. 104; but cf. Rudolph, *Esra und Nehemia,* p. 110.

exilic city enclosed both the eastern and western hills.[2] Nothing is left of the walls and gates inspected by Nehemiah on the north and west sides. It is therefore impossible to locate them; they are buried under Herod's platform. The only place where one could make some progress with identification is on the eastern side. Kenyon is of the opinion that the King's Pool can be identified either with the Pool of Siloam or the modern Birket el-Hamra.[3] *The valley* into which he turned is definitely to be identified with the Kidron Valley. *There was no place for my animal to pass*. Excavations have shown a tumbled mass of stones which could have blocked the way of Nehemiah.[4] The ruins were worse here because the buildings were terraced down into the valley so that when the wall which kept the terraces in position was destroyed, all the buildings fell down the slope and created a wholesale devastation.[5] Archeological evidence reveals further that Nehemiah had decided to abandon that part of the town on the eastern slope and to build the wall on the eastern crest of the hill.[6] This is most revealing, and for the first time some certainty can be obtained about the actions of Nehemiah. It is to be accepted that the city in Nehemiah's time was smaller than the city of preexilic times.[7]

I inspected (from the Hebrew root *śbr*) occurs in the Qal form only in vv. 13 and 15 in the OT. In the Piel form it has the meaning "hope" or "expect."[8] In some of the old versions *śbr* in the Qal form is translated "inspect." This makes good sense in the context here.[9] The meaning, however, is not at all certain. *Jackal's Well* (Heb. *'ên hattannîn*). Some want to translate it "Dragon's Well."[10] This is also possible, because the Hebrew can mean either "jackal" or "dragon." The location of this well is disputed. It is generally identified with En-rogel,[11] but lately Braslavi has argued cogently for Siloam.[12]

16–18 Nehemiah's inspection was done in secret. He did not inform the Jewish officials of his intention. Cf. the discussion of v. 11.

2. Cf. K. Kenyon, *Jerusalem: Excavating 3000 Years of History* (New York: 1967), p. 107.
3. Cf. *ibid.*
4. *Ibid.*, pp. 107–108.
5. *Ibid.*, p. 108.
6. *Ibid.*
7. Cf. also M. Avi-Yonah in Y. Yadin, ed., *Jerusalem Revealed* (New Haven: 1976), p. 9.
8. Cf. Gesenius and Buhl, *Handwörterbuch*, p. 778.
9. Cf. for another view J. Heller, "Die abgeschlagene Mauer," *CV* 11 (1968), pp. 175–78.
10. Myers, *op. cit.*, p. 104.
11. *Ibid.*
12. Cf. J. Braslavi, "En-Tannin (Neh. 2:13)," *ErIs* 10 (1971), pp. 90–93.

The officials (Heb. *s^e^gānîm*) were probably representatives who were chosen by the congregation.[13] We are not informed about their task. That Nehemiah emphasized their role by referring to them first shows that they were regarded as very important. *Citizens* (Heb. *ḥôrîm*) might also be translated "noblemen." It is not a nobleman in the real sense of the word, however. It is a person with certain rights. "Citizen" would then be more to the point. *Anyone else* (lit. "and for the rest"). Nobody was informed. Some think that *anyone else* refers to the laborers who were going to rebuild the walls, but we cannot deduce this from the Hebrew.[14]

After Nehemiah had finished his inspection and made his decision about what to do, he summoned all the people enumerated in the preceding verse. Nothing is said of the timespan between vv. 16 and 17. It might have been the morning following his nighttime inspection. For the first time since his arrival in Jerusalem, Nehemiah disclosed the real purpose of his visit, namely, to rebuild the walls of Jerusalem. He stated that the Jews were in trouble because the defense walls were in ruins and the gates burned down. The skill and persuasion with which Nehemiah put his case comes out clearly in the use of the first person plural. After only a few days he had already identified himself completely with the cause of the inhabitants of Jerusalem. The defenseless city was a great danger to the Jews, especially with all the enemies around them. The word *trouble* (Heb. *hārā'â*) is a strong word. An evil could come upon them because of the poor state of the defenses. Nehemiah selected his words carefully in order to achieve the maximum effect on his audience.

He was also a man of action. His sketch of the poor state of the defenses was followed by an appeal to them to start the rebuilding of the wall. The reason for this is that they could no longer live in disgrace. We may presume that all the important cities around them had their defenses, but the city in the heartland of Judah, the religious center of the Jews, had nothing to protect it. It was a disgrace not only to the city, but to the Jews.

Nehemiah made it clear to them that he was not an upstart who wanted to bring them trouble by acting without permission. In the first place the favor of God was on him (cf. Ezra 7:6). God had sent him on this mission. It was religiously motivated. But in the second place he had also the permission of Artaxerxes to rebuild the walls. This gave him a double authority that was impossible to oppose. The credentials of Nehemiah were now on the table and nobody would be so bold as to gainsay

13. Widengren, *Israelite and Judaean History,* pp. 522–23, although not referring to the *s^e^gānîm*.

14. Cf. H. Kaupel, "Der Sinn von *'ōśēh hamm^e^lā'ḵâ* in Neh 2, 16," *Bibl* 21 (1940), pp. 40–44.

them. His speech had its favorable effect. The congregation undertook to do the work. *So they encouraged themselves for the good cause*—literally "and they strengthened their hands for the good thing." The sense of the Hebrew is not quite clear. It might also mean that they started preparing themselves for the work. Others think that they had already started on the work (JB) or now gave their support to the work.[15] Our translation is given in the light of the preceding expression, *Come, let us rebuild.* With these words they were strengthening their hands, that is to say, they were encouraging themselves.

19–20 When Nehemiah's intention became known to his adversaries, they started scorning the Jews. We must accept, as we shall see later on, that the enemies were well informed, quite probably by traitors in Jerusalem.[16] Their weapon was scorn and ridicule. The term used for *scorned* (Hiphil of *lāʿag*) is a strong word meaning "irreligiously deride." They did not expect much of the Jews, and they wanted to frighten them out of their wits. On Sanballat and Tobiah cf. the discussion of v. 10. A third enemy has been added here, namely, *Geshem the Arab.* This name is now also known from extrabiblical sources. Probably the same person is mentioned in Lihyanite and Aramaic inscriptions as "king of Kedar."[17] At the end of Iron Age II Arabs came into the Negev and Transjordan. The name Geshem is also found in a much later inscription at Beth-shearim.[18]

Two scornful questions were asked by the enemies, quite probably in writing, because in the next verse we have Nehemiah's reply. One of the questions was used to frighten the Jews. They are asked if they are rebelling against the king. This question has a history, because in Ezra 4:12 this argument was used to persuade Artaxerxes to stop the Jews from rebuilding the walls. At that state they were successful, but now they knew fairly certainly that Nehemiah had permission to do it. It was part of their tactics to dishearten the Jews. They had no higher authority to back them, only their own authority.

The reply of Nehemiah is clear. He did not appeal to his authority as granted to him by the king. They knew about it; cf. our discussion of v. 10. Nehemiah gave his religious motivation for this step and he made a careful choice of words. He spoke of *the God of heaven,* a well-known

15. Cf. the translation of Myers, *op. cit.,* p. 103.
16. Cf. also the discussion of W. Th. In der Smitten, "Nehemias Parteigänger," *BiOr* 29 (1972), pp. 155–57.
17. Cf. W. F. Albright, *The Archaeology of Palestine* (Baltimore: [4]1960), p. 145; Brockington, *Ezra, Nehemiah and Esther,* p. 110.
18. Cf. F. Vattioni, "L'inscription 177 de Beth Sheʿarim et le livre de Néhémie," *RB* 80 (1973), pp. 261–63.

expression in the Persian court. The Persian king knew that Nehemiah stood in the service of this God. In the name of God they were going to rebuild the walls. This objective should not be scorned.

Nehemiah concluded his reply with certain important legal remarks. Jerusalem was the city of the Jews and the enemies had no legal authority over it. *Legal share* (Heb. *ḥēleq*) refers to a share in the constellation of the Jewish nation. If somebody said that he had no share in a certain nation, he was declaring a revolt (cf. 2 Sam. 20:1; 1 K. 12:16).[19] This term with the negative thus means that they were not part of the Jews. *Right* (Heb. *ṣᵉḏāqâ*) refers to the fact that they had no legal right over Jerusalem. Nehemiah was appointed governor by the king, and what he was doing was none of their business. *A cultic memorial* (Heb. *zikkārôn*) is a difficult term. It quite probably refers to the cult in Jerusalem.[20] They had no right over the cultic practices (cf. Ezra 4:3). Both Sanballat and Tobiah were also serving the Lord, but in an illegitimate way. They had no jurisdiction over the pure religion of the exiles. With this reply Nehemiah clearly drew the dividing line between himself and his opponents.

E. WORK ON THE WALL (3:1–32)

1 *Then Eliashib the high priest and his companions the priests built the Sheep Gate and consecrated it. They put its doors in. As far as the Tower of Hundred and up to the Tower of Hananel they consecrated it.*

2 *Next to him the men of Jericho built. Next to them Zaccur the son of Imri built.*

3 *The descendants of Hassenaah built the Fish Gate; they laid its beams and put in its doors, bolts, and bars.*

4 *Next to them Meremoth the son of Uriah, the son of Hakkoz, did restoration. Next to him Meshullam the son of Berechiah, the son of Meshezabel, did restoration. Next to him Zadok the son of Baana did restoration.*

5 *Next to him the people of Tekoa did restoration, though their magnates did not submit themselves to the work of their lords.*

6 *Joiada the son of Paseah and Meshullam the son of Besodeiah did restoration on Jeshanah Gate; they laid its beams and put in its doors, bolts, and bars.*

7 *Next to them Melatiah of Gibeon and Jadon of Meronoth as well as the men of Gibeon and Mizpah did restoration up to the quarters of the governor of Trans-Euphrates.*

19. Brockington, *op. cit.*, p. 110.

20. Cf. W. Schottroff, *"Gedenken" im Alten Orient und im AT.* WMANT 15 (Neukirchen: 1964), p. 314. So already F. Horst, *RGG* II, p. 1405.

8 *Next to them Uzziel the son of Harhaiah of the goldsmiths did restoration. Next to him Hananiah of the perfumers did restoration. They repaired Jerusalem to the Broad Wall.*

9 *Next to them Rephaiah the son of Hur, ruler of half of the territory of Jerusalem, did restoration.*

10 *Next to him Jedaiah the son of Harumaph did restoration opposite his own house. Next to him Hattush the son of Hashabneiah did restoration.*

11 *Malchijah the son of Harim and Hasshub the son of Pahath-moab did restoration on a second section and on Oven Tower.*

12 *Next to him Shallum the son of Hallohesh, ruler of half of the territory of Jerusalem, did restoration, he and men from the small towns.*

13 *Hanun and the inhabitants of Zanoah did restoration on the Valley Gate. They built it and put in its doors, bolts, and bars, and also a thousand cubits of the wall up to the Dung Gate.*

14 *Malchijah the son of Rechab, ruler of the territory of Beth-haccherem, did restoration on the Dung Gate. He built it and put in its doors, bolts, and bars.*

15 *Shallum the son of Col-hozeh, ruler of the territory of Mizpah, did restoration on the Fountain Gate. He built it, covered it, and put in its doors, bolts, and bars, and also the wall of Shelah Pool at King's Garden as far as the steps that go down from the city of David.*

16 *After him Nehemiah the son of Azbuk, ruler of half of the territory of Beth-zur, did restoration to the point opposite the tombs of David and to the Artificial Pool and to Hero House.*

17 *After him the Levites did restoration: Rehum the son of Bani; next to him Hashabiah, ruler of half of the territory of Keilah, did restoration on behalf of his own territory.*

18 *After him their companions did restoration: Bavvai (Binnui) the son of Henadad, ruler of half of the territory of Keilah;*

19 *next to him Ezer the son of Jeshua, ruler of Mizpah, did restoration on a second section opposite the slope of the Armory at the Angle.*

20 *After him Baruch the son of Zabbai did (zealous) restoration on a second section, from the Angle as far as the door of the house of Eliashib the high priest.*

21 *After him Meremoth the son of Uriah, the son of Hakkoz, did restoration on a second section, from the door of the house of Eliashib as far as the end of Eliashib's house.*

22 *After him the priests of the rural area did restoration.*

23 *After them Benjamin and Hasshub did restoration opposite their house. After them Azariah the son of Maaseiah, the son of Ananiah, did restoration beside his house.*

24 *After him Binnui the son of Henadad did restoration on a second section, from the house of Azariah to the Angle and the Corner.*
25 *(After him) Palal the son of Uzai (did restoration) opposite the Angle and the Tower projecting from the upper house of the king at the Court of the Guard. After him Pedaiah the son of Parosh*
26 *and the temple servants who stay at Ophel (did restoration) to a point opposite the Water Gate on the east and the projecting tower.*
27 *After them the people of Tekoa did restoration on a second section opposite the great projecting tower to the wall of Ophel.*
28 *From the Horse Gate onward the priests did restoration, each before his house.*
29 *After them Zadok the son of Immer did restoration before his house. After him Shemaiah the son of Shecaniah, the keeper of the East Gate.*
30 *After him Hananiah the son of Shelemiah and Hanum the sixth son of Zalaph did restoration on a second section. After him Meshullam the son of Berechiah did restoration opposite his living place.*
31 *After him Malchijah, one of the goldsmiths, did restoration as far as the house of the temple servants and of the merchants opposite the Muster Gate and up to the upper room of the corner.*
32 *Between the upper room of the corner and the Sheep Gate the goldsmiths and merchants did restoration.*

As we have said in the previous chapter, the identifications of the wall and defenses prior to the excavations of K. Kenyon can be regarded as antiquated. The city of Nehemiah was much smaller than accepted previously;[1] it was limited to the eastern hill or ridge and only to its summit. The northern extension of Solomon was also included in this postexilic city. It is somewhat uncertain when the northern part of the western hill was included in the city. On account of this, Kenyon is of the opinion that it is a waste of time to try to correlate the biblical description of Nehemiah's northern and western walls with the topographical features.[2] It is amazing how little has been discovered in Jerusalem from the Persian period.[3] The description of Neh. 3 can only be corroborated to a certain extent with archeological discoveries insofar as it mentions the eastern wall. The restorations of the Valley Gate, Dung Gate, and Fountain Gate fit the archeological evidence, which shows that at the central valley the preexilic city was still confined to the summit. We may therefore presume that the ruins of the wall and gates could be recognized easily.[4] On the eastern side the biblical description, if closely inspected, shows a clear correlation with

1. Cf. Kenyon, *Jerusalem,* pp. 108ff.
2. *Ibid.*, p. 110. Cf. also M. Avi-Yonah in *Jerusalem Revealed,* p. 22.
3. Cf. N. Avigad in *Jerusalem Revealed,* p. 44.
4. Kenyon, *op. cit.,* p. 110.

the archeological discoveries. In Neh. 3 it is stated clearly that the wall was built opposite the house of, for example, Eliashib. Nothing is said of the old wall or the gates. Archeological evidence shows that the preexilic city on the eastern slope was abandoned and that Nehemiah had built a new wall along the eastern ridge of the eastern hill. This wall was built solidly, about eight feet thick. It was a rough construction, however, quite probably done rapidly.[5] This is an excellent example of the corroboration of archeological results with the biblical description.

It is probable that this description was made from archival material at the author's disposal. It is a careful description giving important detail of which much is today unintelligible. The whole plan of reconstruction was worked out thoroughly. About forty sections of unequal length were chosen and each section allotted to certain persons. Nehemiah was an excellent organizer to divide up all this work and to ensure that the work was carried out properly. We may presume that the work started immediately, because of the deplorable state in which the inhabitants lived with an open city around them.

Another important piece of evidence from this chapter concerns the social structure of the Jews in the time of Nehemiah. Some of the professional groups or guilds also partook in the building operations. Three different groups are mentioned, namely, the goldsmiths, the perfumers, and the merchants or businessmen. This shows that certain guilds existed and that commercial activities took place. In the social stratification they formed the middle class. We must realize that they were not the only professional guilds, because a community without bakers or potters is unthinkable. These three guilds, however, are mentioned in connection with work which was time-consuming and possibly expensive. Two reasons may account for only these three groups being mentioned. First, their regular work was of a more leisurely type, and therefore they could spare time to do the work on the wall. The bakers' guild had to provide bread to the people and could not be occupied by another kind of work. Second, the members of these three professions might have been more wealthy than those of the other professions.[6] They could thus easily afford to do the work.

We must accept the probability that a complete list is not given here. We can derive this from the fact that in the list it is stated that a certain person worked on a second section, but the first section of his work is nowhere mentioned, e.g., Malchijah in v. 11. It was obviously not the

5. *Ibid.*, p. 111.
6. For the professions cf. R. de Vaux, *Ancient Israel* I, pp. 76–79. A thorough diachronical description of Israelite and Jewish professions is still to be made.

intention of the author to supply us with a complete list, but to give an overall picture of the restoration of the wall.[7] He might have felt that it was not necessary to burden his readers with details which were well known to them.

1 It is important to note that Nehemiah started his list with Eliashib the high priest. The most important person is named first. Nehemiah wanted to show that he received the cooperation of the high priest and thus also that of the other priests. Eliashib was the grandson of Jeshua, the high priest in the time of Zerubbabel. The work of the priest was concentrated on the northeastern part of the wall, because it was close to the temple. *Consecrated it.* Some scholars want to emend *qiddᵉšûhû* to *qērûhû* (cf. v. 6),[8] "put in beams." If we accept this emendation, we must also accept that *qiddᵉšûhû* later in this verse is a scribal error.[9] However, two scribal errors of the same word in the same sentence seem unlikely. It is noteworthy that this word is only used in connection with the work of the high priest and his companions. It shows that after the buildings were finished, they were consecrated to the Lord.

2 *Next to him* (Heb. *wᵉ'al-yāḏô*). This expression is used up to v. 12 and then once in v. 19. From v. 16 onward, with the exception of v. 19, "after him" *('aḥᵉrāyw)* is used. The third person suffix attached to *yaḏ* is only sometimes used in accordance with the number of the preceding persons. It is difficult to explain this phenomenon. Some scholars want to emend the text to fit in with the number of persons to which it refers. *The men of Jericho.* Because no names are given, some think that the genealogy of these men was not known.[10] In vv. 5 and 27, in the same manner, reference is made to the people of Tekoa. Other towns mentioned are Gibeon (v. 7), Mizpah (v. 7), Zanoah (v. 13), Beth-haccherem (v. 14), Beth-zur (v. 16), and Keilah (v. 17). In some of these cases the names of the leaders are given. That no names are supplied in a few cases can be ascribed to omission, because a complete description is not given, as we have seen already.

3 *They laid its beams* (Heb. *qērûhû*). This is a term from the root *qrh* in the Piel that refers to the putting up of a roof or the finishing of a house (Ps. 104:3). The finishing of a house would mean that the roof is finished. *They laid its beams* would then mean that they put the finishing touches to their construction. This explanation is substantiated by the fol-

7. Myers, *Ezra. Nehemiah*, pp. 112–13.

8. Rudolph, *Esra und Nehemia*, p. 114; Myers, *op. cit.*, p. 107; Brockington, *Ezra, Nehemiah and Esther*, p. 111 (the latter wants to read *qērᵉšûhû*).

9. Rudolph, *op. cit.*, p. 114.

10. Cf., e.g., *ibid.*, p. 111.

lowing expression: *put in its doors, bolts, and bars*. After the construction was finished, the doors were hung and their accessories put in.

4 *Did restoration* (Heb. *heḥezîq*). The term is also translated "repaired," "reconstructed," or "built." It is clear that they worked on the destroyed wall and gates. Actually they were doing restoration work. *Meremoth the son of Uriah*—cf. the discussion of Ezra 8:33. He is the one person we can identify as known to both Ezra and Nehemiah.

5 *Though their magnates did not submit themselves to the work of their lords*—literally "and their magnates[11] did not bring their necks in service of their lords [or "the Lord"]." It is an enigmatic expression. Who were the magnates? They might have been representatives elected by the people. This verse shows that not all the Jews were enthusiastic about the rebuilding of Jerusalem's defenses. *Tekoa* to the southeast of Jerusalem in an arid area was open country and could easily be attacked by Geshem the Arab. Was this the reason for their unwillingness to help?

6 *Jeshanah Gate*—also translated "the gate of the new quarter" (JB), but Jeshanah was a town,[12] and the gate might have pointed in the direction of the town (like the present Jaffa Gate in the direction of Jaffa).

7 *The quarters of the governor of Trans-Euphrates*. The Hebrew is not clear. The problem is the term *kissē'*, "seat." It could be taken figuratively, meaning "authority," and then translated "those who were under jurisdiction of the governor." Or, "the seat" may refer to the house in which the governor resided while visiting Jerusalem. The former interpretation leaves us with the question, Why should the author single out the men of Gibeon and Mizpah as under the jurisdiction of the governor of Trans-Euphrates, and not all the other people mentioned in this chapter? All of them were under his jurisdiction. It is thus better to accept the latter interpretation that it refers to the seat of the governor in Jerusalem.

It is clear from the whole chapter that the author wanted to refer to certain sections of the wall that were restored. The men of Gibeon and Mizpah did restoration as far as the residence of the governor. But it must be noted that the preposition *le* is used instead of *'aḏ*, the preposition generally used in the rest of the constructions. If our surmise is correct, it is interesting to note that the governor of Trans-Euphrates had a residence in Jerusalem. This would mean that he used the residence while visiting Judah, one of his minor provinces.

8 On the goldsmiths and perfumers cf. our discussion above. *They repaired* (Heb. *wayya'azeḇû*). This term is from the second Hebrew root

11. Widengren's translation, *Israelite and Judaean History*, p. 522.
12. Myers, *op. cit.*, p. 110. Cf. esp. F. M. Abel, *Géographie de la Palestine* II, p. 364.

of *'zb* (cf. also Exod. 23:5). In Ugaritic *'db* has the meaning "to prepare" or "to make."[13] In the context here and in accordance with its usage in Northwest Semitic, the verb means "repair." *Broad Wall.* By emending the text to *hārᵉḥōḇ* some want to translate it "Wall of the Square" (JB). In favor of this emendation is the reference in Neh. 8:16 to a square at the Ephraim Gate. The Broad Wall may only refer to a special reinforced wall for better defense at that particular place.

9 *Half of the territory of Jerusalem* (Heb. for "territory" is *peleḵ*). The term *peleḵ* is used here and in vv. 12, 14, 15, 16, 17, and 18. It refers to Jerusalem, Beth-haccherem, Mizpah, Beth-zur, and Keilah. What does *peleḵ* mean? It is usually translated "district" and it is then accepted that it refers to the different districts in the province of Judah.[14] The term is probably a cognate or loanword from the Akk. *pilku.*[15] It denotes a delimited area, a territory. It is thus the adjacent countryside of a town or city. In Nehemiah's time these areas already had rulers or magistrates. Thus the province of Judah was subdivided into smaller governmental areas. The bigger territories, like Jerusalem and Keilah, had two rulers. It is also clear that the province of Judah consisted of a small area, stretching to the south not even as far as Hebron and to the north barely as far as Bethel.[16] It was a small extent of territory from which Nehemiah recruited his volunteers.

10 *Opposite his own house* might refer here to the work on the eastern wall on the slope which was not restored, but newly built. Cf. our discussion above. The same Hebrew root that was used in v. 4 for restoration, *ḥzq,* however, is used here as well. The verb actually means "strengthen" and could refer to any kind of building activity, although the impression is created that restoration is meant.

11 *A second section.* Heb. *middâ šēnîṯ* denotes that the first section is already restored and that they are working on a second section. Malchijah's name, however, is not associated with the previous work; it is nowhere mentioned. As we have seen above, the description of the work in this chapter is not complete. Some want to translate it "another section," hence not referring to a second section of work by the same people.[17] But there are cases in which the same person is mentioned twice, e.g., Meremoth in vv. 4 and 21, and in the second instance it is said that he did

13. Cf. *WUS,* p. 227. Cf. also C. G. Tuland, "*'zb* in Nehemiah 3:8," *AUSS* 5 (1967), pp. 158–180.
14. Rudolph, *op. cit.,* p. 115.
15. For the meaning in Akkadian cf. *AHW* II, p. 863. Cf. also M. Dietrich and O. Loretz, *UF* 4 (1972), pp. 165ff.
16. Cf. the discussion of S. Herrmann, *A History of Israel in OT Times,* p. 315.
17. Brockington, *op. cit.,* pp. 114–15.

restoration on a second section. This is enough proof to interpret the Hebrew expression as "second section."

12 *Men from the small towns.* This phrase is indeed difficult to explain. In Hebrew we have *ûḇenôṯāyw,* "and his daughters." Most scholars take the Hebrew at face value and accept that the extraordinary fact is stated here that Shallum's daughters helped him.[18] Others want to emend the text and read "sons" (e.g., JB).[19] The term *bānôṯ* may refer in Hebrew to the smaller towns around a city. The problem with this explanation is that the third-person suffix on *bānôṯ* is masculine and not feminine. Had it been feminine, it would have referred to Jerusalem and then it could definitely have meant smaller towns.[20] The context, however, is very important here. Shallum is called the ruler of half of the territory of Jerusalem. He is placed in the center of argumentation. In such a case it would not be strange to call the villages in his territory *his* daughters. It can thus be explained without changing the text. If we accept that *bānôṯ* refers to his own daughters, it would mean that a ruler of his importance could not muster enough volunteers for the work, a strange situation indeed for a ruler of half of the territory of Jerusalem.

13 *Zanoah* lies southwest of Jerusalem. A *thousand cubits* are approximately 1500 feet. This is a large section of the wall. It might have been easy to repair, but we must also take into account that the inhabitants of Zanoah worked on it. They might have been a large group. *Dung Gate*—the Hebrew has an obvious scribal error here, viz., *hāšapôṯ* instead of *hā'ašpôṯ* as in v. 14.

14 *Beth-haccherem* was situated a few miles south of Jerusalem.[21]

15 *Mizpah* was situated approximately 8 miles north of Jerusalem.[22] *Covered it.* The Hebrew *wîṭalelennû,* from the root *ṭll,* is a hapax legomenon in the OT. In Palmyrene Aramaic it means "to cover."[23] Here in Hebrew it might mean that they had put a roof on the Fountain Gate. Then this term is a close parallel to the Piel of *qrh*; cf. our discussion above. *Shelah Pool.* Some want to identify it with Shiloah or Siloam.[24] *King's Garden* was possibly situated at the southern end of the Kidron

18. Pelaia, *Esdra e Neemia,* p. 146; Rudolph, *op. cit.,* p. 117; Brockington, *op. cit.,* p. 115.
19. The view of Vincent; cf. Pelaia, *op. cit.,* p. 146.
20. Cf. the discussion of Rudolph, *op. cit.,* p. 117. Cf. also Coggins, *The Books of Ezra and Nehemiah,* p. 83.
21. Cf. Y. Aharoni, *IEJ* 6 (1956), pp. 152–56. He is of the opinion that it could have been Ramat Rachel, situated a few miles south of Jerusalem.
22. Cf. F. M. Abel, *op. cit.,* pp. 388–390.
23. Cf. *DISO,* p. 101.
24. Brockington, *op. cit.,* p. 116.

Valley. The *city of David* was a limited and small city, stretching from a little northwest of the Gihon Spring on the eastern hill to the southern slope of this hill.[25]

16 *Nehemiah* refers here to another Nehemiah. *Beth-zur* was situated about 13 miles south of Jerusalem. The *tombs of David* have not been discovered yet, but they might have been near the King's Garden.[26] *Artificial Pool,* Heb. *habbᵉrēḵâ hā'ᵃśûyâ,* "the pool which is made (by men)." *Hero House (bêṯ haggibbōrîm)* might refer to the heroes of David (cf. 2 Sam. 23:8ff.). *On behalf of his own territory.* Hashabiah did restoration not as a Levite, but as the ruler of his territory. It is of interest that a Levite had been promoted to a ruler of a territory. Is this Hashabiah to be identified with the Levite in Ezra 8:19?

18–24 *Bavvai (Binnui).* The name Bavvai is unknown in Hebrew. It is probably a scribal error for Binnui[27] (cf. v. 24, where Binnui is called "the son of Henadad," as Bavvai is in this verse). Verse 24 also states that he had restored a second section, implying that he had already worked on a previous section, perhaps the section mentioned in v. 18. *Keilah* was situated about 15 miles southwest of Jerusalem (cf. also v. 17). *Ruler of Mizpah.* In v. 15 Shallum is mentioned as ruler of the territory of Mizpah. Here in v. 19 it is said that Ezer was ruler of Mizpah. The difference lies in the mention of territory in v. 15. Shallum was ruler of the whole territory around the town, while Ezer was only ruler of the town of Mizpah. *The Angle* (v. 19) might have been a sharp turn in the wall. *The Corner* (v. 24) is clearly distinguished from the Angle. *Did (zealous) restoration* (v. 20). The term in parentheses is a translation of the Heb. *heḥᵉrâ*. It means "heated." It might have been dittography of *heḥᵉzîq,* "did restoration," which stands after it,[28] or of *'aḥᵃrāyw,* "after him," which stands immediately before it.[29] In v. 20 with the mention of Eliashib's house we can reconstruct to a certain extent the building operations on the eastern wall, thanks to archeological results. Cf. our discussion above. *Of the rural area* (v. 22, Heb. *'anšê hakkikkār*) refers to a circuit around Jerusalem (cf. 12:28). It is thus not the city itself, but the rural area around it. *Opposite their house* (v. 23)—did they possess the same house? Was it a semidetached dwelling? Or must we take *house* collectively? The last possibility is perhaps to be preferred.

25 It is conceivable that in v. 25 "after him" and "did restoration" were somehow omitted. We cannot explain it. These words may have been

25. Cf. Kenyon, *op. cit.,* pp. 28ff., and the plan of Jerusalem on p. 29.
26. Myers, *op. cit.,* p. 114.
27. Rudolph, *op. cit.,* p. 118; Myers, *op. cit.,* p. 111.
28. Brockington, *op. cit.,* p. 117.
29. Rudolph, *op. cit.,* p. 118.

left out elliptically since it becomes obvious they were repeated in the previous verses. But why then are they repeated in v. 25b? *Upper house of the king* might have been an alternative residence of the king in preexilic times. *Court of the Guard* is mentioned in Jer. 32:2.

26 *The temple servants who stay at Ophel* is regarded by some scholars as a gloss which has crept in from 11:21.[30] But we have no textual evidence to delete it. The *Water Gate* was close to the Gihon Spring. This gate was quite probably part of the wall, and thus not outside the city, as Rudolph claims.[31] Rudolph has a problem with the expression *opposite the Water Gate*. It is likely that we have here at the northeastern part of the wall a turn in the wall so that a section of the wall might be regarded as opposite the Water Gate. *Projecting tower*. It is not clear whether the projecting tower of v. 25 is to be identified with the ones mentioned in vv. 26 and 27.

28 *Horse Gate* is problematical. In 2 K. 11:16 and 2 Chr. 23:15 it is mentioned in connection with the area between the palace and the temple. Jer. 31:40, however, refers to it as a city gate, the same as here in v. 28.[32] This problem is not yet solved, but the restoration of an inner gate would seem strange. We accept that the Horse Gate was a gate in the city wall,[33] probably one of the main thoroughfares of the city.

29 *Keeper of the East Gate*. The East Gate was one of the temple gates (Ezek. 40:6, 10). Work was not done on this gate, but the text only states that the keeper did restoration on a section of the city wall.

30 *Sixth son*. This is unusual, but we may deduce from this reference that Hanum was Zalaph's own son, while in most cases "son of . . ." refers to the family name. *His living place*, Heb. *niškāṯô*, can also be translated "chamber" and might refer to a chamber in the temple[34] (cf. 12:44 and 13:7). For the *goldsmiths* and *merchants* cf. the previous discussion.

31 *The house of the temple servants*. In v. 26 it is stated that the temple servants are living opposite Ophel. It is thus another house that is mentioned here. This may have been a house which they occupied while doing duty at the temple. *Of the merchants*. The house of the merchants might have been a business house where they stayed while in Jerusalem.[35] This house was near the temple where important business was done in the

30. *Ibid.*, p. 120; Brockington, *op. cit.*, p. 118.
31. Rudolph, *op. cit.*, p. 119. But cf. Myers, *op. cit.*, p. 115.
32. Cf. K. Galling, *PJB* (1931), p. 52; Myers, *op. cit.*, p. 115.
33. Rudolph, *op. cit.*, p. 119.
34. Brockington, *op. cit.*, p. 119; Rudolph, *op. cit.*, p. 119.
35. For the role of the merchant in the Old Babylonian times cf. W. F. Leemans, *The Old-Babylonian Merchant* (Leiden: 1950).

olden days. *Muster Gate,* Heb. *šaʿar hammipqāḏ,* might also be translated "Watch Gate" (JB), though some take it with the LXX as a name, "Miphkad Gate" (GNB). The Hebrew root *pqd* has a large semantic field. In Jer. 52:11, e.g., we have *bêṯ happᵉquḏôṯ* from the same root in the meaning "prison."[36] It is thus not impossible that here in v. 31 the same idea prevailed, namely, "Prison Tower." It seems to be more likely, however, that at this Tower the people or men were mustered for conscription.[37]

32 *Sheep Gate.* The description of the restoration starts with the Sheep Gate in v. 1 and now, with the completion of the project, ends at the Sheep Gate. The full circle of activities has thus been completed.

F. SAMARITAN OPPOSITION (3:33–4:17 [Eng. 4:1–23])

1. Reaction of the Enemies (3:33–35 [Eng. 4:1–3])

33 (4:1) *When Sanballat heard that we were rebuilding the wall, he became very angry and heaped scorn on the Jews.*
34 (4:2) *He said in the presence of his companions and the army of the Samaritans: "What are these miserable Jews doing? Are they indeed repairing (the walls) for themselves? Are they going to offer there? Can they complete the work today? Can they revive the stones from the rubbish heaps where they were burned?"*
35 (4:3) *Tobiah the Ammonite said at his side: "Yes, what are they building! If a fox jumps (against it), their stone wall will have a breach."*

In the Hebrew Bible these verses continue as part of ch. 3. In the different translations, however, these verses start with ch. 4. In the Hebrew Bible, with these verses as part of ch. 3, the reaction of the enemies is directly connected to the building activities. There is a kind of progression in the reaction of the enemies. In these verses their reaction is still confined to scorn and ridicule, while in 4:1–2 (Eng. 7–8) they have decided on hostile action.

33–35 (4:1–3) When this rumor reached Sanballat, the Jews had actually just started on their project. Sanballat is mentioned first every time. He is thus designated as the main instigator of trouble against the Jews. *We are building* is the participle (Heb. *bônîm*), which means that the rebuilding was in progress, that they were busy working on it. *He became very angry*—literally "he was angry and very enraged" (Heb.

36. Cf. M. Greenberg, *IDB* III, p. 892.
37. Cf. E. A. Speiser, "Census and Ritual Expiation in Mari and Israel," in *Oriental and Biblical Studies* (Philadelphia: 1967), pp. 175ff., for the place of *pqd* in its Near Eastern setting.

wayyiḥar lô wayyiḵ'as harbēh), which we take as a hendiadys. The different moods of Sanballat in Nehemiah are described in an interesting fashion. In 2:10 the root *r''* describes his indignation; in 2:19 the roots *l'g* and *bzh* describe his scorn and ridicule, and here the roots *ḥrh* and *k's* sketch the intensification of the atmosphere. It is the anger of people who were uncertain what to expect or what to do. They could not complain about it to the Persian king, because Nehemiah did the work with his permission. They were helpless spectators of events of which they did not approve. *Heaped scorn on the Jews.* This translation is an attempt to give expression to *l'g + 'l,* while in 2:19 it is *l'g + lᵉ*.

The army of the Samaritans (Heb. *ḥêl šōmᵉrōn*). Some think that *ḥayil* does not refer to an army, because Samaria was not a military colony.[1] It is possible that the term *ḥayil* has a wider connotation and denotes the lords *(Oberschicht)* who were in command of Samaria, but this does not exclude the military.[2] We must recognize that Samaria had an army for defensive purposes for aiding the Persian king if necessary. Cf. the discussion of Ezra 4:23.

Sanballat addressed his nobles and his army, possibly to prepare them for future action. It was the beginning of a propaganda campaign against the Jews. He used five questions, some of them subtly phrased to require a negative answer. The audience could reach only one conclusion: These Jews were good for nothing. *Miserable Jews* (Heb. *hayyᵉhûḏîm hā'ᵃmēlālîm*). The Hebrew root *'mll* is occasionally used in the OT to denote the fading or withering of a plant (Isa. 16:8; 24:7; etc.). It is also used of people without any hope (Isa. 19:8; Hos. 4:3). It is employed here in Nehemiah to ridicule the Jews. They are a withering lot of people. How could they do anything worthwhile! *Repairing* is Heb. *ya'azᵉḇû,* from the second root of *'zb;* cf. our discussion of 3:8. *For themselves*—the *lᵉ* is taken as *dativus ethicus*.[3] *To offer there.* It is not quite certain what is meant by this expression. It might refer to a foundation offering,[4] or to an offering of thanksgiving for the completion of the task. The consecration of 3:1 might have been in the form of an offering. *Complete the work today* or "complete the work in one day." With this kind of remark Sanballat wanted to ridicule their ability to complete their work in a short time. Furthermore, they are unable to revive[5] the stones in the ruins to new life, to build them in a new construction. At the back of his mind might have been the thought that the stones blackened with fire were cursed

1. Myers, *Ezra. Nehemiah,* p. 123; Rudolph, *Esra und Nehemia,* p. 121.
2. Alt, *KS* II, pp. 322ff.
3. GKC, § 119s.
4. Brockington, *Ezra, Nehemiah and Esther,* p. 120.
5. Cf. also the inscription of Yehimilk where *ḥwy* is used to denote a renovation of buildings in Byblos. Cf. *KAI* II, p. 6.

and could not be reused as building material. Tobiah was obviously a close ally and friend of Sanballat, because at this important meeting he was at Sanballat's side. His ridicule is clothed in a beautiful image. What kind of construction are they erecting? It would be useless. If a fox jumps against it, it will show a breach. *Will have a breach* (Heb. *pāraṣ*). The quality of the construction will be so poor that even a touch of a fox's paw will create a breach in the wall. We must keep in mind that in warfare a breach in a city wall could be made only after prolonged efforts with siege weapons. The wall of the Jews will be so poorly built that a fox can break it. This is the height of scorn and ridicule combined with contempt.

2. *Nehemiah's Prayer; Continuation of the Work (3:36–38 [Eng. 4:4–6])*

36 (4:4) *"Hear, our God, how we are despised. Turn their taunt down on their own heads and give them over as plunder in a land of captivity.*
37 (4:5) *Because they have insulted the builders, please do not forgive their iniquities and sins. Let it not be blotted out."*
38 (4:6) *And so we rebuilt the wall and the whole wall was joined together up to half its height, because the people were inspired by the work.*

36–38 (4:4–6) When he heard about the scorn of the enemies and especially their ridicule heaped on the builders, Nehemiah prayed to God. It is a prayer of vindication, because the enemies despised the work which was being done in the name of God. There was no doubt that God inspired the work and that it was his will to carry it out. Opposition to the work was opposition to God.[1] The prayer for vindication is couched in strong language.[2] *Turn their taunt down on their own heads,* i.e., bring on them what they have wished for us. We may presume that they on their part will be scorned and ridiculed. Heb. *ḥerpâ, taunt,* can also be translated "reproach," "ridicule," "sneer," or "insult." It has a wide variety of meanings. *Taunt,* however, seems to be the best translation here. The next phrase asks the Lord to deliver Sanballat and his companions to their enemies so that they could become plunder or booty and could be taken into captivity or exile, i.e., they should be taken from their country and transferred to another country. *Plunder* is Heb. *bizzâ*, from the root *bzz,* but some want to derive it from the root *bûz* in the meaning "contempt" or "shame" (JB). Cf. also the word *bûzâ* in this same verse and *bûz* in 2:19. The term *bizzâ* is well attested in postexilic OT Hebrew, however (e.g., 2 Chr. 14:13 [Eng. 14]; 25:13; Esth. 9:10, 15, 16). The use of *bûzâ* and *bizzâ* in such

1. Myers, *Ezra. Nehemiah,* p. 125.

2. It may have close relationship with the psalms of the accused; cf. U. Kellermann, *Nehemia,* pp. 84–88.

a connection might be wordplay, namely, we are despised *(bûzâ),* but they will become plunder *(bizzâ). Because they have insulted the builders* stands in the Hebrew at the end, but could be changed around easily to the beginning to emphasize it. This phrase is not clear because of *l^eneged* between the verb "insult" and "builders." Thus some hold the opinion that "insult" from the root *k's* should mean "provoke anger" and that God is the object. The translation is then "for they have provoked thee to anger before the builders."[3] But if we take it literally, "For they insulted before the builders,"[4] our translation becomes obvious. *Forgive their iniquities.* The Hebrew for "forgive" is from the root *ksh,* "to cover." To cover iniquities and sins is to forgive them, to forget about them. The same thought of covering up sins and blotting them out occurs in Jer. 18:23.[5] If it is a citation, it is made freely, not word for word. We should not make too much of the similarities between this verse in Nehemiah and that of Jeremiah. It could have been merely common usage in those times. Nehemiah requested the Lord not to forgive the enemies their sins, committed by deriding the abilities of the builders, not to blot them out, wash them off, or sweep them away. The iniquities and sins were committed by sneering at the work God had commanded. The prayer was thus not vindictive because the Jews were insulted, but because God's work was ridiculed. Thus the prayer was religiously and not nationalistically motivated.

In v. 38 (Eng. 4:6) Nehemiah states that the work went ahead in spite of the insults from the enemies. From this we may conclude that the ridicule was meant to stop the building activities but was not successful. *The whole wall was joined together up to half its height.* The Hebrew is not as clear as this translation. The problem is with *half its height.* The Hebrew states only "up to its half" or "to its middle." This could also refer to half of the length of the wall, or even half of the width.[6] It seems better to take it as height, however, and to accept that the whole wall was built up to half its height when Sanballat and his friends heard about it.[7] The speed with which it was done was due to the inspiration of the builders for their task. *The people were inspired by the work*—literally "and the heart of the people was to do the work"; their heart was set on it. "The heart of

3. Brockington, *Ezra, Nehemiah and Esther,* p. 121.
4. Rudolph, *Esra und Nehemia,* p. 123.
5. *Ibid.,* p. 121.
6. Myers, *op. cit.,* p. 123.
7. Rudolph, *op. cit.,* p. 123, wants to delete *kl,* "whole," because he regards it unlikely that at a certain stage the whole wall, of which the height of the ruins varied, could reach the same height. But we must keep in mind that in the spoken language such expressions are common. It is not an exact description, but conveys the general idea.

the people"—we are reading here *lēḇ hā'ām* with some manuscripts[8] instead of *lēḇ lā'ām,* "the heart for the people."

3. Action Planned by the Enemies and Measures Taken by Nehemiah (4:1–17 [Eng. 7–23])

1 (7) *When Sanballat, Tobiah, the Arabs, the Ammonites, and the Ashdodites heard that the walls of Jerusalem were mended and that the breaches were filled up, they became very angry.*

2 (8) *All of them conspired to go and fight against Jerusalem and to create confusion.*

3 (9) *But we prayed to our God and put out a watch against them day and night.*

4 (10) *Judah said: "The strength of the carriers is failing and the rubbish is too much, we are not able to build the wall."*

5 (11) *Our enemies said: "They will not know or become aware of it until we come among them and kill them, and so put a stop to the work."*

6 (12) *When the Jews who lived near them came, they said ten times to us: "From everywhere they are coming against us."*

7 (13) *Then, at the open spaces inside the wall, away from the lowest places, I placed the people according to their families, with their swords, spears, and bows.*

8 (14) *I inspected them and said to the important citizens, the leaders, and the ordinary people: "Be not afraid of them. Think of the Lord who is great and terrible. Defend your brothers, your sons, your daughters, your wives, and your homes."*

9 (15) *When our enemies heard that it became known to us, God frustrated their plans. So all of us went back to the wall, each one to his work.*

10 (16) *From that day on, half of my men were working on the project and the other half were holding spears, shields, bows, and breastplates. The leaders (stood) behind the house of Judah*

11 (17) *who were rebuilding the wall. The carriers carrying the burden were doing the work with their one hand and with the other they were holding a weapon.*

12 (18) *The builders, each with his sword fastened to his side, were building. A trumpeter was at my side.*

13 (19) *I said to the important citizens, the leaders, and the ordinary people: "There is much work and it is widely spread and we are separated on the wall far from each other.*

14 (20) *At the place where you hear the sound of the trumpet, gather there around us. Our God will fight for us.*

15 (21) *We were doing the work and half of them were holding the spears from the break of day until the stars came out.*

8. Cf. *BHS*.

16 (22) *At that time I also said to the people: "Let everyone with his servant spend the night in Jerusalem so that they can guard us at night and work in the day time."*

17 (23) *Neither I, nor my companions, nor my servants, nor my guard, no one of us took off our clothes, each one with his weapon in his right hand.*

1–2 (7–8) The numbers of the enemies of the Jews grew rapidly. They were upset by the progress of the work. Their derision and taunts were of no avail. Nehemiah and his workers were adamant to continue the work and to complete the project. So the enemies joined together and plotted to attack Jerusalem. They might have thought of the former days when they had stopped the work with the help of the Persian king (Ezra 4:23). *The Arabs* came in Persian times to the southern part of Transjordan and the Negev.[1] So they were the southern neighbors of the Jews. *The Ammonites* were the eastern neighbors who also had a foothold on the western bank of the Jordan.[2] *The Ashdodites* were the western neighbors. Their territory consisted of the whole area where the Philistines once lived.[3] To the north were the Samaritans with their leader Sanballat. From a bird's-eye view Nehemiah gives the four neighboring provinces of the Persian empire. The plot against Nehemiah was contrived by all his neighbors, a grave situation indeed. Judah was totally isolated, cut off from the caravan routes from South Arabia and from the Mediterranean Sea to the west. *The walls of Jerusalem were mended.* The Hebrew for "mend" is *'ᵃrûḵâ,* from the root *'rk,* which is occasionally used in the OT for the healing of a wound, the growing of the skin over a wound. It can also be translated "repair" or "rebuild." *The breaches were filled up.* The Hebrew for "fill up" is from the root *stm* and is used only here in the Niphal. It has the meaning "to lock up," "to seal," and "to fill up." Its meaning here is clear from the context: the breaches in the wall were filled up with stones and mortar. *To create confusion*—literally "to create to him confusion." The term *lô,* "to him," is problematic. It could not be the city, because cities in Hebrew are feminine and a feminine suffix should then be expected. Some want to read *lî,* "to me," or *lānû,* "to us."[4] In the light of the first person plural of the next verse, we must consider *lānû* as a likely emendation.

3–6 (9–12) Rudolph refers to the motto of medieval monks, *ora et labora,* as a good summary of v. 3 (Eng. 9).[5] The Jews prayed, but at

1. Cf. W. F. Albright, *The Archaeology of Palestine,* pp. 144–45.
2. Cf. Alt, *KS* II, pp. 341–42.
3. Cf. *ibid.,* pp. 342–43.
4. Rudolph, *Esra und Nehemia,* p. 124.
5. *Ibid.,* pp. 123–24.

the same time they put out a watch so that they were not trapped unawares by the enemies. It was indeed a dangerous situation. According to v. 4 (Eng. 10) it seems as if the propaganda of the enemies had its effect. In the form of a song, in the lamentation or qinah rhythm,[6] the Jews expressed their anxieties. It might have been a popular song of the workers. These verses show that the initial enthusiasm had died down under the onslaught of propaganda. It was a time of great uncertainty. The enemies could attack at any moment. Filled up with dust and rubble, the ruins of many years were becoming too much for the workers. Nehemiah was facing a crisis among his own people. This was the right moment for the enemies to spread fresh rumors and to dishearten the workers to such an extent that the work would stop. Then it would not be necessary to carry out the planned attack. In v. 5 (Eng. 11) such a rumor is given. The enemies will sneak into the city and kill the workers before they notice the attack. The Jews who lived near the enemy border witnessed their preparations for the attack on Jerusalem.

They are coming against us. The Hebrew is obscure here. The problem is *tāšûḇû,* "you return," which does not make any sense in this context. Various emendations have been proposed. Some are of the opinion that we must read *kol-hamm^{e}zimmôṯ* with the meaning "all the evil designs."[7] Another proposal is to read *yēš^{e}ḇû,* "they live," instead of *tāšûḇû.*[8] Still another possibility is *ya'^{a}lû,* "they are coming up" (JB). The text is so corrupt that it is impossible to restore it properly. The context seems to imply that the enemies were gathered for an attack on Jerusalem. In such a case our translation is to be preferred. *Ten times*—time and again. It became common knowledge that the enemies were preparing for an attack.

7–8 (13–14) Facing this danger Nehemiah decided to take precautionary measures. The Jews were organized into an army, ready to defend themselves and their rights. Verse 7 (Eng. 13) describes the gathering of the leaders and ordinary people. They were mustered according to their families. This might be an indication that the family as such played an important role in military matters. The army or host was built around the families. This was already the case in early Israelite history, when the Israelite army consisted of the different *mišpāḥôṯ,* "families" or "clans" (cf. 1 Sam. 10:21). The number of such a unit was approximately 1000 men.[9] The same custom was continued in the time of Nehemiah. From

6. The rhythm is 3+2, 3+2, with the rhyme of *hassabbāl* and *nûḵal.*
7. Rudolph, *op. cit.,* p. 124; Myers, *Ezra. Nehemiah,* p. 124.
8. Brockington, *Ezra, Nehemiah and Esther,* p. 121.
9. R. de Vaux, *Ancient Israel* I, p. 216.

this particular it is clear that an army was organized to cope with the planned hostile action of the enemies.

The Hebrew of v. 7 (Eng. 13) is full of problems and we have to recognize that scribal errors have crept into the text. The first problem is the repetition of *wā'a'ᵃmîḏ*. The first or second one must be regarded as dittography. Some want to change the first verb to *wᵉ'āmᵉḏû* and to continue the sentence of v. 6 (Eng. 12) into v. 7 (Eng. 13), e.g., "they are coming against us and placed themselves at the. . . ."[10] This is a possibility, but the best solution seems to be to take one of the verbs as dittography. Another problem is *open spaces* (Heb. *baṣṣᵉḥiḥîym*). The Qere is here correct by reading *baṣṣᵉḥîḥîm*.[11] A third problem is *mittaḥtîyôṯ*, literally "from under (or "low") spaces." Some scholars want to retain the first *wā'a'ᵃmîḏ* and to emend *mittaḥtîyôṯ* to *mᵉṭê ḥᵃnîṯ*, "spearmen."[12] No textual evidence supports this emendation, but this is occasionally the case in Nehemiah where textual corruption crept in at an early stage of the transmission of the text. Although the Hebrew construction is indeed awkward here, it is possible to explain *mittaḥtîyôṯ* as "away from the lowest places." The reason why Nehemiah avoided the lowest places is unknown to us. The open spaces might have been higher and thus more visible. As we see it, Nehemiah did the mustering of his army openly so that the informers of the enemy could see what was happening. The enemies should take notice that the Jews were prepared for them. *Their swords*. Throughout the history of Israel swords were the principal weapons for close combat. *Spears* were used as a stabbing or thrusting weapon in close range combat. *Bows*—probably the composite bow with a range of about 700 yards, but accurate at 300 to 400 yards.[13] Nehemiah had at his disposal about all the important weapons for a minor war.

The men were assembled and Nehemiah looked at them or inspected them. With the morale of his men low he had to give them fresh courage for their task. It was a time of crisis: from outside the enemies were fuming against the Jews; from inside his own people were frightened by the continuous propaganda of the enemies. Nehemiah, as a devout man, drew his companions' attention to the real strength of the Jews, namely, their great and terrible God (cf. 1:5). Be not afraid of the enemies. Who are they anyhow? Trust in God. But it is not a trust in God without any action. It is not a mystical wait on him. It is trust *and* action. The Jews

10. Brockington, *op. cit.*, pp. 121–22.
11. See *BHS*.
12. Rudolph, *op. cit.*, p. 126; Myers, *op. cit.*, p. 124.
13. Cf. Y. Yadin, *The Art of Warfare in Biblical Lands* I (New York: 1963), pp. 7–8, 10–11; R. Gonen, *Weapons of the Ancient World* (London: 1975), pp. 20ff., 29ff., 43ff.

must defend their families and their property. This call of Nehemiah is a masterstroke of diplomatic language. He got his audience involved emotionally. They must think of their children and wives.

I inspected (Heb. *wā'ēre'*) could simply mean "I looked." In Hebrew the verb has no object, although one can be supplied from the context. It might also be translated "I observed it." Other scholars want to add *yir'āṯām* and translate "I saw their anxiety."[14] This is not impossible, though there is no textual evidence for it.

9 (15) It is easy to attack a city which is unaware of the danger. Nehemiah took precautions in order to defend Jerusalem. This became known to the enemies; the attack would now be no easy task. A war between provinces of the Persian empire would be regarded as a serious matter by Artaxerxes. The adventure of the enemies might be damaging to their reputation, and not least in the light of the fact that the work that they wanted to stop was permitted by the Persian king. Through the speedy action of Nehemiah their efforts were thwarted. Their propaganda of cold warfare did not have its desired effect. For Nehemiah as a religious person it was God who thwarted their schemes. *God frustrated their plans* (Heb. *wayyāp̄er hā'ᵉlōhîm 'eṯ-'ᵃṣāṯām*). God broke up their plans. In Ezra 4:5 the same expression is used to denote the frustrating of the plans of the Jews to rebuild the temple. Here we have the opposite: God frustrated the plans of the enemies of the Jews. With his diplomatic language in v. 8 (Eng. 14) Nehemiah gave his companions fresh courage to continue their work. The song of v. 4 (Eng. 10) died on their lips and they were again body and soul in their work.

10–15 (16–21) But no one could be too sure what the future plans of the enemies were. In these verses Nehemiah describes his organization of the defense of the city and the continuation of the work. His important challenge was to organize his defenses without necessarily neglecting his most important task, namely, that of rebuilding the wall. These two actions do overlap to a degree: A wall around the city would make the defense of the city and its inhabitants easier.

Half of my men. The meaning of the Hebrew term for "men," from *na'ar,* is not clear. In v. 16 (Eng. 22) it refers to "servant." In 5:10, 16, and 13:19 Nehemiah writes about his men. It is possible that Nehemiah regarded the Jews as his subjects, his servants, because he was appointed governor. The impression created by 5:10 and 13:19, however, is that a special group of men is intended, a group distinguished from the general

14. Rudolph, *op. cit.*, p. 125; Myers, *op. cit.*, p. 124. It was first proposed by A. Bertholet, *Die Bücher Esra und Nehemia.* Kurzer Hand-Commentar zum AT (Tübingen: 1902), *in loc.*

Jewish population. These men might have been special favorites or more probably minor officials in his service. If this is the case, the men here in v. 10 (Eng. 16) were a group of officials who also worked on a section of the wall not mentioned in ch. 3. They were under the direct jurisdiction of Nehemiah. Half of these men were standing guard and the other half were working on the wall.

Spears, shields, bows, and breastplates. The arrangement of the offensive weapons and the defensive armor reflects an intimate knowledge of warfare. The shield was carried by the spearmen to defend themselves in close combat.[15] The breastplate or coat of mail was used against an attack of archers.[16]

The leaders (stood) behind . . . who were rebuilding the wall (vv. 10–11 [Eng. 16–17]). This phrase can be differently interpreted, e.g., some want to translate it as follows: "The leaders stood behind the house of Judah. The builders were rebuilding the wall" (Afrikaans Translation). We prefer our translation, which follows almost all modern translations (e.g., RSV, NEB, GNB, JB, the New Dutch Translation). In such a case it is clear that Nehemiah makes a distinction between the work of his own men (v. 10a [Eng. 16a]) and the work of the rest of Judah (vv. 10b and 11a [Eng. 16b and 17a]). *The carriers carrying the burden*—literally "Those that lift up the burden were carrying" (cf. also 1 K. 5:29 [Eng. 15]).[17] *Carrying* (Heb. *'ōm^{e}śîm*). Some want to read with the LXX *ḥ^{a}mušîm,* "armed."[18] But it is possible that the LXX tried to avoid the difficult *'ōm^{e}śîm.* Nehemiah wants to emphasize that the carriers were somehow hindered in their work by holding in one hand the basket and the other hand a weapon. The carriers also did their work on the outside of the wall in more dangerous circumstances. *Weapon* (Heb. *haššālaḥ*). This term is also attested in Ugaritic (Krt 20).[19] Some want to translate it "javelin" or "missile."[20] It would seem quite natural for men who work among the rubble to pick up a stone (missile) and carry it in one hand to defend themselves. In v. 12 (Eng. 18) the second group of workers is mentioned, namely, the builders or masons. They had their swords fastened to their sides, ready for combat. The builders had to use both hands for their work and thus could not, like the carriers, hold a weapon in one of their hands. Nehemiah was a practical person. His workers were spread out all along

15. For the shield cf. Gonen, *op. cit.,* pp. 59ff.
16. Cf. Yadin, *op. cit.,* p. 8.
17. Cf. M. Noth, *Könige* I. BKAT (Neukirchen-Vluyn: 1968), p. 87.
18. Rudolph, *op. cit.,* p. 126; cf. Myers, *op. cit.,* p. 123.
19. Cf. *WUS,* pp. 305–306; F. C. Fensham, "Remarks on certain difficult Passages in Keret," *JNSL* 1 (1971), p. 21.
20. KB, p. 976.

a lengthy extent of wall, and were consequently thinned out in numbers. An attack on them could be successful. Nehemiah saw this danger and did not want to give the enemy any opening for an easy attack. He formed a plan to avoid this difficulty. A trumpeter followed him. He must have been well informed of what was happening at every section of the work. If trouble with the enemies should break out somewhere, his trumpeter would sound the trumpet and all the Jews had to rally around him to ward off the danger. This was an ingenious plan to cope with the problem of men working far away from one another.

Our God will fight for us. This does not mean that the Jews should not fight, but that God would assist them in their fighting. They were fighting for the cause of God. It was his will that the holy city should have defenses, that his people should live in safety. Therefore their war was his war. They could rely on him. Nehemiah obviously wanted to boost their morale. They had a mighty Ally on their side. The religious motivation of the whole project and for the plans for its defense breaks through occasionally.

One interpretation of v. 15 (Eng. 21) is that Nehemiah gives a short summary of what he had said in the previous section. Another is that in this verse he again refers to the work of his own men, described in v. 10 (Eng. 16). The use of the first person plural *(we were doing the work)* and the reference to the fact that half of the men were armed might imply that Nehemiah referred to the work on his own section of the wall. He further stressed that they worked long hours, from the break of day until it became dark in the evening. This information sketches the zeal with which the task was undertaken.

16–17 (22–23) Another practical emergency measure was taken. The people coming from the rural areas and villages preferred to spend the night in their homes. This created a situation of movement into the city early in the morning and out of the city late in the evening. This could be dangerous for two reasons: the people going to and fro might be attacked by the enemies, and it was not easy to check on the people arriving. The enemies might easily have the opportunity to sneak in (cf. v. 5 [Eng. 11]). It was important to have all the men around in case the enemies should venture a night attack; they could guard the city at night and work during the day. This does not mean that nobody got any sleep, but that the guarding of the city was properly organized. Nehemiah emphasizes one thing, however: in such dangerous circumstances one has to sleep with one's clothes on and one's weapon ready at hand, because when the enemy attacks, one must be ready to fight immediately. Nehemiah and his men (cf. v. 10 [Eng. 16]) set the example.

It is of interest that in v. 17 (Eng. 23) a distinction is made between his *companions ('aḥay)* and his *servants* or men *(n^e'ārāy).* The companions were probably the higher officials in his service who were on an equal footing with him while the other men were minor officials. Or do we have here real servants as in the previous verse?

His weapon in his right hand. At the end of this verse the Hebrew cannot be understood. Literally it reads: "each one his weapon water." It is possible that the word water *(hammāyim)* is a corruption for "right hand" *(hayyāmîn).*[21]

G. ECONOMIC AND SOCIAL PROBLEMS (5:1–19)

1. The Problem of Slavery (5:1–5)

1 *From the people and their wives there was a serious outcry against their Jewish brothers.*
2 *There were some of them that said: "We have numerous*[1] *sons and daughters and we must procure grain to eat in order that we may stay alive."*
3 *Others said: "We have to mortgage our fields, vineyards, and houses to procure grain in the famine."*
4 *Still others said: "We have to borrow money for the royal tax on our fields and vineyards."*
5 *"Now we are from the same flesh as our brothers, their children are like our children, but we have to submit our sons and daughters to servitude. Some of our daughters have already been submitted. We have no power over it; our fields and vineyards belong to others."*

1–5 In these verses Nehemiah tells about the poverty in the province of Judah. This poverty had two causes. First, Judah was cut off from its neighbors through their hostility. It is probable that commercial ties were cut at this time between Judah and its neighbors. The normal flow of commercial activities was suspended. Second, the demands of Nehemiah for rebuilding the wall and the defenses of Jerusalem were stern. According to 4:16 (Eng. 22) Nehemiah expected that the farmers from the rural areas would stay in Jerusalem. In such circumstances farming became

21. Cf. Rudolph, *op. cit.,* p. 127; Myers, *op. cit.,* pp. 123, 124.

1. *BHS* suggests reading *'ōr^{e}ḇîm,* "barter," for *rabbîm,* "numerous." Then the text would read: "We are having to barter our sons and daughters." The Hebrew text does seem awkward (lit. "Our sons and our daughters, we are numerous"), and *'ōr^{e}ḇîm* does occur in v. 3. But the MT is not impossible; until we have further textual evidence the MT is to be preferred. Cf. Rudolph, *Esra und Nehemia,* p. 128; Myers, *Ezra. Nehemiah,* p. 128; Brockington, *Ezra, Nehemiah and Esther,* p. 123.

impossible. The high ideals and precautionary measures of Nehemiah had their effect, and the heaviest burden was on the people of the rural areas. It is important to note that their complaint was not leveled at Nehemiah, but against their Jewish brothers. They probably accepted the measures of Nehemiah as necessary. They leveled their attack on the wealthy Jews who misused their disposition to enrich themselves. *A serious outcry* (Heb. *ṣᵉʿāqâ* + *gᵉḏôlâ*), "a loud cry," refers to a cry made in distress (cf. Exod. 14:10). They were in serious trouble. Their problems were so serious that even their wives joined them in their complaint.[2] This is unusual, because in Ezra-Nehemiah women stay very much in the background.

They gave three reasons for their trouble. First, they had big families. With all the work they had to do for Nehemiah, they were not able to produce enough grain to stay alive. They had to buy the grain, and because they were poor it was difficult to pay for it. Second, their problem of lack of grain was solved by mortgaging their property. The term mortgage (from the Hebrew root *ʿrb*) is used only here in Nehemiah in this sense. Other meanings are "barter" (Ezek. 27:9, 27) and "surety" (Gen. 43:9; Prov. 11:15; 22:26; etc.). The latter meaning is by far the most common. *Fields, vineyards, and houses*—their real estate was mortgaged. *Fields* refers to their tilled soil on which the grain was grown. *Vineyards*—Judah was famous for its wine production. Gibeon, which formed part of the province of Judah, was a very important center of wine production during Iron Age II. In the excavations at Gibeon very little was found that could be dated in Persian times, in the second part of the sixth century B.C.[3] This is true not only of Gibeon, but also of many other sites in the Holy Land, although lately more and more material from Persian times has turned up and a more careful study of the types of pottery could be made.[4] The lack of material during Persian times might indicate that a very small settlement existed. Third, the farmers had to borrow money to pay the royal tax on their estates. For *tax* cf. our discussion of Ezra 4:13. Taxation on real estate or "ground tax" was probably taken over by the Persian kings from the Babylonians, who called it *ilku*. It is of interest that in this connection only the fields and vineyards are mentioned. Darius

2. This is probably the beginning of a court case. The complaint is the starting point. The Akk. *šasû*, used in similar contexts, can mean "to call out" or "to complain"; cf. A. Walther, *Das altbabylonische Gerichtswesen* (1917, repr. 1968), p. 215.
3. Cf. J. B. Pritchard, *Winery, Defenses, and Soundings at Gibeon* (Philadelphia: 1964), p. 38.
4. Cf. P. W. Lapp, "The Pottery of Palestine in the Persian Period," in A. Kuschke and E. Kutsch, eds., *Archäologie und AT.* Festschrift K. Galling (Tübingen: 1970), pp. 179–197.

instituted a tax on the past yield of the fields combined with the amount of crops they yielded. This became a heavy burden on the farmers.[5] Tax was thus levied only on fields with produce.

In these three complaints their Jewish brothers are not mentioned, but we may presume that their lands were mortgaged to wealthy Jews and that they borrowed money for their taxes also from them. This is substantiated by the summary of their position in v. 5. The result of their disposition was that their children were taken into slavery, debt slavery (cf. Exod. 21:1–11).[6] The children of the debtor were taken into the service of the creditor and had to work for him until the debts were paid.

The case of the daughters was in certain circumstances different. They could be taken into the service of the creditor as a second wife of the household. *Some of our daughters have already been submitted* (cf. Heb. *nik̲bāšôt̲*)—this may refer to a position where a daughter was taken as second wife.[7] In such a case the repetition of the plight of the daughters is not a mere repetition, but wants to convey the idea that the daughters were submitted to another kind of humiliation. *We have no power over it*—literally "there is no power for our hands" (cf. for a positive expression Gen. 31:29; Mic. 2:1; and for the negative Deut. 28:32). Deut. 28:32 states that the sons and daughters of the Israelites shall be given to a foreign nation and the Israelites will have no power over it. In Nehemiah it is not a foreign nation, but their own Jewish brothers. The fact was that the Jewish farmers had lost their rights on their property, an unhealthy situation indeed. With all the trouble the Jews were in it would be sheer madness to liquidate the agricultural backbone of this small community.

2. *Nehemiah's Measures against Slavery (5:6–13)*

6 *I was very angry when I heard their outcry and these facts.*
7 *I contemplated it carefully and then I brought charges against the important citizens and leaders. I said to them: "Everyone of you imposes a burden (loan) on his brother." Then I summoned the great assembly against them.*
8 *I said to them: "We were able to redeem our Jewish brothers who were sold to foreign nations, but you too are selling your brothers.*

5. Frye, *The Heritage of Persia,* p. 108. Cf. also for the OT economy R. P. Maloney, "Usury and Restrictions on Interest-Taking in the Ancient Near East," *CBQ* 36 (1974), pp. 1–20; O. Loretz, "Die prophetische Kritik des Rentenkapitalismus. Grundlagen-Probleme der Prophetenforschung," *UF* 7 (1975), pp. 271ff.
6. Cf. the discussion of N. P. Lemche, "The 'Hebrew Slave'," *VT* 25 (1975), pp. 128–144. Cf. now I. Cardellini, *Die biblischen "Sklaven"-Gesetze im Lichte des keilschriftlichen Sklavenrechts*. Bonner biblische Beiträge 55 (Bonn: 1981), pp. 323ff.
7. Although it is possible to detect some nuance of sexuality in this word, the translation of JB, "rape," goes beyond the sense.

As far as we are concerned, they are sold." They were silent and had nothing to say.

9 *"What you have done is wrong," I continued. "You ought to walk in the fear of our God to prevent the foreign nations, our enemies, from sneering (at us).*

10 *I, my companions, and my servants have also lent them money and grain. Let us absolve this loan!*

11 *Return now their fields, their vineyards, their olive groves, their houses, and a hundredth of the money, grain, wine, and oil you have lent them."*

12 *They replied: "We will return it. We will claim nothing of them. We shall do as you say." Then I summoned the priests and made them take an oath to fulfil it.*

13 *Furthermore, I shook out my gown and said: "May God shake out from his house and property everyone who does not keep this promise. So may he be shaken out and with nothing left." And the whole congregation said: "Let it be so." They praised the Lord and kept their promise.*

6–13 Nehemiah immediately realized the danger of the situation. On the one hand the economic infrastructure of the province of Judah was in danger. On the other hand it was a shame that wealthy Jews should act with such inconsideration toward their brothers. It was thus the peaceful coexistence in the Jewish community which was also in danger. The thought that one Jew could act like this against another Jew enraged Nehemiah. He acted speedily. *I contemplated it carefully* (from the Hebrew root *mlk* II, which is probably a Babylonian loanword with the meaning "to think over," "to contemplate").[1] Nehemiah had to make a plan to reverse the fortunes of the poor Jews. He was thinking the whole situation over, because his ablest men were involved. If he should act with too little strength, the problem would remain. He decided on drastic measures. He confronted them with his charges and came with a lawsuit against them. We derive this from the verb *rîḇ*.[2] But it could not be brought before an ordinary court in which the important citizens and leaders were the judges. They were the accused. He summoned a great assembly of all the people,[3] even those who suffered under the leaders. Before this congregation Nehemiah

1. Cf. *AHW* II, pp. 593ff.

2. Cf. B. Gemser, "The *rîb*- or controversy-pattern in Hebrew mentality," in M. Noth and D. W. Thomas, eds., *Wisdom in Israel and the Ancient Near East* (*VTS* 3, 1955), pp. 120–137; H. J. Boecker, *Redeformen des Rechtsleben im AT.* WMANT 14 (Neukirchen-Vluyn: 1964), p. 54 n. 2.

3. Against Brockington, *Ezra, Nehemiah and Esther*, p. 123, who wants to derive *q*ᵉ*hillâ* from an Arabic root meaning "rebuke." We must be very cautious in using a language as late as Arabic for explaining difficulties in the OT.

made his accusation against the wealthy people. It must have taken courage to take this step. He might have tried to persuade them to stop their activities before he summoned the congregation (v. 7), but it was of no avail. The important point in the accusation of Nehemiah is their practice of debt slavery. *Redeem our Jewish brothers*—we bought them back. It is not clear whether *foreign nations* refers to the Persians or to the neighboring nations. The latter is quite probably the case. Such an action is nowhere described in Ezra-Nehemiah. We may presume that wealthy landowners of the people of the land could have become creditors of poor Jewish families and taken their children into debt slavery. They were redeemed at one stage or other through a concerted effort by the Jews. But now the Jews were doing exactly the same to their brothers: they were buying their brothers and subjecting them to humiliation. *As far as we are concerned, they are sold.* The Hebrew of this phrase is difficult. Some want to emend "sold" *(nimkᵉrû)* to "buy" *(nik̲ᵉrû)*.[4] This is a possibility. Literally we have "They are sold for us." We take *lānû,* "for us," in the meaning "concerning us," thus *as far as we are concerned.* In such a case Nehemiah emphasized that even if they were sold to Jews, they were still sold. This was clearly wrong. The accused had no reply to the accusation. They were thus pleading guilty.

In v. 9 we have their conviction. They had acted wrongly. The people of God are expected to walk in fear of him. They should live according to his commandments. It is a fact, however, that in Exod. 21:1–11 debt slavery of a Hebrew slave is allowed (cf. also Deut. 15:12). Release after seven years is prescribed.[5] In the time of Zedekiah such a release was proclaimed, but after a while the released debt slaves were taken back again into slavery (Jer. 34:8ff.). Here in Nehemiah we also have a release from debt slavery. We may presume that the legal stipulation of the release, after six years, was not kept. This was wrong and contrary to the law of God. There was also another reason why this custom should be abolished, namely, that the custom gave the enemies of the Jews the opportunity to sneer at them. *To prevent the foreign nations, our enemies, from sneering (at us)*—literally "away from the sneers of the nations, our enemies." At Nehemiah's time, with all its problems, it was necessary that exploitation of fellow Jews should be stopped.

It is amazing how candidly Nehemiah was handling this problem. He confessed in front of the congregation that he, his companions, and his servants had lent money and grain to the farmers. It is important to note

4. Rudolph, *Esra und Nehemia,* p. 130, with Vulgate.

5. Cf. F. C. Fensham, *Exodus,* pp. 146–47. Cf. R. Noth, *Sociology of the Biblical Jubilee* (Rome: 1954), pp. 205ff., who thinks that Lev. 25 is important here.

that nothing is said of debt slavery in his confession (v. 10). We may presume that he and his associates had not taken any Jew into debt slavery, but still they had also contributed by their loans to the serious disposition of the farmers. *Let us absolve this loan.* These words reflect the involvement of Nehemiah in the whole problem. He was ready to absolve the loans he had made. At the same time he expected all the persons present to do likewise. They must restore immediately all the lands which were pledged to them.

Olive groves. This is not mentioned in the complaints of the farmers (cf. vv. 3–5), but we should understand that olive groves were also involved because this was another important agricultural enterprise in Judah. *And a hundredth of . . .* (Heb. *ûmᵉ'aṯ*). This is indeed difficult. Most scholars regard it as a scribal error for *maššа'ṯ,* "loan," referring to Deut. 24:10.[6] There is no textual evidence to support it, however. If we accept the difficult reading of the MT, the *hundredth* might refer to interest of a hundredth a month.[7] They could not produce anything for the reasons we have discussed above, and now to meet their bare necessities money, grain, wine, and oil which they borrowed must be given to them free of charge. It is interesting that grain, wine, and oil correlate precisely with the fields, vineyards, and olive groves mentioned in the first part of the verse. This shows where the problem lies. The farmers, as a result of their involvement in the rebuilding of the wall, could not till their fields properly, and consequently they had to borrow these commodities to stay alive.

The guilty persons had no choice and pledged to return what they had lent the farmers. There would be no further claims against them. They were willing to do exactly as Nehemiah had demanded. The problem was solved.

The role of the congregation in this whole matter is not clear. Were they judges or were they witnesses? They might have been witnesses, because Nehemiah as a Persian official functioned as judge and gave the verdict. The priests were then summoned to take the oath to act according to what Nehemiah had decided. *And made them take an oath* (Heb. *wā'ašbî'ēm*). This clause is not clear. Who are the *them?* According to the immediate context it could only be the priests. The verb has the first person as subject (Nehemiah) and the object is the third person plural (the priests?). In such a case the priests were the guilty; they were the landowners who oppressed the people.[8] Other scholars are of the opinion that the priests

6. Rudolph, *op. cit.*, p. 130; R. North, *op. cit.*, p. 205.

7. Brockington, *op. cit.*, p. 124. Cf. also E. Neufeld, "The Rate of Interest and the Text of Nehemiah 5.11," *JQR* 44 (1953/54), pp. 194–204; A. van Selms, *OTWSA* 17/18 (n.d.), p. 85.

8. R. North, *op. cit.*, p. 206.

were summoned to let the oath be taken by the guilty leaders.[9] They might have been witnesses of the oath.[10] In the light of the broader context (cf. v. 7) it seems as if the important citizens and leaders were charged. Can the citizens and leaders be identified with the priests? This is most unlikely. We must understand therefore that the priests had some function with the oath taking, but we cannot define it precisely.

In v. 13 a symbolic act of Nehemiah is described. In those days people kept some of their personal belongings in the folds of their gowns or garments. We may call it the pocket of the gown. Nehemiah emptied the pocket before the people, shaking out everything. This became now a symbol of a curse, a kind of rite he performed to illustrate the curse.[11] It was shown to the people in its empty state to signify that, if they should fail to keep the promise, they would be shaken out in the same manner and they would have nothing left.[12] This implies that the Lord in whose name the oath was taken would shake them out of any possession they had. This rite had the necessary effect. *Let it be so* (Heb. *'āmēn*)—they said "Amen." They were taking the consequences if the oath should be broken. They were relieved from all the tension that had been built up on account of their wrongful acts. Relieved, they praised the Lord for what had happened, and they kept the oath. Nehemiah's drastic measures were thus successful. It is obvious that Nehemiah and Ezra followed different courses with the people. Nehemiah, with the authority of a governor, could accuse the guilty, convict them, and consequently take penal measures. He acted on his own. Ezra, on the contrary, left the decisions to the leaders and then acted on what they had decided. He had a more restricted commission from the Persian king, namely, to apply the law of God.

3. *Nehemiah as Administrator (5:14–19)*

14 *Furthermore, from the time the king appointed me governor in the land of Judah, from the twentieth to the thirty-second year of Artaxerxes the king, for twelve years I and my companions never made use of the food allowance of the governor.*

15 *The former governors, my predecessors, laid a heavy burden on the people and took from them food and wine, also forty shekels of silver. Even their servants ruled the people, but I did not do it from fear of God.*

9. Rudolph, *op. cit.*, p. 130; cf. A. Médebielle, *Esdras-Néhémie. La Sainte Bible* (Paris: 1952), p. 344.
10. Myers, *op. cit.*, p. 131; Brockington, *op. cit.*, p. 124.
11. Cf. W. Schottroff, *Der altisraelitische Fluchspruch.* WMANT 30 (Neukirchen-Vluyn: 1969), p. 161.
12. Myers, *op. cit.*, p. 131.

16 *I also kept myself to the work on the wall and bought no land. All my servants were gathered there for the work.*
17 *Jews and leaders, a hundred and fifty men, besides those who came to us from the surrounding nations, were at my table.*
18 *We prepared every day one ox and six of the best sheep. Fowls were also prepared for me and every ten days skins of wine in abundance. In spite of this I never demanded the food allowance of the governor because the service weighed heavily on this people.*
19 *"Remember me in favor, my God, for all I have done for this people!"*

14 Important historical facts are given in this verse. First, Nehemiah was appointed (lit. "commanded") governor of Judah. The exact timespan of this appointment is also given—twelve years, from 445 B.C. to 433 B.C.[1] Second, Nehemiah and his companions did not make use of their right to claim a food allowance from the people. A governor, like a satrap, had the right to collect taxes not only for the central treasury, but also for his own treasury.[2] *Governor* (Heb. *peḥām*) is difficult. It is quite probably a scribal error for *peḥâ*. One manuscript and the Vulgate as well as the Peshitta have this reading.[3] *My companions* (Heb. *'aḥay*)—literally "my brothers." As we have already seen, this term refers to higher officials in the service of the governor, Nehemiah.

15–16 Another important historical fact is given in these verses. The former governors of Judah exercised their right to levy taxes for their own use. Who were the former governors (plural of *peḥâ*)? We know of Sheshbazzar (Ezra 5:15) and Zerubbabel (Hag. 1:1, 14; 2:2, 21), but no names of governors in the time between Zerubbabel and Nehemiah are supplied. They were not regarded as important enough. This reference by Nehemiah might be aimed at his immediate predecessors, who laid a heavy burden of taxes, including a food and wine allowance, on the people in order to live a luxurious life. *Also forty shekels of silver.* The Hebrew preposition *'aḥar* is difficult. It means "after." Perhaps here it means that forty shekels were claimed first, and then in addition food and wine, again corresponding with fields and vineyards (cf. the discussion of v. 4). *Even their servants ruled the people*. The servants, as we have seen (4:16), were probably minor officials in service of the governor. The governor permitted these minor men to play lord over the people. With this we have quite probably a reference to tax collecting. The minor officials levied the taxes in a harsh manner in order to collect enough for the Persian king, the satrap, themselves, and the governor. It became a heavy burden. Out of

1. Brockington, *Ezra, Nehemiah and Esther*, p. 124, does not regard it probable that twelve years' leave was given in 2:6.
2. Frye, *The Heritage of Persia*, p. 109.
3. See *BHK*.

reverence for God, because it was his people who were burdened, Nehemiah refrained from this practice. His minor officials were not sent out to collect taxes, but they were occupied with the work on the wall. Here again (v. 16) we have a clear reference to Nehemiah's direct involvement in building a section of the wall (cf. our discussion of 4:16).[4] *Bought no land.* Nehemiah emphasizes with these words that he, in spite of his high authoritative position, did not become a landowner. This confirms what we have written on v. 10. Nehemiah and his officials did not own land and thus could not by procuring land take people in debt slavery.

17–18 According to the Persian custom, as governor of Judah Nehemiah had to entertain a number of people at his table. In the Persian court the nobles were usually at the table of the king.[5] *A hundred and fifty men:* the heads of the families who were a separate body above the congregation of the people, and who had executive powers.[6] *Those who came to us from the surrounding nations.* Nehemiah, the governor and Persian official, had to receive other officials of the Persian empire who were appointed in surrounding countries; for example, any official from Egypt could stay in Jerusalem on his way to the Persian court. For this entertainment at his table Nehemiah had to slaughter every day one ox and six of the best sheep. *The best sheep* might also be translated "select sheep" or "choice sheep." *B^e^rurôṯ,* from the Hebrew root *brr,* means "selected," "hand-picked." *Ṣipp^o^rîm* refers probably to fowls, but it may be wild birds. Fowls were known in the Holy Land from the end of the seventh century B.C. onward.[7] *Skins of wine in abundance*—literally "from all the wine in abundance." We accept with almost all modern scholars that MT *b^e^ḵol* is a scribal error for *nēḇel,* "skin," referring to the containers of wine.[8] These containers were refilled every ten days. It is not said from where all these commodities were supplied. It is possible that Nehemiah bought them. But he makes it clear that they were not supplied by taxes. *The service* (Heb. *hā'^a^ḇōḏâ*) may refer to the work on the wall. In the context here it is better to think of it as referring to the heavy taxation levied for the treasury of the Persian king and the satrap. Nehemiah decided therefore not to add insult to injury and to refrain from claiming his rightful portion of taxes. In this respect Nehemiah set an example as a Persian official

4. Against Brockington, *op. cit.,* p. 124. Cf. Rudolph, *Esra und Nehemia,* p. 133.
5. Rudolph, *op. cit.,* p. 133.
6. Widengren, *Israelite and Judaean History,* p. 525.
7. Cf. the seal published by W. F. Badè, "The Seal of Jaazaniah," *ZAW* 51 (1933), pp. 150–56, discovered at Tell Nasbeh. It has a cock on it, ready for fighting. For a totally different approach to *ṣprm* see A. Kahan, *Beth Mikra* 12 (1966/67), pp. 139–140.
8. Rudolph, *op. cit.,* p. 132; Myers, *Ezra. Nehemiah,* p. 133.

without precedent in the Persian empire as far as we know. He wanted to stress the fact that, contrary to what the Jewish leaders did (v. 7), he himself endeavored to promote the welfare of his people.

19 Here we have another prayer of Nehemiah. What he did was not out of charity; he did it to receive the favor of God. The Jews were God's own people, the carriers of his revelation. To promote their welfare was to promote the cause of God. Nothing must be done to thwart the plan of God for his people. Nehemiah's action was thus motivated religiously and was not done for purely humanitarian reasons. This is difficult to understand in the light of modern conceptions. One is apt to suspect Nehemiah of egoistic tendencies. It might be partially true, but we must remember that Nehemiah and the Jews were at that moment the sole bearers of the true religion. What they were doing for themselves, they were doing on behalf of the maintenance of their religion.

H. ATTEMPTED PLOTS AGAINST NEHEMIAH; COMPLETION OF THE WALL (6:1–19)

1. Attempted Entrapment (6:1–4)

1 *When Sanballat, Tobiah, Geshem the Arab, and our other enemies were informed that I had built the wall and that not a breach in it was left—though at that time the doors of the gates were not hung—*

2 *Sanballat and Geshem sent to me the following message: "Come, meet us in Hakkephirim, in the Valley Ono." But they were conspiring to harm me.*

3 *Then I sent messengers to them saying: "I am busy with an important task, I cannot go down. Why should the work stop while I leave it to go down to you?"*

4 *They sent this message four times to me and I replied to them with the same message.*

1–4 After discussing internal problems Nehemiah is now back to the external dangers with which he had to cope. Sanballat and the enemies were informed that the wall was completed. Only the doors at the gates were not yet finished. Nehemiah's work was progressing beyond their expectations. So they had to make fresh plans as to how to stop the work. The only possibility was to remove the person who had been responsible for the whole project. They decided to lure him to a place of their choice and to eliminate him. Nehemiah, however, understood what they were intending to do and refused to leave his important work. *Tobiah.* Some scholars regard this proper name as a gloss here, because the preposition is omitted before the name while it occurs before both the names of Sanballat and Geshem.[1] We must keep in mind that a preposition which is obvious could be omitted in Biblical Hebrew. The name Tobiah is used so frequently with that of Sanballat in Nehemiah that the occurrence of such a gloss is highly doubtful.[2] *The doors . . . were not hung*. In Neh. 3 it is stated that the doors of the gates were finished. We must not regard this as a contradiction to what we have here. In ch. 3 the finishing of the work is seen as a whole. The moment of completion, however, is described in Neh. 6:15–16. With Neh. 6:1–4 we are at a stage between the finishing of the wall and the completion of the project as the doors were hung.

Sanballat and Geshem. Here the name Tobiah is omitted. It is clear from this chapter that Geshem started to play an important role in the plots against Nehemiah. *Hakkephirim*. An unknown place, the name of which means "lions." R. Schiemann's attempt to connect it to a kind of covenanting in which this term means "princes" is not convincing.[3] *The Valley Ono* is about twenty-seven miles northwest of Jerusalem. Brockington is of the opinion that it was on the extreme edge of Judah and thus part of the Persian province of Judah.[4] A. Alt, however, has held the opinion that Valley Ono was neutral territory between the provinces of Ashdod and Samaria.[5] In the eighth century B.C. it was part of Philistine country. The smaller villages were conquered by Josiah in the second half of the seventh century, but not the bigger cities.[6] It is therefore clear that Nehemiah's enemies wanted to lure him away from Jewish territory. Valley Ono was for centuries neither Israelite nor Jewish territory. It was probably hostile to the Jews.

Nehemiah suspected foul play. It is possible that he had received certain information which uncovered their plot; perhaps both sides made use of informers. It is noteworthy that the enemies were well informed about the progress on the wall and Nehemiah was fully informed about their plans.

Nehemiah's reply to their overtures was an emphatic no in diplomatic language. He did not want to go down to them, because his first priority was the finishing of the city wall, precisely the work they detested so much. But they did not take no for an answer. Four times they repeated their request, but to no avail. Nehemiah was determined to stay out of

1. Rudolph, *Esra und Nehemia*, p. 134.
2. Myers, *Ezra. Nehemiah*, pp. 137–38.
3. Cf. R. Schiemann, "Covenanting with the Princes: Neh. VI 2," *VT* 17 (1967), pp. 367–69.
4. Brockington, *Ezra, Nehemiah and Esther*, p. 125.
5. Cf. A. Alt, "Judas Gaue unter Josia," *PJB* 21 (1925), pp. 110ff.; *idem*, *KS* II, p. 343 n. 4.
6. Cf. Alt, *KS* II, p. 287.

trouble. This repeated message of the enemies was a sign of their desperation.[7] They were trying anything to stop the work on the wall. Jealousy played a not unimportant role in their reactions.

2. Threat and Accusation (6:5–9)

5 *Then Sanballat sent for the fifth time his servant with the same purpose with an open letter in his hand to me.*

6 *In it was written: "There is a rumor among the nations and Gashmu confirms it that you and the Jews are conspiring to rebel—that is why you are rebuilding the wall. According to these rumors you want to become king over them.*

7 *You have appointed prophets to proclaim concerning you in Jerusalem: 'He is king of Judah!' Now the king will be informed about these matters. Come, let us meet one another."*

8 *I sent to him the following message: "We have nothing to do with the things you are mentioning. You are fabricating them out of your own imagination."*

9 *All of them were trying to frighten us, saying to themselves: "They will leave the work and it will not be done." On the contrary, it strengthens my hands.*

5–7 *His servant* (Heb. *na'ᵃrô*). Probably one of Sanballat's minor officials. Sanballat made frantic attempts to lure Nehemiah to Valley Ono. He reverted to his earlier tactics by referring to the intent of rebellion (2:19). In his message here his tactics are more comprehensively worked out. He refers to rumors among the neighboring nations that the real purpose of the wall was to rebel and to proclaim Nehemiah as king. This rumor was spread with a complete awareness of Jewish religious conceptions. The prophets were brought in to show that a messianic movement was on the way.[1] The Jews expected the restoration of the kingdom of Judah with a Davidic king over them. Facts about Nehemiah's lineage, however, are lacking. We do not know whether he was a Davidide or not, quite probably not, or else it would have been mentioned somewhere. For Sanballat this was not important; he wanted to stress that in Jerusalem, according to his information, a messianic movement was started to make Nehemiah king. The guile with which Sanballat did it is obvious—it could be true. In such circumstances the Persian king must be informed that his high ideals for his cupbearer had failed. Nehemiah was rebelling against him, again a piece of perfect guile, because in the Persian empire confidants of the king

7. Myers, *op. cit.*, p. 138.

1. Cf. W. Vischer in *Probleme biblischer Theologie*, pp. 606–607; Coggins, *The Books of Ezra and Nehemiah*, p. 96.

occasionally rebelled against him.[2] This charge of high treason against Nehemiah was serious indeed.

At the end of his message Sanballat betrayed himself by insisting on a meeting. If Nehemiah was busy with a revolt, why should a governor of another province want to meet him? It could be interpreted immediately by the Persian authorities as collaboration. Why should a Samaritan be interested in the welfare of the Jews? The scheming of Sanballat became clear to Nehemiah. Another proof of Sanballat's dishonest intentions is that he sent *an open letter,* i.e., not sealed, as was the custom in those days. With the open letter, which could be read by anyone on the way, he was responsible for the further spreading of the rumor. Why then did he want to meet Nehemiah in private?[3]

Gashmu confirms it. Gashmu is the correct spelling of this proper name. Geshem is a later development in the Hebrew spelling. Some scholars accept that Gashmu was responsible for this dangerous rumor.[4] The Hebrew has literally "and Gashmu is saying." From the context it is clear, however, that the rumor was heard everywhere and that Gashmu simply confirmed it. He was also spreading the same rumor. Some scholars regard *Gashmu* as dittography for the preceding *nišmā'*. But this is improbable, despite the support of LXX^{A,B}.[5] *Among the nations.* Some are of the opinion that this term was inserted by Nehemiah,[6] i.e., Nehemiah gives here a free rendering of the message of Sanballat. This is not impossible. But it is dangerous to build such a surmise only on the term *gôyim,* and accept that it always denoted "heathens" in the book of Nehemiah. The OT uses it in quite a few instances with the meaning "nations." The term *'am* is usually used for blood relationship of people while *gôy* is used for a territorial community.[7] That *gôyim* was used elsewhere for heathens or foreign nations does not mean that this is the primary meaning of the term.[8] It could have been used by Sanballat without any difficulty for the neighboring nations of the Jews.

8–9 Nehemiah saw through all the plans of Sanballat. The serious charges of Sanballat were dismissed in a few words. *We have nothing to do with the things you are mentioning*—literally "we are not according to

2. Pelaia, *Esdra e Neemia,* p. 168 refers to the role played by Megabyzus.
3. Rudolph, *Esra und Nehemia,* p. 135.
4. Cf. Vischer, *op. cit.,* p. 606.
5. Cf. the discussion of Rudolph, *op. cit.,* p. 134. Note that *BHS,* unlike *BHK,* does not suggest deletion.
6. *Ibid.*
7. Cf. E. A. Speiser, "'People' and 'Nation' of Israel," *JBL* 79 (1960), pp. 157–163 (=*Oriental and Biblical Studies* [1967]), pp. 160–170.
8. Cf. R. E. Clements, *TDOT,* II, p. 432.

these things which you are saying." The rumors are without any base. It is a short and curt reply. Nehemiah added to this another short remark to show that he was well aware of the origin of the rumors. *You are fabricating them out of your imagination*—literally "from your heart you are fabricating [or imagining] them." "Heart" (Heb. *lēḇ*) has a wide semantic field in Biblical Hebrew. It is used occasionally for intellectual activities, as in this case.[9] *Fabricating* (Heb. *bôḏā'm* from the root *bd'*) is used only twice in the OT. 1 K. 12:33 states that Jeroboam had instituted a religious festival which he himself had imagined *(bāḏā')*. Here *bāḏā'* is also used with *lēḇ*, "heart," if we follow the Qere.[10] In Imperial Aramaic there is one uncertain example of *bāḏā'* in Aḥiqar 30 where Aḥiqar refers to "his son, who was not his son," who had "devised" *(bāḏā')* a falsehood. The reading and interpretation are uncertain, however.[11] From these examples it is clear that something unpleasant is associated with this verb. "Fabricating," with its unpleasant overtones, seems the best translation. JB translates it aptly in the modern idiom: "it is a figment of your own imagination." Nehemiah cut off the diplomatic negotiations curtly by referring to the absolute worthlessness of their accusations. It would be of no value to negotiate on accusations that they had concocted themselves.

Nehemiah also discovered the real motive of their actions. With the rumors they wanted to frighten the people so that they would stop working on the wall. We have already seen how this continuous propaganda had its effects on the Jews (4:4–6 [Eng. 10–12]). It was disheartening to work in such circumstances. The strong leadership of Nehemiah thwarted this attempt.

The last remark of Nehemiah in v. 9 is enigmatic. Literally the MT can be read either as "and now, strengthen my hands," or "and now to strengthen my hands." The first possibility refers to a short prayer, which is not uncommon in Nehemiah.[12] It is strange, however, that the appellation "God" is not used. The second possibility takes "strengthen" as an infinitive construct, but without the initial l^e. In such a case our rendering is the best. Yet another possibility is open, namely, to read with the LXX the first person of the verb, *ḥizzaqtî*.[13] The translation of this is "and now I have strengthened my hands." The interpretation is uncertain. It is clear, however, that Nehemiah was not frightened by all the attempts of his

9. For a discussion of *lēḇ* cf. F. H. von Meyenfeldt, *Het hart (LEB, LEBAB) in het Oude Testament* (1950); F. Stolz, *THAT* I, pp. 861–67, esp. pp. 862–63; H. W. Wolff, *Anthropology of the OT* (E.T. 1974), pp. 40–58, esp. pp. 46–51.
10. Cf. M. Noth, *Könige* I, pp. 290, 295.
11. Cf. *AP*, pp. 213, 221, 229. Cf. also *DISO*, p. 32.
12. Cf. Brockington, *op. cit.*, p. 126.
13. Cf. the discussion of Rudolph, *op. cit.*, p. 134.

enemies to stop the work. He stood his ground against them. Again, this attempt of his enemies had failed, like all their previous attempts. But they did not take no for an answer.

3. Plot Using False Prophets (6:10–14)

10 *Now when I came to the house of Shemaiah, the son of Delaiah, the son of Mehetabel, who was restricted (to his house), he said:*
"Let us meet at the temple of God,
in the inside of the sanctuary;
let us lock the doors of the sanctuary;
for they are coming to kill you,
they are coming to kill you tonight."
11 *Then I replied: "Will a man like me take flight? Will I enter the sanctuary to stay alive? I shall not go!"*
12 *I realized that it was not God who sent him, but he spoke the oracle to me because Tobiah and Sanballat had hired him,*
13 *in order to frighten me so that I would act accordingly and commit a sin. This would give me a bad name among them so that they could humiliate me.*
14 *"Remember, my God, Tobiah and Sanballat for what they have done, and also Noadiah the prophetess and the other prophets who tried to frighten me."*

10–13 The enemies now started to use Nehemiah's own people against him. This tactic shows that in Jerusalem some of the people were against the measures of Nehemiah. This is understandable in the light of the stern steps he had taken (cf. esp. ch. 5). This time his enemies tried to make a major breakthrough by hiring a prophet or prophets to lure Nehemiah into the temple. Nehemiah as a layman was not allowed to enter the temple. We must keep in mind that he was probably a eunuch and was therefore excluded from any religious participation in the temple (Lev. 21:17–24; Deut. 23:1). A person was allowed to flee to the altar to seek asylum (Exod. 21:13–14; 1 K. 1:50–53; 2:28ff.),[1] but asylum was restricted to certain definite cases, and flight from a foreign enemy was not one of them. The whole purpose of the enemies and the false prophet was to incite him to commit a ritual transgression. This would discredit him in the eyes of his own people, and consequently they would not be willing to cooperate with Nehemiah in finishing the wall.

Shemaiah. We know nothing about him except the reference in this verse. *Who was restricted (to his house)* (Heb. *'āṣûr*). This is indeed difficult to interpret. Various proposals have been made to explain this term.

1. Myers, *Ezra. Nehemiah,* p. 139.

Some have suggested that Shemaiah was somehow unclean and thus restricted to his house. In such a case his prophecy would not make sense. He said: "Let us meet at the temple." Could an unclean person make such a proposal?[2] It is rather improbable. Others believe that Shemaiah had an ecstatic experience and that *'āṣûr* refers to it. But nowhere in the OT does the root *'ṣr* describe an ecstatic experience.[3] Still others hold that by the use of this term Nehemiah wants to point out that he as governor went to the house of the prophet while the prophet did not take the trouble to visit him.[4] Another possibility is that Shemaiah performed a symbolic act to restrict himself to his house. He wanted to illustrate symbolically that, as he restricted himself to his house, so they had to lock themselves up in the temple.

The oracle of Shemaiah is given in poetic form.[5] The repetition of "to kill you" is not only a poetic device, but is also intended to frighten Nehemiah out of his wits. But Nehemiah was not so easily frightened; they underestimated his strength of character and his intelligence. He saw immediately through their whole conspiracy. He refused to enter the temple and commit a transgression. There might have been another reason for his refusal, namely, that it would have been a humiliation to him as governor to flee from his enemies in such an undignified manner. *Will I enter the sanctuary to stay alive?* The last word (Heb. *wāḥāy*) can also be translated "and stay alive." It would mean that Nehemiah could have been killed for entering the temple as a layman and eunuch. This is not possible, however, in the light of v. 13 in which Nehemiah says that the whole plot was planned to humiliate him and not to kill him. It is thus better to interpret the *waw* as expressing purpose.

In v. 12 Nehemiah describes his uncovering of the plot. Shemaiah was a false prophet, hired by Tobiah and Sanballat. Some want to delete Sanballat, because the usual sequence of the names is reversed here and because the verb "hire" is in the third person singular.[6] By placing Tobiah first Nehemiah wants to draw the attention to the fact that Tobiah was the main instigator of this plan. In such a case the singular of the verb is not strange. The attempt of the hired prophet failed, and the enemies were

2. Rudolph, *Esra und Nehemia,* p. 135.
3. Cf. the discussion of Rudolph, *op. cit.,* p. 137.
4. *Ibid.*
5. Again in the lamentation form *(qinah)* 3+2, 3+2, 3. The last three beats are probably to be regarded as a shortened verse form *(Kurzvers)*; cf. G. Fohrer, "Über den Kurzvers," *ZAW* 66 (1954), pp. 205–207; E. Sellin and G. Fohrer, *Introduction to the OT* (E.T. 1968), pp. 46–47.
6. Rudolph, *op. cit.,* p. 136.

unable to discredit Nehemiah. With his firm stand against the so-called word of God spoken by a false prophet, he won the day.

14 Here we have a second short or hurried imprecatory prayer. The treacherous plot of the enemies to stop the work on the wall, work commanded by God, must not pass unpunished. At the same time the prophets who were specially called by God to pronounce his will and who were prophesying contrary to his will must be punished. It is again a religious approach which dominates the thoughts of Nehemiah. *Noadiah the prophetess.* We know nothing of her. She belonged probably to a group of prophets who opposed the work and plans of Nehemiah. Thus in the time of Nehemiah a group of visionaries was around, but their spiritual standards were indeed low.

4. *Completion of the Wall (6:15–16)*

15 *So the wall was finished on the twenty-fifth of Elul, in fifty-two days.*
16 *When all our enemies heard of it and all the neighboring nations were frightened, their high opinion of themselves received a serious setback, and they acknowledged that this work was from God.*

15–16 These verses continue the theme of v. 1. This section describes the consummation of the whole task of Nehemiah. He came to Jerusalem to rebuild its walls. It was not an easy task; enemies from inside and outside tried to stop the work. Serious internal economic problems developed. In spite of all these attacks and setbacks the wall was finished in the remarkably short time of fifty-two days. Some scholars regard this as improbable and want to follow Josephus (*Ant.* xi.5.8), who refers to a period of two years and four months, but the timespan mentioned by Josephus is uncertain, because some scholars think that here a scribal error has crept in.[1] The period of fifty-two days for rebuilding the wall is short, but we must accept it as it stands. The following arguments in its favor can be mentioned. First, as we have already seen, restoration work was done. It was only a question of filling up the breaches and building the wall higher. Only the eastern wall was built from its foundation. To the north, west, and south the ruins of the old wall were used. Second, the wall was built with great speed. In special circumstances when people are aware of the dangers around them, they are able to work much more rapidly than in normal circumstances. Vischer refers to the building of a wall around Athens in just one month (Thucydides i.93).[2] Third, Jerusalem was much smaller

1. Cf. J. Bewer, "Josephus' Account of Nehemiah," *JBL* 43 (1924), pp. 224–26.
2. Vischer in *Probleme biblischer Theologie,* p. 606. In 447 A.D. an earthquake wrecked the defense wall of Constantinople while the Huns were attacking the Eastern Romans. By a concerted effort the massive wall was rebuilt in 60 days; cf. E. A. Thompson, *A History of Attila and the Huns* (1948), p. 91.

than generally accepted. According to the calculation of K. Kenyon the circuit of the wall was probably 2600 meters. It is uncertain whether the northern end of the western hill was included. If so, the circuit was approximately 4150 meters.[3] Fourth, the excavations on the eastern hill have shown that the wall was a rough construction, executed rapidly.[4] This confirms the view that the work was done speedily and that only the bare necessities for a wall were executed. *Twenty-fifth of Elul* — the beginning of October, 445 B.C. It is thus clear that within six months after he had heard of the plight of Jerusalem, Nehemiah had finished his commission to rebuild the wall.[5] He was a man of action.

The Hebrew of some parts of v. 16 is obscure. As we have taken it, the enemies heard about the finishing of the wall; all the neighboring nations were struck with awe at the tremendous speed with which the work was done. They were frightened by the thought that the Jews could achieve this objective in such a short time. The Arabs had become an important factor in the Holy Land. Their sense of superiority over the Jews received a serious setback. Finally they acknowledged that the God of the Jews was responsible for the miracle that happened. This interpretation follows the MT to a great extent. There are, however, other possibilities.

Nations were frightened. Some want to derive the Heb. *yr'w* not from the root *yr'*, "frighten," like the MT, LXX, Vulgate, etc., but from *r'h*, "see."[6] The translation would then be: "the nations saw it," i.e., the nations saw the wall. In our approach we have considered the fact that in this chapter the idea of frightening plays an important role. In vv. 9, 13, and 14 it is said that the enemies wanted to frighten Nehemiah. But now in v. 16 the climax is reached. Nehemiah is not frightened, but the neighboring nations are. The prayer of 4:4 is fulfilled: their scorn is turned down on their own heads. *Their high opinion of themselves received a serious setback,* Heb. *wayyippᵉlû mᵉ'ōḏ bᵉ'ênêhem,* literally "and they fell much in their eyes." Some want to read *wayyippālē'* instead of *wayyippᵉlû* and translate "it was a wonderful thing in their sight."[7] "In their eyes" can also be differently interpreted. The third person plural suffix to the noun can refer either to the enemies or to the Jews.[8] The latter possibility would then mean that the fear which the Jews had for the nations was removed,

3. Cf. K. Kenyon, *Jerusalem,* p. 110.
4. *Ibid.,* p. 111.
5. Brockington, *Ezra, Nehemiah and Esther,* p. 127.
6. Rudolph, *Esra und Nehemia,* p. 137; Myers, *Ezra. Nehemiah,* p. 140.
7. Brockington, *op. cit.,* p. 127. Originally proposed by Klostermann; cf. Rudolph, *op. cit.,* p. 137.
8. Myers, *op. cit.,* p. 140.

because they had a city with defenses. We should expect a clearer formulation if this meaning was intended, however.

5. *Correspondence with Tobiah (6:17–19)*

17 *Also in those days a number of letters from the important citizens of Judah were sent to Tobiah, and those of Tobiah were coming back to them,*
18 *for many a person was bound by oath to him, because he was a son-in-law of Shecaniah the son of Arah, and Tobiah's son Jehohanan had married the daughter of Meshullam the son of Berechiah.*
19 *They even mentioned his good deeds to me and they reported back to him what I had said, but Tobiah sent letters to frighten me.*

17–19 We should expect these verses after v. 14. Verses 15–16 should then stand before the beginning of ch. 7. This is the logical sequence.[1] On the other hand there might have been logic in the arrangement as we have it in the MT that escapes us now. It is possible that the events of 6:17–19 took place after the nations experienced the failure of their plans to stop the work on the wall (vv. 15–16). In vv. 17–19 it is no longer a question of stopping the work, but of diplomatic negotiations to reconcile Nehemiah with Tobiah. Some of the important citizens of Jerusalem were against the isolation of Judah, perhaps for commercial reasons. They corresponded with Tobiah, one of Nehemiah's enemies.

The reason why Tobiah was chosen is given in v. 18. Some of the important citizens had a pact with him. *Bound by oath,* Heb. *ba'ᵃlê šᵉḇû'â,* cannot refer only to the marriages mentioned in this verse.[2] Such an interpretation would be contrary to *many a person*. The two cases of intermarriage mentioned in v. 18 are only the most important examples of how Tobiah succeeded in binding certain Jewish families to him. *Son of Arah*—cf. Ezra 2:5. *Meshullam the son of Berechiah*—cf. Neh. 3:4, 30. If we place Ezra before Nehemiah, it is clear that the measures taken against marriages with foreigners (Ezra 10) were soon forgotten. The important citizens who were bound to Tobiah acted as mediators between Nehemiah and Tobiah. At first they wanted to persuade Nehemiah of the good intentions of Tobiah. To them Tobiah was not such a bad person. *Good deeds.* Some want to point the Hebrew differently with *ṭibbôṯāyw* instead of *ṭôḇōṯāyw* and translate it "rumors."[3] But the MT makes perfect sense. Nehemiah was open for persuasion, and in fact he started negotiating with

1. Cf. the arrangement of Myers, *op. cit.,* pp. 137, 140, and his discussion on p. 139.
2. Cf. Akk. *bēl adē; AHW* I, p. 119. It was used in Late Babylonian.
3. Cf. Myers, *op. cit.,* p. 137.

Tobiah through the Jewish intercessors. Soon it became clear that Tobiah misused his friendship with certain Jews to influence Nehemiah into capitulation. Nehemiah was not frightened by his negotiations and threats. Here again we meet a man of firm belief in his ultimate destiny. He was not willing to make pragmatic concessions.

IV. REPOPULATION OF JERUSALEM; GENEALOGY OF RETURNEES (7:1–72a)

A. APPOINTMENT OF OFFICERS OVER JERUSALEM (7:1–3)

1 *When the wall had been rebuilt and I had hung the doors, gatekeepers (singers and Levites) were appointed.*
2 *I appointed my brother Hanani and Hananiah the officer of the citadel over Jerusalem. Hananiah was a trustworthy man and more devoted to God than many others.*
3 *Then I said to them: "The gates of Jerusalem must be opened before the sun is hot, and while they are still standing (guard) the doors must be shut and barred. Appoint guards from the inhabitants of Jerusalem, the one to his position and the other before his own house."*

1–3 These verses are to be connected to 6:15–16. The wall was finished and the doors were put in their places. Now was the time for the appointment of personnel. It is noteworthy that in these three verses three different verbs for "appoint" are used, namely, in v. 1 a verb from the root *pqd,* in v. 2 a verb from the root *ṣwh* (cf. 5:14), and in v. 3 a verb from the root *'md.* The appointment in v. 1 was probably made by representatives of the people, the one in v. 2 by Nehemiah as governor (the same verb is used for the appointment by the king), and in v. 3 it was made by the two officials selected by Nehemiah. So the three verbs have different shades of meaning. *Singers and Levites.* Scholars regard these words as a gloss which crept in from vv. 43ff.[1] This is quite probably correct because the appointment of singers and Levites at the gates seems indeed strange. Singers and Levites were appointed for service at the gates of the temple and not for the gates of the city.

The Hebrew of v. 3 is not clear at all. As we have it, Nehemiah appointed his brother Hanani (cf. our discussion of 1:2) and another person with almost the same name, Hananiah, over Jerusalem. Some scholars

1. Rudolph, *Esra und Nehemia,* p. 138; Myers, *Ezra. Nehemiah,* p. 141; Brockington, *Ezra, Nehemiah and Esther,* p. 127.

think that one of the names is an error of dittography.[2] The problem with this idea is that v. 2 says: "Then I said *to them*." The Hebrew here refers to more than one person. *Hananiah was a trustworthy person*—literally "*he* was a trustworthy person." From the context it is clear that Hananiah is meant. Nehemiah gave Hananiah his recommendation. He was faithful and a devoted religious man and therefore trustworthy in all respects. The reason for this recommendation was probably that some doubt existed about his capabilities.

Neh. 3:9 states that Rephaiah was ruler of half of the territory of Jerusalem, and 3:12 that Shallum was ruler of the other half. In our discussion of 3:19 we pointed out that rulers of territories were not appointed over cities. We must therefore recognize that now for the first time two administrators were appointed over the city of Jerusalem.

Verse 3 is problematic. As we have taken it, following the MT, Nehemiah commanded the two administrators of Jerusalem to open the gates well after sunrise. His next command is uncertain in meaning. *While they are still standing (guard) the doors must be shut and barred*—literally "and until they are standing, they must shut the gates and bar it." The term "shut" from the root *gwp* is a hapax legomenon in the OT. The term "bar" is related to the Aram. *'ḥd* in this same sense.[3] The real problem is "and until they are standing," Heb. *w^{e}'aḏ hēm 'ōm^{e}ḏîm*. Who are the "they"? As we have taken it, "they" refers to the guards. This might either be the two administrators or a guard appointed by them. Some want to emend the text and read *w^{e}'ôḏ hû' 'ōmēḏ*, "and he (the sun) still stands," that is to say, while the sun is still high in the sky. Another possibility is to read *w^{e}'ōḏ haḥōm 'ōmēḏ*, "and the warm one (the sun) still stands." These proposals want to reach the logical consequence of the preceding phrase.[4] The two phrases thus mean "before the sun gets hot and while it is still high in the sky." The guards who are appointed according to v. 3b formed a kind of home guard. They were to guard the more important strategic places and others would guard their homes. It is clear that Nehemiah was still not certain that the enemies were going to leave them alone. The city should therefore be guarded properly.

B. GENEALOGY OF THE SPARSE POPULATION (7:4–5)

4 *The city was stretched out and large, while the people in it were few and not enough houses were built.*

2. Brockington, *op. cit.*, pp. 127–28; Myers, *op. cit.*, p. 141.
3. Cf. *BMAP*, pp. 236–37, 241 (9:13); *DISO*, p. 10.
4. Cf. also the discussion of G. R. Driver, "Forgotten Hebrew Idioms," *ZAW* 78 (1966), pp. 1–7.

5 *God inspired me to assemble the important citizens, leaders, and ordinary people in order to draw up a genealogy. Then I discovered a book with the genealogy of those that arrived first and I found written in it:*

4–5 After the wall was finished, Nehemiah gave his attention to internal problems. One of the major problems was the small population in the large city of Jerusalem. We might imagine how small the population was when we consider that Nehemiah's Jerusalem was much less extensive than the preexilic city or the one of later years. The returned Jews were settled mainly in the rural areas. *And not enough houses were built*—literally "and there were not houses built." This seems awkward. Some scholars propose that the word "houses" must be taken as "families."[1] This is a possible solution (cf. Deut. 25:9; Ruth 4:11; Prov. 24:27). It seems, however, that the Hebrew expressions *yēš,* "there is" (cf. Judg. 19:19),[2] and *'ayin,* "there is not," may sometimes denote "there is enough" and "there is not enough." *God inspired me*—literally "God gave it to my heart." This expression is used to point out that it was God who inspired him and not Satan, as in the case of David (1 Chr. 21:1). He wanted to draw up a genealogy of the people to see where the different families were living in order to place some of them in Jerusalem (cf. 11:3ff.). Then he discovered a very important genealogical list.

C. LIST OF RETURNEES (7:6–72a)

6 *These are the people of the province who came back from captivity and exile in which Nebuchadnezzar the king of Babylon had carried them. They returned to Jerusalem and Judah, each one to his own city.*
7 *They came with Zerubbabel, Jeshua, Nehemiah, Azariah, Raamiah, Nahamani, Mordecai, Bilshan, Mispereth, Bigvai, Nehum, and Baanah. This was the number of the people of Israel:*
8 *The descendants of Parosh 2172;*
9 *the descendants of Shephatiah 372;*
10 *the descendants of Arah 652;*
11 *the descendants of Pahath-moab, of the descendants of Jeshua and Joab 2818;*
12 *the descendants of Elam 1254;*
13 *the descendants of Zattu 845;*
14 *the descendants of Zaccai 760;*

1. Rudolph, *Esra und Nehemia,* p. 140.
2. Implied by the discussion of R. G. Boling, *Judges.* AB 6A (Garden City: 1975), p. 276.

15 *the descendants of Binnui 648;*
16 *the descendants of Bebai 628;*
17 *the descendants of Azgad 2322;*
18 *the descendants of Adonikam 667;*
19 *the descendants of Bigvai 2067;*
20 *the descendants of Adin 655;*
21 *the descendants of Ater and of Hezekiah 98;*
22 *the descendants of Hashum 328;*
23 *the descendants of Bezai 324;*
24 *the descendants of Hariph 112;*
25 *the men of Gibeon 95;*
26 *the men of Bethlehem and Netophah 188;*
27 *the men of Anathoth 128;*
28 *the men of Beth-azmaveth 42;*
29 *the men of Kirath-jearim, Chephirah, and Beeroth 743;*
30 *the men of Ramah and Geba 621;*
31 *the men of Michmas 122;*
32 *the men of Bethel and Ai 123;*
33 *the men of the other Nebo 52;*
34 *the descendants of the other Elam 1254;*
35 *the descendants of Harim 320;*
36 *the men of Jericho 345;*
37 *the men of Lod, Hadid, and Ono 721;*
38 *the men of Senach 3930.*
39 *The priests: the descendants of Jedaiah from the house of Jeshua 973;*
40 *the descendants of Immer 1052;*
41 *the descendants of Pashhur 1247;*
42 *the descendants of Harim 1017.*
43 *The Levites: the descendants of Jeshua, of Kadmiel of the descendants of Hodevah 74;*
44 *the singers: the descendants of Asaph 148;*
45 *the gatekeepers: the descendants of Shallum, of Ater, of Talmon, of Akkub, of Hatita, and of Shobai 138.*
46 *The temple servants: the descendants of Ziha, the descendants of Hasupha, the descendants of Tabbaoth,*
47 *the descendants of Keros, the descendants of Sia, the descendants of Padon,*
48 *the descendants of Lebana, the descendants of Hagaba, the descendants of Shalmai;*
49 *the descendants of Hanan, the descendants of Giddel, the descendants of Gahar,*
50 *the descendants of Reaiah, the descendants of Rezin, the descendants of Nekodah,*

51 *the descendants of Gazzam, the descendants of Uzza, the descendants of Paseah,*
52 *the descendants of Besai, the descendants of Meunim, the descendants of Nephushesim,*
53 *the descendants of Bakbuk, the descendants of Hakupha, the descendants of Harhur,*
54 *the descendants of Bazlith, the descendants of Mehida, the descendants of Harsha,*
55 *the descendants of Barkos, the descendants of Sisera, the descendants of Temah,*
56 *the descendants of Neziah, and the descendants of Hatipha.*
57 *The descendants of Solomon's servants: the descendants of Sotai, the descendants of Sophereth, the descendants of Perida,*
58 *the descendants of Jaala, the descendants of Darkon, the descendants of Giddel,*
59 *the descendants of Shephetiah, the descendants of Hattil, the descendants of Pochereth-hazzebaim, and the descendants of Amon.*
60 *All the temple servants and the descendants of Solomon's servants were 392.*
61 *These were those who came up from Tel-melah, Tel-harsha, Cherub, Addon, and Immer, but they were not able to give evidence of their fathers' genealogies and their descendants whether they were of Israel:*
62 *the descendants of Delaiah, the descendants of Tobiah, and the descendants of Nekoda 642.*
63 *Also of the priests: the descendants of Hobaiah, the descendants of Hakkoz, and the descendants of Barzillai who took a wife from the daughters of Barzillai the Gileadite and was called by their name.*
64 *These searched for their registration in the genealogies, but they could not be located; therefore they were considered unclean and were excluded from the priesthood.*
65 *The governor said to them that they should not eat from the most holy food until a priest stood up with the Urim and Thummim.*
66 *The whole assembly together was 42,360,*
67 *besides their male and female servants, who were 7337; and they had 245 men and women singers.*
68 *(Their) camels were 435; their donkeys were 6720.*
69 *Some of the heads of the families gave to the work. The governor gave to the treasury a thousand darics of gold, fifty basins, and five hundred and thirty priests' garments.*
70 *Some of the heads of families gave to the treasury of the work twenty thousand darics of gold and two thousand two hundred minas of silver.*
71 *The other people gave twenty thousand darics of gold, two thousand minas of silver, and sixty-seven priests' garments.*

72a *Now the priests, the Levites, the gatekeepers, the singers, some of the people, the temple servants, and all Israel lived in their cities.*

The list of Ezra 2 is inserted in a historical description. The list here was used to ascertain which families had returned, and to reorganize the population of the province of Judah.[1] The differences between Ezra 2 and this list are mainly in connection with numbers, the order of certain family names, the spelling of various names, and certain omissions and additions. For a discussion of the reasons for these differences cf. our remarks on Ezra 2.

V. FURTHER REFORMS OF EZRA (7:72b–10:40 [Eng. v. 39])

A. READING OF THE LAW (7:72b–8:12)

7:72b *With the coming of the seventh month the Israelites were in their cities.*

8:1 *All the people gathered as one man on the square in front of the Water Gate and they requested Ezra the secretary to bring the book of the law of Moses which the Lord had commanded for Israel.*

2 *Ezra the priest brought the law before the congregation, consisting of men and women as well as all who could understand. It was on the first of the seventh month.*

3 *He read from it in front of the square, in front of the Water Gate, from dawn until the early afternoon before the men, women, and those who could understand. All the people listened to the book of the law.*

4 *Ezra the secretary stood on a wooden platform made for this purpose. Beside him on his right stood Mattithiah, Shema, Anaiah, Uriah, Hilkiah, and Maaseiah; on his left stood Pedaiah, Mishael, Malchijah, Hashum, Hashbaddanah, Zechariah, and Meshullam.*

5 *Then Ezra opened the book in the sight of all the people, for he was higher than all the people. When he opened it, all the people stood up.*

6 *Ezra praised the Lord, the great God, and all the people replied: "It is so, yes, it is so!" While uplifting their hands, they bowed down and worshipped the Lord with their heads bowed down to the ground.*

7 *Jeshua, Bani, Sherebiah, Jamin, Akkub, Shabbetai, Hodiah, Maaseiah, Kelita, Azariah, Jozabad, Hanan, and Pelaiah, the Levites, interpreted the law for the people while the people remained in their places.*

1. Myers, *Ezra. Nehemiah,* p. 146.

8 *They read from the book of the law of God and translated it, giving the meaning so that the people understood what was read.*
9 *Nehemiah the governor and Ezra the priest and secretary, as well as the Levites who interpreted for the people, said to all the people: "This day is sacred to the Lord your God. You must not mourn or weep." For all the people were weeping while they listened to the precepts of the law.*
10 *He said to them: "Go, eat of the best, drink of the sweetest, and send a portion to him who has nothing ready, for today is sacred to our Lord. Be not dejected, because the joy of the Lord is your strength."*
11 *The Levites calmed all the people by saying: "Be silent, because this day is sacred. Be not dejected!"*
12 *All the people went away to eat and drink and send portions over and celebrate with great joy, for they understood the meaning of that which was brought to their attention.*

We may have here a careful description of the liturgical ritual of public worship in the postexilic times,[1] namely, the people coming to form a congregation, the request to read the law, opening of the book of the law, the rising of the congregation, the benediction of the congregation, reply of the congregation, kneeling down to hear the word (Gk. *proskynéō*), the sermon(?), reading from the law, oral transmission by translation, and dismissal for a festival.

7:72b Because this sentence does not occur in Ezra, it is generally accepted that it forms part of the next chapter which describes the reading of the law by Ezra. There is some difference of opinion how Neh. 8–10 is to be connected to Neh. 1–7 and how this is linked to the book of Ezra. Some scholars think that the original place of Neh. 8–10 is after Ezra 10, because it obviously forms part of the memoirs of Ezra.[2] Others hold the opinion that Neh. 2–10 must come after Ezra 8.[3] Another view is that Neh. 8–10 was inserted by the Chronicler, who gives us here a free rendering of a part of the memoirs of Ezra.[4] Still another view is that these chapters must follow Neh. 13.[5] The whole position is obscure. The best of these proposals seems to be that the Chronicler composed these chapters from the memoirs of Ezra. The connection in time between Neh. 7:1–5 and 7:72b is thus very difficult to determine. The seventh month was the time for the celebration of the Atonement (Lev. 16:29; 23:27; 35:9) and

1. Cf. In der Smitten, *Esra*, p. 40.
2. Cf. the discussion of Widengren, *Israelite and Judaean History*, pp. 491–92.
3. Cf. Schaeder, *Esra*, pp. 17ff.
4. Cf. O. Eissfeldt, *The OT: An Introduction*, p. 548; In der Smitten, *Esra*, pp. 35–36.
5. Cf. Pavlovský, *Bibl* 38 (1957), pp. 436–39.

the Festival of the Tabernacles (Lev. 23:34, 39).[6] It was the right month to have a reading of the law.

8:1–3 *All the people gathered as one man.* The reason for this assembly of all the people is not given. But we may deduce from Lev. 23:24 that they gathered on the first of the seventh month because it was regarded as a day of rest and sacred to the Lord. This day must be proclaimed with a trumpet call. We may presume that it was intended as a day of joy. It was probably the New Year's festival.[7] *On the square in front of the Water Gate.* It was thus not at the temple, because the congregation consisted of men, women, and all who could understand. In the temple precincts only men were allowed. For the Water Gate cf. our remarks on 3:26. *The book of the law of Moses.* Quite probably part of the Pentateuch. It could not have been the whole Pentateuch, because Ezra read from it *(bô),* and only for half a day.[8] *All who can understand* (Heb. *w^ekōl mēḇîn*). The usage of the root *bîn* is not clear in this chapter. In vv. 7, 8, and 9 this term is used for interpreting the law to the people. It is therefore not impossible that it could mean in vv. 2 and 3 "interpreters." We take it, however, in the sequence men, women, and all who could understand, as referring to children who have reached the stage of understanding.

4–5 The congregation summoned Ezra to read the law to them. In order to do it effectively a wooden structure was erected (Heb. *migdāl*). The Hebrew term is used only here in the OT with this meaning; for the rest it is employed in the sense of "tower." It was thus a kind of wooden pulpit or platform. On it he was visible to everyone and could be heard better. It is of interest that all the people stood up when he started reading. This was a sign of reverence for the word of God.[9] They remained standing until the reading was finished. Ezra had to his right six persons and to his left seven, thirteen altogether. This number is regarded with suspicion by scholars, because in the Greek translations the names are not uniformly transmitted.[10] One would expect that the helpers of Ezra would have been twelve. It is hazardous, however, to try to reconstruct the real names to reach either the number twelve or fourteen.[11] Another problem is that only the names are given, without any reference to who they were, namely, priests or Levites. Some are of the opinion that they were Levites and even speak of this platform as the Levites' platform.[12] But this is still more

6. See further Myers, *Ezra. Nehemiah,* p. 153.
7. Cf. K. Elliger, *Leviticus.* HAT (Tübingen: 1966), pp. 317–18.
8. Myers, *op. cit.,* p. 153.
9. Rudolph, *Esra und Nehemia,* p. 147; Myers, *op. cit.,* p. 151.
10. For a comparison of these lists see Myers, *op. cit.,* p. 151.
11. Coggins, *The Books of Ezra and Nehemia,* p. 108.
12. Kapelrud, *The Question of Authorship in the Ezra-Narrative,* pp. 81–82.

uncertain, because in the other list given in this chapter the Levites are mentioned clearly[13] and the Levites' platform only in 9:4. All we can accept is that the persons mentioned here in v. 4 were important, quite probably leaders of the community.

6 In this verse we have the benediction pronounced by Ezra and the response of the people to it by saying twice "Amen." *The great God.* An appellation well known in the OT (Deut. 10:17; Jer. 32:18; Dan. 9:4; Neh. 1:5; 9:32). It was a general appellation in the ancient Near East for an important god; cf. Akk. *ilu rabū,*[14] and it was known also in Persian religion.[15] *While uplifting the hands* (Heb. *b^{e}mōʻal y^{e}ḏêhem*). *Mōʻal* is a noun from the root *ʻlh* and is used only here in the OT. This was a general prayer gesture in the ancient Near East;[16] cf. our discussion of Ezra 9:5. *They bowed down and worshipped* (Heb. *wayyiqq^{e}ḏû wayyištaḥ^{a}wû*). These two verbs are used occasionally with one another in the OT (e.g., Gen. 24:26; Exod. 34:8; Num. 22:31; etc.).[17] It is clear from this description that the congregation stood in awe and fear before God. They were supplicating.

7–8 In v. 7 thirteen names, the same number as in v. 4, are mentioned. These thirteen persons were Levites who were responsible for the interpretation of the law. How it was done is not said. Every one of them might have taken a group of the congregation to explain the law. The Levites played here approximately the same role as that ascribed to them in 2 Chr. 17:7–9. Much has been written on the term *m^{e}pōrāš* in v. 8. We have translated it "translate," opting for the solution proposed by H. H. Schaeder.[18] The root *prš* means "to break up" and this may refer to the breaking up of the language while it is translated.[19] We must recognize that the Jews who spoke Aramaic needed someone to translate the Hebrew of the law for them in their own vernacular. Some modern scholars are not convinced, however, that *m^{e}pōrāš* denotes translation.[20] They accept that the Jews in Judah could understand enough Hebrew to follow the reading of Ezra. It is thus either translating or interpreting. In v. 8, how-

13. Rudolph, *op. cit.*, p. 147.
14. Noted by Myers, *op. cit.*, p. 151; cf. *AHW* II, p. 937.
15. Cf., e.g., in the Avesta, Nyāyišn 5:20. Cf. F. Wolff, *Avesta* (1910), p. 144.
16. Cf. H.-J. Kraus, *Psalmen* I. BKAT XV (Neukirchen: 1960), p. 230.
17. Kapelrud, *op. cit.*, p. 83.
18. Cf. Schaeder, *Iranische Beiträge* 1, pp. 204ff. Cf. also M. McNamara, *Targum and Testament* (Grand Rapids: 1972), pp. 79–80.
19. Brockington, *Ezra, Nehemiah and Esther*, pp. 132–33.
20. Cf., e.g., K. F. Pohlmann, *Studien zum dritten Esra*. FRLANT 104 (Göttingen: 1970), p. 133; In der Smitten, *Esra*, p. 42. But cf. M. McNamara, *The New Testament and the Palestinian Targum to the Pentateuch* (Rome: 1966), pp. 155ff.

ever, it seems that a distinction is made between translating *(prš)* and interpreting *(bîn)*. In such a case our rendering is to be preferred.

9 This is one of the most important verses in Ezra-Nehemiah, but full of problems. On face value this verse mentions Nehemiah and Ezra, and thus shows that they were contemporaries. This is very important for a better understanding of the relationship between Nehemiah and Ezra. It is one of the mysteries of the books of Ezra-Nehemiah that according to the description Nehemiah the governor and Ezra the secretary acted on their own without the aid of the other. The book of Ezra describes the history of the Jewish exiles before Nehemah arrived. So the omission of Nehemiah's name in Ezra is understandable. But the description in the book of Nehemiah reports events which could have happened while Ezra was in Jerusalem (cf. the discussion in the Introduction). In the memoirs of Nehemiah up to this chapter Ezra is strangely absent. Suddenly, now, in v. 9 Nehemiah and Ezra are both mentioned, partaking in the same act. It is furthermore pointed out by scholars that although both Nehemiah and Ezra are mentioned in this verse as subjects of the verb, the verb is in the singular. On account of this the name Nehemiah and the mentioning of the Levites are regarded as secondary.[21] Other scholars, however, regard the name Ezra as secondary and Nehemiah as original.[22] The use of a verb in the singular with a plural subject is, however, not impossible in Hebrew, although not normal.[23] What is the textual position? In 3 Esd. 5:40 the name of Nehemiah is omitted, but instead of "governor" *(tiršāṯā')* the word Attharates is read. It shows that the author of 3 Esdras had the word *tiršāṯā'* before him and probably the name Nehemiah.[24] In the LXX, on the other hand, the name Nehemiah occurs, while *hû' hattiršāṯā'* is omitted. From this we may deduce that at an early stage the name Nehemiah occurred in the Hebrew text. In spite of the difficulty with the singular of the verb, we take the position that both Nehemiah and Ezra are mentioned in this text and that not enough textual-critical evidence can be presented to delete either name. For *tiršāṯā'* cf. our discussion of Ezra 2:63.

The reading of the law and its explanation to the people had its effect. They became aware of their sins and wept. Instead of a joyous gathering, they were mourning. This reaction is not according to the char-

21. Rudolph, *op. cit.*, p. 148; In der Smitten, *Esra*, p. 43. In der Smitten holds that the term *the Levites* is not secondary.

22. Cf. M. Noth, *Überlieferungsgeschichtliche Studien*, p. 130.

23. Cf., e.g., C. Brockelmann, *Hebräische Syntax* (Neukirchen: 1956), p. 51. Cf. also Neh. 9:4.

24. Cf. Rudolph, *op. cit.*, p. 148; Kapelrud, *op. cit.*, p. 85. Cf. also R. Hanhart, *Text und Textgeschichte des 1. Esrabuches*, p. 55.

acter of this festival, which should be an occasion of joy. The reading had the wrong effect on them.

10–12 This festival had to receive its real character as a day of joy. So the people were sent to their homes to eat and drink, because it must be a day of rejoicing. The people should realize that in their joy in the Lord would lie their strength. *Eat of the best,* literally "eat of the fat," which means the choicest and thus the best. *Drink of the sweetest.* The Hebrew for "sweetest" is *mamtaqqîm*. In Cant. 5:16, its only other occurrence, *mamtaqqîm* might refer to kissing, as in Ugaritic.[25] In Neh. 8:10 sweetness may allude to the effect of the drink on the palate. Some think the drink was wine, and the Vulgate has *mulgum,* wine mixed with honey.[26] But certainty is not possible. *Send a portion.* For those who were unable to prepare anything for the festival, a portion must be sent out of generosity. The recipients might be the poor, as interpreted by the LXX. *Your strength,* Heb. *mā'uzzeḵem,* means "mountaintop," "bulwark," and in the prophets "protection."[27] The people must realize that in spite of their sins the Lord will be their strength, their protection during the coming year.

The Levites succeeded in calming the people down. Afterward the people went to their homes for the festival. What kind of meal at home is intended here? Could it be an *agápē*-meal?[28] It is difficult to tell. They went to their homes and feasted with great joy, rejoicing in the Lord. We should expect that it was a meal of thanksgiving for what they had received. That is why a portion was sent to poor neighbors. The Lord gave them all the things they possessed. In the coming year he would give them again what they needed.

B. CELEBRATION OF THE FESTIVAL OF TABERNACLES (8:13–18)

13 *On the second day the heads of the families of all the people, the priests, and Levites gathered round Ezra the secretary to study the precepts of the law.*

14 *They discovered written in the law which God had commanded Moses that the Israelites must stay in booths during the festival of the seventh month.*

15 *Then they made it known and sent a message through all their cities and Jerusalem saying: "Go out to the mountains and bring branches*

25. Cf. M. H. Pope, *Song of Songs.* AB 7C (Garden City: 1977), p. 549.
26. Wine mixed with honey was well known in the ancient Near East. Cf. in Ugaritic Krt 72; cf. F. C. Fensham, "Remarks on Keret 59–72," *JNSL* 4 (1975), pp. 19–20.
27. Kapelrud, *op. cit.,* pp. 86–87.
28. In der Smitten, *Esra,* p. 40.

of olive, wild olive, myrtle, palms, and other leafy trees to make booths as it is written."

16 *The people went out, brought them, and made for themselves booths, each one on his roof and in their courtyards, in the courtyard of the temple of God, and on the squares of the Water Gate and the Ephraim Gate.*

17 *The whole congregation who had returned from captivity made booths and dwelt in the booths. From the time of Jeshua the son of Nun until that day the Israelites had not done so. There was a very great rejoicing.*

18 *Every day, from the first to the last day, Ezra read from the book of the law of God. They celebrated the festival for seven days and on the eighth there was a solemn assembly as prescribed.*

13–14 On the second day of the seventh month, the day after the one described in vv. 1–12, a special Bible study group, consisting of the heads of families, priests, and Levites, was instructed by Ezra. This was a more select group than that of the previous day. We might presume that the celebration of the Feast of the Tabernacles had been completely forgotten, because now for the first time they became aware of it. Ezra 3:4 describes such a feast held just after the arrival of the first group of exiles. It is thus apparent that this feast fell into disuse. On the Feast of Tabernacles cf. our discussion of Ezra 3:4.

15–16 The leaders of the Jewish community took immediate steps to reinstitute the feast. We know that this feast should begin on the fifteenth of the seventh month. So from the second to the fifteenth the people had enough time for preparations. *And sent a message.* The same expression is used in Ezra 10:7. Cf. our discussion there. We should probably delete *'ᵃšer* of *wa'ᵃšer* at the beginning of v. 15 as dittography of the *'ᵃšer* in the previous verse,[1] or else we must regard it as a continuation of the cognate clause in the previous verse.[2] But the latter option seems awkward. They could not have discovered in the law that it must be made known that a message had to be sent through the cities. It is thus better to delete *'ᵃšer* in v. 15. *Wild olive.* Some translate "pine" (JB).[3] It refers, however, to the small tree *Elaeagnus angustifolia,* which is plentiful in the Holy Land.[4] The *myrtle* is not a tree, but a shrub, *Myrtis communis,* which is a popular evergreen with fragrant leaves.[5] The people brought the branches to Jerusalem, the proper place for this festival. Deut. 31:11 states that this

1. See *BHK*.
2. Kapelrud, *op. cit.*, p. 88.
3. By placing "pine" first and "olive" second GNB has made an obvious mistake.
4. Cf. F. N. Hepper, *NBD*, p. 1294.
5. Cf. R. K. Harrison, *NBD*, p. 1006.

festival must be held at a place selected by the Lord. In the time of Ezra it was obviously Jerusalem. *Water Gate*. Cf. our discussion of 3:26. *Ephraim Gate*. Some accept that this gate opened in the direction of Ephraim to the northwest. It is not mentioned in Neh. 3, however.

17–18 These verses describe the celebration. The exiles held a special Feast of Tabernacles. Never since the time of Joshua (Jeshua) was such a feast celebrated. What is the meaning of this? Was it now for the first time since Joshua that this feast was celebrated? This could not be the case, because in Ezra 3:4 it is stated that this feast had been celebrated. It might refer to the spirit in which it was celebrated. For the first time since Joshua this feast was held in the same spirit as that of ancient times. It is important to note, however, that the theme of reference to an early occasion on which a feast was held occurs also in 2 K. 23:22; 2 Chr. 30:26; 35:18.[6] Some of the Israelite authors were fond of referring back into history to a certain festival and comparing it with their own. On every day of the seven days of the feast Ezra read from the Pentateuch, as prescribed in Deut. 31:11. It shows that Ezra had followed precisely the precepts of Deuteronomy and also of Leviticus.[7] *A solemn assembly* (Heb. *'aṣereṯ*) or "closing ceremony."[8] This term is also used in 2 K. 10:20; Isa. 1:13; Jer. 9:1; Joel 1:14; Amos 5:21. In Lev. 23:36 and Num. 29:35 this solemn assembly on the eighth day of the Feast of Tabernacles is prescribed. This gives immediately the clue to the term "as prescribed" *(kammišpāṭ)* at the end of v. 18. It was done according to the law.

C. DAY OF FASTING (9:1–5)

1 *On the twenty-fourth of the same month the Israelites gathered with fasting, in sackcloth, and with dust on their heads.*

2 *Israel's stock was separated from all foreigners. Then they stood up and confessed their sins and the iniquities of their ancestors.*

3 *While they remained standing in their places, it was read from the book of the law of the Lord their God for a quarter of a day, and for another quarter they confessed and worshipped the Lord their God.*

4 *On the platform of the Levites stood Jeshua, Bani, Kadmiel, Shebaniah, Bunni, Sherebiah, Bani, and Chenani. They cried out loudly to the Lord their God.*

5 *The Levites Jeshua, Kadmiel, Bani, Hashabneiah, Sherebiah, Hodiah, Shebaniah, and Pethahiah said:*

6. Myers, *Ezra. Nehemiah,* p. 157.
7. For Leviticus cf. Kapelrud, *op. cit.*, pp. 91–92.
8. Brockington, *Ezra, Nehemiah and Esther,* p. 134.

"Come, praise the Lord your God
for ever and ever.
May your glorious name be praised,
be exalted above all blessing and praise."

On the precise place of Neh. 9 in the books of Ezra-Nehemiah there exists some difference of opinion among modern scholars. One of the problems is that in Neh. 8 the congregation is requested to have a feast of joy, while in Neh. 9 in the same month a day of fasting and confession of sins is proclaimed.[1] How can one explain this? Another problem is the mentioning of the separation from foreigners. In the preceding chapters nothing is said of such a separation. One proposed solution to these problems is to postulate that Neh. 9 has been displaced. According to some scholars it should be placed immediately after Ezra 10.[2] We must keep in mind that the position of Neh. 9 is not easy to understand.[3] In der Smitten is correct in stating that it is hazardous to try to solve the problems of Neh. 9 by regarding it as displaced.[4] His solution is that Neh. 9:1–5a is to be regarded as parallel to Neh. 8:1–18, but between Neh. 9 and Ezra 9:6–15 too many differences appear to link these two pericopes with each other. He suggests that Neh. 9 must be regarded as edited by a redactor of the post-Chronicler period.[5] In der Smitten's arguments are unfortunately built on the assumption that the memoirs of Ezra do not form part of Neh. 8, an assumption which is unacceptable. He is, however, correct in urging that we must make the most of the present position of Neh. 9 in the books of Ezra-Nehemiah.

The first problem, namely, that we have a sudden change from joy to confession of sins, can be solved if we keep in mind that the Israelites were already weeping and mourning on the first of the month after they had heard the law. The Levites requested that they celebrate a feast of joy, but after this feast it would be natural for them to think again of their sins and iniquities. These sins were not yet atoned for. The problem with the approach of modern scholars is that they want to link every assembly of the people to a prescribed festival in the Pentateuch. We can think here of the Day of Atonement, but this day was celebrated on the tenth day. The best solution is to regard this assembly as something unique which hap-

1. Rudolph, *Esra und Nehemia,* pp. 153ff.
2. *Ibid.,* p. 154; Myers, *Ezra. Nehemiah,* p. 165.
3. For discussions on the problems of this chapter see A. C. Welch, "The Source of Nehemiah IX," *ZAW* 47 (1929), pp. 130–37; M. Rehm, *BZ* N.F. 1 (1957), pp. 59–69.
4. In der Smitten, *Esra,* p. 48.
5. *Ibid.,* p. 51. Cf. also Kellermann's arguments against Rudolph (Kellermann, *Nehemia,* p. 36).

pened on that occasion under special circumstances. The separation from foreigners can be explained as quite natural, because their participation in the confession of Israelite sins would have been impossible. We must concede that in Neh. 9:1–5 Ezra is not mentioned, which is indeed strange. The close relationship between Neh. 8 and 9 in their liturgical approach[6] shows, however, that these chapters come from the same background.

1–5 *In sackcloth, and with dust on their heads*. This was the general sign of mourning and of displaying the frailty of mankind. It is of interest that the congregation did not only confess their own sins, but also those of their ancestors. This is a recurring theme in the books of Ezra-Nehemiah. They felt their solidarity with past generations. This becomes now the theme of the prayer of Neh. 9:6–37. *While they remained standing* (cf. Neh. 8:8). This verse creates a problem for those scholars who accept that Neh. 9 is dislocated. It is then regarded as a post-Chronicler gloss.[7] The approach by which problematic parts of Scripture that do not fit into the preconceived assumption are eliminated is totally unacceptable. In spite of this the problem remains that two lists of Levites are supplied of which only five names are the same. We must conclude that we have two groups of Levites who quite probably executed two different functions, the first group as petitioners and the second as chanters.[8] As in the case of Neh. 8:4 the meeting lasted for half a day. *It was read* (Heb. *wayyiqr*$^{e'}$*û*). We take it as impersonal and thus passive, as occurs many times in Biblical Hebrew.[9] *On the platform of the Levites*. *Platform* is Heb. *ma'*^{a}*leh,* which might mean the steps of an edifice higher than the position of the people. It is not to be confused with the pulpit of Ezra described in Neh. 8:5. *Be praised*. We are reading with the Peshitta *way*^{e}*ḇōraḵ* instead of *wîḇār*^{e}*ḵû;* instead of "may they praise . . . ," read "may your glorious name be praised."[10] It is also noteworthy that the first verb of v. 4, *stood,* is in the singular and not plural as we might expect; cf. our discussion of this phenomenon at 8:9.

At the end of v. 5 we have a hymn which forms the *introitus* to the prayer of penitence of vv. 6–37. In modern scholarship this part, like vv. 6–37, is quite correctly regarded as poetic.

D. PENITENTIAL PRAYER (9:6–37)

6 *You alone are the Lord,*

6. Cf. J. L. Liebreich, "The Impact of Nehemiah 9:5–37 on the Liturgy of the Synagogue," *HUCA* 32 (1961), pp. 227–237.
7. Rudolph, *op. cit.*, p. 156.
8. Brockington, *Ezra, Nehemiah and Esther,* p. 136.
9. In der Smitten, *Esra,* p. 49.
10. Myers, *op. cit.*, p. 164.

you have made the heaven,
the heaven of heavens with all its host,
the earth and everything on it,
the seas and everything in them.
You give life to all of them,
the host of heaven worships you.
7 *You are the Lord, the God*
who chose Abram,
brought him from Ur of the Chaldees
and gave him the name Abraham.
8 *When you found him faithful of heart,*
you made a covenant with him
to give him the land of the Canaanites,
the Hittites, and the Amorites,
the Perizzites, Jebusites, and the Girgashites,
to give it to his descendants.
You kept your word,
because you are just.
9 *You perceived the affliction of our ancestors in Egypt,*
you heard their cry at the Sea of Reeds.
10 *You gave signs and miracles against the pharaoh,*
against his servants and all the people of his land,
for you knew that they acted insolently against them.
You made a name for yourself up to this day.
11 *You divided the sea before them;*
they went through the sea as on dry ground.
Their pursuers you hurled into the depths
like a stone in mighty waters.
12 *With a pillar of cloud you led them by day*
and with a pillar of fire by night
to illumine for them the way
on which they should go.
13 *On Mount Sinai you came down*
and spoke with them from above.
You gave to them
judgments that are just,
laws that are reliable,
statutes and commandments that are good.
14 *Your holy sabbath*
you made known to them.
You charged them with your commandments, statutes, and law
through Moses your servant.
15 *Food from heaven you gave for their hunger;*
water from a rock you brought out for their thirst;
you told them to go

and conquer the land
which you had sworn
to give to them.
16 *But they, our ancestors, grew insolent,*
became stubborn, and did not obey your commandments.
17 *They refused to obey,*
did not remember your wonders
which you did for them;
they became stubborn
and determined to go back to their servitude in Egypt.
But you are a God of forgiveness,
gracious and loving,
patient and with much covenant love,
you never abandoned them.
18 *When they made for themselves*
a molten calf
and said: "This is your god
who brought you out of Egypt,"
and committed serious blasphemies,
19 *you in your bounteous love*
did not abandon them in the desert.
The pillar of cloud did not depart from them
by day to lead them on the way,
nor the pillar of fire by night
to illumine for them the way
on which they should go.
20 *Your good Spirit*
you gave to them to instruct them.
Your manna you did not withhold from their mouths
and water you gave to them for their thirst.
21 *For forty years you provided for them*
in the desert; they lacked nothing;
their garments did not wear out;
their feet were not swollen.
22 *You gave to them*
kingdoms and nations
and allotted them as a boundary;
they conquered the land of Sihon king of Heshbon
and the land of Og king of Bashan.
23 *Their children you multiplied*
like the stars of heaven
and brought them into the land
which you promised to their ancestors
to enter and conquer.
24 *The children entered*

and conquered the land.
Before them you subdued
the inhabitants of the land, the Canaanites.
You gave them into their power,
their kings and the nations of the land,
to do to them as they pleased.
25 *They captured fortified cities*
and rich soil.
They took in possession houses
full of pretty things,
hewn cisterns, vineyards, and olive groves,
fruit trees in abundance.
They ate, were filled, and became rich;
they revelled in your great goodness.
26 *But they were disobedient and rebelled against you;*
they cast your law away from them.
They killed your prophets
who warned them
to return to you.
They committed serious blasphemies.
27 *You gave them into the power of their adversaries,*
who oppressed them,
but in the time of their oppression
they cried to you
and you heard them from heaven.
According to your great love
you gave to them saviors
who saved them from the power of their adversaries.
28 *When they had peace,*
they again committed evil before you;
then you gave them over into the power of their enemies;
again they cried to you,
and you heard them from heaven,
and according to your love you saved them many times.
29 *You warned them*
to bring them back to your law,
but they became insolent
and did not obey your commandments,
they sinned against your judgments
by which man finds life if he keeps them;
they turned a stubborn shoulder;
they were stubborn and did not obey.
30 *You bore them for many years;*
and warned them by your Spirit,
through your prophets,

but they would not listen.
So you gave them into the power of the people of the countries.
31 *Through your great love*
you did not eliminate them completely;
you did not abandon them,
for you are a gracious and loving God.
32 *Now, our God, great God,*
mighty and terrible,
keeper of the covenant and covenant love,
do not regard all the miseries as insignificant
which overtook us, our kings, our leaders,
our priests, our prophets,
our ancestors, and all our people
from the time of the kings of Assyria
to the present day.
33 *You are just*
in everything that has befallen us,
because you acted faithfully
while we acted wickedly.
34 *Our kings and our leaders,*
our priests and our ancestors
did not keep your law;
they did not pay attention to your commandments
and your warnings that you gave them.
35 *Even in their own kingdom*
and with the many good things
you gave them,
and in the wide and rich country
you gave them,
they did not serve you
and did not turn away from their evil deeds.
36 *Now we are slaves,*
and the country you gave to our ancestors
to eat its fruits and good things,
we are slaves in it.
37 *Its abundant products are for the kings*
whom you appointed over us for our sins.
They rule over our bodies
and over our cattle as they please.
We are in great distress.

If we have here the redactional work of the Chronicler, it is interesting that it is one of his favorite methods to insert a prayer for purposes of exhortation.[1] But this is uncertain. The prayer is intended to instruct the readers. It gives us a survey of the history of Israel with emphasis on certain events

1. Myers, *Ezra. Nehemiah,* p. 166.

in the life of the Chosen People. This approach is comparable to that of Pss. 78, 105, 106, 135, and 136. Ps. 78 has as introduction a wisdom theme.[2] The historical emphasis in the rest of this Psalm is probably designed to instruct Israel about its history.[3] In Ps. 105 we have a hymnic introduction and a thanksgiving theme. This whole psalm is regarded as a cultic hymn[4] to express Israel's thanksgiving for the Lord's acts in history. With Ps. 106 we are moving closer to the theme of Neh. 9. It extols the Lord's mighty acts, but emphasizes at the same time the unfaithfulness of Israel, a theme well known in Deuteronomic literature.[5] In Ps. 135 we have another typical parallel to Neh. 9: a theme is taken from Scripture and then it is woven in poetic form into a psalm.[6] In Ps. 136 we have another thanksgiving poem composed in an antiphonal style.[7] Thus two types of historical psalms occur,[8] namely, those with a thanksgiving theme and those with a penitential theme. Neh. 9 forms part of the latter. Parts of Scripture, mainly from the Pentateuch, are used as a base on which to build the position of the author. This view is that Israel had been unfaithful to the Lord in spite of his great acts of salvation. Only on account of God's patience and grace did he refuse to abandon them. What had happened to them was due to their own ingratitude.

The composition of this hymn is as follows: The praising of God as Creator (v. 6), the covenant with Abraham (vv. 7–8), the great and wonderful acts of God in Egypt (vv. 9–11), the care of God in the desert (v. 12), Mount Sinai and the desert wandering (vv. 13–21), the conquering of the Holy Land (vv. 22–25), the unfaithfulness of Israel and God's patience in the Holy Land (vv. 26–31), and the confession of sin (vv. 32–37).

The exhortational character of Neh. 9 is clear. The author felt his solidarity with the history of unfaithfulness of his forebears. He also felt the burden of sins of his own time weighing down on his people. True to their history the Jews repaid the mercy and good acts of the Lord with ingratitude on every occasion. After they were punished by the Lord, they

2. Cf. R. E. Murphy in J. L. Crenshaw, ed., *Studies in Ancient Israelite Wisdom* (Ktav: 1976), p. 464.
3. Cf. H.-J. Kraus, *Psalmen* I, pp. 540–41.
4. *Ibid.*, II, p. 719.
5. *Ibid.*, p. 727.
6. *Ibid.*, p. 895.
7. *Ibid.*, pp. 900–901.
8. Cf. also Acts 7. The recapitulation of the history of Israel became a popular theme in later Jewish writings, e.g., the book of Jubilees and the Qumran literature. Cf. F. Baumgärtel, "Zur Liturgie in der 'Sektenrolle' vom Toten Meer," *ZAW* (1953), pp. 263–65; A. G. Lamadrid, *Los descrubrimientos del mar Muerto* (1973), p. 158.

would be faithful for a while, but as soon as they were prosperous, they became again unfaithful to the Lord. This is an ancient theme, familiar throughout the entire OT. The author has rediscovered a general truth which is real even today.

6 This is a beautiful hymn praising the Lord as Creator and Preserver of his creation. *The heaven of heavens.* This is a well-known way of expressing the superlative in Hebrew. *Its host.* This refers either to the stars or to the angels, but quite probably to the stars. The creation theme is present in Ps. 95:5; 104; 136:5–9. In Ps. 136 the creation theme is used as introduction, as in this case. It is then followed by the deliverance from Egypt (Ps. 136:10ff.). The sequence of events is a little different. In Ps. 136 it is the creation and then the history in Egypt; in Neh. 9 it is the creation, the history of Abraham, and then the salvation from Egypt.

7–8 The next topic of this prayer is the election of Abraham. It is a reference to the patriarchal period. For Ur cf. Gen. 11:31 and 15:7, and for the change of Abram's name cf. Gen. 17:5. *You made a covenant.* This refers to Gen. 15:17–21 and 17:4ff. *Canaanites . . . Girgashites.* All six mentioned here in Nehemiah occur also in Gen. 15:19–21, but four are left out (cf. also our discussion of Ezra 9:1). It is interesting to note how the faithfulness of Abraham in v. 8a is balanced with the righteousness of the Lord at the end of this verse (Heb. *ne'ᵉmān* with *ṣaddîq*). It shows that Abraham was faithful and had faith in the Lord; he had set a fine example for his descendants. In Ps. 105:5ff. the history of Abraham is described after the introductory hymn, as in this case.

9–12 The acts of the Lord in Egypt were regarded as one of the most important saving events in the history of Israel. Accounts occur in Ps. 78:12ff.; 105:23ff.; 106:7ff.; 135:8ff.; 136:10ff. It was thus a common theme in the poetical description of Israel's history. *Signs and miracles.* Cf. Exod. 7:3. For v. 11 cf. Exod. 15:4, 5, 19. For v. 12 cf. Exod. 13:21ff. If we compare these verses with the descriptions in the Pentateuch, it is obvious that the author has used a few expressions as a base for outlining a short, compact history of those events he has deemed important for his arguments. The significance of the saving event is emphasized at the end of v. 10 with the phrase *you made a name for yourself up to this day.* The great and wonderful acts of God were still remembered in the days of the author. It is important for people in affliction to remember the power of their Lord over a mighty enemy like the Egyptians in times when they need salvation themselves.

13–14 For v. 13 cf. Exod. 19 and for v. 14 Exod. 31:13–17. In v. 13 the giving of the law is accentuated. It is of interest that the covenant is only mentioned in connection with Abraham. The patriarchal covenant is accentuated because of its promissory character (cf. v. 8). In both vv. 13 and 14 nothing is said of the Sinai covenant, but the stipulations are emphasized. The Davidic covenant (2 Sam. 7) is also not mentioned. The Sinai covenant is not regarded by the Chronicler as important, but he regards the Davidic covenant as very significant.[9] Thus it is rather strange that David and the Davidic covenant are not mentioned in this prayer. *Judgments* (Heb. *mišpāṭîm*) may refer to customary law sanctioned by the Lord at Sinai. Customary law might have developed from verdicts given by local judges in the city gates. Only the judgments which are just were sanctioned by the Lord. *Laws* (Heb. *tôrôṯ*). This term has a large variety of meanings in the semantic field in which it is used in the OT.[10] It refers quite probably to the written part of the law of God that expresses his will. *Statutes* (Heb. *ḥuqqîm*) are not only the obligations which God has given to his people, but are also closely connected to the promise.[11] *Commandments* (Heb. *miṣwōṯ*) are the direct commandments of the Lord.[12] The use of the whole list of legal terminology as we have it here is typical of Deuteronomy (cf., e.g., Deut. 30:10). The parallel use of statutes and judgments occurs frequently in Deuteronomy (cf., e.g., Deut. 4:1; 5:1; 6:1; 7:11, etc.), while the same is true of the parallel use of statutes and commandments (cf., e.g., Deut. 6:2; 8:10; 10:13; etc.). The Chronicler frequently adds *laws* to the list (e.g., 2 Chr. 19:10).[13] The whole catalog signifies the legal prescriptions in their entirety.

15–21 In these verses the main theme of the prayer is developed. The prayer describes alternatively the great acts of God and the disobedience of his people. Even after their salvation from Egypt and in spite of the fact that the Lord provided food and water the Israelites grew insolent and stubborn. Their gravest sin is also described, namely, the making of the molten calf. In spite of all their ingratitude and sins, the Lord never abandoned them. For v. 15 cf. Exod. 16:4. For v. 18 cf. Exod. 32. For v. 21 cf. Deut. 8:4 and 29:5. *Food from heaven*. This is a familiar expression in poetic descriptions of Israel's history (cf. Ps. 78:24; 105:40). It is also

9. Cf. D. J. McCarthy, *OT Covenant: A Survey of Current Opinions* (Richmond: 1972), p. 47.

10. Cf. G. Liedke and C. Petersen, *THAT* II, pp. 1032–43.

11. Cf. G. Liedke, *THAT* I, p. 631. For a general discussion of *ḥōq* see R. Hentschke, *Satzung und Setzender. Ein Beitrag zur israelitischen Rechtsterminologie*. BWANT 5, 3 (Stuttgart: 1963), *passim*; P. Victor, "A Note on *ḥōq* in the OT," *VT* 16 (1966), pp. 358–361; G. Liedke, *Gestalt und Bezeichnung alttestamentliche Rechtssätze. Eine formgeschichtlich-terminologische Studie*. WMANT 39 (Neukirchener: 1971), pp. 154ff.

12. Cf. J. Morgenstern, *HUCA* 33 (1962), pp. 59ff.; Liedke, *Gestalt und Bezeichnung alttestamentliche Rechtssätze*, pp. 187ff.; *idem*, *THAT* II, pp. 530ff.

13. Cf. Liedke, *THAT* I, p. 632; *THAT* II, p. 535.

an important theme in the NT (cf. John 6:22–40; Rev. 2:17).[14] *Conquer* (from the Hebrew root *yrš*) can also mean "to possess." In the wider context here it obviously refers to the conquering of the Holy Land (cf. also vv. 22, 23, and 24), but in v. 25 it means "to take into possession."[15] *Which you had sworn,* literally "you lifted up your hand."[16] *Grew insolent* (Heb. *hēzîḏû*). It is interesting that in v. 10 the same verb is used to denote the insolence of the Egyptians against the Israelites. It means to act in total disregard of someone. If this someone is the Lord, then the gravity of their transgression becomes apparent. *Determined,* literally "and they gave a head (or leader)" (Heb. *wayyittᵉnû rō'š*). Some have taken this to mean "they appointed a leader," referring to Num. 14:4.[17] But here we have obviously a Hebrew idiom meaning "determined," or, "they set their minds on it."[18] *In Egypt* (v. 17). The MT has *bᵉmiryām,* which means "in their rebellion." The *ṣ* of *miṣrayim,* "Egypt," has obviously been omitted.[19] *Your good spirit* (v. 20). Cf. Ps. 143:10. It stands in contrast to evil spirit; cf. 1 Sam. 16:14–16. Some scholars want to discover in the term "good spirit" a Persian influence,[20] but the dualism between the spirit of the Lord and evil spirit or a spirit of deceit (cf. 1 Sam. 16:14; 2 K. 22:23ff.) shows that this kind of terminology was used long before the Persians could have exercised any influence on the Jews.[21]

22–25 Here we have a description of the conquest of the Holy Land. The author emphasizes that the Lord gave them the land. Nothing is said of the valor and guile of Joshua. This is typical of OT tradition. People were important only insofar as the Lord had used them. The real conqueror of the land was the Lord. He fulfilled his will through the history of his people. That is the reason for this prayer, for he is still the God of history. *As a boundary* (Heb. *pē'â*; v. 22). The phrase is not clear. Does it mean that some of the conquered kingdoms later became a boundary,

14. Cf. F. C. Fensham, *Exodus,* p. 104; B. S. Childs, *The Book of Exodus.* OTL (Philadelphia: 1974), pp. 283ff.; and for the NT P. Borgen, *Bread from Heaven: An Exegetical Study of the Manna in the Gospel of John and the Writings of Philo.* Supplements to Novum Testamentum X (Leiden: 1965), *passim.*
15. For a discussion on *yrš* see H. H. Schmid, *THAT* I, pp. 778ff. In Ugaritic *yrṯ* can either mean "take into possession" or "inherit"; cf. *WUS,* p. 137.
16. In Akkadian we have *nīš ilim,* "the oath by the god"; see *AHW* II, pp. 797ff.
17. Brockington, *Ezra, Nehemiah and Esther,* p. 137; GNB.
18. Rudolph, *Esra und Nehemia,* p. 158; Myers, *Ezra. Nehemiah,* p. 160; JB.
19. See *BHS;* Rudolph, *op. cit.,* p. 158; Brockington, *op. cit.,* p. 137. But cf. G. W. Coats, *Rebellion in the Wilderness* (Nashville: 1968), pp. 70, 78, for the acceptance of the MT.
20. Cf. P. Volz, *Der Geist Gottes* (Leipzig: 1910), pp. 175ff.
21. Cf. H.-J. Kraus, *Psalmen* II, p. 938.

that is to say, became neighboring nations? The mentioning of Heshbon and Bashan in this verse might indicate that this was the presumption.[22] *Sihon king of Heshbon.* The Hebrew indicates obvious dittography, because in the MT we have "the land of Sihon and the land of the king of Heshbon." The *waw* might be explicative, in which case we could translate: "the land of Sihon, namely, the land of the king of Heshbon." But this is rather improbable.[23] *Sihon . . . Og.* These two kings are also mentioned in Ps. 135:11; 136:19–20. It is apparent that the mention of these two kings was popular in the poetic description of Israelite history at a certain stage. For v. 22 cf. Num. 21:10–35; Deut. 29:7ff. *Stars of heaven* (v. 23). Cf. Gen. 15:5; 22:17; Exod. 32:13; Deut. 1:10. *Promised to their ancestors.* Here fulfilment of the promise to Abraham is mentioned (cf. v. 8). The Lord kept his covenantal promise to Abraham. We have here two of the most important promises to Abraham, namely, the multiplication of the descendants and the conquering of the Holy Land, themes which were taken up again strongly in postexilic times (cf. also Isa. 51:2).[24] *Subdue* (from the Hebrew root *kn'*). Cf. Deut. 9:3. *The Canaanites.* This is the general term for all the inhabitants of the Holy Land before the Israelite conquest.[25] For *fortified cities* cf. Deut. 1:28; 9:1. For *rich land* (Heb. *'ᵃḏāmâ šᵉmēnâ*) cf. Num. 13:20. *Became rich* (Heb. *wayyašmînû* from the root *šmn*). Cf. Deut. 32:15. It may mean "to become fat." But the meaning "to become rich" has been proposed by H. M. Barstad, which seems acceptable.[26] *Revelled* (Heb. *wayyiṯ'addᵉnû* from the root *'dn*) is a hapax legomenon in the OT. The meaning is uncertain.

26–31 The central theme is developed further in this pericope. It is the contrast between the Lord's love and care and the disobedience of his people. We have here general references to the attitude of his people, e.g., the killing of the prophets (cf. 1 K. 18:4, 13; 19:10, 14; 2 Chr. 24:21) and their reaction to the warnings of the Lord issued throughout the history of Israel. It is a history of disobedience and total neglect of the commandments of the Lord (v. 29). Of this the Israelites could not have been

22. For Ugar. *pat* see *WUS*, p. 252. It has virtually the same semantic field as the Hebrew.
23. Rudolph, *op. cit.*, p. 160.
24. For a discussion of these promises see C. Westermann, *The Promises to the Fathers: Studies on the Patriarchal Narratives* (E.T. 1980), pp. 149–155.
25. For an archeological description of the settlement of Amorites and Canaanites in the early history of the Holy Land, see K. Kenyon, *Amorites and Canaanites* (London: 1966), *passim*, although one cannot agree with all her assumptions. Cf. also A. R. Millard, "The Canaanites," in D. J. Wiseman, ed., *Peoples of OT Times* (Oxford: 1973), pp. 29–52.
26. Cf. H. M. Barstad, "En bemerkning til Deuteronomium 32:15," *NThT* 2 (1975), pp. 103–106.

proud. Every time they were saved by the Lord, and every time they became prosperous, they deviated from the Lord's prescribed ways. *They cast your law away from them,* literally "they cast your law behind their backs," a sign of contempt. *They committed serious blasphemies.* Some scholars want to delete this as possible dittography of the same expression in v. 18.[27] But this deletion is unacceptable because strong textual evidence favors retention of the expression. *Saviors* (Heb. *môšî'îm* from the root *yš'*) in v. 27 probably refers to the judges (cf. Judg. 3:9, 15).[28] For v. 28 cf. Judg. 3:11, 12, 30; 4:1; 6:1.[29] For vv. 29–30 cf. 2 K. 17:13ff. *By which man finds life if he keeps them.* Cf. Lev. 18:5; Ezek. 20:11. It is possible that this kind of expression refers to the admittance of a person to the temple or sanctuary.[30] Real life which is worthwhile for the Jew is to have the right, by keeping the law, to enter the temple as a righteous person. *Gracious and loving God.* Cf. v. 17.

32–37 In these verses the author confesses the sins of his people, past and present. Again the feeling of solidarity with his people becomes apparent. The totality of sins through the ages forced the Lord to take steps against his people. The Israelites were delivered into the hands of foreign kings, who oppressed them and made slaves of them. In this pericope the theme of cause and effect is visible: the sins of the Israelites were the cause for action by the Lord; the effect was their servitude. Sins would be punished. The history of Israel gives evidence of this punishment. Religious apostasy was not condoned. At the same time the people of God were never abandoned by him, because of his *covenant* and *covenant love* (v. 32). We may presume that the patriarchal covenant is intended here. The leading covenant partner, the Lord, kept his covenant by his special interest in his people. They had broken the covenant, but the Lord was still faithful to it. It was the same kind of situation as the one described in Exod. 32–34. The Sinai covenant was broken by the Israelites, but the patriarchal covenant still existed. So they were not abandoned by the Lord (cf. vv. 18–19). *Terrible.* Cf. Neh. 1:5. *Kings of Assyria.* This might be a reference to the Assyrian kings Tiglath-pileser III, Shalmaneser V, Sargon II, and especially Sennacherib. Another possibility is that it is simply a pseudonym for the Persian kings. *You are just.* Cf. Ezra 9:15.

27. Rudolph, *op. cit.*, p. 164.
28. Cf. O. Grether, *ZAW* 57 (1939), pp. 110–121. Cf. also F. C. Fensham, *OTWSA* (1959), p. 20; W. Beyerlin, "Gattung und Herkunft des Rahmens in Richterbuch," in E. Würthwein and O. Kaiser, eds., *Tradition und Situation. Studien zur alttestamentlichen Prophetie.* Festschrift A. Weiser (Göttingen: 1963), p. 7.
29. Cf. Beyerlin, *op. cit.*, p. 11.
30. Cf. W. Zimmerli, *Ezekiel* I, p. 410.

When *just (ṣaddîq)* is applied to God it refers to his righteousness in contrast to the unrighteousness of his people.[31] For v. 35 cf. Deut. 28:47.

Some scholars think that vv. 36–37 testify against the authorship of Ezra, because reference is made to kings who were appointed over the Jews to rule over their bodies and their cattle. It is then held that Ezra would not have referred in this way to the Persian kings, because they had assisted the Jews.[32] We must keep in mind, however, that the Jews were subjects of the Persian kings. They had to pay taxes to them. If Nehemiah could call Artaxerxes "this man" (Neh. 1:11) in his prayer, it is quite acceptable to maintain that Ezra could have used the terminology of vv. 36–37.

E. COVENANT CONFIRMED (10:1–40 [Eng. 9:38–10:39])

1. The Covenant (10:1 [Eng. 9:38])

1 (9:38) *Because of all this we made a firm covenant and wrote it down. Our leaders, Levites, and priests set their seal to it.*

In the Hebrew Bible this verse quite correctly forms part of the next chapter. There is some difference of opinion as to whether Neh. 10 stands in its original position.[1] It is clear, however, from the expression *because of all this* (Heb. *ûḇᵉḵol-zō'ṯ*) that this chapter is connected to the previous one, whether or not an editor may have been responsible for this phrase.[2]

1 (9:38) The author describes here a covenant renewal. After the confession of sin in ch. 9, this approach to the solving of the problem is understandable.[3] They must come into a new relationship with the Lord. *Made a firm covenant,* literally "We cut a firmness," which is a surrogate for making a covenant.[4] *Set their seal to it,* literally "And on the seal were our leaders. . . ."[5]

31. For *ṣdq* cf. the discussion of K. H. Fahlgren, *Ṣedaḳa, nahestehende und entgegengesetzte Begriffe im AT* (1932); A. Jepsen, "*ṣdq* und *ṣdqh* im AT," in H. G. Reventlow, ed., *Gottes Wort und Gottes Land.* Festschrift H. W. Hertzberg (Göttingen: 1965), pp. 78–89, esp. p. 87.
32. Rudolph, *op. cit.,* pp. 156ff.; Myers, *op. cit.,* p. 170.
1. Myers, *Ezra. Nehemiah,* pp. 174–75; Galling, *Die Bücher der Chronik, Esra, Nehemia,* p. 242.
2. Rudolph, *Esra und Nehemia,* p. 172; K. Baltzer, *The Covenant Formulary,* p. 43; A. Jepsen, "Nehemiah 10," *ZAW* 66 (1954), pp. 87–106; In der Smitten, *Esra,* pp. 51ff.
3. Baltzer, *op. cit.,* pp. 43ff.
4. Myers, *op. cit.,* p. 173.
5. Cf. S. Moscati, "I sigilli nell'Antico Testamento: Studio esegetico-filologico," *Bibl* 30 (1949), pp. 314–338, esp. p. 320.

2. *Signers of the Pledge (10:2–28 [Eng. 1–27])*

2 (1) *On the sealed document (were the names) of Nehemiah the governor, the son of Hacaliah, and Zedekiah,*
3 (2) *Seraiah, Azariah, Jeremiah,*
4 (3) *Pashhur, Amariah, Malchijah,*
5 (4) *Hattush, Shebaniah, Malluch,*
6 (5) *Harim, Meremoth, Obadiah,*
7 (6) *Daniel, Ginnethon, Baruch,*
8 (7) *Meshullam, Abijah, Mijamin,*
9 (8) *Maaziah, Bilgai, and Shemaiah: they were the priests.*
10 (9) *The Levites were Jeshua the son of Azaniah, Binnui from the descendants of Henadad, and Kadmiel.*
11 (10) *Their companions were Shebaniah, Hodaviah, Kelita, Pelaiah, Hanan,*
12 (11) *Micah, Rehob, Hashabiah.*
13 (12) *Zaccur, Sherebiah, Shebaniah,*
14 (13) *Hodiah, Bani, and Beninu.*
15 (14) *The leaders of the people were Parosh, Pahath-moab, Elam, Zattu, Bani,*
16 (15) *Bunni, Azgad, Bebai,*
17 (16) *Adonijah, Bigvai, Adin,*
18 (17) *Ater, Hezekiah, Azzur,*
19 (18) *Hodiah, Hashum, Bezai,*
20 (19) *Hariph, Anathoth, Nebai,*
21 (20) *Magpiash, Meshullam, Hezir,*
22 (21) *Meshezabel, Zadok, Jaddua,*
23 (22) *Pelatiah, Hanan, Anaiah,*
24 (23) *Hoshea, Hananiah, Hasshub,*
25 (24) *Hallohesh, Pilha, Shobek,*
26 (25) *Rehum, Hashabnah, Maaseiah,*
27 (26) *Ahijah, Hanan, Anan,*
28 (27) *Malluch, Harim, and Baanah.*

2 (1) *On the sealed document,* literally "and on the seals." The usage of the plural here, while in 10:1 (Eng. 9:38) the singular is used, is puzzling. Does it refer to the signing of names on different sealed documents? In this verse the names of two leaders are mentioned. *Nehemiah the governor, the son of Hacaliah.* Cf. our discussion of 1:1. The position of the term *governor (tiršāṯā')* between the name Nehemiah and the patronymic is regarded as strange, but various examples of the same phenomenon appear in extrabiblical texts.[1] It is therefore clear that Nehemiah was the first to sign the renewed covenant. Why is Ezra not mentioned? This is difficult

1. Myers, *Ezra. Nehemiah,* p. 173, offers some references.

to explain; cf. our discussion of 8:10. *Zedekiah.* The special position of this person is not explained. No title is given, and it is the only place in Ezra-Nehemiah where he is mentioned. Some think that Zedekiah might have been the secretary of Nehemiah.[2] This is not impossible, but cannot be proved. He was most probably an official acting in an unstated capacity.

3–9 (2–8) In these verses the priests are mentioned quite probably according to their family names. Twenty-one names are listed.[3] Certain of these names do not occur either in 12:1–7 or 12:12–21. To suggest that a reduction of the number of priests was made from the time of Zerubbabel onward is unacceptable. Some think that the presence of Harim in this list, but its omission in Neh. 12, confirms such a reduction, but this theory relies too much on the listing of people.[4] Names could have been omitted. We have seen already that not all the work on the wall of Jerusalem is described in Neh. 3, so the same could have happened with lists of names. Many scholars hold the opinion that this list of Neh. 10 is earlier than any other of the lists of the Chronicler or Ezra-Nehemiah.[5] It is difficult to prove, however, because any attempt to systematize the names of the different lists is futile.

10–14 (9–13) The names of the Levites are supplied. It is clear that we have here names of individuals and not of families.[6] To illustrate how hazardous it is to compare the names of this chapter with names of Levites in other lists we refer to Ezra 2 (= Neh. 7) where only three families are listed, while in Neh. 9:4–5 sixteen names are given, some of which are the same as here. In Neh. 12:8–9 we have again eight names of which four are the same as in Neh. 10, but in Neh. 12:24–25 only three names are supplied. It is clearly difficult to derive from these lists the information that in the time of Nehemiah there were additions to the Levites.[7] We may presume that families grew larger and that some of them broke up into several more families, but it cannot be proved from the lists.

15–28 (14–27) Here the names of lay families are given. It is obvious that vv. 14–19a follow the list of Ezra 2, because fourteen of the names are the same.[8] From v. 19b onward we have an expansion. Ac-

2. *Ibid.*, p. 176; Brockington, *Ezra, Nehemiah and Esther*, p. 139.

3. Brockington, *op. cit.*, p. 139, refers to the possibility that originally twenty-four names might have been given, "representing the twenty-four priestly courses or family divisions of priests" (cf. 1 Chr. 24:1–19).

4. Cf. E. Auerbach, "Der Aufstieg der Priesterschaft zur Macht im alten Israel," *VTS* 9 (1962), pp. 246–47.

5. Cf. A. Jepsen, *ZAW* 66 (1954), pp. 87–106; *idem*, "Nehemia 10," *TLZ* 79 (1954), pp. 305–306; Myers, *op. cit.*, p. 176.

6. Rudolph, *Esra und Nehemia*, p. 175; Myers, *op. cit.*, p. 176.

7. Myers, *op. cit.*, pp. 176–77.

8. Brockington, *op. cit.*, p. 141.

cording to Myers this expanded list shows that the community had grown through the addition of those who had not gone into exile, or who had returned to the land from hideouts during the Babylonian invasion.[9] His reasons for the growth are not acceptable, for it is clear that those Jews who were not exiles were not regarded as part of the religious community. The second reason, namely, that they had returned from hideouts, is also not very plausible. Is it possible that after more than a century people were still returning from hideouts in the country? It is more satisfactory to presume that the numbers had grown by the natural increase of the population. Things had changed for the Jewish families since the arrival of Sheshbazzar, for even the local names of towns, like Anathoth and Nebai, were now accepted as family names. Larger families had divided themselves into several smaller family units. Even those names which are missing from lists might point to the fact that the people concerned no longer existed because no male descendants had been born—a fairly common phenomenon in genealogies.

3. Oath to Keep the Covenant (10:29–30 [Eng. 28–29])

29 (28) *The rest of the people, the priests, Levites, gatekeepers, singers, and temple servants, namely, all who had separated themselves from the people of the lands to (keep) the law of God, their wives, sons, and their daughters, all who are able to understand,*

30 (29) *joined their important companions and took (on themselves) a curse and oath to follow the law of God which was given through Moses the servant of God, to keep and practice all the commandments of the Lord, our God, and his judgments and statutes.*

29–30 (28–29) The signing of the document is finished and now the next step in contracting the covenant is fulfilled, namely, the ceremony of taking an oath. This was an integral part of making a covenant. The minor partner or partners had to take an oath to keep the stipulations of the treaty or covenant.[1] Interesting in this respect is the mention of the curse (Heb. *'ālâ*). The curse is closely connected to the oath. When the oath is broken, the curse will come into effect.[2] It is a question of cause and effect. The breaking of the oath of the covenant automatically results in the curse.

9. Myers, *op. cit.*, p. 177.
1. Cf. D. J. McCarthy, *OT Covenant*, pp. 65–66. For the oath see M. R. Lehmann, "Biblical Oaths," *ZAW* 81 (1969), pp. 74–92.
2. Cf. W. Schottroff, *Der altisraelitische Fluchspruch*, pp. 28–29; J. Scharbert, *TDOT* I, pp. 261–66, esp. p. 264. Cf. also H. C. Brichto, *The Problem of "Curse" in the Hebrew Bible*. JBL Monograph Series 13 (Philadelphia: 1963), pp. 22–76; J. Scharbert, *Bibl* 39 (1958), pp. 2–5; C. A. Keller, *THAT* I, pp. 148–152.

Curse *('ālâ)* is sometimes so closely related to covenant that it functions as a synonym of covenant (cf. Deut. 29:20).[3]

Some scholars are of the opinion that v. 29 (Eng. 28) is to be connected directly to 10:1 (Eng. 9:38) and that 10:2–28 (Eng. 1–27) is inserted later.[4] The problem is the infinitives of v. 30 (Eng. 29), but these are not contrary to the style of Ezra-Nehemiah. We must admit that the list of categories of Jews with a clause inserted in between, with the verb at the beginning of v. 30 (Eng. 29) and the whole of v. 29 (Eng. 28) as subject, is a little awkward. But why should we have a difference of opinion with a biblical author about his style? As it stands it makes perfect sense.

It was an important oath that the Jews had taken. All in the community who were clean and thus separated from the foreigners took on themselves to keep *and* practice the law of God, the Pentateuch. With the renewal of the covenant they came into a renewed relationship with God, a relationship of obedience to the precepts of his law.

4. *Stipulations of the Covenant (10:31–40 [Eng. 30–39])*

31 (30) *We shall not give our daughters in marriage to the people of the land nor shall we allow our sons to marry their daughters.*

32 (31) *When the people of the land will bring their wares and any grain on the sabbath to sell, we shall not buy it from them on the sabbath, the holy day. We will forego (farming products) in the seventh year and also debts from anyone.*

33 (32) *Furthermore, we take on ourselves the following obligations: To give a third of a shekel yearly for the service of the temple of God*

34 (33) *for the showbread, the perpetual meal offering, the perpetual burnt offering, the sabbaths, the new-moon festivals, for feasts, sacred foods, the sin offerings to atone for Israel, and for all the work of the temple of our God.*

35 (34) *We have cast our lot for the priests, Levites, and people in connection with the wood offering, to bring it into the temple of our God according to families at appointed times every year to burn on the altar of the Lord our God, as it is written in the law;*

36 (35) *also to bring the firstfruits of our soil and the firstfruits of every fruit tree each year to the temple of the Lord,*

37 (36) *and also the firstborn of our sons and our cattle as is written in the law, and the firstborn of our herds and flocks, to bring them to the*

3. Cf. the discussion by P. C. Craigie, *The Book of Deuteronomy*. NICOT (Grand Rapids: 1976), p. 359. In Phoenician an example of *'lt* means "covenant"; *KAI* II, p. 45.

4. Brockington, *Ezra, Nehemiah and Esther,* p. 143; JB; Baltzer, *The Covenant Formulary,* p. 43.

temple of our God for the priests who are serving in the temple of our God.

38 (37) *We shall also bring the best of our dough, our products, the fruit of every tree, wine, and oil to the priests, to the chambers of the temple of our God, and a tithe of our soil to the Levites. The Levites will collect the tithes in all our farming cities.*

39 (38) *An Aaronite priest must be present when the Levites collect the tithes. The Levites must take up to the temple of our God a tithe of the tithes to the treasury chambers of the temple.*

40 (39) *The Israelites and Levites must bring up to the chambers the produce of grain, wine, and oil. It is at this place where the sacred vessels, the serving priests, the gatekeepers, and the singers are. We shall not neglect the temple of our God.*

These stipulations lay the emphasis on religious and cultic practices. The small Jewish community is reorganized to meet the obligations of their religion. Most of the stipulations are intended for the maintenance of the temple service. For a time the Persian king took the responsibility for the provision of necessary funds to maintain the temple cult. According to the stipulations of this pericope, the Jews under strong leadership accepted responsibility for continuing the temple service from their own means. This was a heavy burden for a relatively small and poor community, but it was obvious that at some stage they had to face their responsibilities. The religious inspiration born out of the new relationship with the Lord gave them the courage to carry this heavy burden. In this they were united from the highest official to the lowest in the social structure.

31 (30) The mixed marriages are a recurrent theme in Ezra-Nehemiah (cf. Ezra 9–10; Neh. 13:23–28). Some scholars have drawn attention to the problem that in this verse the people undertake not to marry foreigners, but in Neh. 13 foreign marriages are a major problem. Is it possible that the Jews could have forgotten their solemn pledge so soon? It is important, however, to note that the pledge was made only by those who had separated themselves from the foreigners. It is quite probable that those who had already married foreign women had been dealt with earlier.[1] For the problems in connection with mixed marriages cf. our discussion of Ezra 9–10.

32 (31) In the Ten Commandments, the keeping of the sabbath as a day of rest which is sacred to the Lord is prescribed (cf. Exod. 20:8–11; Deut. 5:12–15). For a small religious community in a larger world of heathens who did not hold the sabbath law, it became more and more difficult to keep it. The foreign merchants arrived in Jerusalem on

1. Myers, *Ezra. Nehemiah*, p. 178.

the sabbath and wanted to do business (cf. Neh. 13:16). The way of least resistance was for the Jews to accommodate themselves to these foreign customs. But in this verse the Jews put themselves under obligation to withhold from participating in any transactions on the sabbath. *The sabbath, the holy day.* We take the *waw* before "on the holy day" as explicative.[2]

The command to hold a sabbatical year occurs in Exod. 23:10–11; Lev. 25:2–7. It is interesting to note the connection of the sabbatical year with the *debts from everyone* (literally "debts in every hand"). This is quite probably taken over from Deut. 15:1–3. Exod. 23:10–11 says nothing of debts or pledges.[3] It is probably inserted here as a result of the problems described in Neh. 5. This would mean that from now on debts or pledges should be suspended in the sabbatical year. It is of interest, however, that nothing is said of debt slavery.[4]

33–34 (32–33) These two verses mention the necessities for the daily functioning of the temple service. *A third of a shekel.* In Exod. 30:13 half a shekel is prescribed as a yearly contribution. The change to a third of a shekel can be attributed to a different monetary system in the Persian empire.[5] *Showbread,* literally "The bread which is set in rows," a typical postexilic term for "the bread of presence" (cf. 1 Chr. 9:32; 32:29; 2 Chr. 13:11). For *the perpetual meal offering* cf. Num. 28:1–8. *The perpetual burnt offering* consisted of one lamb each for morning and evening (cf. Exod. 29:38–42). The priority of meal offering over burnt offering in this verse might point to the growing importance of the meal offering.[6] *The sabbaths . . . feasts.* Cf. Num. 28:9–31; 29:1–39. For *sin offerings* cf. Lev. 4:1–5:13; Num. 15:22–29. *All the work of the temple.* This refers to the maintenance of the building of the temple.

35 (34) The casting of the lot to make a person responsible for a specific task is known in the OT (1 Sam. 10:19ff.). In Lev. 1:17 and 6:12ff. the wood and the fact that enough wood must be present is mentioned, but nothing is said about families who were held responsible for supplying the wood. On these verses of Leviticus a new obligation was built to divide the responsibility for the delivery of wood (cf. Mishnah *Taanith* 4:5). This was a practical measure, typical of Nehemiah, to ensure the continual delivery of this important commodity of the temple service.

36–40 (35–39) Not only must the regular sacrifices to the Lord be continued, but also the maintenance of temple service itself. The most

2. It is then unnecessary to include all holy days like Myers, *ibid.*
3. For a discussion see R. North, *Sociology of the Biblical Jubilee,* pp. 181ff.; H. Weill, *AHDO* 2 (1938), p. 171.
4. Cf. North, *op. cit.,* p. 38.
5. Myers, *op. cit.,* pp. 178–79.
6. Brockington, *Ezra, Nehemiah and Esther,* p. 144.

important part of this is the temple personnel. For them food must be provided. This explains the meaning of the bringing of firstfruits and the firstborn to the temple. This is then supplemented further with the delivery of tithes. For the *firstfruits* cf. Exod. 23:19; 34:26; Deut. 26:1–11. The firstborn child could be redeemed by paying five shekels of silver (Exod. 13:13; 34:20). For the firstborn of cattle and sheep cf. Exod. 13:12; Num. 18:17; Deut. 12:6. For the firstborn of a donkey redemption by a lamb is prescribed, or else its neck must be broken (cf. Exod. 13:13). In addition to all these, the best products of the house and farm must be brought for the temple personnel. *Our products* (Heb. *t^e^rûmōṯênû*). The Hebrew term is usually translated "contributions," but if we compare it with the same term in v. 39, namely, *the produce of grain,* it becomes clear that products from house and farm are meant. *Tithes.* According to Lev. 27:30 the tithes are sacred to the Lord, and according to Num. 18:21 the tithes belong to the Levites. Here in Nehemiah they are not only the recipients, but also the collectors of the tithes. At other times it was expected of individuals that they would bring the tithes to the temple (Deut. 14:23ff.; Amos 4:4; 2 Chr. 31:12).[7] It is possible that Nehemiah enacted this measure in accordance with tax-collecting procedures in the Persian empire.[8] The supervision of the collecting of tithes by a priest might also be connected to practices in the Persian empire where an overseer *(šaknu)* was appointed to supervise the tax collecting.[9] *Farming cities* or rural cities—all the towns with farms around them are meant here.[10]

It is obvious that the temple is the central theme of this whole pericope. The temple was very important for Nehemiah.[11] The continual maintenance of the temple cult and personnel was a necessity as a binding factor uniting all the loose elements of Jewish families who had returned from exile. It bound them to the service of God, but also to one another. In every religious community this is one of the most important characteristics. It was not only a legal obligation, but a living reality to them, because with the renewal of the covenant they came into a living relationship with the Lord.

7. *Ibid.*, p. 145.
8. Frye, *The Heritage of Persia*, p. 108.
9. *Ibid.*
10. Myers, *op. cit.*, p. 180, thinks of "cult cities," but this is not acceptable.
11. Rudolph, *Esra und Nehemia*, p. 180.

VI. FURTHER ACTIVITIES OF NEHEMIAH; GENEALOGIES (11:1–13:3)

A. PEOPLE SETTLED IN JERUSALEM (11:1–24)

1. The Repopulation of Jerusalem (11:1–2)

1 *The leaders of the people lived in Jerusalem. The rest of the people cast lots in order to bring one out of every ten to live in Jerusalem, the holy city, while the other nine remained in the (other) cities.*
2 *The people praised all the men who were willing to stay in Jerusalem.*

1–2 These verses and this chapter are closely connected with Neh. 7:1–5, especially v. 4. In 7:4 the sparse population of Jerusalem is mentioned. Then Nehemiah started an investigation into the genealogies of the returnees (Neh. 7:6–72a). Here the solution to the problem of 7:4 is given. We are not certain as to whether the leaders set the example and were the first to settle in Jerusalem[1] or whether they were already living in Jerusalem.[2] The verb from the root *yšb* could have both meanings. It is, however, better to assume that the leaders already lived in Jerusalem and that measures for the resettlement of the other people were being taken. *Cast lots*. Cf. 10:34. Lots were cast to select one out of every ten persons to live in Jerusalem. From this we may deduce that circumstances were such that some were in effect forced to go to Jerusalem. In such a case the reference in v. 2 to their willingness to stay in Jerusalem is uncertain. This problem can be solved either by understanding that in v. 2 another group is mentioned, a group of volunteers, or that those selected by the lot accepted it gladly.[3] The people regarded their selection by the sacred lot as the will of God, and were thus satisfied and glad to do his bidding. For this positive attitude they were praised by the rest of the people. The religious motivation lies below the surface, but it is there, e.g., the reference to Jerusalem as the holy city points to an accentuation of the religious cult performed there. It was for them a privilege to live so close to the temple where the special presence of the Lord was felt. *The holy city* (cf. Isa. 48:2; 52:1; Neh. 11:18; Dan. 9:24). This is mainly a postexilic appellation for Jerusalem.[4] *The other nine* (Heb. *w^{e}ṯēša‘ hayyāḏôṯ*), literally "and nine

1. Rudolph, *Esra und Nehemia*, p. 181; Brockington, *Ezra, Nehemiah and Esther*, p. 146.
2. Myers, *Ezra. Nehemiah*, p. 186.
3. Brockington, *op. cit.*, p. 146.
4. Rudolph, *op. cit.*, p. 181; Myers, *op. cit.*, p. 184; W. Vischer in *Probleme biblischer Theologie*, p. 608; Pelaia, *Esdra e Neemia*, p. 205.

parts[5] (or hands)." The remaining nine were to stay in the rural cities or towns in order to maintain farming activities. Nehemiah saw to it that the agricultural work was not hampered unnecessarily by his measures. His action in this respect is characterized by a thorough awareness of the practical implications. At the same time his decision to execute it by the casting of the lot betrays his intimate knowledge of the religious convictions of his people. By casting the lot it is no longer Nehemiah who forces them to live in Jerusalem, but it is the will of God. So they could not bear a grudge against him.

2. *Laity Living in Jerusalem (11:3–9)*

3 *There were the leaders of the province who lived in Jerusalem, but in the cities of Judah everyone lived on his own property in their cities, the Israelites, priests, Levites, temple servants, and descendants from Solomon's servants.*

4 *In Jerusalem there lived some of the Judeans and some of the Benjaminites. Some of the Judeans were Athaiah the son of Uzziah, the son of Zechariah, the son of Amariah, the son of Shepathiah, the son of Mahalalel, from the descendants of Perez;*

5 *Maaseiah the son of Baruch, the son of Col-hozeh, the son of Hazaiah, the son of Adaiah, the son of Joiarib, the son of Zechariah, a descendant of the Shilonites;*

6 *All the descendants of Perez who lived in Jerusalem were 468 able men.*

7 *These were the Benjaminites: Sallu the son of Meshullam, the son of Joed, the son of Pedaiah, the son of Kolaiah, the son of Maaseiah, the son of Ethiel, the son of Jeshaiah;*

8 *after him Gabbai and Sallai, 928.*

9 *Joel the son of Zichri was in charge of them, and Judah the son of Hassenuah was second in command over the city.*

There are several problems with this list from vv. 3ff. The first is the number of similarities between this list and that of 1 Chr. 9:2ff. Is the one dependent on the other? Rudolph is of the opinion that the list of 1 Chr. 9 is dependent on the list of Neh. 11.[1] His main argument is built on the fact that the Chronicler also makes use of the Nehemian redactional addition of v. 3. Other scholars, however, think that both Nehemiah and the Chronicler made use of a list in the archives, or else both made their copies

5. Cf. F. C. Fensham, "Remarks on Keret 54–59," *JNSL* 3 (1974), p. 29.

1. Rudolph, *Esra und Nehemia*, pp. 183–84.

from archival material.[2] Even if we accept Rudolph's surmise, the problem of the many differences between the lists remains unsolved. A comparison of the two lists shows that the one of 1 Chr. 9 is much longer. For example, in connection with the Benjaminite line the Chronicler lists another three families which are omitted in Nehemiah. A glaring difference is seen in the names listed for the sons of Perez in 1 Chr. 9:4 and here in Neh. 11:4.

These differences are enigmatic and very difficult to explain. We might presume that various genealogical lists were present in the archives. Each author made use of it in his own way, omitting material which he did not regard as relevant and adding new material to bring the list up to date. It is also clear that with the transmission of genealogical lists many scribal errors had crept in. The same hazards existed then that are still well known in modern research on genealogies. So it is wise to refrain from producing solutions which are built merely on assumptions. This list in Nehemiah provides us with the names and descent of those leaders who were living in Jerusalem. The city wall was built, and now a new measure to safeguard the city was instituted, namely, to repopulate it. It was typical of postexilic times that not only were the names of persons supplied, but also their genealogical descent to show that they were of pure Jewish extraction.

3 This is a redactional note inserted by Nehemiah as an introduction to the list. The parenthetical clause *but in the cities . . . in their cities* makes the reading and translation awkward. The meaning and purpose, however, are quite clear. Nehemiah mentions the leaders in Jerusalem, but then he reminds himself of the people still living outside Jerusalem. After drawing attention to them, he continues with the different categories of Jews who are listed, namely, Israelites (laity), priests, Levites, etc.

4–9 Two groups of heads of families are given, one from Judah and the other from Benjamin. Of the Judeans, the family which traced their origin back to Perez (Gen. 38:29), one of the sons of Judah, is placed first. The second family is in the Shilonite line. Only a total for the descendants of Perez is given. It shows, as we have seen, that certain information is omitted.[3] Of interest is that in the Benjaminite line the ancient ancestor is not given. This omission might be due to the early history of Benjamin, when almost the whole tribe was killed (Judg. 19–21).[4]

The beginning of v. 8 is not clear. *After him*. This may refer to the

2. Myers, *Ezra. Nehemiah,* p. 185; H. Schneider, *Die Bücher Esra und Nehemia.* HSAT 4/2 (Bonn: 1959), *in loc.* Cf. also U. Kellermann, "Die Listen in Nehemia 11 eine Dokumentation aus den letzten Jahren des Reiches Juda?," *ZDPV* 82 (1966), pp. 209–227, for a possible early date of this list.

3. Brockington, *Ezra, Nehemiah and Esther,* pp. 147–48.

4. *Ibid.*, p. 148.

two persons following Sallu. Some want to read "his kinsmen" instead of "after him."[5] Others want to change the names of Gabbai and Sallai to read *gibbôrê ḥayil,* "able men," as in v. 6. But it is noteworthy that the name Sallai occurs in 12:20 and in the Elephantine papyri.[6] The best course is to accept the MT.

It is not clear whether Joel and Judah in v. 9 were Benjaminites or Judeans. Some scholars think that they were not Benjaminites;[7] others maintain that they were.[8] Because no clear lineage is given of these persons, we shall never know. As we have translated it, Joel was in charge of Jerusalem as administrator and Judah was second in command. This stands in contradiction to Neh. 7:2, but some time might have elapsed between the appointment of Hanani and the administration of Joel. At least they appear to have had the same office.

3. *Priests (11:10–14)*

10 *Of the priests there were Jedaiah the son of Joiarib, Jachin,*
11 *Seraiah the son of Hilkiah, the son of Meshullam, the son of Zadok, the son of Meraioth, the son of Ahitub, the overseer of the temple of God,*
12 *and their companions administering the work of the temple, 822; and Adaiah the son of Jeroham, the son of Pelaliah, the son of Amzi, the son of Zechariah, the son of Pashhur, the son of Malchijah,*
13 *and his companions, leaders of the families, 242; and Amashsai the son of Azarel, the son of Ahzai, the son of Meshillemoth, the son of Immer,*
14 *and their companions, able men, 128. Zabdiel the son of Haggedolim was in charge of them.*

10–14 This list is full of problems, and corruption of the text occurred with its transmission. The first problem is the name Jachin without the phrase "the son of" in front of it. One solution is to regard *yāḵîn* as a scribal error for *bēn,* "son."[1] This would mean that we have a long genealogical list of Jedaiah. It would furthermore mean that Jedaiah, as overseer of the temple of God, is the high priest. Other scholars, however, retain the name Jachin and maintain that five priestly families are mentioned.[2] Some scholars hold that "the son of" before Joiarib is an intrusion and

5. See *BHS*.
6. Cf. *AP,* p. 55 (18:2), where the name *sly'* appears.
7. Myers, *op. cit.*, p. 187.
8. Brockington, *op. cit.*, p. 149.
1. Rudolph, *Esra und Nehemia*, p. 184.
2. Myers, *Ezra. Nehemiah*, p. 187.

must be deleted.[3] The textual evidence is uncertain. Another problem is the name *Amashsai*, which is impossible to explain from the Hebrew. Some think that it is an error for Amasiah, others hold that it must be Amasai. In 1 Chr. 9:12 the name Maasai is read. The reading here in Nehemiah might be a combination of Amasai and Amaśai (Heb. *ʿ^{a}māsāy* and *ʿ^{a}māśāy*).[4] This may explain the readings *s* and *ś* (read as *š*). The next problem is the name *Haggedolim* ("the great ones"). It occurs nowhere else in the OT. It must be a scribal error, but it is impossible to determine its significance. It is difficult to ascertain the precise difference or similarity between *nāgîḏ* ("overseer")[5] in v. 11 and *pāqîḏ* ("in charge of") in v. 14. Is it possible that two different persons could have held the high-priestly office? Alternatively, *pāqîḏ* might refer to an administrative office below the level of high priest.

4. *Levites (11:15–18)*

15 *Of the Levites there were Shemaiah the son of Hasshub, the son of Azrikam, the son of Hashabiah, the son of Bunni.*
16 *Of the leaders of the Levites Shabbethai and Jozabad were responsible for the work outside the temple of God.*
17 *Mattaniah the son of Micah, the son of Zabdi, the son of Asaph, was the leader of the praise songs; he also intoned the thanksgiving for the prayer songs. Bakbukiah was second in command among his companions. There was also Abda the son of Shammua, the son of Galal, the son of Jeduthun.*
18 *All the Levites in the holy city were 284.*

15–18 In this list Levites and singers are mentioned. This is contrary to the approach of Ezra and Nehemiah elsewhere (cf. Ezra 7:7) where they are separated.[1] In this list we have six families. The family of Shemaiah is approximately the same as in 1 Chr. 9, the only difference being in the name *Bunni* at the end of Shemaiah's family tree. Some scholars think that *Bunni* is a scribal error for "the son of" and that the name Merari is left out, comparing it with 1 Chr. 9 (cf. also Ezra 8:19).[2] This is possible, although in such a case one has to realize that there was also dittography of *ben*, "son of." *The work outside the temple*. Some scholars are of the

3. See *BHK* with one ms. and in comparison with 1 Chr. 9:10; cf. also Myers, *op. cit.*, p. 187.
4. Rudolph, *op. cit.*, p. 184.
5. Cf. C. Westermann, *THAT* II, p. 34; W. Richter, "Die *nāgîd*-Formel," *BZ* N.F. 9 (1965), pp. 71–84.
1. Brockington, *Ezra, Nehemiah and Esther*, pp. 150–51; Myers, *Ezra. Nehemiah*, p. 188.
2. Rudolph, *Esra und Nehemia*, p. 186.

opinion that this refers to the outside appearance of the temple.[3] Another possibility is that this outside work entails the collecting of the tithes, the temple taxes (10:38–40 [Eng. 37–39]).

From the Levitic singers two or three families are listed. *The son of Asaph.* As we have noted already, "son of" does not always denote the immediate son, but occasionally a person in the family lineage. Alternatively we must accept that Mattaniah was the grandson of Asaph. *Praise song.* We are reading with the Lucianic version and Vulgate *tᵉhillâ,* "praise," instead of *tᵉḥillâ,* "beginning," of the MT.[4] *Intoned the thanskgiving* (Heb. *yᵉhôḏê*). In postexilic literature the Hebrew roots *ydh* and *hll* were used almost as synonyms.[5] It is quite difficult to express this fact in translation. *Second in command.* For singing this would mean a stand-in or substitute. For *Jeduthun* cf. 1 Chr. 16:42. The number of Levites is still relatively small in comparison with the other groups.

5. *Other Groups (11:19–24)*

19 *The gatekeepers were Akkub, Talmon, and their companions who kept watch at the gates. They were 172.*

20 *The rest of the Israelites with the priests and Levites were in all the cities of Judah, each one in his inheritance.*

21 *The temple servants lived at Ophel, and Ziha and Gishpa were over the temple servants.*

22 *In charge of the Levites in Jerusalem was Uzzi the son of Bani, the son of Hashabiah, the son of Mattaniah, the son of Micah, descendants of Asaph who were responsible for the singing in the temple of God,*

23 *for they were under command of the king and a contract existed for the singers for their day-by-day attendance.*

24 *Pethahiah the son of Meshezabel, from the descendants of Zerah the son of Judah, was the king's representative concerning matters of the people.*

19 We probably have two family names here. For Akkub and Talmon cf. Ezra 2:42; 1 Chr. 9:17. They were gatekeepers of the temple and should not be confused with the gatekeepers of the city gates (cf. Neh. 7:3).

20 Some scholars hold the opinion that this verse belongs to vv. 25ff. and is therefore out of place here.[1] This is possible, because this verse would make better sense before v. 25. On the other hand, it is also

3. *Ibid.*
4. *BHS;* Rudolph, *op. cit.,* p. 186; Myers, *op. cit.,* p. 185; Brockington, *op. cit.,* p. 151.
5. Cf. C. Westermann, *THAT* I, p. 681.
1. Rudolph, *Esra und Nehemia,* pp. 186–87.

conceivable that Nehemiah wanted to draw attention to a fairly large group of Jews who lived outside Jerusalem, as he does in 11:3. He might have reasoned that the reader of this list might receive the wrong impression, namely, that all the Jews lived in Jerusalem. So occasionally he draws attention to those who lived outside the city. The position of this verse, we must admit, is indeed awkward.

21–24 Rudolph regards these verses as a later addition by a knowledgeable author.[2] His arguments in favor of his surmise seem to be cogent. The problematic text is v. 22, where the descendants of Asaph are again listed (cf. v. 17) and another leader, Uzzi, is mentioned. According to this genealogy Uzzi was the great-grandson of Mattaniah, who is mentioned in v. 17. It is obvious that in this later addition the genealogy of the Asaphites was brought up to date, making it considerably later than the list of v. 17. *Command of the king.* This might refer to King David (Neh. 12:24; 1 Chr. 25), but it is more likely that it refers to the Persian king who was interested in the continuation of cultic practices (cf. Ezra 4:8–10; 7:21–24). V. 24 gives the name of the Jewish ambassador at the Persian court. This official was appointed by the king to give him advice in connection with Jewish affairs, an office remarkably close to that of Ezra,[3] although the latter was sent to Judah to initiate certain reforms. *The king's representative,* literally "at the hand (or side) of the king."

B. CITIES OF JUDAH AND BENJAMIN (11:25–36)

25 *Concerning the rural areas and their farms — some of the Judeans lived in Kiriath-arba and its villages, in Dibon and its villages, in Jekabzeel and its hamlets,*
26 *in Jeshua, Moladah, Beth-pelet,*
27 *in Hazer-shual, in Beersheba and its villages,*
28 *in Ziklag, in Meconah and its villages,*
29 *in En-rimmon, Zorah, and Jarmuth,*
30 *Zanoah, Adullam, and their hamlets, Lachish and its farms, Azekah and its villages. They settled from Beersheba up to the Valley of Hinnom.*
31 *The Benjaminites were in Geba, Michmash, Aijah, Beth-el and its villages,*
32 *Anathoth, Nob, Ananiah,*
33 *Hazor, Ramah, Gittaim,*
34 *Hadid, Zeboim, Neballat,*
35 *Lod, Ono, and the Valley of Craftsmen.*

2. *Ibid.*, p. 186.
3. *Ibid.*, p. 187.

36 *Some of the Levites assigned to Judah were given to Benjamin.*

25–36 Much has been written on the origin of this list of cities. All the names of the Judean cities with the exception of Dibon, Jeshua, and Meconah appear in Josh. 15. Some scholars think that this list is influenced by the Levitical city lists of Josh. 21:8ff. and 1 Chr. 4:54ff., because of the prominent role of the Levites in this chapter (cf. v. 36).[1] It is also of interest that Hebron (Kiriath-arba) is mentioned first in the Levitical lists, as in v. 25. But there are also several important omissions in Nehemiah's list that show that it was not directly copied from the Levitical lists. According to Albright this list of Nehemiah is a partial list of towns of Simeon reoccupied in the fifth century B.C.[2] A. Alt has held that Neh. 11:25ff. is an excerpt of Josh. 15, but independent of any other list.[3] According to him the list of Josh. 15 comes from the time of Josiah, but this is rightly questioned by various scholars.[4]

The real problem with this list is that it creates the impression that the Jews lived in a much larger area than expected (cf. our discussion of Neh. 3). The question is whether this list delineates the limits of the Persian province of Judah. Some scholars think that it indeed gives the outer borders of the province.[5] But a problem arises with such an assumption, since the cities in the Negev that were quite probably occupied by Geshem and the Arabs are mentioned. Another city, Ono of Valley Ono, was in neutral territory. How can we explain this? It seems better to assume that some of the cities listed refer to areas with a partially Jewish population. The Jews were citizens of the Persian empire and could move to and fro in the different provinces.[6] The list does not describe the border of the province Judah—it is nowhere claimed—but gives us the names of areas with a fairly large Jewish population. Even so it does not provide us with a complete list. It is a partial one with emphasis in the first part (vv. 25–30) on the Levitical cities. *Its villages* (Heb. *b^e^nōṯêhā,* lit. "her daughters"). Cf. Neh. 3:12. *Its hamlets*. This refers to a very small settlement.[7] *Lachish and its farms* (or fields). This reflects an intimate knowledge of the situation of Lachish in a rich farming area. The mentioning of the Levites in v. 36 might refer again to their task of collecting tithes. Because the tithes were

1. Myers, *Ezra. Nehemiah,* p. 189.
2. Cf. W. F. Albright, *JPOS* 4 (1924), pp. 149ff.
3. Cf. Alt, *KS* III, p. 419.
4. Cf., e.g., F. M. Cross and G. E. Wright, "The Boundary and Province Lists of the Kingdom of Judah," *JBL* 75 (1956), pp. 224–26.
5. Brockington, *Ezra, Nehemiah and Esther,* p. 153.
6. Myers, *op. cit.,* p. 191.
7. Cf. Alt, *KS* III, p. 421.

intended for the temple service, a purely Jewish institution, they could be collected among Jews who even lived outside the province of Judah.

C. VARIOUS LISTS OF PRIESTS AND LEVITES (12:1–26)

1. Priests and Levites Who Returned with Zerubbabel (12:1–9)

1 *These were the priests and Levites who came with Zerubbabel the son of Shealtiel, and Jeshua: Seraiah, Jeremiah, Ezra,*
2 *Amariah, Malluch, Hattush,*
3 *Shecaniah, Rehum, Meremoth,*
4 *Iddo, Ginnethoi, Abijah,*
5 *Mijamin, Maadiah, Bilgah,*
6 *Shemaiah, and Joiarib, Jedaiah,*
7 *Sallu, Amok, Hilkiah, and Jedaiah. These were the leaders of the priests and their companions in the time of Jeshua.*
8 *The Levites were Jeshua, Binnui, Kadmiel, Sherebiah, Judah, Mattaniah—he and his companions were in command of the singing (praise songs),*
9 *while Bakbukiah and Unni with their companions were opposite them in the services.*

1–9 It is obvious that in this list family names, and not names of individuals, are supplied. The method employed is as follows. The author had at his disposal lists from the time of the high priests Joiakim and Eliashib, thus from a time slightly before the arrival of Nehemiah and contemporaneous with Nehemiah.[1] Joiakim was a little before Nehemiah, and Eliashib was a contemporary of his. From these archival materials the author had drawn up a list of family names of priests whom he regarded as contemporaries of Zerubbabel and Jeshua, that is to say, those who had returned immediately after Cyrus's edict. For the list of Levites (v. 8) the author made use of the list of Ezra 2:40 with a few additions.

An explanation for the additional names is very difficult to give. Mattaniah in v. 8, as with all the names in this verse, is intended as a family name. The problem, however, is that the addition of v. 8b tends to make this the name of an individual. The solution proposed by certain scholars is that vv. 8b and 9 are a later addition when an individual Mattaniah was the choirmaster of the singers in the temple.[2] This might be true, because v. 8b is obviously connected to 11:17. If we regard the position described in 11:17 as occurring in the time of Nehemiah, it would be problematical to think of Mattaniah holding the same position in the

1. Rudolph, *Esra und Nehemia,* p. 191; Myers, *Ezra. Nehemiah,* p. 196.
2. Rudolph, *op. cit.,* p. 192.

time of Zerubbabel. This could only have been the case if there had also been a Mattaniah who was contemporary with Zerubbabel, but the role of Bakbukiah in v. 9 is comparable to the role of Bakbukiah in 11:17. It would be exceptional to have both a Mattaniah and a Bakbukiah in the time of Zerubbabel and Nehemiah.

Another feature of the list of priests is the *and* before the name *Joiarib* (cf. also v. 19). It is generally accepted that the names after *and* are later additions.[3] It is thus clear that to both lists of priests and Levites certain later additions were made.

Iddo is the same name as that of the prophet Zechariah's father. It might have been a family name. *In command of the singing (praise songs)*. *Hôḏôṯ* should be read instead of *'al-huy^{e}ḏôṯ*.[4] Cf. Neh. 11:17.

2. *Genealogy of High Priests (12:10–11)*

10 *Jeshua was the father of Joiakim, Joiakim of Eliashib, Eliashib of Joiada,*
11 *Joiada of Jonathan (Johanan), and Jonathan of Jaddua.*

10–11 Here we have a list of high priests from Jeshua to Jaddua, from 538 B.C. to well after 400 B.C.[1] Some want to regard *Jaddua* as a contemporary of Alexander the Great (c. 330 B.C.).[2] One thing is certain, namely, that this list was compiled after the time of Nehemiah. *Jeshua* was the contemporary of Zerubbabel. We know nothing about *Joiakim* save what is said of him in this list and in vv. 12 and 26. *Eliashib* was a contemporary of Nehemiah (cf. Neh. 3:1, 20, 21). We know nothing of *Joiada* except the notice in 13:28 that one of his sons was a son-in-law of Sanballat. *Jonathan* is here quite probably a scribal error for Johanan (cf. v. 22).[3] Josephus (*Ant.* xi.8) tells the story that Johanan murdered his brother Jesus, who was a favorite of the Persian governor Bagoas. Johanan is also mentioned in the Elephantine papyri (c. 410 B.C.). To equate this Johanan with the one mentioned in Ezra 10:6 is highly questionable (cf. our discussion of Ezra 10:6). This list gives additional material to supplement the one in 1 Chr. 5:27–41.

3. *Ibid.;* Brockington, *Ezra, Nehemiah and Esther,* p. 155.
4. See *BHK;* cf. *BHS;* Rudolph, *op. cit.,* p. 190.
1. Rudolph, *Esra und Nehemia,* p. 193.
2. For the whole problem of this list cf. *BMAP,* pp. 100–110; H. H. Rowley, "Sanballat and the Samaritan Temple," *BJRL* 38 (1955/56), pp. 166–198 (= *Men of God* [New York: 1963], pp. 246–276); cf. the remarks of J. Bright, *A History of Israel,* pp. 398–99.
3. Cf., e.g., H. H. Rowley, "Nehemiah's Mission and Its Background," *BJRL* 37 (1954/55), p. 552 (= *Men of God,* p. 233); Myers, *Ezra. Nehemiah,* p. 195.

3. *Priests and Levites in the Time of Joiakim (12:12–26)*

a. List of priests (12:12–21)

12 *In the time of Joiakim the heads of priestly families were of the family of Seraiah, Meraiah; of Jeremiah, Hananiah;*
13 *of Ezra, Meshullam; of Amariah, Jehohanan;*
14 *of Malluchi, Jonathan; of Shebaniah, Joseph;*
15 *of Harim, Adna; of Meraioth, Helkai;*
16 *of Iddo, Zechariah; of Ginnethon, Meshullam;*
17 *of Abijah, Zichri; of Miniamin; of Moadiah, Piltai;*
18 *of Bilgah, Shammua; of Shemaiah, Jehonathan;*
19 *and of Joiarib, Mattenai; of Jedaiah, Uzzi;*
20 *of Sallai, Kallai; of Amok, Eber;*
21 *of Hilkiah, Hashabiah; of Jedaiah, Nethanel.*

12–21 This list of priests is closely connected to the list of vv. 1–7. In vv. 1–7 the family names are given, probably taken over from this list or else the list of vv. 1–7 and coming from the same archival source. We want to draw attention to some differences between these two lists. Here only twenty-one families are listed while in vv. 1–7 twenty-two are mentioned. The family of Hattush (12:2) is missing. There are also differences in spelling between the two lists and differences in names. Cf. the following: Shecaniah (v. 3)—Shebaniah (v. 14); Rehum (v. 3)—Harim (v. 15),[1] Meremoth (v. 3)—Meraioth (v. 15); Ginnethoi (v. 4)—Ginnethon (v. 16); Mijamin (v. 5)—Miniamin (v. 17); Maadiah (v. 5)—Moadiah (v. 17); Sallu (v. 7)—Sallai (v. 20).[2] It is obvious that a name after Miniamin has dropped out. These differences should caution us about making any far-reaching conclusions concerning the names on lists which are obviously not well transmitted. It is also very difficult to ascertain when the errors had crept in. We might assume that the list was copied carefully, but with the transmission over centuries scribal errors made the text corrupt at various places.

b. Levites (12:22–26)

22 *Concerning the Levites—in the time of Eliashib, Joiada, Johanan, and Jaddua, they were registered as heads of families, as also with the priests during the reign of Darius the Persian.*
23 *The Levites, heads of families, were registered in the Book of the Chronicles up to the time of Johanan the son of Eliashib.*
24 *The heads of the Levites were Hashabiah, Sherebiah, and Jeshua the son of Kadmiel, and their companions, directly opposite them*

1. Cf. at 10:6 our discussion of the view of Auerbach, *SVT* 9 (1962), p. 247.
2. Myers, *op. cit.*, p. 198; Brockington, *Ezra, Nehemiah and Esther*, pp. 156–57.

to intone praise and thanksgiving songs according to the prescription of David the man of God, division corresponding to division.
25 *Mattaniah, Bakbukiah, and Obadiah (were the singers), while Meshullam, Talmon, and Akkub were the gatekeepers who stood at the storehouses of the gates.*
26 *These lived in the time of Joiakim the son of Jeshua, the son of Jozadak, and in the time of Nehemiah the governor and Ezra the priest and secretary.*

22–26 The author worked from archival material. His short notices, however, are confusing and sometimes enigmatic. As we interpret it, he gives in v. 22 a form of superscription concerning the Levites. He then continues to refer to the time in which the Levites were registered, namely, from the time of Eliashib to the time of Jaddua. It is probably from c. 450 B.C. to well into the fourth century.

Verse 22b refers to the registration of priests. It is difficult to determine which *Darius* is meant here. It could be Darius the Great, Darius II (Nothus), or Darius III (Codomanus). This reference may be a historical one, that is to say, that from the time of Darius I it was expected of the priests to register.

In v. 23 the author describes what he has discovered in the Book of the Chronicles, the archival document in the temple, and not to be confused with the biblical books of the same name. In archival material the registration was only taken up to the time of Johanan the high priest (c. 400 B.C.). In v. 22 the author indicates that he has material at his disposal which takes the registration up to the time of Jaddua (well after Johanan), but this later material is not as yet copied in archival documents of the temple.[1] *The son of Eliashib.* This man is actually the grandson of Eliashib. Cf. our discussion of the term "son of" (cf. Ezra 5:1).

In v. 24 the names of the Levites are given. *The son of Kadmiel.* This is obviously a scribal error, because Jeshua was not the son of Kadmiel. Something went amiss with the text and a family name was confused with "son of."[2] Verses 24b and 25a are difficult to interpret. It is possible, as JB takes it, that *their companions* are to be identified with Mattaniah, Bakbukiah, and Obadiah. Alternatively, we have to supply *were the singers* as we have done (cf. 11:17). The MT might imply that Mattaniah and the rest of the persons mentioned in v. 25 were gatekeepers. This would mean that singers were also employed as gatekeepers, but for this we have no evidence. It is therefore better to make a division between Obadiah and Meshullam. The first group were singers and the second gatekeepers. The

1. Rudolph, *Esra und Nehemia*, p. 194.
2. E.g., Brockington, *Ezra, Nehemiah and Esther*, p. 158.

gatekeepers were thus regarded as Levites.[3] For *according to the prescription of David* cf. 1 Chr. 16:4; 23:30; 2 Chr. 29:25.

In v. 26 the author gives a general chronological indication of when these Levites were active. It was in the time of the high priest Joiakim, Ezra, and Nehemiah, from roughly 460 to 445 B.C. Some scholars have problems with this chronological reference.[4] According to them Joiakim was not a contemporary of Nehemiah, since in the time of Nehemiah, Eliashib was the high priest. This is quite correct, of course, but in this verse it is nowhere claimed that all three persons were contemporaries. The passage under examination refers to a timespan. It is quite possible that some of the Levites mentioned in vv. 24–25 were active c. 460 B.C. and were still officiating in 445 B.C. That Nehemiah is placed before Ezra does not mean that Nehemiah has been before Ezra in time. They were only mentioned in their official order of importance.

D. DEDICATION OF THE WALL OF JERUSALEM (12:27–13:3)

1. Preparation of the Levites and Priests (12:27–30)

27 *With the dedication of the wall of Jerusalem the Levites were sought from all their dwelling places and brought to Jerusalem to perform the dedication with joy, with thanksgiving songs, and songs with cymbals, harps, and lyres.*
28 *The singers gathered from the rural areas around Jerusalem and from the hamlets of the Netophathites,*
29 *from Beth-haggilgal and the farms of Geba and Azmaveth, for the singers had built for themselves hamlets around Jerusalem.*
30 *The priests and Levites purified themselves, the people, the singers, and the wall.*

Scholars generally accept that 12:27–43 stems from the memoirs of Nehemiah, but that the Chronicler had a strong hand in it, adding to and reformulating the material of Nehemiah. This is possible, of course, though the role of the Chronicler in this respect has yet to be demonstrated.

27–30 According to various scholars, vv. 27–29 are from the Chronicler, because of his preference for material on the Levites,[1] although it is also possible that this was a general tendency in postexilic times and could have been the view of Nehemiah as well. Because the Levites play

3. Cf. R. de Vaux, *Ancient Israel* II, p. 285.
4. Rudolph, *op. cit.*, p. 195.
1. Rudolph, *Esra und Nehemia*, p. 195.

such an important role in Chronicles, it is an unnecessary restriction to hold that in all instances where the role of the Levites is stressed it should be ascribed to the work of the Chronicler. We should realize that general tendencies in postexilic times also influenced people other than the small circle of the Chronicler. One may ascribe a certain phenomenon which only existed in the time of the Chronicler as actually typical of the thought pattern of the Chronicler. But the role of the Levites comes out clearly in sections which do not form part of the editing of the Chronicler, as we have seen in the memoirs of Ezra (cf., e.g., Ezra 8:18–20; Neh. 9:4–5).

It is clear that 12:27ff. is to be connected to either 11:36 or quite probably 6:15. It is difficult to tell how much time had elapsed between the finishing of the wall and its dedication. Some scholars think that the wall was dedicated almost immediately after its completion.[2] On the other hand, it is quite possible that the impression created by the book of Nehemiah is correct, that Nehemiah first wanted to solve the problem in connection with his enemies and also certain issues related to the repopulation of Jerusalem before the dedication took place. As a practical man he wanted to safeguard Jerusalem, and this was a higher priority than the dedication ceremony.

From vv. 27–29 it is clear that some of the Levites had settled in the rural areas and were farming. The district from which the Levites came is of interest, being described in terms of *Netophah,* southeast of Bethlehem, *Geba,* and *Azmaveth,* Benjaminite cities about six miles north of Jerusalem.[3] *Beth-haggilgal* is probably to be identified with Gilgal near Jericho. *Cymbals* (Heb. *m*ᵉ*ṣillayim*) is a later word for *ṣelṣ*ᵉ*lîm,* which occurs only in Chronicles and Ezra-Nehemiah. *Harps*. Heb. *n*ᵉ*ḇālîm* refers to a large stringed instrument comparable to a harp. *Lyres* (Heb. *kinnōrôṯ*) are smaller stringed instruments comparable to the lyre.[4]

Verse 30 represents the beginning of the dedication ceremony. Some think that this must stand at the end of the ceremony, but it is quite probable that all the participants would have been ritually clean before the ceremony itself started. The purification itself is not described. For the clergy it might have been fasting, abstaining from sexual intercourse, and

2. *Ibid.*
3. Cf. A. Alt, *PJB* 28 (1932), pp. 9ff.; *KS* II, p. 299.
4. Cf. D. G. Stradling, *NBD,* pp. 852ff. Our knowledge of musical instruments and music of the ancient Near East has grown immensely over the last decade; cf. R. D. Barnett, *Iraq* 31 (1969), pp. 96–103; A. D. Kilmer, *IDBS*, pp. 610–12. For almost the same Ugaritic terminology see M. Dietrich, O. Loretz, and J. Sanmartin, "Der 'Neujahrspsalm' RS 24.252 = Ug. 5 S 551–557 Nr. 2," *UF* 7 (1975), p. 115 (RS 29.252:3–4).

a sin offering, and for the laymen the washing of garments, bathing, etc.[5] What is meant by the purification of the wall is not clear.

2. *People Going to the Right (12:31–37)*

31 *Then I made the leaders of Judah ascend the wall and appointed two large groups as thanksgiving choirs. One went in procession to the right on the wall, to the Dung Gate.*
32 *Following them were Hoshaiah and half of the leaders of Judah,*
33 *namely, Azariah, Ezra, and Meshullam,*
34 *Judah, Benjamin, Shemaiah, and Jeremiah,*
35 *and of the priests with trumpets: Zechariah the son of Jonathan, the son of Shemaiah, the son of Mattaniah, the son of Micaiah, the son of Zaccur, the son of Asaph,*
36 *and his companions: Shemaiah, Azarel, Milalai, Gelalai, Maai, Nethanel, and Judah and Hanani with the musical instruments of David the man of God. Ezra the secretary went in front of them.*
37 *At the Fountain Gate they ascended the stairs of the city of David and went on top of the wall above the house of David to the Water Gate on the east.*

31–37 These verses describe one of the processions (we are reading *w^{e}hā'aḥaṯ hōleḵeṯ* instead of *w^{e}ṯah^{e}lūḵōṯ* in v. 31),[1] which turned to the right in the direction of the Dung Gate. This procession was accompanied by a choir of Levites (here called priests) under the direction of Zechariah (cf. our discussion of 11:17). *Milalai, Gilalai, Maai.* These names occur only here and might be some kind of assonance with *-ai* at the end. *Ezra the secretary went in front of them.* Some scholars regard this as a later insertion from an editor who wanted to make Ezra and Nehemiah contemporaries.[2] It is totally unacceptable to eliminate a certain expression to fit in with a preconceived idea as to how the history of Ezra and Nehemiah should be interpreted. This is an important piece of evidence that Ezra and Nehemiah were indeed contemporaries. That Ezra walked in front of the procession shows his importance.[3]

The procession walked on top of the wall. This might have a ritual meaning which is no longer known to us.[4]

5. Myers, *Ezra. Nehemiah,* pp. 202–203.

1. Brockington, *Ezra, Nehemiah and Esther,* p. 159; Myers, *Ezra. Nehemiah,* p. 201. Cf. v. 38.

2. Brockington, *op. cit.*, p. 160.

3. Cf. N. H. Snaith, "Nehemiah XII 36," *VT* 17 (1967), p. 243.

4. The view of van Selms, *Ezra en Nehemia, in loc.*, that it is to ward off evil spirits and any evil which could befall the wall, is an attempt to explain the meaning of the procession but cannot be proved.

3. *People Going to the Left (12:38–39)*

38 *A second thanksgiving choir went to the left. I and half of the people followed them on the wall, above the Tower of the Ovens up to the Broad Wall*
39 *and above the Ephraim Gate and by the Jeshanah Gate, Fish Gate, Hananel Tower, and Tower of the Hundred to the Sheep Gate. They came to a halt at the Guard Gate.*

38–39 This procession under the leadership of Nehemiah went to the north and the east. It is clear from the verses that the thanksgiving choir walked at the head of the procession, followed by the officials in order of their importance. *To the left.* Heb. *l^emô'l* is certainly a scribal error for *liśmō'l,* "to the left." Cf. *to the right* in v. 31. For the gates and towers cf. Neh. 3. For *the Ephraim Gate* cf. 8:16. *Guard Gate* is only mentioned here and could be the Muster Gate; cf. 3:31. *They came . . . Guard Gate.* This phrase does not occur in the LXX,[1] but there is not enough textual evidence to delete it.[2]

4. *Dedication Ceremony at the Temple (12:40–43)*

40 *The two thanksgiving choirs came to a standstill in the temple of God, and I with half of the leaders with me.*
41 *The priests were Eliakim, Maaseiah, Miniamin, Micaiah, Elioenai, Zechariah, and Hananiah with trumpets,*
42 *and Maaseiah, Shemaiah, Eleazer, Uzzi, Jehohanan, Malchijah, Elam, and Ezer. The singers in charge of Jizrahiah sang.*
43 *On that day they sacrificed great offerings and they rejoiced because God gave to them great joy. The women and children also rejoiced so that the joy of Jerusalem could be heard from afar.*

40–43 With the dedication ceremony in the temple the laity is separated from the clergy. We may derive this from vv. 40 and 41. The priests had to perform the sacrifices. It is of interest that Nehemiah mentions only his half of the leaders *(s^egānîm)* and not the other half under the leadership of Ezra. He probably takes this for granted in the light of his description of vv. 31–37. Some scholars maintain plausibly that Ps. 147 originated from this dedication ceremony; cf. especially Ps. 147:2, 13.[1] This ceremony was held with great joy (the term *joy* appears five times in v. 43). The final consummation of Nehemiah's work had been reached. The city was protected by a wall and could resist any attempt of the neighboring

1. Brockington, *Ezra, Nehemiah and Esther,* p. 160.
2. Rudolph, *Esra und Nehemia,* p. 197. For the topography of Neh. 12:31–43 see M. Burrows, "The Topography of Nehemiah 12:31–43," *JBL* 54 (1935), pp. 29–39.
1. Cf. H.-J. Kraus, *Psalmen* II, p. 956; Rudolph, *Esra und Nehemia,* p. 199.

nations to attack it. This was one of the main reasons for the joy. The other was that the people had demonstrated that they could perform a major task as a unit, and this proved to be a great stimulus to their morale. As in the case of the completion of the foundations of the temple (Ezra 3:13), the joyful shouts could be heard from afar. It is also of interest that Nehemiah emphasizes that the Lord gave joy to the people. In the last but must important place, they had the Lord to thank for their success.

5. *Willing Contribution to the Service of God (12:44–47)*

44 *At that time men were appointed to take charge of the treasury chambers, the products, the firstfruits, and the tithes, and to collect for themselves from the farms of the cities portions prescribed by the law for the priests and Levites, for Judah rejoiced in the priests and Levites who were performing their duties.*

45 *because they, the singers, and the gatekeepers performed the service of their God and the rite of purification according to the prescription of David and his son Solomon.*

46 *From the time of David and Asaph, from long ago, there were conductors of singers and praise and thanksgiving songs for God.*

47 *So the whole of Israel in the times of Zerubbabel and Nehemiah were giving regular daily portions to the singers and gatekeepers. They gave to the Levites their sacred contributions, and the Levites gave their sacred contributions to the Aaronites.*

44–47 Some scholars call this pericope idealistic and not true of any time in Jewish history.[1] It could have happened after the joy of the dedication ceremony, however. Although this pericope is generally ascribed to the Chronicler, he could have written it with a good knowledge of what happened after the dedication. At that time the people, laymen as well as clergy, were strongly motivated to keep the prescriptions of the law. This pericope is to be connected to 10:28ff. In ch. 10 the institution of the collecting of firstfruits, tithes, etc. is described. In 12:44–47 the fact is stressed that it is functioning well. Men were appointed for the treasury chambers. The Levites went out to the rural areas to collect the tithes. They were performing their duties in an exemplary fashion. The Jews were proud of them. Much is made of the fact that in Neh. 13 no such idealistic situation is reflected.[2] But we must keep in mind that Neh. 13 describes a much later situation, after the second return of Nehemiah to Jerusalem.

It is of interest that special attention is given to the singers and gatekeepers. This may point to the fact that singing with the services had

1. E.g., Myers, *Ezra. Nehemiah,* p. 206.
2. Rudolph, *Esra und Nehemia,* p. 201.

become more and more important. It was thus a specific development in postexilic times, as indicated by v. 47. The mentioning of *Zerubbabel* and *Nehemiah* is not strange, because they were the only well-known governors of postexilic times. The stressing of the importance of the singers comes out clearly in v. 46 where Asaph is placed alongside David, the great hero-king.

To the prescription of David and his son Solomon. Cf. 1 Chr. 23–26 and 2 Chr. 8:14. *The rite of purification.* Cf. Lev. 11–15; 1 Chr. 23:28; Neh. 12:30. *There were conductors of singers and praise and thanksgiving songs,* literally "heads (or head) of singers and praise song and thanksgiving." In v. 47b the tithes are described as sacred (from the Hebrew root *qdš*), especially set aside for the Levites, while they in their turn must give the priests their fair share (cf. 10:39). Everything was now well organized and the people were satisfied with the situation.

6. *Exclusion of Foreigners (13:1–3)*

1 *At that time there was a reading from the book of Moses to the people. It was discovered written in it that no Ammonite or Moabite should ever come into the congregation of God,*
2 *because they did not come to meet the Israelites with food and water. They even hired Balaam to curse them, but our God turned the curse into a blessing.*
3 *When they heard the law, they excluded all foreigners from Israel.*

Scholars have some problems in detecting the author of this pericope. Rudolph, although uncertain, thinks that it might have been the Chronicler, because these verses are intended to take the stress off the rest of ch. 13, where the transgressions of the people are described.[1] It is quite probable that the Chronicler made use here of the memoirs of Nehemiah.[2]

1–3 These three verses are a good introduction to what follows. With the regular reading of the law it was discovered that foreigners could not be allowed in the congregation of God. *Congregation of God* (Heb. *q*ᵉ*hal hā'*ᵉ*lōhîm*). This is the only place in the OT where *qāhāl* is connected with *'*ᵉ*lōhîm*. Elsewhere it is connected with the Lord (Yahweh). It refers here to the cultic congregation of God[3] and obviously alludes to Deut. 23:3–6. In the light of this it is wrong to take *'ēreḇ* in v. 3 as meaning people of mixed blood, since *Ammonite* and *Moabite* testify against it. It is therefore obvious that *'ēreḇ* refers to foreigners. After the law was heard, foreigners were excluded from the Israelite cult. Or was the reading

1. Rudolph, *Esra und Nehemia,* pp. 202–203.
2. Myers, *Ezra. Nehemiah,* p. 207.
3. Cf. J. D. W. Kritzinger, *Q*ᵉ*hal Jahwe,* p. 47.

interpreted in a wider sense to exclude the presence of any foreigner in the Israelite community? This might have been the case if we consider the measures taken against marriages with foreigners. It is also true that Ezra and Nehemiah were opposed to anything which could endanger the purity of religion.

VII. REFORMS OF NEHEMIAH'S SECOND ADMINISTRATION (13:4–31)

A. ACTION AGAINST ELIASHIB AND TOBIAH (13:4–9)

4 *Before this, Eliashib the priest, who was appointed over the chambers of the temple of our God and who was close to Tobiah,*
5 *arranged for him to have a large chamber in which they previously placed the food offering, frankincense, the vessels, and the tithes of grain, wine, and oil which were given by command to the Levites, the singers, and gatekeepers as well as the products for the priests.*
6 *While all this happened, I was not in Jerusalem, for in the thirty-second year of Artaxerxes king of Babylon I went to the king. After some time I asked the king leave*
7 *and I went back to Jerusalem and discovered the evil which Eliashib had done to arrange for Tobiah to have a chamber inside the court of the temple of God.*
8 *I became very angry and I threw all the household belongings of Tobiah out of the chamber.*
9 *Then I commanded that they should purify the chambers, and I brought back all the vessels of the temple of God, the food offering, and frankincense.*

4–9 After twelve years in Jerusalem (445–433 B.C.), Nehemiah left Jerusalem for the Persian court. His leave of absence had expired. He had to ask the king permission to return to Jerusalem, because he obviously felt that his mission to reform his people had not yet been accomplished. How true this was is illustrated by the case of the priest Eliashib. During Nehemiah's absence, in his capacity as overseer of the chambers of the temple, Eliashib granted a spacious chamber to Tobiah, the Ammonite.[1] Eliashib has the same name as the acting high priest, but he must be someone different, because it would be strange to mention that he was an overseer of the chambers if he was the high priest.[2] It is also important to

1. For a discussion see H. H. Rowley, *BJRL* 38 (1955–56), pp. 166–198 (= *Men of God,* pp. 246–276).
2. Cf. S. Herrmann, *A History of Israel in OT Times,* p. 316; W. Vischer in *Probleme biblischer Theologie,* p. 608; Rudolph, *op. cit.,* pp. 203–204.

note that Eliashib was allowed to bring Tobiah into the temple precincts. The acting high priest would not have been ignorant of it. If we keep in mind that the grandson of Eliashib the high priest had married the daughter of Sanballat (13:28), such permissiveness is understandable. In Nehemiah's absence certain prominent Jewish leaders were bringing their pure religion into danger.

It is not said for how long Nehemiah was absent from Jerusalem. When he arrived and discovered the presence of Tobiah in a temple chamber, he took action immediately. He threw Tobiah's personal belongings into the street and commanded that this chamber and adjacent chambers which could have been contaminated should be purified. For Nehemiah, Tobiah's presence as a heathen, though he probably believed in the Lord but in an unorthodox way, meant contamination of everything which was holy. A person like Tobiah could not be allowed to enter the temple area. The room which was given to him was a storage room for all kinds of products intended for the cult and for the support of the priests and Levites. These products were regarded as sacred (12:47). It was thus an act of desecration to bring into a sacred chamber a profane person such as Tobiah. The chamber was restored immediately to its original usage by Nehemiah. For *frankincense* as an offering cf. Exod. 30:34ff. For *king of Babylon* cf. our discussion of Ezra 5:13.

With this incident Nehemiah set the example of his new approach to an unnecessarily close relationship with foreigners. The purity of religion had to be maintained at any cost. This was absolutely necessary if the small community, beset as it was with all the temptations of paganism, was to be prevented from reverting to a compromise with the neighboring nations and bringing their ancestral religion into danger.[3]

B. REORGANIZATION OF THE LEVITES (13:10–14)

10 *I discovered also that the portions of the Levites were not given to them so that every one of them, as well as the singers responsible for the work, had gone to their farms.*

11 *Then I brought a case against the leaders, saying: "Why is the temple of God abandoned?" So I gathered them and reinstated them in their positions.*

12 *The whole of Judah brought the tithes of grain, wine, and oil for the treasuries.*

13 *I appointed over the treasuries Shelemiah the priest, Zadok the secretary, and Pedaiah from the Levites, and as their aide Hanan the*

3. Cf. Herrmann, *op. cit.*, p. 316.

son of Zaccur, the son of Mattaniah, for they were regarded as reliable men to make the distribution to their companions.

14 *"Remember me, my God, for all this and do not wipe out my good deeds which I have done for the temple of my God and its services."*

10–14 The Levites had to live on the tithes which were given to them (Num. 18:21). According to 11:15ff. Nehemiah brought some of the Levites to Jerusalem for the temple service. In 12:27ff. some of the Levites lived in certain cities of Judah and were farming there. The regular delivery of the tithes was ensured (12:44ff.). People granted their tithes willingly because they were proud of the Levites. Combined with other taxes (cf. ch. 5), however, the tithes became a heavy burden for the Jews, and they were unable to keep it up. In Nehemiah's absence the giving of tithes had ceased somehow. Thus the Levites could not perform their duties at the temple. So they moved out to their allotted rural areas (12:28–29) to do some farming in order to stay alive. *Had gone away* (from the Hebrew root *brḥ*). This means actually that they fled to the country, being forced to do it. All the goodwill described in 12:44ff. was gone. With Nehemiah's return the whole service of the temple was reorganized and the Levites restored to their earlier tasks.

In v. 11, as in 5:7, we have, according to the usage of the Hebrew verb *rîḇ*, a court case between Nehemiah and the leaders. He as governor accused them of evading their responsibilities. They were subservient to him, and thus responsible to him for their conduct. *The temple of God abandoned.* The proper functioning of the cult had been neglected.

I appointed over the treasuries. Some scholars propose to read *wā'ᵃṣawweh*, "I have appointed," with the LXX instead of *wā'ôṣᵉrâ*, "I have made treasurers," regarding this word as dittography for the next word *'ôṣārôṯ*, "treasuries."[1] This is quite probably correct. *Zadok the secretary.* Does this mean that Ezra, the secretary, was no longer present in Jerusalem?

Verse 14 is another of the short prayers of Nehemiah. His main purpose in all his reforms was to organize the cult in the temple properly. In this verse he asked God not to wipe out all his good deeds. *Good deeds* (from Heb. *ḥeseḏ*). We have translated *ḥeseḏ* elsewhere "covenant love." In this case it obviously refers to care for the temple and its services, but also to his love for the temple. He felt his solidarity with the temple of God and its cult. We must remember that at that time the temple was regarded as the place where God was present. Care for the temple meant also care for God.

1. Rudolph, *Esra und Nehemia*, p. 206.

C. RESTORATION OF THE SABBATH (13:15–22)

15 *In those days I saw in Judah the treading of winepresses on the sabbath; others were bringing heaps of grain loaded on donkeys. Also wine, grapes, figs, and all kinds of loads they were bringing on the sabbath to Jerusalem. I warned them not to sell food on that day.*

16 *Tyrians who stayed in the city were bringing fish and all kinds of merchandise, and were selling it on the sabbath to the Jews in Jerusalem.*

17 *Then I brought in a court case against the leaders of Judah and I said to them: "What is this evil thing you are doing in profaning the sabbath?*

18 *Your ancestors did the same and our God brought over us this catastrophe and also over this city. You are bringing fresh wrath on Israel by profaning the sabbath."*

19 *Then when the shadows began to fall (on) the gates of Jerusalem before the sabbath, I commanded them to shut the gates and further commanded that they should not be opened until after the sabbath. Some of my servants I appointed to be in charge of the gates so that no burden could be brought in on the sabbath.*

20 *The merchants and sellers spent the night once or twice outside Jerusalem.*

21 *Then I warned them: "Why do you spend the night before the wall? If you do it again, I shall lay my hands on you." From that time onward they did not come on the sabbath.*

22 *I commanded the Levites to purify themselves and to come and guard the gates in order to keep the sabbath sacred. "Remember this, my God, and spare me according to your great covenant love."*

15–22 On his visits to the rural areas of Judah Nehemiah had noticed that the Jews did not observe the sabbath as a sacred day. He visited the province of Judah, quite probably as governor, soon after his return as part of his official duty. He saw that the Jews were continuing their daily work on the sabbath. They were making wine, carrying their loads of grain by donkeys into Jerusalem, as well as doing business as on every other day. The Tyrians, the famous Phoenician merchants (Ezek. 27:12–36; 28:16), were selling fish and other kinds of merchandise to the Jews on the sabbath. This business was quite probably done at the Fish Gate.[1] The sabbath law was totally forgotten. The real meaning of the sabbath, a day to acknowledge the Lord as Creator and to give all the honor to him for a successful week, had been abandoned. The sabbath was celebrated to show that man's

1. Cf. B.-Z. Luria, "Wehaṣṣōrîm yāsebû bamebî 'îmdāg wekol-meker," *Beth Mikra* 15 (1970), pp. 363–67; Brockington, *Ezra, Nehemiah and Esther,* p. 163.

existence as a creation was more important than his fight for survival.[2] It is one of the significant phenomena which distinguished the Jews from other nations. Because of their need, the Jews were conducting their business on that day like the neighboring heathen.

With his excellent knowledge of Scripture (cf. Jer. 17:27; Ezek. 20:12ff.) Nehemiah warned them against this practice. He instructed them not to sell food. The term for *food* (Heb. *ṣayiḏ*)[3] is probably chosen deliberately to remind the Jews of the manna episode in the desert during the wilderness wanderings (cf. Exod. 16:22ff.). The Lord provides food for the sabbath; it is wrong and a sin to buy or sell food on that day. It seems as if the warning of Nehemiah was not taken seriously. Then he immediately started a *rîḇ,* a court case against them. He summoned the leaders and told them that through this negligence of the sabbath law they were adding to the wrath of God on Israel. Here in v. 18 we have again the solidarity between the Jews and historical Israel (cf. Neh. 9). Because of the sins of the ancestors in profaning the sabbath, this catastrophe of exile and servitude had befallen the Jews.

The next step taken by Nehemiah again proves his practical nature.[4] If the Jewish people did not want to heed his warnings, precautions should be instituted to ensure the observance of the sabbath. From the beginning of the sabbath (Friday evening) to its end (Saturday evening), the gates of Jerusalem were closed so that no burden could be brought into the city on the sabbath. Initially Nehemiah appointed some of his servants or minor officials (cf. 4:10, 17; 5:10, 16) to guard the gates on the sabbath. In the meantime the merchants came, as the custom was, with their merchandise to Jerusalem, but found the gates closed and then camped for the night outside the wall. We may presume that this became a fresh temptation for the inhabitants of the city to go out to them and buy their wares. Nehemiah realized immediately the new danger and warned them to move away or else they would be removed by force. As governor he had the power to remove them. This warning was enough to frighten them away.

After the initial steps, Nehemiah decided to place the guarding of

2. Cf. W. Vischer in *Probleme biblischer Theologie,* p. 609; H. W. Wolff, *Anthropology of the OT* (E.T. 1974), p. 141.
3. The term *ṣayiḏ* has two spheres of meaning in Hebrew, viz., "food" or "provisions" (cf. Ps. 78:25; 132:15) and "sacrifice of game." In Ugaritic (e.g., Krt 79) the latter meaning predominates; cf., e.g., J. C. de Moor, *UF* 2 (1970), p. 347; H. P. Rüger, *UF* 2 (1970), p. 203. But some Ugaritic scholars think that it should mean "food"; cf. J. Gray, *The KRT Text in the Literature of Ras Shamra* (Leiden: 1964), p. 38; B. Margulis, *UF* 2 (1970), p. 133. Cf. also F. C. Fensham, *JNSL* 6 (1978), pp. 19–24.
4. Cf. Vischer, *op. cit.,* p. 610.

the gates on a permanent footing. The Levites as clergy were appointed, after purifying themselves, to guard the gates. The sabbath was sacred to God and only persons from the sacred sphere could guard the sacredness of the sabbath properly. This explains Nehemiah's whole approach to religious matters. He was not a priest—quite probably only a maimed member of the laity—but still a very religious man. It shows, furthermore, what can be achieved by one devoted man in the face of the religious negligence of his people.

Then when the shadows began to fall (on) the gates, literally "when they threw shadows, the gates." Some want to connect *ṣālᵃlû,* "they threw shadows," to a Syriac word meaning "to become clean" or "emptied."[5] This is uncertain, however, because no contemporary meaning in Aramaic has as yet turned up.[6] As we have translated it, we understand that a preposition must be read before "gates," but this presents no difficulty since an obvious preposition is occasionally omitted in Hebrew. Or else we may translate: "when the gates threw shadows." What is the meaning of this? The gates, we may presume, threw shadows throughout the day.

The pericope is concluded with another short prayer. The term *spare* (from Heb. *ḥûs*) is not clear. It might mean either "spare," "excuse," or "have compassion," "have pity." It is clear, however, that Nehemiah besought the Lord to give special attention to what he did. He wanted to receive through his deeds the love of God. Again it is clear that what he did was not so much for the people's sake or even out of nationalistic considerations, but was firmly centered in his religious convictions.

D. THE PROBLEM OF MARRIAGES TO FOREIGNERS (13:23–29)

23 *Also in those days I saw Jews who had married Ashdodite, Ammonite, and Moabite women.*

24 *Half of their children spoke Ashdodite or the language of the other peoples, and they could not speak the language of the Jews.*

25 *Then I brought a court case against them, cursed them, struck some of the men, pulled out their hair, and made them take an oath by God: "You must not marry your daughters to their sons or marry your sons to their daughters or marry them yourselves.*

26 *Solomon the king of Israel committed a sin in this regard. Among the many nations there was not a king like him. He was loved by his God, and God made him king over the whole of Israel. The foreign women caused him to sin.*

5. Rudolph, *op. cit.*, p. 207; Myers, *Ezra. Nehemiah,* p. 213.
6. The one possible example is doubtful; cf. *DISO*, p. 245.

27 *Concerning you, must we hear now that you have committed this grave evil to act treacherously against our God by marrying foreign women?"*
28 *One of the sons of Joiada, the son of Eliashib the high priest, was a son-in-law of Sanballat the Horonite. I chased him from me.*
29 *"Remember them, my God, for the defilement of the priesthood and the covenant of the priesthood and Levites."*

23–27 Another continual problem was the marriages to foreigners (cf. Ezra 9–10; Neh. 6:18; 10:31 [Eng. 30]). On his arrival, Ezra had tackled this problem. Drastic measures were taken and the foreign wives and their children were sent away. But when Nehemiah came, the problem was still not resolved, as we learn from Neh. 6:18. As part of the covenant renewal described in Neh. 10 the marriages are again mentioned. The people solemnly undertook not to marry foreigners. In Neh. 13:1–3 the presence of Ammonites and Moabites in the cultic congregation is strictly forbidden. So after Nehemiah's departure to the Persian court this problem must have developed again. If we take the view that everything was under control when Nehemiah left Jerusalem, we may deduce from the fact that the children spoke a foreign dialect that quite a time had elapsed between his departure and arrival. Soon after his arrival he discovered that children of foreign wives of Jews spoke Ashdodite, Ammonite, and Moabite. We know from inscriptions that Moabite was closely related to Hebrew.[1] We may presume that Ashdodite and Ammonite were languages very similar to Aramaic.[2] This is substantiated to a certain extent by the discovery of an ostracon in Nebi Yunus that is written in Aramaic.[3] *Ashdodite:* for Ashdodites cf. our discussion of 4:7. *The language of the Jews* (Heb. *y^e^hûḏîṯ*): this is quite probably Hebrew. If we take all this into consideration, we may presume that there was little linguistic difference between Hebrew and Moabite. The vernacular of the Jews was probably Aramaic, so that some difference between this and Ashdodite and Ammonite would exist. What was then precisely the difference? No doubt dialectal differences were involved as well as the different pronunciation of sounds.[4]

1. Cf., e.g., F. M. Cross, "Notes on the Ammonite Inscription from Tell Sīrān," *BASOR* 212 (1973), pp. 12–15; J. Hoftijzer, *De ontcijfering van Deir-'Alla-teksten* (1973); H. J. Franken, "Texts from the Persian period from tell Deir 'Allā." *VT* 17 (1967), 480–81. For the Ammonite text cf. J. Hoftijzer and G. Van der Kooij, *Aramaic Texts from Deir 'Alla* (1976).
2. Rudolph, *Esra und Nehemia*, pp. 208–209.
3. Cf. D. N. Freedman, *IDBS*, p. 72. Some scholars think that Ashdodite was a Philistine language mixed with Canaanite elements; cf. H. H. Schaeder, *Iranische Beiträge* I, p. 29; van Selms, *Ezra en Nehemia, in loc.* But we have no proof for this.
4. Myers, *Ezra. Nehemiah,* p. 217.

Nehemiah was able to distinguish between the language spoken by children of foreign women and by regular Jewish children. Because Hebrew was the language of the cult, people with such a different language could not be permitted to participate in Jewish religious life. For the religion it was therefore a new and dangerous development. Nehemiah tackled this problem vehemently. He brought in a court case *(rîḇ)* against his people before the Lord (cf. 5:7; 13:11, 17).

But there was also some further action. Nehemiah cursed them, not in the modern sense of the word, but in terms of the pronouncement of a religious curse. In Neh. 10 the forming of a covenant is described with the stipulation that foreign marriages are out. If the covenant should be broken, the religious curse would come into effect. This is what we have here.

Nehemiah also had a fight with some of the transgressors. He struck them and pulled out their hair. He received his authority from the Persian king, and could thus take drastic action. It is also clear that he received strong opposition, although he did not demand from them, as Ezra did, that they should divorce their foreign wives. For the second time the Jews had to take an oath not to marry foreigners (cf. also 10:30 [Eng. 29]).

Nehemiah was well versed in the history of early Israel, and in a short summary he gives the main facts of Solomon's sin with his foreign wives (cf. 1 K. 3:12ff.; 2 Sam. 12:24ff.; 1 K. 4:1; 11:1–6). Like Solomon, the Jews in Nehemiah's time acted treacherously against God; they were traitors to their religion. This, of course, is the important point: they were neglecting the religious tongue, Hebrew, and were bringing the purity of their religion into danger.

28–29 It was not only the ordinary people who had committed this crime against their religion, but among the leaders of the community the same thing had happened. The grandson of the high priest, Eliashib, had married the daughter of Sanballat the Horonite.[5] Lev. 21:14 prohibits the high priest from marrying a foreigner. Any person in the high-priestly lineage could become high priest. It was thus a dangerous situation. On the other hand, Sanballat was the archenemy of Nehemiah. Such an act as that of Eliashib's grandson was a direct challenge to the authority of Nehemiah. So it was regarded as the highest form of religious apostasy. Nehemiah *chased him* away, which means that Nehemiah expelled him from the Jewish religious community. The story of Josephus that Manasseh, the son of Johanan, brother of the high priest Joiada, had married Sanballat's daughter, that he was expelled by Nehemiah, that he went to Sanballat, and that Sanballat had built a temple for him on Gerizim, is

5. Cf. also H. H. Rowley, *BJRL* 38 (1955–56), pp. 166–198.

probably a reflection of the time of Alexander the Great. It was a Jewish story to explain the presence of a Samaritan temple.[6]

Verse 29 is another of the short prayers of Nehemiah. This time the Lord must remember in wrath those who defiled the priesthood. *The covenant of the priesthood.* Some scholars think that this refers to the contract of marriage, but in the light of Neh. 10:29ff. (Eng. 28ff.) it seems more probable that it refers to the covenant taken at that time in which it was undertaken not to marry foreign women.

E. SUMMARY OF NEHEMIAH'S REFORMS (13:30–31)

30 *I cleansed them from everything foreign and instituted the duties of the priests and Levites, everyone in his work,*
31 *as well as the delivery of wood on appointed times and also the firstfruits. "Remember this, my Lord, in my favor."*

30–31 This is a short summary of some of the important work of Nehemiah in connection with the cult. Because he refers to the cultic reforms only, nothing is said of the rebuilding of the walls that played such an important role in the first part of Nehemiah. In a certain sense this is a short peroration of Neh. 10. For steps against foreign marriages cf. 10:31 (Eng. 30) and 13:23ff. For the duties of priests and Levites cf. 10:38–40 (Eng. 37–39); 12:44–47; 13:12–13. For the delivery of wood cf. 10:35 (Eng. 34) and for the firstfruits cf. 10:36ff. (Eng. 35ff.). Nehemiah only reorganized the cultic functions which had fallen in disuse after his departure to the Persian king.

The book of Nehemiah concludes with a short prayer. He asks the Lord to remember all these things which he had done in his favor. Everything was done for the Lord. He had disciplined his people to serve the Lord according to the prescriptions of the law. A new era of Jewish worship has started, worship according to prescribed legal principles. It was only with the coming of Christ and the interpretation of his coming by Paul that another new era was commenced in which the legal burden was removed from the shoulders of mankind and the center of religion placed in his vicarious suffering on the cross. It is the new era of faith and love in Jesus Christ.

6. Cf. H. G. Kippenberg, *Garizim und Synagoge,* pp. 50ff.; Josephus *Ant.* xi.7–8.

INDEXES

I. SUBJECTS

II. AUTHORS

INDEX OF AUTHORS

III. PERSONS

As far as possible we have tried to distinguish the different categories of people named in this list. It is sometimes difficult to determine to which category a person belongs. In such a case we have made no distinction. It is also possible that one name can represent more than one person, that a different name could have been used for the same person, or that a nickname could have been used in one place and the real name in another place. Where we have certainty about the identification of a person with more than one name or with a different spelling of the name, we have put one of the names in parentheses.

Tattenai (Persian official), 28, 79, 80, 81, 82, 83, 85, 86, 89
Tiglath-pileser III (king), 51, 233
Titus (Roman general), 93
Tobiah (Ammonite), 27, 29, 164–65, 168–69, 181, 199, 200, 205, 208, 209, 260–61
Tyrians, 62, 263

Udjeharresne (Egyptian), 103
Ugbaru (Persian), 42
Urhai (layman), 112
Uriah (priest), 121, 174
Ushtani (Persian), 79
Uzzi (singer), 248

Xerxes (king), 5, 12, 14, 15, 28, 69–71, 74, 75, 130
Yaḫdun-Lim (king), 91
Yahu (the Lord), 105, 114, 163
Yahweh (the Lord), 25, 27
Yehimilk, 180
Zababa (god), 55
Zabad (layman), 26
Zabbud (layman), 122
Zabdi (singer), 26
Zaccai (layman), 51, 144
Zaccur (layman), 112
Zadok (high priest), 24
Zadok (priest), 99
Zalaph, 178
Zattu (layman), 112
Zechariah (priest), 256
Zechariah (prophet), 11, 28, 49, 50, 78–79, 92, 114, 251
Zedekiah (secretary), 236
Zedekiah (king), 75, 194
Zerubbabel (governor), 5, 11, 21, 23, 25, 29, 46, 47, 49, 50, 56, 59, 63, 78, 85, 89, 92, 111, 152, 173, 197, 236, 250, 251, 259
Ziha (temple servant), 54

IV. PLACES

Ahava River, 113, 116, 120
Ai, 52
Akkad, 84
Anathoth, 52, 237
Anshan, 42
Arad, 136
Ashdod, 200
Asia Minor, 10, 11, 12, 42
Assyria, 73, 96, 233
Athens, 13, 14, 15, 206
Athos, 13
Azmaveth (Beth), 52, 255

Babylon, 4, 9, 10, 25, 42, 45, 48, 56, 84, 85, 86, 96, 98, 100, 101, 103, 104, 105, 106, 108, 112, 114, 115, 118, 120, 129, 261
Bactria, 149
Bashan, 232
Beeroth, 52
Benjamin, 138, 244
Bethel, 16, 52, 70, 175
Beth-haccherem, 173, 175, 176
Beth-haggilgal (Gilgal), 255
Bethlehem, 52, 255
Beth-shearim, 168
Beth-zur, 50, 173, 175, 177
Black Sea, 13

Casiphia, 114
Chephirah, 51, 52
Constantinople, 206
Corinth, 14

Dan, 16
Dibon, 249

Ecbatana, 86
Egypt, 9, 10, 11, 13, 15, 21, 70, 77, 90, 103, 104, 105, 122, 130, 149, 150, 156, 198, 229, 231
Elam, 52, 73
Elephantine (Yeb), 8, 9, 43, 54, 80, 82, 86, 89, 90, 99, 104, 105, 114, 136, 245, 251
Erech, 73
Erertria, 13
Euphrates, 73, 113
Europe, 13

Geba, 255
Gerizim, 267
Gibeon, 50, 52, 70, 99, 131, 173, 174, 191
Greece, 12, 14, 77, 140

Hadid, 51, 52
Hakkephirim, 200

Index of Places

V. SCRIPTURE REFERENCES

OLD TESTAMENT

VI. NONBIBLICAL TEXTS

HEBREW

RABBINICAL SOURCES

UGARITIC

ARAMAIC

30:1 51
30:2 43
30:5 105
30:14 91
30:18 136
30:19 163
30:26 90
30:27 43
31:1 51
31:2 43
31:17 136
32:3 43
32:8 85
38:3 43
80:7 72
81:31 51

BMAP
2:2 105
3:23 80
3:23b 72
9:13 210
10:19 72
11:14 72
12:34 72

Driver, *Documents*
4:4 100
6:6 100
7:10 100
8:6 100
9:3 100
10:5 100

Hermopolis Papyri
1:12 80

JEWISH-GREEK SOURCES

3 Esdras
2:24 76
5:40 218
7:6 93

Josephus *Antiquities*
xi.2 68
xi.4–7 93
xi.5 163
xi.5.8 206
xi.7–8 268
xi.8 251

2 Maccabees
1:18–36 150

Tobit
1:22 157

GREEK SOURCES

Herodotus *History*
iii.34 157

Thucydides *History*
i.93 206

Xenophon
Anabasis i.6.4–5 105
Cyropaedia viii.6.22 86, 150

PERSIAN

Avesta
Nyāyišn 5:20 217

VII. HEBREW WORDS

'^{a}g̱art^{e}lîm 46
'^{a}ḏōnāy ('^{a}ḏōnî) 135
'āḥ 114, 115, 190, 197
'^{a}ḥašdarp^{e}nîm 122
'ayin 211
'ālâ 237–38
'mll 180
'āmēn 196
'ôṣārôṯ 262
'rk 184
'ašpôṯ 176

b^{e} 22, 59, 216
bd' 203
bhl 68
b^{e}hēmâ 165
bûzâ 181, 182
bzh 180
bizzâ 181, 182
bîn 113, 216–18
bayiṯ 64
blh 68
bēn (b^{e}nê) 50, 245, 246, 253
bānôṯ 176, 249
ba'^{a}lê š^{e}ḇû'â 208
brḥ 262
b^{e}rîṯ 134, 154
brk 223
brr 198
bšlm 71–72

gibbôrê ḥayil 245
gāḏēr 130–31
gôyim 202
gwp 210
gešem 139

hôḏôṯ 251
h^{a}lō' 132

wayyāḇî' 22
wā'ôṣ^{e}râ 22
waw 42, 60, 114, 115, 117, 205, 232

zeh 64
zûḏ 231
zikkārôn 169

ḥûs 265
ḥôrîm 167
ḥzq 175, 203
ḥāy 205
ḥayil 180
ḥēleq 169
ḥeseḏ 64, 130, 154, 262
ḥōṣ^{e}ḇîm 62
ḥōq 230
ḥrh 180
ḥrm 138
ḥerpâ 181
ḥārāšîm 62

ṭll 176
ṭap̱ 116

ydh 247
yāḏôṯ (yaḏ) 242–43
y^{e}hûḏîṯ 266
ysd 61–62, 64, 101
yāṣā' 45, 134
y^{e}hôḏeh 22
yr' 154, 187, 207

VIII. ARAMAIC WORDS

IX. WORDS OF OTHER LANGUAGES